MILTON STUDIES

XXV

MILTON STUDIES

XXV ❧ *Edited by*

James D. Simmonds

UNIVERSITY OF PITTSBURGH PRESS

MILTON STUDIES

is published annually by the University of Pittsburgh Press as a forum for Milton scholarship and criticism. Articles submitted for publication may be biographical; they may interpret some aspect of Milton's writings; or they may define literary, intellectual, or historical contexts — by studying the work of his contemporaries, the traditions which affected his thought and art, contemporary political and religious movements, his influence on other writers, or the history of critical response to his work.

Manuscripts should be upwards of 3,000 words in length and should conform to the *MLA Style Sheet*. Manuscripts and editorial correspondence should be addressed to James D. Simmonds, Department of English, University of Pittsburgh, Pittsburgh, Pa. 15260.

Milton Studies does not review books.

Within the United States, *Milton Studies* may be ordered from the University of Pittsburgh Press, Pittsburgh, Pa. 15260.

Overseas orders should be addressed to Baker & Taylor International, 1114 Avenue of the Americas, Fifth Floor, New York, N.Y. 10036-7794, U.S.A.

Library of Congress Catalog Card Number 69-12335

ISBN 0-8229-3625-9

US ISSN 0076-8820

Published by the University of Pittsburgh Press, Pittsburgh, Pa. 15260

Baker & Taylor International, London

Manufactured in the United States of America

CONTENTS

MILTON STUDIES

XXV

MILTON PLAYING WITH OVID

John K. Hale

T HEORIES OF LITERARY influence are distinguished by their central metaphors as much as by their methods and conclusions. Harold Bloom sees influence as "anxiety," Joseph Wittreich as "illumination," Thomas Greene as "dialogue."[1] Commentators record "borrowings" or "echoes" or "ingredients." Mention of "ingredients" calls up the self-conscious metaphor of "chutney-making" in Salman Rushdie's novel, *Midnight's Children*[2]: metaphors of influence, then, are not merely readers' abstractions but may be conscious, even deliberate, on the writer's part. By metaphors we find things out, and — very usefully — make words say more than one thing at once. Metaphors may produce our best insights, though equally they will limit what we can see and will cause characteristic errors of seeing.

The case of Milton has particular interest in this debate. He was exempted — specifically and exceptionally — from the "anxiety" model of influence by Harold Bloom (pp. 34, 50). Be that as it may, Milton remains a most literary and indebted poet, as the reader of secondary epic expects. So a different model of influence has been sought, with all the more energy of late because of Bloom's exempting. Thus Richard DuRocher considers the instance of Milton and Ovid.[3] He images as "admiring antagonism" the relation between the mature English poems of Milton and the Ovid which they use. This is a fine study, yet it sees only certain possibilities in a relationship that began early and altered much.

To extend our sense of the relationship I adopt a different heuristic metaphor and apply it to another group of Milton's poems. The metaphor is that of "playing," and the poems are his Latin elegiacs. Because there is general agreement that these poems are his most influenced ones, they tend to be dismissed as mere Ovidian exercises. DuRocher, for example, gives them five pages and sees them as simply "youthful imitation of Ovid according to contemporary grammar-school methods" (p. 38). I propose, instead, to view them in the light thrown by the metaphor of influence as playing a game, and thus to see, more clearly than existing models of influence allow, what is distinctive and worthwhile in the *Elegiae*.

To play a game, one first learns its rules. In the "game" of Ovidian elegiacs, rules abound and may at first constrict the player; but once learned, they cease to constrain and instead engender a style of playing (whether strenuous or casual, detached or passionate) that approaches self-expression. One finds value intrinsic in the playing, and one is partly changed by it. Some play the game with their usual personality, but with more of it. Some use attributes they seldom otherwise show: pacifists make aggressive snowballers, bank managers shine at I Doubt It. Some players suspend their habitual self or turn it upside down. To the spectator, accordingly, the player's playing can be revealing, startling, and — to the degree that we do not share the spirit and style of the game — puzzling.

When the young Milton plays with Ovid, we *shall* be puzzled if we do not enter into the game and its spirit. Conversely, if we do accept the premises and rules and valuation of this "game," we may understand the differentia of the young Milton; exploratory, eristic, and multiple; unaware before some playings what self will be found.

Our inquiry should pursue him in an analogous spirit, nimble and flexible. I take over ideas from the French theorist of human play, Rogier Caillois, who distinguishes four elements of playing: agon, or contest of skill; the opposite, alea, or chance; mimicry; ilinx, or a deliberately sought vertigo.[4] Of these, the paramount one is the contest with Ovid, by mimicry of him, though a kind of vertigo and some pursuit of luck come into local effects. But I take in other features of play: the putting-on of masks (drama is play); the analogy of playing music; the presence or absence of competitors in the playing; the analogues of arena and audience for the play. Let us in fact bring to these Latin poems the interconnected semantic field of the metaphor of "play"; for it cannot be accidental that the same connections turn up in many languages and cultures. Without listing all the suggestive senses, and without tediously applying them all, I believe the semantic field of "playing" — playing games, playing roles, playing music — wins the best understanding for these poems.

1

First, Milton had to learn how to play, how to obey the rules of prosody and of imitation. As to prosody, the sound patterns which give elegiac rhythm are quantitative, made up of long and short syllables, with accentual stress important only in a secondary or counterpointing way. From the practice of the classical exemplars, especially Ovid, but also Catullus, Propertius, Tibullus, and Martial, elaborate rules were codified.

Ordinary phonological rules determine vowels as long or short by nature (thus *patere*, to lie open, has a long *e* where *patera*, a saucer, has a short *e*). But in some circumstances prosodic rules may override phonology, and vowels become lengthened or shortened "by metrical position." So, in *longus miles* the *u* will lengthen because a pair of full consonants follows; and the final long *o* may at times shorten where only one consonant follows (speech-stress aiding in this case) — hence, a short *o* in *nec puto multum*.

The elegiac couplet consists of dactylic hexameter alternating with dactylic pentameter; schematically,

$$| -uu| -uu| - ||uu| -uu| -uu| - \!-$$
$$| -uu| -uu| - || -uu| -uu| - |.$$

In the hexameter, any of the first four feet may replace a dactyl with a spondee. (The fifth foot is always a dactyl, and the sixth always a spondee.) In practice, naturally, not all these options are taken up at once. The following line, for example, has spondees in its third and fourth feet:

Terra tri-| bus scopul-| is || vast-| um pro-| currit in | aequor.

The caesura is normally as shown, but may be varied with the pattern

$$| -uu| - ||uu| -uu| - ||uu| -uu| - \!- |$$

thus,

Inde toro || pater Aeneas || sic orsus ab alto.

As for the pentameter, it consists of a doubling of the dactylic colon ("limb") which precedes the caesura in the normal hexameter:

$$| -uu| -uu| - || -uu| -uu| - |.$$
Trinacris | a posi- | tu || nomen a- |depta lo-| ci.

As if to confirm the departure from hexameter after its caesura, no spondees whatever are admitted there; and Ovid restricted the options as to word-lengths in this final colon (it may finish only with a dissyllable).[5]

So much for the rules of the game: what, once learned, did they enable? Hexameters, like English blank verse, allow a long-striding march of thought. They make up into units of a period or verse paragraph, aided by the tendency to enjamb across line endings into verse paragraphs but equally by the many special mimetic effects which the choice between dactyl and spondee in the first four feet facilitates. Elegiac couplets, like the English heroic couplet, arise from the higher style of continuous hexameters by *refusing* the momentum of enjambment in favor of a neat two-line stanza. They pause more often and more symmetrically than hexameter. The effects thus allowed are again many: witty, epigrammatic, rhetorical-pleading, epistolary, abusive — in fact, most of the effects of the heroic couplet, with others.

To speak from personal experience, the rules of prosody are fewer and more bearable in hexameter than in elegiac composition. If, however, one begins the game young and spends many hours in school making them into second nature — as Milton did at St. Paul's School — then the rules solve one's problems of expression instead of being the problem.[6] The problems are solved above all by intuition based on thorough practice and continual reading — continual *hearing* — of Ovid.

2

Whereas the prosodic rules governed composition in countless small respects, the rules of imitation governed it equally at levels of greater generality. While acquiring the rudiments of prosody and then developing some powers of *copia* and *inventio*, one would copy the models slavishly. One might, for example, translate a Latin poem into English and then retranslate it, ideally, into its original words, thinking Ovid's words after him. But once sufficient fluency and correctness had been gained, the rules would be reversed: slavish fidelity, the saying of Ovidian things in no language and rhythm but those already used by Ovid, became a fault. One must now do something of one's own. The purpose of the game became to "wade further," to "stand on the shoulders of the giants"; not to replicate but to "digest" the work of the exemplar; to renew his life in the vitality of one's own work. (The case of translation was akin.) Imitation was, in one word, emulation.[7]

So far, then, the rules governing imitation accord with the nature of playing, since emulation is playing insofar as it is agon: a striving or wrestling with what is respected and admired. And Ovid held particular fascination for the emulative humanist for two reasons. His fluency was phenomenal, even among Romans: "I lisped in numbers, for the numbers came."[8] Yet his life had been trivial and lubricious, its end had been woeful and degrading. Could the humanist emulate the fluency? Could he live better without jeopardizing the art?

Nevertheless, emulation is not the entire explanation of Ovidian imitation as "playing." Obviously, the vying with Ovid among ancient exemplars could have been easily condemned as frivolous if not also corrupting — he is the last exemplar one would expect of that earnest epoch. Yet Ovid held his own, and with ease. That fact deserves explanation; and the best explanation is our metaphor of influence as play since it gives the sufficient *psychological* reason.

Ovid was fun. He told stories. He gave religious earnestness a holiday with his myths of glamorous remote beings in the throes of love. Love, sex, the battle of the sexes, this subject matter had to receive expression for students in some way. The tense prescriptiveness of the pulpit would not slake their curiosity, ignoring as it did their bodily changes along with the intractable facts of sexuality and women's difference. Ovid did not ignore these. He rejoiced in them and made a game of them; and all the more a game, because his treatment of sex shares central qualities of game-playing. It is reductive and hypothetical and intrinsic. We play *as if* nothing else mattered, knowing somewhere that that is not so.

And to the person who asks, "Why play games (or music, or roles in drama)?" the reply can only be, "Why ask such a silly question?" This is our human nature. And while it is receiving expression in a fiction — the fiction of poetry or that of game, and most of all in gamesome poetry — it does no one harm. It does oneself good. It gives the imagination a workout, hence teaches us empathy and empowers the self to "go walkabout." For the qualities required of good poetry, such playing offers a way to intensity, freedom, experiment, and variety. For the meeting of selfhood and poetry in composition, this playing with Ovid had a most liberating and educative impact upon Milton. It allowed an intensity of engagement with what was utterly different in tone and ethic. It encouraged him to try out varying forms of emulation; varying roles as elegiac poet; varying relationships with the classical master. This in turn satisfies me that "playing" is a good heuristic metaphor of literary influencing: it explains the relationship between apparent aliens as precisely one of the freedom to follow, revise, reject, extend, subvert, mock, follow *ad absurdum*.

I see a complete appropriateness to one another of Ovid's subjects and manner, the grammar school curriculum, Milton's emergent imagination, and the self-sufficiency of playing. Milton himself felt this, even in after years when the trivial pursuits of his youth had become puzzling to him: "the smooth Elegiack Poets, . . . Whom both for the pleasing sound of their numerous writing, which in imitation I found most easie; and most agreeable to natures part in me, and for their matter, which what it is, there be few who know not, I was so allur'd to read, that no recreation came to me better welcome. For . . . it was then those years in me which are excus'd."[9] To speak of "nature's part in me" may be coy or obscure, but it is right enough: to play and grow like this is natural.

3

Next, let us watch the young Milton learning the rules of the game in elegiacs composed about the age of fifteen.[10] Milton first wrote "Surge age surge leves iam convenit arcere somnos" ("Get up, come on, get up, now is the time to shed slumbers that are valueless"). But since *arcere* (infinitive from *second*-conjugation verb) scans with the middle syllable long, it infringes the requirement of a dactyl in the fifth foot of the hexameter. It is an interesting error for two reasons. Milton could have been expected to know how *arcere* must scan: was he concentrating on some other aspect of the game — as he might, since the opening of any poem is important? His solution, to substitute *excute*, changes an infinitive depending on *convenit* to an independent imperative, with the result that *convenit* is demoted, syntactically, into a parenthesis while the new verb continues a set of imperatives in the line. I conclude that the revised line is better, not merely in metrical correctness, but in sound and syntax. The expressive force resulting has more energy and agitation; and the eventual manuscript pointing — with five commas instead of the original three — makes this more noticeable. By this recovery, Milton indeed gives his poem an awakening, mimetic beginning.

Correctness did occupy him at this time. In bringing back the first two lines as the close of his poem, he made the same change again. He also changed *somnum* in line 15 to the *somnos* needed for agreement with *languentes* preceding. And even so, blemishes remain. It is not skillful to end three hexameters out of ten with the same word, *somnos*. Nor is it clear why *segnes* in line 13 should be plural, except that the expected singular would not have produced the required spondee: "Segnes invenias molli vix talia lecto" ("You sluggards, you would hardly find such things by staying in your soft bed"). He is heeding the rules to excess: he depends too much on them.

Similar overdependence is detected in the adjective-noun combinations. Overdependence should not be inferred simply from their number, twenty-two in the twenty lines, for that accords with the preferences of Latin verse and of Ovid's elegiacs, but from the fact that (as Douglas Bush notes) seventeen of the combinations are found in the verse writer's manual, the *Epithetorum Epitome* of Ravisius Textor.[11] Whether or not Milton took them thence, they occur in Textor and in this poem because they occur in Ovid and the ancients, and their re-use is formulaic and dependent.

Should we in fact conclude that the topic is to blame, and recognize that only limited music can be found in five-finger exercises? The theme is a hoary old one, coming immediately to Milton from Lily's *Grammar:*

Mane citus lectum fuge comes thence, to appear as the title of Milton's prose theme done at the same time as these elegiacs.[12] Nor is the message adjusted well to the model, Ovid: Ovid's lovers are more likely to linger in bed. All that the proverbial topic conjoined with the elegiac medium offered to Milton was a speech situation and the opportunity for some exempla and maxims: he had not enough to work on, because not enough to play with, in the desired spirit of strenuous emulation.

4

The next elegiacs to be considered, *Elegia Prima,* are transitional again, but to different effect; and these, as opposed to the preceding ones, Milton preserved for publication. The poem is not a commissioned exercise but a voluntary self-expression — a letter to his friend Diodati, the earliest of several such letters — and the rules of elegiac are not so much observed as transcended. When I checked for prosodic inaccuracy or infelicity, I found nothing of significance. But I had to *make* myself check up; one does not instinctively feel any need to, here.[13] The verses move with sureness and create a trusting attention in the reader. To put it more relevantly, there is too much else happening, and one must keep up with the play.

The poem has been well termed a "cross-comparison" of Ovid's literal and hated exile with Milton's metaphorical and delightful "exile" from university.[14] This perception gives us the clue to its whole emulation. Milton tends to replace Ovid's levity with Christian or humanist gravity. But here — because Ovid took his own exile with unprecedented gravity (to the degree that his writing stance altered forever in the poems of exile) — for that very reason Milton does the opposite. He moves Ovid from gravity to levity. This is the key to the poem's address to its subject, and to its entire strategy of *aemulatio.*

Let us examine some small-scale acts of emulation, since out of these grows the single larger emulation; and in these we can see more exactly how Milton plays and contends with his exemplar. Ovid had declared that Rome has as many nubile girls as the sky has stars: "Quot caelum stellas tot habet tua Roma puellas" — so let the man who is being addressed get amongst them, let him give chase![15] Milton echoes the passage, in idea rather than language:

> Non tibi tot caelo scintillant astra sereno
>> Endymioneae turba ministra deae
> Quot tibi conspicuae formaque auroque puellae
>> Per medias radiant turba videnda vias.

Elegia Prima, 77–80

["There are not as many stars glinting in the calm sky, the crowd of attendants on Endymion's goddess, as the beautiful gold-adorned girls who crowd radiantly through the middle of London, most worthy to be seen."]

He has expanded the idea and slowed it down. And why not? It is no longer an inciting to sexual conquest which happens to be in Rome, but a praise of the city, London, for the female beauty within its walls. This slower pace of thought suits the reading of the visual-mythological pageant. The comparison has shifted in a further way, from the girls' numbers (Ovid's sole point) to their brightness and beauty, joined in the glimpse of deity; something of the vehicle (*deae*) is absorbed into the tenor. We need not judge this fuller version better than Ovid's, which one might well prefer for swiftness and prodigality of invention; but we do need to note how Milton composes — by absorbing Ovid, then imitating, matching, and overgoing (or overdoing) him. He does it well, assimilating an erotic suasion into a patriotic panegyric, the city and its beauties enhancing one another. Moreover, it is only through Ovid's presence that we know London pleased Milton because he could see pretty girls there: a clear case of the need of imitation releasing sides of his personality and taste which seldom received expression elsewhere.

Thus the contest with Ovid explains what Milton is seeking. Play is discovery for him. It is the beginning of self-discovery. And the reader can understand these things only by empathy with the process. For us, as for him, the metaphor of playing and contesting is heuristic and crucial.

5

A veritable crux will prove this claim, the notorious final line of the elegiac poem on the death of the Bishop of Winchester (Lancelot Andrewes): "Talia contingant somnia saepe mihi" (Elegia III, 68). "May I often have such dreams as this!" means in context that he has been rapt into a vision of heaven by seeing the good bishop there among the saints of the new Jerusalem. But the allusion is to Ovid's line, "Proveniant medii sic mihi saepe dies" ("May many such mid-days come my way!"), where he exults over a lusty midday bedroom encounter. Do we find this audacious, absurd, doctrinaire, or what?

In the first place, the whole poem — not simply its close — depends on erotic passages of Ovid for turns of phrase. The poet's serious and ultimately visionary sleep is systematically dependent on Ovid for diction concerned with bed, sleep, clothes, gems, gold, wings of angels as celebrants of love, and so on. Ovid provides elegiac diction for the vision of heavenly love because he is the supreme celebrant of erotic love: the two loves, qua love, are alike (just as iconographically the cherubs attending in naked sportive innocence upon heavenly love became cupidinized in the Renaissance). A similar connection is made at the close of the *Epitaphium Damonis*. If we so lack the taste for this sort of thing that we find it "startling" or "audacious," we must recover the humanist sense that *amor*, whether sacred or profane, was a continuum. To establish the continuity was a laudable enterprise, suitable and distinctive to the humanist as inheritor of both Ovid and the Bible — what only he could do, and could do best.

But a second explanation comes nearer to our specific concern with the element of playing in elegiac. The passage about Corinna in her delightful midday deshabille was a favorite with the Elizabethans. Marlowe translated it as "Corinnae Concubitus" (and Milton must have read that version). It even entered a pop song, "While sweet Bessy sleeping lay": this hinges on the same final point ("And since this trance begun / She sleeps *every* afternoon"). Consequently, though modern critics are not wrong to notice the allusion to Ovid and to wonder about it, they should credit the poet with knowing what they know themselves since the elegy is often and willingly read by boys at school. And what then is Milton doing with it? The *aemulatio* is of that frequent kind which transposes Ovid into an opposite mood and meaning. Just as the topos of exile was controverted into levity, so this lewd levity is claimed for the gravity of epitaph. From this viewpoint of playing and contest it is what we should expect.

This is not altogether to reject Bush's temperate view, that "The pleasure of recognizing an ancient jewel in a new setting is sometimes attended by something of a shock because of the radical and even violent change it has undergone."[16] But I suggest that the poet is here taking up a challenge to his Christian humanism that lies implicit in the imitating of Ovid, the thoroughly secular pagan. Boldness might therefore be thought a natural option, causing shock because using it.

The attempt can be seen in other details, and in the shape of the whole poem. First, a detail: the "winged squadrons" (*aligerae . . . turmae*, Elegia III, 65) touch their harps in music-making for the bishop's soul once it has been welcomed into the company of heaven; the word for the harps is the unusual *nablia*. It occurs in Ovid, but is commoner in (Christian) neo-Latin; it actually comes from Hebrew.[17] Seizing on one of rather few loan words from Hebrew in Latin — few, since in the Roman stereotype the Jews were a despised and "atheistic" race — Milton seizes a fine opportunity. Even Ovid made some contact — verbal and imaginative, though inadvertent — with the religion of Yahweh. Let this, then, make part of his emulation by appropriation, the appropriating of Ovid to a religious purpose.

Such appropriation is the key to the whole poem, and to other poems (*Elegia Quarta*, for one). The opening hinges on a desolate vision, just as the end is a beatific one. A dismal procession of the great and good dead is seen; a march-past of the victims of Libitina: the ancient Italian goddess of corpses here symbolizes the pagan despair of any worthwhile afterlife. She expresses the bankruptcy (as Christendom saw the matter) of paganism, "without God in the world." But if so, the ending brings even Ovid, Ovid in his lewdness, into the countervailing vision. This makes the transition, from forlorn death-absorbedness into the hope of the life of the Resurrection, as extreme and forceful as possible. Once again, when one sees the poem as an *aemulatio* in these terms, one sees why it is as it is. This is at least a precondition, if not a fulfillment, of the critical endeavor with regard to these poems.

6

Is Milton, indeed, sometimes so involved in the "playing" with Ovid that he is pushing its limits? Does he test how much of Ovid can be annexed and reclaimed? Does he therefore appropriate him at his most outrageous? The example of *Elegia Quinta* inclines me to think so, once again, both in the large terms of its mood and meaning and in its virtuoso detail. We can view the former in the latter.

The poem celebrates nature naturing, in joyous — erotic — detail:

"Te manet Aeolides viridi venator in herba
        Surge tuos ignes altus Hymettus habet."
Flava verecundo dea crimen in ore fatetur
        Et matutinos ocyus urget equos.   (51–54)

["The Aeolid hunter awaits you on the green grass: get up! Lofty Hymettus has your flame waiting. The blonde goddess shows on her shamed face that she admits guilt, and presses her horses of the morning to go more quickly."]

The shepherd calls on Aurora, the personified dawn goddess, to leave her aged husband Tithonus and hurry to her human lover, Cephalus. Her "shame" (*verecundo*) is not for this extramatrimonial intercourse, but for being slow to complete it. Although Milton is thwarting a conventional moral expectation to fulfill a humanist decorum, is he not doing it extravagantly? He goes on:

Exuit invisam Tellus rediviva senectam
        Et cupit amplexus Phoebe subire tuos
Et cupit et digna est quid enim formosius illa
        Pandit ut omniferos luxuriosa sinus.   (55–58)

["Earth comes alive again, strips off her loathed senescence, and yearns to undergo your embraces, Phoebus. Yes, she yearns for them, and deserves them; for she is surpassingly lovely as she sensually bares her fertile bosom."]

He is being explicit in a visual way, for she desires to be underneath him (*subire*) as he embraces her,[18] and she "sensually exposes her fertile breasts" to him — these being the loveliest features of her beauty (line 57 leads into mention of them). The sensuality is nature's, hence natural, but is presented so anthropomorphically that the naturalness seems to extend to the natural in man. Moreover, these vernal impulses have been connected in advance to the stirrings of new life in the poet himself (5–24). Particularly if the new imaginative life is that realized in the present poem, he is doubly committed to the sensual inspiration.

Paganism is unwavering in this poem. It even becomes more explicit toward the close when he imagines both local and general polytheism: "Dii quoque non dubitant caelo praeponere sylvas / Et sua quisque sibi numina lucus habet (131–32) ("The gods, too, do not hesitate to prefer the woods to heaven, every grove possesses its own deities"). And, with another of the ecstatic repetitions which are a feature of the elegy, he turns statement into prayer: "Et sua quisque diu sibi numina lucus habeto / Nec vos arborea dii precor ite domo" (133–34) ("And long may every grove possess its own deities. You gods, I pray you to stay in your woody homes"). The sense of pursuing a hypothesis and its decorum to the utmost is of the essence of the poem and its conviction. And it is a pagan conviction. This time, he plays the game *within* the Ovidian postulates.

Playing with Ovid has here carried Milton away, carried him outside his previous and usual range. Nothing but the playing with Ovid could have produced this masterly poem.

7

Not the most masterly thing in the poem, but its most fascinating instance of emulative playing, occurs where Milton envisages the satyrs appearing: "Sylvanusque sua cyparissi fronde revinctus / Semicaperque deus semideusque caper" (121–22) ("And garlanded with leaves of cypress Sylvanus, the god who is half-goat, the goat who is half-god"). Ovid has the line (describing the Minotaur), "Semibovemque virum semivirumque bovem" ("the man who is half-ox, the ox who is half-man"). His friends objected to this line: it must have seemed in some way excessive to them; yet not to Ovid himself.[19] The excess would surely be the otiosity in the sense, the too-evident pursuit of balance and pattern.

The defense would be partly the same as the critique: the symmetries of sound and sense and rhythm were irresistible—especially in that by their very transparency and redundancy of sense they brought out the inner shape of the beloved pentameter, the line in its pure entelechy. Later poets thought so too. (Sannazaro has Milton's line, but in reverse order.[20]) Our question is why Milton should imitate and vie with the notorious line *just here*.

Several considerations suggest themselves, all arising from our metaphor of "playing" with Ovid. First, whereas Ovid's description of the Minotaur was an incidental self-indulgence, Milton's description suits Sylvanus, and the theme of the poem, and the particular point which the argument is reaching. In satyrs and Sylvanus, goat and god have mingled: the interlacing of *deus* and *caper*, therefore, mimics that nature. The poem concerns interpenetration, of human and divine, cosmic and earthly: so if gods and men cohabit and gods and earth (51–54, above), why not gods and animals?—and why not mimic this, by a dance of vocabulary with syntax and meter? Finally, the poem is at this point intensifying. The picture of evening (*crepuscula surgunt*, 119) realizes the return of an even older world—the gods of place, hidden from men even in the days of the sway of the Olympians. A special effect of language is apt here, for it draws attention by subtler, stylistic means to the rarity of the theophany.

Whatever may be the case elsewhere, then, the form which the playing takes in this poem is that of going to extremes. Nothing succeeds like excess.

8

From this perspective we see that Milton has varied the manner and purpose of his playing with Ovid. What else does he do?

In *Elegia Quarta* he takes another leaf out of Ovid's book as he personifies the letter he is sending to a friend overseas. When it transpires that the friend is "banished" to Hamburg for religious causes, the poem moves dexterously into a second Ovidian motif, that of exile. That motif is repeated from *Elegia Prima*, of course, but in a fresh way, since the letter to Diodati and Ovid's letters had been sent *from* exile. Then the poem changes gear again: from Ovid copied then Ovid reversed to Ovid transcended as the thought moves (by way of the religious cause of the exile, and resultant danger to Young in Hamburg from the Thirty Years War) to much graver issues. Very gradually, without ceasing to use Ovid's language and to inhabit Ovid's world of *amicitia*, the poem expands its range of spiritual reference to the struggles within England, the cruel *patria* (87), then wider still to the wars of religion sweeping the continent. These, moreover, are likened to the life-and-death struggles within ancient Israel and in the life of Jesus and the Church. All is done without lapse of decorum, for the verse adjusts its intensity to each transition in the thought. It is a fine, strong poem, all the more so through starting from Ovid and keeping in contact with him. The poem gravitates into sonorities alien to Ovid, and all the more impressive for that since it stays true (like a dutiful convert) to its pagan as much as to its Christian parent. By the end, the effect is not exactly playful: more like a wrestling bout.

Elegia Sexta shows something of the same thing, also something of the self-referential quality of *Elegia Quinta*. (It was singled out for praise by E. K. Rand in his excellent essay, "Milton in Rustication."[21]) Here again is a picture of friendship, with something Roman — perhaps Horatian, says Rand — about it. Here again is a powerful transition, power *from* transition, between the pagan pleasures of life on earth and the poet's imaginative self-discovery. Only the latter is not now seen in Ovidian or even Roman terms, but in those of an epic asceticism, something more like the self-image of bard as priest found in Homer and Pindar. Greek enters Milton's Latin much more in this elegy than in any before it. And (as befits the language of the New Testament), Greek is felt in a context of writing about the birth of Christ: the poem's climax is the news that Milton has just finished the Nativity ode (81–88).

Each elegy is a new playing, a new exploration of this ancient and versatile medium. The form and momentum of each are varied. Here, the ending opens outward, into a poem in another language, expressing a different self. Languages cohabit in this poem, singularly.

Elegia Septima, last of the numbered series though not necessarily the last written,[22] is in some respects most Ovidian of all. Its subject is the poet's defiance of Cupid, followed by Cupid's revenge: the poet falls in love, all the more helplessly because he omits to accost the fair lady and she passes on out of his sight and his ken. Since the story depends entirely on a personified Cupid and his habits with arrows, one could say it is just like Ovid, yet not Ovid alone, since of course the sonnet tradition is full of such conceits. And the story is not altogether like Ovid, in that Ovid would not have had his lover give up the chase so early and pusillanimously.

A note of reservation has appeared. This poem is a playing which includes the element of limitation, of mere play — play which serves a contest of manner only, and does not serve emulation since the subject is even smaller than Ovid's. It is playing around. And yet that is Milton's point, too. He ends this poem with a recantation or palinode:

Haec ego mente olim laeva studioque supino
Nequitiae posui vana trophaea meae
Scilicet abreptum sic me malus impulit error
Indocilisque aetas prava magistra fuit
Donec Socraticos umbrosa Academia rivos
Praebuit.[23]

["In time past, with perverse mind and supine zeal, I set up these verses as the vain trophies of my frivolous contesting. Obviously error and unsoundness led me astray then and impelled me, my stubborn youth was a bad teacher, until the shady Academy offered me Socratic streams to drink."]

This recantation is itself Ovidian, since Ovid has many such "codas," passages in elegiac meter but of the length of epigram which round off and revise or recant the longer elegiac poem preceding.[24] I suggest that the key to *Elegia Septima* and the coda is to take them together and read them as jointly another taking of Ovid to extremes. On this occasion the game is to take him to two successive opposite extremes: an extreme of erotic frivolity (lighter and more mannerist even than Ovid), then an extreme of recantation (more severe and final than Ovid's are). My new suggestion is to see the poem as composed in two parts, of which the second is designed to answer the first but contrariwise the first is made such as to earn rejection from the second. The "diptych" is another playing with the Ovidian repertoire of possibility.

9

The poem makes a more general point, too. What most resembles Ovid in it is a certain mannerism, the prominence and importance of manner as distinct from thought. It shows a mannerist sense of style and what style is for: not for larger ends, but for leisurely attention to detail, for rhetoric of defiance and plaining. Because the manner is in higher relief and more emphatic than in other *Elegiae*, the manner *is* the subject, and as a result, peculiarly like Ovid himself.

It is time to generalize how elegiac is composed, heard, and read. Where *aemulatio* is concerned, does the whole effect or the local effect matter more? "Matter" to the imitator first, then to the reader? The answer to this question of principle will not be identical for all modes of poetry. For epic, and for high styles in general, the effect of the whole matters more than that of any part. For epigram, the question barely arises: the conciseness ensures that part and whole are synonymous, a single act of attention by the reader. For Ovidian elegiac, though, which is a somewhat extended mode yet falls far short of epic amplitude, the preceding discussion has confirmed my intuition: the moment-by-moment reading experience tends to outweigh the experience of the whole. And exactly this is the nature of playing. Normal people play a game for the sake of the moment-by-moment enjoyment of the playing itself, not out of a passion for winning (or why would losers go on playing?). Musicians play for the joy of the playing, the entering into pure relations between people and sound and silence. In the self-sufficiency of the moments occurs the joy and freedom of the playing. As in other forms of playing, so in the playing with Ovid's elegiac — the choice of mode and model sanctioning it.

Milton is thus vying with Ovid in pursuit of the inner nature of the medium. The playing is teleological: it seeks to give fullest possible actualization to the nature of the given material. Style, the happy conjoining in elegiac of topic with words and of both with the tight little stanza form, matters supremely. Style is in high relief: it is almost the subject itself. The pleasures of wrestling with the stringent demands of the form are more self-sufficient in this mode than in most others.

And as elegiacs are written, so should they be read. For the reader the moment-to-moment pleasures are the greatest: they approach self-sufficiency. I mean such pleasures as seeing the problem neatly solved — solved again and again, solved in varying ways, solved in defiance of the laws of probability (this mode of poetry, after Ovid had tightened its rules still further, should have been impossible). To put it another way, whereas in epic we read for story and profound meaning, or in tragedy for the complex pleasure of pity and fear held in balance, in elegiac we read for straightforward pleasures like sprightly puzzle-solving and self-renewing inventive play. Though the medium can give more than this, and Milton sometimes makes it do that, he knows that it does not have to do so. He knows that giving this "more" is itself part of the self-renewal of play.

Consequently, the last elegy proves climactic after all. It is the most self-displaying of the emulations of Ovid (and goes on displaying its emulation by its palinode). In the main poem he writes "teleologically," in a manner as Ovidian as he then knew how (being still young in years and younger in the ways of men with women). In the recantation he says his "Goodbye to all that." In the two together, culminating the series of seven elegiac performances, he says, "Vos plaudite." And because the moment-by-moment pleasure has been intense and invigorating, and has also preponderated over the effects of whole poems and worries about moral issues, we do applaud. He has played well.

University of Otago

NOTES

1. Harold Bloom, *The Anxiety of Influence: A Theory of Poetry* (New York, 1973); Joseph Anthony Wittreich, Jr., *Angel of Apocalypse: Blake's Idea of Milton* (Madison, Wis., 1975); and Thomas M. Greene, *The Light in Troy: Imitation and Discovery in Renaissance Poetry* (New Haven, Conn., 1982).

2. Salman Rushdie, *Midnight's Children* (London, 1981). See, for example, his last few pages on the "chutnification of history."

3. Richard J. DuRocher, *Milton and Ovid* (Ithaca, N.Y., 1985).

4. Rogier Caillois, *Les jeux et les hommes* (Paris, 1967). The first element is stressed throughout this paper. The second, alea, contributes little. The third, mimicry, is a constant in that Ovid is the object of a sort of mimicry throughout the *Elegiae*. Ilinx, the enjoyment of deliberately sought vertigo or the defiance of it, enters in whenever the mimicry leads Milton and his reader into unorthodox contemplations — as often happens, and because of Ovid.

5. See L. P. Wilkinson, *Golden Latin Artistry* (Cambridge, 1963), pp. 133–34.

6. See D. L. Clark, *John Milton at St. Paul's School* (New York, 1948).

7. Among a copious literature, I have used especially C. T. Prouty, *The Sources of "Much Ado about Nothing"* (New Haven, Conn., 1950) for its lucid statement of the basic principle of "wading further," as enunciated by the Elizabethans; and the recent study by G. W. Pigman III, "Versions of Imitation in the Renaissance," *Renaissance Quarterly* XXX, no. 1 (1980), 1–32, most valuable for its recognition of differing, equally authoritative models of imitation. DuRocher, *Milton and Ovid*, pp. 42–43, is a succinct summary of the essentials.

8. "Sponte sua carmen numeros veniebat ad aptos / Et quod temptabam dicere versus erat" (*Tristia* IV, x, 25–26).

9. Milton is writing in 1642, *An Apology Against a Pamphlet Called a Modest Confutation of the Animadversions upon the Remonstrant Against Smectymnuus*, in *Complete Prose Works of John Milton*, 8 vols., ed. Don M. Wolfe et al. (New Haven, 1953–82) vol. I, p. 889.

10. Dating discussed by A. J. Horwood introducing *A Common-place Book of John Milton* for the Camden Society (1877); Clark, *Milton at St. Paul's*, pp. 178–80, 230–37; and commentators, for once unanimously. The verses were found with other verses and prose all on the one theme — the need to rise early — in the same box of papers as the Commonplace Book. From the evidence of the St. Paul's curriculum, and internal evidence such as handwriting and the inexpertness of some Greek quoted in the theme, it is agreed that the three works are school exercises of Milton's done at the age of fifteen or sixteen and in the last year or two of school. A similar conclusion can be reached from our present study of how he plays the game of elegiacs, whether we look for infractions of the rules of quantity or at the wider powers of invention and the quality of the emulation.

11. See the introduction to *The Latin and Greek Poems*, vol. I of *A Variorum Commentary on the Poems of John Milton*, ed. Douglas Bush (New York, 1970), p. 11and n. 8.

12. *The Latin and Greek Poems*, p. 333n1.

13. A checking of the commentaries, some of which delight to fault Milton's prosody, confirms his advance in correctness in Elegia Prima.

14. R. W. Condee, "Ovid's Exile and Milton's Rustication," *PQ* XXXVII (1958), 498–502.

15. See *Ars Amatoria*, I, 59.

16. See Bush, introduction to *The Latin and Greek Poems*, p. 14. A suggestion simi-

lar to mine is made by Gordon Campbell, "Imitation in *Epitaphium Damonis*," in *Milton Studies*, vol. XIX, ed. James D. Simmonds (Pittsburgh, 1983), p. 169.

17. See Amos vi, 5, Psalm xxxiii, 2, 1 Kings x, 12.

18. Under *subire* (1.d), the *Oxford Latin Dictionary* gives "to go under (so as to submit to the action of)." Though apparently not used by classical Latin in an erotic application, the sense fits the *amplexus* of Phoebus in the text perfectly.

19. Seneca, *Controversiae* (II, ii, 12), tells the story. Ovid was asked by his friends to delete three lines from his poems, lines which they will appoint. He agrees, provided he may first appoint three lines which are not to be deleted. They turn out to be thinking of the same three lines, of which the one about the Minotaur is one.

20. Bush, *Commentary*, p. 109, citing similar attempts with other compounds to cap Ovid's notorious line.

21. Edward K. Rand, "Milton in Rustication," *SP* XIX (1922), 109–35.

22. See, e.g., *Milton: The Complete Shorter Poems*, ed. John Carey (London, 1984), p. 69.

23. Some scholars think the palinode repudiates the erotic or frivolous parts of Elegies I and V as well as just the poem it follows. This seems a clumsy and unlikely hypothesis to me, and unlike Ovid's own practice (see next note).

24. Douglas Parker, "The Ovidian Coda," *Arion* VIII (1969), 80–97. See p. 96, "The coda . . . in creating a context for the work . . . yields a detachment" by which "the ceaseless competence of the verse . . . contrasts with the disorder of the situations it presents."

SALVATION HISTORY, POETIC FORM, AND THE LOGIC OF TIME IN MILTON'S NATIVITY ODE

M. J. Doherty

I

THE POETIC LOGIC of Milton's handling of time in the Nativity ode has presented a critical problem since the eighteenth century.[1] The reader's rhetorical experience of the duration of the ode — the time it takes to announce, to request, and to fulfill the request for a devout Christmas hymn — is an experience of poetic order. Milton, however, has framed such coherence in complex references to the twelve days of Christmas, 25 December through 6 January — the "month" and "happy morn" of the Nativity, the "Now" in which the Muse presents a hymn of welcome, the moment of Epiphany when the star "Hath fixt her polisht Car" and brought the wise men to Bethlehem — and with multiple allusions to various events in salvation history, events which are commemorated typologically in worship. The Christmas-Epiphany time frame of the ode should be obvious to any reader familiar with the scriptural readings used in the liturgy in that season of the church year.[2] If the young Milton was already critical of Anglican ecclesiology and liturgical practice, the use to which he puts temporal liturgical reference in his poem on the Incarnation of the Son of God nevertheless points to his scriptural interest in the significance of the Epiphany. The feast of the revelation to the Gentiles is an historical event that Milton sees as still having effect in the conversion of contemporary England to Protestantism.[3] Milton has further complicated the logic of time in the ode by certain internal devices of expression, as readers have often noted: ungrammatical shifts of verb tense, anachronistic juxtapositions of scriptural events, use of the time-eternity paradox. The internal complexity of the poem has, therefore, made critical formulation of its unity difficult. Even the best essays on the structural disposition of the ode in five parts, that is, the essays of Barker and Rajan, convey a sense of dissatisfaction with the craft of the young Milton and with scholarly perceptions of the architectonic whole of the poem; moreover, these essays do not satisfactorily address the textual evidence of Milton's use of certain rhetorical figures to shape

21

the ode.[4] Bernard S. Adams, on the other hand, in his fine study of Milton's "Ramist invention" and the way contrastive images negate time and develop the "atmosphere" of timelessness, does consider Milton's dialectical invention of *discordia concors* in the ode, but resorts to a simple division of the hymn proper into two sections and does not inquire into the structural implications of Milton's logic of time.[5]

This essay proposes a new view of the text, context, and disposition of the ode. A truer evaluation of the verbal "architecture" of the poem — the relation of the parts to the whole in its rhetorical disposition and the significance of Milton's particular kind of eloquence in relation to his invention — follows from critical awareness of the intellectual and moral interests of Milton the student-poet. In the same way, as Rosemond Tuve once suggested, the ode ought to be read as a liturgical encomium, a welcoming act of worship for the infant God, a *hymn* emerging from the devout character of the young poet. In the language and form of the Nativity ode one perceives not only the university man but also, in retrospect, Milton the boy of Saint Paul's School where students were trained in a humanist program of both learning and piety and, in prospect, Milton the mature Puritan scholar who would envision salvation history in new ways.[6] The university man was literally at home and familiar with the militant singing of "Englished" psalms that promoted a nationalistic political interpretation of the traditional Christ/David/Israel typology.[7] Likewise, the Christian humanist schoolboy had his literary imagination trained by the Alexander Gills, father and son, to appreciate the value of an *ars poetica Christiana* in which Apollo and the muses were rejected as "deaf nobodies" compared to a Christian poet's imitative singing of the Word.[8] The psalm used in the communion service of Epiphany, the feast that marks the journey of the wise men to Bethlehem and the revelation of Christ to the nations, asks the worshipper to "Sing unto the Lord a newe Song" and to "bring an offring," to enter into the courts of the great Lord in comparison to whom "all the gods of the peoples are idoles"; so Milton composed a new poetic hymn for the infant Son, incarnated as the New Song, who drives out the old oracles and idols of the classical world — types of contemporary religious abuse for Milton, especially Roman Catholic ones — and offers his poem as a "present" to the infant God.[9] But the ode also looks forward to the learned Milton of political tracts and encyclopedic poems, who sought in salvation history the kind of wisdom that could transform the knowledge of the liberal arts into the spiritual value of a truly free mind. For all of these reasons, a primary consideration for the reader-critic of the Nativity ode may be the student Milton's fascination with the nature, organization, and scope of the arts and sciences. The young Milton's effort to dominate metaphysics, logic, ethics, politics, and science through expressive language defined for him a poetic master craftsmanship that could serve, in turn, a unifying theological end.[10]

The argument of this essay observes such a consideration. The young Milton poetically organized his ode as a definition of time and history according to various types of knowledge, including the sacred knowledge of salvation expressed historically in the songs and fables of Holy Scripture. Time is defined by grammar, by logic, by rhetoric; time is defined by astronomy, by music, by arithmetic and geometry; time is defined by mythology, by scriptural typology, and by the practices of religious devotion. The formal unity of the poem depends on the complex set of correspondences that Milton invents among these various definitions based on various types of knowledge. Time itself, in short, is the principle of master craftsmanship showing the architectonic unity that Milton devised for his poem as the union of trivial and quadrivial forms; and such time is fundamentally the symbolic representation of salvation history in both the liturgical design of the church calendar and also the poetic arrangement of rhetorical figures. The use of a variety of definitions for the same idea is, of course, a standard means of amplification in rhetoric; such accumulation of proofs and arguments from the commonplaces gives the speaker a way to generate *copia* while exhibiting eloquence to good, forceful purpose, as Erasmus had noted.[11] What is unusual about Milton's rhetorical variations on the nature of time, however, is that his principle of poetic invention reflects also a visionary principle of philosophical unity among the arts and sciences.[12]

In the following pages I shall particularly discuss Milton's analogical adaptations of quadrivial knowledge — arithmetic, music, geometry, and astronomy — to the supreme logic of salvation history through his manipulation of the liturgical calendar of the church year, a calendar traditionally worked out from year to year by simple astronomical calculations. As a poet, Milton simultaneously dovetails that scientific knowledge with a rhetorical patterning of the word of God that surpasses trivial knowledge — grammar, logic, and rhetoric — as classically conceived. This rhetorical patterning confirms the analysis of the ode into five parts, but not in the measure that readers have so far perceived. Milton's disposition of the ode is as exact as the division of the weeks of the liturgical seasons of the church year, 1629–30, in which the ode was written; similarly, Milton's rhetorical patterns effect the persuasive composition of a solemn musical strain while confirming the analysis of the ode into the specific disposition of stanzaic sections that the calendar of 1629–30 marks off. The poem formally addresses exactly its own moment in history, its present composition as an English poet's musical offering to the infant God and for an English nation still learning to hear revelation. *This* is the month in which the Son brings redemption from above, "For so the holy sages once did sing" (1–5).

II

Milton's poetic transformation of liturgical time into private, devotional time in the Nativity ode is the means by which he integrates his knowledge of the quadrivial sciences and shapes the proportions of the poem. Proportion — or relation, correspondence — is a form of analogy, and Milton's use of quadrivial knowledge serves his creation of an elaborate analogy less as a species of verbal "building" than as a form of musical thought.[13] The first three sources of his sense of the proportions of time in arithmetic, music, and geometry are certain parallels: (1) the broad flow of salvation history as a progression, a numerical or chronological sequence of events as recorded in the stories and prophecies of Scripture; (2) the specific lessons and psalms assigned liturgically to the services of the Christmas season as the ongoing holy song in which the significance of the birth of Christ is repeatedly communicated; and (3) the power of typology "optically," that is, by the laws of geometry used visually, to telescope the twelve days of Christmas into one day of the Incarnation, and one day into all of history, and all of history into the everlasting moment of eternity, just as the Word who is light enters all of history at once and just as "holy Song" can "enwrap" the fancy, making time "run back, and fetch the age of gold" (135). The fourth and formally determining proportion draws on the laws of astronomy to establish the exact measure of the church year, which always begins with four weeks of Advent textually commemorating Old Testament prophecy, and proceeds through the seasons of Christmas, Lent, and Easter, which observe the milestones of the life of Jesus, and moves to Sundays after Trinity to denote the believer's progress in the imitation of Christ toward the end of time and Last Judgment. In 1629–30, the seasons of Christmas, Lent, and Easter contained eight, ten, and eight weeks respectively, and the major division of the year, First Advent, 29 November 1629, through Trinity, 23 May 1630, and First Trinity, 30 May 1630, through the twenty-sixth Sunday after Trinity, 21 November 1630, was an even split of twenty-six Sundays each.[14] The hymn proper follows the eight, ten, eight divisions and observes the even split.

The first three proportions — salvation history, scriptural readings of the ecclesial season, and typological interpretation — have become criti-

cal commonplaces in the study of Milton's poetry, in this case, the ode.
Milton's ungrammatical mingling of verb tenses, or the rhetorical figure
of *solescismus* — "And then at last our bliss / Full and perfect is, / But
now begins" (165-67) — has been understood to disrupt rules of sequentiality in order to illustrate the relationship of time to eternity, for instance. Breaking the rules of chronology conveyed by verb tense makes
poetic sense in a poem that expresses the inexpressible mystery of the Incarnation, or divine intervention in human history. Likewise, salvation
history, the chronological record of God's intervention in human history,
provides the Christian imagination with an elaborate temporal metaphor, with an understanding of the counting of the ages as itself a type
of poem.[15] The metaphor allows a poet like Milton — and every believer —
to celebrate the idea, for example, that Christ came once in the historical past, that he comes again and again in the present of one's own devotion, and that he will come again in the fullness of time before the Last
Judgment. In the ode, when readers who are aware of this metaphoric
arithmetic of the numbers of the years see "Smiling Infancy" and the "bitter cross" side by side in lines 152 and 153, apparently out of chronological sequence, and with "the trump of doom" (156) thundering close by,
they have the authority of Saint Augustine and of centuries of biblical
exegesis to interpret Milton's poetic synthesis: the elevation of all of time
to the perspective of eternity in Christ's act of atonement.[16] At the same
time, Milton starts the hymn proper with clear references to the scriptural ordering of time, that is, to Genesis. "It was the Winter wild" in
which Nature, as fallen as Eve, has doffed her "gaudy trim" to stand
in "naked shame" (stanzas 1-2); winter, or the seasons' difference, as
Shakespeare's Duke Senior observed in *As You Like It*, is the "penalty
of Adam." Almost immediately, however, Peace begins gently to slide
down through the spheres, "meek-ey'd," "with Olive green," "with Turtle
wing," like Noah's dove (stanza 3). As distinctly, the next stanzas re-
capitulate the age of prophets and kings (stanza 4) and lead to Milton's
amplification of the peace of Augustus (stanzas 5-7), which the eighth
stanza, the image of the shepherds at Bethlehem, punctuates. Such historical "arithmetic" as Milton's handling of salvation history from Eden
to Bethlehem is actually a rhetorical figure shaping the first section of
the hymn. Inscribing the descent of Peace, the first eight stanzas com-
prise a *chronographia*, the vivid representation of a time.[17]

Milton's sense of number and order in the course of salvation history reaches, finally, the status of music, the science of moving number
that even borrows its terminology from the trivial arts.[18] Readers of the
Nativity ode are invited by Milton's rhetorical patterning not only to com-

pose instants of time in salvation history according to their sequentiality but also to expand and to contract those moments with regard to the theological fullness of time. In such a perspective, centuries of prophets and kings do not count much more than the one moment of the shepherds on the lawn who "Or ere the point of dawn / Sat simply chatting in a rustic row" (85–87). Such rhetorical expansion and contraction of time parallels receding and advancing sound. And so, in the next section of the hymn proper, stanzas 9 through 18, Milton writes of the angelic choir that sang at Bethlehem, taking the shepherds' souls in "blissful rapture", and "With thousand echoes still prolongs each heavenly close" (98–100). In present tense, then, without any logical disjunction from the past tense of the image of the shepherds, Milton asks the constellations and the "Crystal spheres" formed at the beginning of time to ring out their "silver chime" now, to "Move in melodious time" (124–28). The arithmetical and musical point of Milton's handling of salvation history is, consequently, also the logical and rhetorical one of the time-eternity paradox. As Milton's contemporary Sir Thomas Browne put it, alluding to Saint Paul's ecstasy, the contemplation of such a paradox can lift a person "to the third heaven" since "those continued instants of time which flow" from unknown beginnings to unknown ends are present to God's eternity as "one permanent point without succession, parts, flux, or division." "Who can speake of eternity without a soloecisme, or thinke thereof without an extasie? . . . in eternitie there is no distinction of Tenses."[19] Neither is there distinction in the meaning of Milton's tenses in the "ninefold harmony" of the celestial spheres (131): "For if such holy Song / Enwrap our fancy long, / Time will run back, and fetch the age of gold" (133–35). In the structure of the ode as well as in the structure of paradox, the central line of the hymn proper is that pivotal statement, "Time will run back" (line 107 of the 216 lines of the hymn proper; line 135 of the entire ode); for the moment in which past, present, and future are coterminous is characteristically the moment of divine intervention in human history, that is, the Incarnation.

In even more obvious ways, Milton formally uses the specific texts of salvation history assigned to the liturgical season of Christmas to organize the significance and form of his poem. Although the ode contains allusions to the full scope of salvation history, Genesis through Apocalypse, this scope is articulated specifically with reference to readings from Isaiah, from seasonal psalms in morning and evening prayer, and from the Christmas epistles and gospels. Such themes as the putting on of light and the overcoming of darkness, the destruction of the idols and the second coming of Christ, are the focus of these readings. It is light that inscribes space according to the laws of optics, the geometric science of the genesis and propagation of light; and the movement of light in the heavenly bodies of the sun, moon, and stars measures out light astronomically. Milton especially designs the geometric and astronomical proportions of his poem by drawing on the readings for two days, 25 December and 6 January, Christmas and Epiphany, the two days that mark off the twelve days of Christmas. The lessons of Christmas morning prayer, for example, paralleling "this the happy morn" of the first line of the ode, are from Isaiah, chapter ix, the announcement that a child is born to us, the Prince of Peace, and from Luke, chapter ii, the Bethlehem story.[20] The psalms of morning prayer on Christmas explain that the heavens shall reveal their glory and that the sun shall run (Ps. xix), that God is King and that the writer's tongue is a pen to sing his praises (Ps. xlv), and that Mercy and Truth, Peace and Justice (the "four daughters of God") shall be reconciled (Ps. lxxxv). To see the parallels in the ode one has only to recall how Milton urges his Muse to produce his own announcement, or "print of the approaching light" (20), the "rude manger" (31), the "meek-ey'd Peace" (46), the "Prince of light" (62), the kings sitting still "with awful eye, / As if they surely knew their sovran Lord was by" (59–60), the sun that "withheld his wonted speed" (79) because the greater Son had appeared and because the special "sun" of the star is racing across the sky, and the meeting of Peace with Truth, Justice, and Mercy (stanza 15). It helps that Milton's Muse, like the prophet of Isaiah, chapter vi, joins an "Angel Choir, / From out his secret Altar toucht with hallow'd fire" (27–28). The same kind of poetic parallelism to the liturgical readings of Epiphany shows up in the themes of the coming of the Incarnate Son as the Light and the singing of the New Song who casts out idols.[21] The Lord is everlasting light (Luke iii), the light to the Gentiles (Isa. xlix) that comes at the acceptable time on the day of salvation, the light which, by the leading of the star, subordinates all kings and all nations to itself. In Milton's terms the genesis and propagation of light in both the natural and the moral universe is the movement of "That glorious Form, that Light unsufferable, / And that far-beaming blaze of Majesty" to choose with us "a darksome House of mortal clay" (8–14). Thus the fullness of time suggested by all of salvation history is compressed into the lessons of one liturgical season; and the Christmas season itself, from the first sunday of Advent through the Epiphany, is telescoped into the one point of the Incarnation and human worship of it, in much the same way the whole creation is recapitulated in the genesis of light. The Nativity ode reflects an "optical" analogy for a religious event insofar as Milton's Muse acts the part of angelic messenger, star,

and song, announcing the instant of the coming of the light and poetically "measuring" out in verses its propagation.[22]

Milton's assimilation of the laws of optics to the making of his metaphors does not stop at the inscription of space by light. The geometry
of light that determines the shapes and forms of things becomes the astronomy of light; for Milton's figures move through space, through the
grand silence of the heavens, with a knowledge that dominates the allegorical mythology of the legendary silencing of the oracles, the idols, and
the pagan gods in all of their secret places and perverse temples. The
last section of the hymn proper, then, stanzas 19 through 26, rhetorically
conveys the silencing of the oracles by means of a *topographia*, the lively
description of a place or places. That is, Milton demonstrates the coming of the light by describing the evacuation of darkness, the emptying
out of the places of the gods in the earth, from the inmost places of
material substance—"And the chill Marble seems to sweat, / While each
peculiar power forgoes his wonted seat" (195–196)—to the outermost
boundary of the "mooned Ashtaroth" (220). From the arched roof of the
heavens and the shrine of Apollo at Delphos to the humblest evacuated
urn, Christ's light penetrates space, completely expunging darkness. As
Milton describes the pagan places of Egypt, the power of hell is contracted
into one spot, Memphis, in Osiris's complete perversion of religion: but
in his "sacred chest" Osiris can no longer be at rest because the holy infant reigns. So, too, finally, the inverted spiral of hell, the perversion
of moving light imaged in "Typhon huge ending in snaky twine" (226),
is countermanded by the spiral of true Light, the babe in his swaddling
bands (228). As stanza 8 ended the first section of the hymn proper by
contracting the descent of Peace and punctuating the *chronographia* with
the humble, local icon of the rustic shepherds, so stanza 26 contracts
the expansive geography of the cessation of the oracles into the reductive
scene of the sun in bed, pillowing his chin.[23] The two eight-stanza sections of the ode symmetrically surround the ten-stanza central section
of cosmic music with forms of silence; in the first section the stillness informs historical time, and in the third section the stillness informs geographical space. Peace descends as light comes; noise ceases as darkness
vanishes.

The revelation to the Gentiles is at the center of Milton's harmoniz-
ing of time and space, sound and vision in his imagistic contrasts. Thus
the Eve-like Nature's "lusty paramour," the sun, must give way to the
"greater Sun," the new Adam, the true Light that comes into the world.
Milton moves the reader from the physical measure of light and darkness
in Genesis, chapter i, the beginning of the Old Testament, to the new

measure in the appearance of the Word in John, chapter i, which also starts "In the beginning." This intertextual shift makes the race of time the medium of a divine Providence that allows the devout "Gentile" informed by the grace of revelation to "prevent" in meditation on 25 December the arrival of the "Star-led Wizards" on 6 January.[24] The propagation of light had long been a metaphor for the gift and reception of grace, and Milton's own university was rapidly gaining fame for its wizardries in the sciences of optics and astronomy.[25] In the ode, Milton seems to be demonstrating that poetic speech was at least as graceful and wise as those sciences and perhaps more so.

What, then, is the poetic disposition of the ode? It is a disposition shaped by a complex understanding of salvation history; knowledge of salvation through the Word of God progresses through human knowledge in time in conjunction with the divine will of Providence. The astronomy of the church year guides Milton's formulation of the parts of the poem. Thus the four stanzas of the proem parallel the four weeks of Advent and numerically total twenty-eight lines in four stanzas of seven lines each, constituting a correspondence to the lunar month.[26] The hymn proper deals not with the moon and the sublunary expectations to which the "blaze of Majesty" descends, but with the sun that withholds his speed (79) and is displaced by the actual appearance of that blaze of Majesty, "a greater Sun" (83), in the created universe. In content the proem, like the liturgical texts of Advent, deals with prophecy and the nature of the announcements of the "holy Sages" (5). In content the hymn proper, like the scope of all of salvation history in the word of God preached through the church year, is a meditation on creation, history, and the end of time seen from the perspective of one event, the Incarnation. Milton has measured the proportions of his stanzas in the hymn proper according to the disposition of the set and moveable feasts in the church calendar of 1629–30, a year of unusual symmetry since the seasons of Christmas and Easter were each eight weeks long. In the ode the hymn proper falls into divisions of eight stanzas, ten stanzas, and eight stanzas, with the twenty-seventh stanza acting as a coda, a musical punctuation.[27] Since the season of Lent in 1629–30 was ten weeks long, the central section of the ode on the heavenly music nevertheless includes the "horrid clang" of human history and the "blast" of Judgment Day (stanza 17) in discordant concord with the "Divinely warbled voice" (stanza 9) that harmonized heaven and earth to begin with. That is, Milton's paralleling of the season with his structural disposition of the center of the poem accounts for the acknowledgment of human sinfulness and proposes its historical transformation through Christ's atonement.[28] The coda not only expresses a sense of restoration, the "order serviceable," from the vantage of the Incarnation, but this order parallels the coming sabbath rest — "But see! The Virgin blest, / Hath laid her Babe to rest" (237–38) — and marks the arrival of the "Gentile" who speaks the poem at his moment of visionary witness.

III

The logic of time in the Nativity ode is quite clear if one takes salvation history — the poet's rule for organizing his knowledge of the liberal arts according to the truth of revelation — as one's rule of interpretation. Rhetorical analysis of the poem further demonstrates that Milton not only used paradox and the inexpressibility topos as the proper language of the Incarnation revealed in salvation history, but designed his poem by means of the figures of speech recommended in the rhetorical handbooks for the development of the topic of subject and adjuncts.[29] Since Milton's subject, the Incarnation, the Word made flesh, is indefinable in its divinity, its "glorious Form," Milton's language of definition for praising the Lord of history is largely adjunctive on the idea of time. A clue to the rationale for Milton's choice of the rhetorical topic of subject and adjuncts may be found in his *Art of Logic* in the entry on the adjunct "time" and the subject "God."

Here [among adjuncts of circumstance] is put *time*, to wit, the duration of things past, present, and future. Thus also God is named, who is, who was, and who is to be (Apocalypse 1.4 and 4.8). But to God everlastingness or eternity, not time, is generally attributed, but what properly is everlastingness except eternal duration, in Greek αἰων as though, ἀεὶ ὄν, *ever existing?*[30]

Milton explains that every adjunct is posterior to the subject except the adjunct of time (*Logic*, p. 87). But time is not properly an adjunct of the subject, God; and God is a subject who exists before time. Time, in short, is pure paradox. God exists before time, but time itself is of God when everlastingness is defined as eternal duration, and the God-Man exists both in time and in eternity. The adjuncts of the God-Man that are not proper to him as infinite, inexpressible God are expressible in their second and third modes, that is, place and the circumstance of time. Thus Milton uses these to shape his poem in its disposition — the description of time in the *chronographia*, the description of place in the *topographia*. Fundamentally, as rhetorical analysis of the ode bears out, the shaping of the ode is a *peristasis*, or amplification of a person or thing, on the Word of God and the Incarnation.[31] In linguistic texture, the ode is full of adjunctive expressions including taxis, epithet, and especially metonymy, the most obvious figure for substituting adjuncts for subjects, because one cannot write a *finitio* for the infinite per se other than that historical *notatio* for God as the One who is, who was, and who is to be.

In all the patterns of speech that the young Milton draws from his rhetorical treasury, his intention to expand the power of language and thought to its limit is evident. Nowhere, however, is it more brilliant than in his use of language both to manipulate the trivial arts of expression to suit the word of God in Scripture and also to dominate the quadrivial sciences of form by means of the superior integrating knowledge of salvation history.[32] Just as the Word of God effects a restorative correspondence between the created and the uncreated light, the created wisdom of Milton's poetic proportioning of the arts and sciences effects a correspondence between human speech and uncreated wisdom. Precise knowledge of the arts and sciences is analogized in Milton's poetic language because of the peculiarly intense, intellectual cast of his vision of the movement of human history. The arts and sciences result from the Fall of Man to mark off the fragmentation of knowledge; they are, nevertheless, also providentially caught up in the restoration of human nature through time, as long as human beings view time as the realization of salvation history. Marjorie Nicolson once commented that to read Milton was to gain a liberal education;[33] I would add only the Erasmian note that such an education is itself unified in the *philosophia Christi* of the holy Word of God in the Scriptures, whose words the image and likeness of God may imitate. Saint Augustine understood that a divine number, weight, and measure that permeated the universe was revealed in the Scriptures; Milton in his youth expressed the possibility that the poetic man could "measure" out in devotional song—already angelic and starlike—a vision similar to prophecy.

This poet's appropriation of all of the arts and sciences in the making of metonymic correspondences leads past Peter Ramus's *Dialecticae institutiones* as a revision of logic, consequently, to Ramus's own larger project in the sixteenth century: the revision of the entire structure of knowledge, especially as it was expressed in the Aristotelian scheme of the arts and sciences. And it leads even further on the Ramistic course in ways that illuminate the disposition or the verbal "architecture" of the ode. In the *Commentariorum de religione Christiana*, which was published posthumously with a life of Peter Ramus appended to it by Theophile de Banos (Banosius) in 1576 and dedicated to Sir Philip Sidney, Ramus took the standard architectural analogy for the organic arts and, having already extended it to the structure of knowledge, applied it to sacred letters as he discussed the "architecture" of the Word of God in creation and in Scripture.[34] In the *Commentariorum* proper, Ramus applied his method for the organization of knowledge to the divine science not by dividing questions into alphabetical categories or precepts, examples, and arguments as, he says, had been done by scholastic thinkers, but by arranging them in constructive order and referring all Christian doctrines to a single head (Book 1, p. 5). In Book 4 Ramus relates the "machine" of the created universe to the Word of God in the idea of a sacred "Logic" that is not only "learned" but "built" on the cornerstone of the Christ who brings all things into congruence and agreement (IV, xiii, p. 315). Ramus finishes his essay by citing Saint Augustine's open attitude to science; the power of God is not a subject of geometry and physics, not even Euclid's geometry and Aristotle's physics but, rather, the truth of the arts and sciences is justified by the truth of God (IV, xv, p. 325). The universe is rhetorically made and scientifically established, in other words, as Scripture is written and the minds of human beings rectified. Milton's practice of a true devotion in the Nativity ode poetically fulfills this kind of intellectual program by subordinating all knowledge to revealed truth — namely the supreme "Logic" or dialectic that is the Word of God threading through human history. Like Ramus in the *Commentariorum*, Milton does not divide what he knows in categories, precepts, examples, and arguments, but arranges all of it in a constructive order under the single head of the doctrine of the divine birth. The "order serviceable" that redeems human time and space deformed in the fall from grace is, finally, the reforming power of the Son who laid aside "That glorious Form" in the humblest self-emptying (Phil. ii), "and here with us to be, / Forsook the Courts of everlasting Day / And chose with us a darksome House of mortal Clay" (8–14).

IV

In Milton's discovery of correspondences among various types of knowledge on the topic of time, we have a foretaste of his poetic method in the great poems to come. As the power of language expands to contain knowledge even beyond "what the mind may well contain" (*PL* VII, 128), the content of various bodies of knowledge is condensed, making *Paradise Lost* an encyclopedic treasury of knowledge and *Paradise Regained* a researching of a "true wisdom" (*PR* IV, 319). The artistry and message of the Nativity ode are an early, simpler declaration of the idea that knowledge, at best, is integrated with and propaedeutic to the only human wisdom possible, that is, in the words of that philosopher of time and memory, Saint Augustine, an act of worship and devotion.[35] To know time in such a way is not only to have grasped the nature of thought in its diverse disciplines but also to "prevent" the wise men. The "prevenient grace" that Milton humbly marks as his own poetic motivation has come beforehand to inspire him to pray poetically, to "make" an act of devotion. The ode records, therefore, Milton's response to the grace of a certain moment in which he sings a song in his own darksome house of mortal clay. But Milton's response, in turn, constitutes the ode as an inspiration that comes to others as a prevenient grace evoking their performance of devotion, too. The poem moves from the public liturgical celebration of the Word in sacrament and preaching to the inward temple of the Word in the more radical Protestant heart that feels compelled to witness to revelation.

Curiously, in a sermon preached at Saint Paul's in London by John Donne — and probably on Christmas day, 1629, the same Christmas of the composition of the Nativity ode — Donne used John, chapter x, verse 10, to articulate a similar sense of prevenience and devotion. He described Christmas as one of the shortest days of the year according to sunlight, but one of the longest according to the measure of the star:

It is a day that consists of twelve dayes; A day not measured by the naturall and ordinary motion of the Sun, but by a supernaturall and extraordinary Star, which appeared to the Wisemen of the East, this day, and brought them to Christ, at Bethlem, upon Twelfe day. That day, Twelfe day, the Church now calles the Epiphany; The ancient Church called this day (Christmas day) the Epiphany. Both dayes together, and all the dayes between, This day, when Christ was manifested to the Jews, in the Shepheards by the Angels, and Twelfth day, when Christ was manifested to the Gentiles in those Wisemen of the East, make up the Epiphany, that is, the manifestation of God to man. And as this day is in such a respect a longer day than others, so, if we make longer houres in this day, then in other dayes; if I extend this Sermon, if you extend your Devotion, or your Patience, it is but a due, and just celebration of the Day.[36]

From the vantage of Milton's piety, perhaps the ode is such an amplification of devotion; from the vantage of his student life and his love of learning, however, the ode expresses the logic of time through a poet's freedom to recreate the unity of the arts and sciences in the workings of salvation history. The combination qualifies an old rhetorical esthetic that compared poetic composition to the building of a house in set proportions and looks forward to Milton's great "unbuilding" of philosophy in the house of intellect that might yet become historically "a Paradise within" (*PL* XII, 587).[37] In the ode Milton's subordination of trivial and quadrivial sciences to the knowledge of salvation makes architectonic form no mere disposition of "architectural" proportions but truly a measure in words of the human mind and spirit touched by the Word.[38] In *Para-*

dise Lost, similarly, as Marvell's commendatory poem put it, "Thy verse created like thy Theme sublime, / In Number, Weight, and Measure, needs not Rime." For the youthful poet, as for the mature one, literary architectonics or the proportion-making of poetry is less a matter of verbal "architecture" and the designing merely of spatial images than the disposing of these forms in an intellectual and moral analogy having to do with the character of the poet at his devotions or in his visions and revelations.

The central doctrine that informs "Ode on the Morning of Christ's Nativity" is the Incarnation; but the doctrine that controls the poetic order of the language that gives the reader the rhetorical experience of the duration of the ode is that of the Epiphany, the revelation to the Gentiles, in the speaker's own witness. Already the poetic form articulated in the ode discloses the emergence of a "voice" that seeks to join itself to the "Angel choir" (27), but does so in the prophetic mode of one touched on the lips by a burning coal (28) and one who reenters the poem self-consciously, by calling his attention both to its time of composition — "Time is our tedious Song should here have ending" (239) — and to his visionary function as a prophetic witness to revelation: "But see!" (237). It is Milton in his very life, his time of history, who makes longer hours of devotion on the Christmas of 1629–30 by writing a poem. It is the biography of his Christian soul, which metonymically searches out the identity of the Son of God in the logic of time and in the logic of the Word, that calls Milton himself to be an adjunct of that divine birth. Indeed, the more mature narrator of *Paradise Lost* will telescope Genesis and Apocalypse together and find himself, and the poet of *Paradise Regained* will bespeak the revelation of the identity of the Son from within Milton's own participation in divine logic. In all the temporal and rhetorical symmetry and paradox of the form of the ode, the extra note of the coda identifies the arrival of the speaker on the scene of revelation as if he were "Heav'n's youngest-teemed Star."

University of Wisconsin, Madison

NOTES

1. For a summary of early criticism, see A.S.P. Woodhouse and Douglas Bush, eds., *The Minor English Poems: A Variorum Commentary on the Poems of John Milton*, gen. ed. Merritt Y. Hughes (New York, 1972), II, ii. All references to the ode are to the Columbia edition, *The Works of John Milton*, 18 vols., ed Frank Allen Patterson et al.,

(New York, 1931–38), vol. I, pp. 1–10, and will be cited by line number in the text. Other references to Milton's work are to *John Milton: Complete Poems and Major Prose*, ed. Merritt Y. Hughes (Indianapolis, 1957).

2. I am indebted to Alex B. Chambers of the University of Wisconsin for directing me to these readings. See his "Christmas in the Liturgy of the Church," *Literary Monographs* VI, 109–53, and Rosemond Tuve, *Images and Themes in Five Poems by Milton* (Cambridge, Mass., 1957), pp. 37–72, esp. p. 70.

3. In Thomas B. Stroup, *Religious Rite and Ceremony in Milton's Poetry* (Lexington, Ky., 1968), Stroup glances at Milton's adaptation of liturgical influences to a Protestant poetics; John R. Knott, Jr., "Milton and the Spirit of Truth," *The Sword of the Spirit: Puritan Responses to the Bible* (Chicago, 1980), pp. 106–30, describes Milton's view that Scripture liberates the devout from strictly prescribed forms of worship, "which he understood as manifestations of the 'bondage of the Law'" (p. 112).

4. Arthur Barker, "The Pattern of Milton's 'Nativity Ode,'" *UTQ* X (1941), 167–81; Balachandra Rajan, "In Order Serviceable," *MLR* LXIII (1968), 13–22. On Milton's expression of time, see Lowry Nelson, Jr., "Gongora and Milton: Toward a Definition of the Baroque," *CL* VI (1954), 53–63; D. C. Allen, *The Harmonious Vision: Studies in Milton's Poetry* (Baltimore, 1954), pp. 24–40; Harriet Frazier, "Time as Structure in Milton's *Nativity Ode*," *Universitas* III (1965), 8–14; Malcolm Ross, "Milton and the Protestant Aesthetic," *UTQ* XVII (1947–48), 346–60; and Rosalie Colie, "Time and Eternity, Paradox and Structure in *Paradise Lost*," *JWCI* XXIII (1960), 127–38.

5. Bernard S. Adams, "Miltonic Metaphor and Ramist 'Invention': The Imagery of the Nativity Ode," in *Milton Studies*, vol. XVIII, ed. James D. Simmonds (Pittsburgh, 1983), pp. 85–102.

6. Tuve, *Images and Themes*, p. 42. See Donald Lemen Clark, *John Milton at Saint Paul's School: A Study of Ancient Rhetoric in English Renaissance Education* (New York, 1948), and Georgia B. Christopher, *Milton and the Science of the Saints* (Princeton, N.J., 1982), pp. 22–29, on the Puritan character of Milton's literary theology and "speech act" in the ode.

7. I am indebted to Margaret P. Hannay for reminding me of these associations and of the political context of Milton's use of the Psalms as models for his own hymn. Mary Ann Radzinowicz's forthcoming study of Milton and the Psalms (Princeton, 1989) is the fullest on the subject.

8. Saint Paulinus of Nola criticizes the muses in his famous verse epistle to his teacher Ausonius on rejecting Apollo for the new God, Christ; Erasmus alluded to Paulinus in the *Antibarbarorum* (1488; rev. ed. 1520), p. 64, to defend learning and to advocate Christian letters. Fabricius anthologized the letters to Ausonius in *Poetarum veterum ecclesiasticorum opera Christiana* (Basle, 1562) and argued the case for presenting school boys with models of Christian eloquence. On the Gills see Arthur Barker, "Milton's Schoolmasters," *MLN* XXXII (1937), 517–36.

9. Psalm xcvi, Geneva Bible. Geneva Psalm xcvi, 3, orders a declaration of God's glory among "all nations," King James Psalm xcvi, 3, "among the heathen." On the use of the Genevan translation in the early seventeenth century and its influence on Milton, see Lloyd E. Berry's introduction to the facsimile edition, *The Geneva Bible of 1560* (Madison, Wis., 1969), pp. 19–20. Saint Clement of Alexandria, *Exhortation to the Greeks*, trans. G. W. Butterworth (London, 1919), personifies Christ as the "New Song" and writes of the nature of the gods, the value of literature and philosophy, and the triumph of the new music of the Word over the idols.

10. See Walter J. Ong, S.J., "Logic and the Epic Muse: Reflections on Noetic Struc-

ture in Milton's Milieu," *Achievements of the Left Hand,* ed. Michael Lieb and John T. Shawcross (Amherst, Mass., 1974), pp. 239–68; Michael Lieb, "Milton and the Metaphysics of Form," *SP* LXXI (1974), 206–74; and *Milton and Scriptural Tradition: The Bible into Poetry,* ed. James H. Sims and Leland Ryken (Columbia, Mo., 1984).

11. Erasmus, *On Copia of Words and Ideas,* trans. Donald B. King and H. David Rix (Milwaukee, Wis., 1963), pp. 66–106.

12. Cf. Adams, "Miltonic Metaphor," pp. 86–89, on Milton's Ramistic organization of units, or visual analogies, in a spatial pattern, and consider Ramus's larger project for all of knowledge, not merely logic. According to Walter J. Ong, S.J., in *Ramus, Method, and the Decay of Dialogue* (Cambridge, Mass., 1958), p. 89, Ramus's *Dialectiae* (1555) and his *Scholae in Liberales Artes* (1569) both established a "method" for knowledge that connected words spatially to geometric patterns.

13. See Sigmund G. Spaeth, *Milton's Knowledge of Music* (Ann Arbor, Mich., 1963); Lawrence Stapleton, "Milton and the New Music," *UTQ* XXIII (1953–54), 217–26, "Milton's Conception of Time in *The Christian Doctrine,"* *Harvard Theological Review* LVII (1964), 9–21, and "Perspectives of Time in *Paradise Lost,"* *PQ* XLV (1966), 734–68; Mother M. Christopher Pecheux, "Milton and *Kairos,"* in *Milton Studies,* vol. XII, ed. James D. Simmonds (Pittsburgh, 1978), pp. 197–211; and John T. Shawcross, "Stasis and John Milton and Myths of Time," *Cithara* XVIII, no. 1 (1978), 3–17. Plato's *Philebus,* sections 16–20 and 66a–d, seems to have direct bearing on Milton's composition. See the *Collected Dialogues,* ed. Edith Hamilton and Huntington Cairns (Princeton, N.J., 1961), pp. 1087–96 and 1148–49. Carol Maddison, *Apollo and the Nine: A History of the Ode* (London, 1960), p. 7, observes that a sense of the eternal and the mythic is at the core of the ode as a poetic form; Milton's "ordered song," reflecting the timelessness of the Incarnation and the eternality of divine revelation, stretches the traditional form beyond its classical mythic bounds. Richard Halpern, "The Great Instauration: Imaginary Narratives in Milton's 'Nativity Ode,'" *Re-Membering Milton: Essays on the Texts and Traditions,* ed. Mary Nyquist and Margaret W. Ferguson (New York, 1987), pp. 3–24, psychologizes Milton's "narrative of development" in the ode, arguing that a temporal collapse threatens to push history backwards "to a state of infantile plenitude" (pp. 10–11) and emphasizing Milton's identification with the infant Son.

14. *The Annotated Book of Common Prayer,* ed. John Henry Blount (London, 1895), comments on the church year in general while providing charts to devise the structure of feasts and liturgical readings in the seasons and weeks of a particular church calendar. From the dates listed by Blount I have extrapolated the following table, which outlines the church calendars for three years—1628, 1629, and 1630—the last church year, 1629–30, being the year of composition of the Nativity ode (see table 1). In these years Easter fell on April 13, 1628; April 5, 1629; and March 28, 1630. The Sundays for each season of the year receive the abbreviation of either the season or the dominant feast:

A = Advent   Ep = Epiphany   Asc. = Ascension
X = Christmas   L = Lent   T = Trinity
E = Easter

15. On these issues, see, e.g., K. J. Woolcombe, "The Biblical Origins and Patristic Development of Typology," *Essays on Typology,* ed. G. Lampe and K. J. Woolcombe (London, 1957); H. R. MacCallum, "Milton and the Figurative Interpretation of the Bible," *UTO* XXXI (1962), 397–415; C. A. Patrides, *Milton and the Christian Tradition* (Oxford, 1966) and "'That great and indisputable miracle': The Cessation of the Oracles," in *Premises and Motifs in Renaissance Thought and Literature* (Princeton, N.J., 1982), pp. 105–23;

TABLE 1. ANGLICAN CHURCH CALENDAR FOR 1628–1630 WITH VARIANTS

Church Calendar for 1627–28

Date	Sunday	Feast	Date	Sunday	Feast
Dec. 2	1st A		June 1	Whitsun	Pentecost
9	2nd A		8	Trinity	
16	3rd A		15	1st T	
23	4th A		22	2nd T	
25		Christmas	24		St. John the
30	1st X				Baptist
Jan. 1		Circumcision	29	3rd T	
6	2nd X	Epiphany	July 6	4th T	
13	1st Ep		13	5th T	
20	2nd Ep		20	6th T	
27	3rd Ep		27	7th T	
Feb. 3	4th Ep		Aug. 3	8th T	
10	7th	Septuagesima	6		Transfiguration
17	6th	Sexagesima	10	9th T	
24	5th	Quinquagesima	17	10th T	
Mar. 2	1st L	Lent	24	11th T	
9	2nd L		31	12th T	
16	3rd L		Sept. 7	13th T	
23	4th L		14	14th T	
25		Annunciation	21	15th T	
30	5th L		28	16th T	
Apr. 6	6th L	Palm Sunday	Oct. 5	17th T	
11		Good Friday	12	18th T	
13	Easter		19	19th T	
20	1st E		26	20th T	
27	2nd E		Nov. 1		All Saints
May 4	3rd E		2	21st T	
16	4th E		9	22nd T	
18	5th E		16	23rd T	
22		Ascension	30	1st A	St. Andrew
25	after Asc.				

Literary Uses of Typology, ed. Earl Miner (Princeton, N.J., 1977); Barbara Lewalski, "Biblical Poetics," *Protestant Poetics and the Seventeenth-Century Religious Lyric* (Princeton, N.J., 1979), pp. 31–144; T. K. Meier, "Milton's Nativity Ode: Sectarian Discord," *MLR* LXV (1970), 7–10; Saint Augustine, *On True Religion*, trans. J. H. Burleigh, in *Augustine: Earlier Writings* (Philadelphia, 1953), xxii, 42–43, pp. 245–46.

16. Augustine, *The City of God*, XXII, 30, trans. Marcus Dods (New York, 1960), p. 867. Cf. Milton's view of the centrality of the act of redemption to the theology of the atonement developed by Saint Gregory of Nyssa, who linked the idea of ransom to the necessity of the Incarnation of his *Oratio catechetica*, chaps. 22–26, and contributed to its classical Protestant formulation.

17. See Sister Miriam Joseph, *Rhetoric in Shakespeare's Time* (New York, 1962), pp. 318–22; and Erasmus, *On Copia of Words and Ideas*, p. 55.

TABLE 1. *Continued*

Church Calendar for 1628–29

Date	Sunday	Feast	Date	Sunday	Feast
Nov. 30	1st A		May 24	Whitsun	Pentecost
Dec. 7	2nd A		31	Trinity	
14	3rd A		June 7	1st T	
21	4th A		14	2nd T	
25		Christmas	21	3rd T	
28	1st X		24		St. John the
Jan. 1		Circumcision			Baptist
4	2nd X		28	4th T	
6		Epiphany	July 5	5th T	
11	1st Ep		12	6th T	
18	2nd Ep		19	7th T	
25	3rd Ep		26	8th T	
Feb. 1	7th	Septuagesima	Aug. 2	9th T	
8	6th	Sexagesima	6		Transfiguration
15	5th	Quinquagesima	9	10thT	
22	1st L	Lent	16	11th T	
Mar. 1	2nd L		23	12th T	
8	3rd L		30	13th T	
15	4th L		Sept. 6	14th T	
22	5th L		13	15th T	
25		Annunciation	20	16th T	
29	6th L	Palm Sunday	27	17th T	
Apr. 3		Good Friday	Oct. 4	18th T	
5	Easter		11	19th T	
12	1st E		18	20th T	
19	2nd E		25	21st T	
26	3rd E		Nov. 1	22nd T	All Saints
May 3	4th E		8	23rd T	
10	5th E		15	24th T	
14		Ascension	22	25th T	
17	after Asc.		29	1st A	

18. In his *De Musica* Augustine maintains that music and grammar are distinct arts, but uses a literary vocabulary to distinguish sounds and their dimensions. (*Patrologia Latina* [Petit-Montrouge: J. P. Migne, 1845], XXXII, i, 1, cols. 1081–83). Cf. Augustine's treatment of music in *On Christian Doctrine*, II, 26–28. The same borrowing of terms appears in Boethius's *De Musica*, strengthening the primacy of grammar and the relation between poetry and music in western thought.

19. Sir Thomas Browne, *Religio Medici*, in *Selected Writings*, ed. Sir Geoffrey Keynes (Chicago, 1968), p. 16.

20. Table 2 shows the scriptural readings of the Christmas season, 1629–30, developed by listing the normal lessons with the annual variants.

21. Sanford Budick, "Patterns of Division in the Nativity Ode," *The Dividing Muse: Images of Sacred Disjunction in Milton's Poetry* (New Haven, Conn., 1985), pp. 13–31,

TABLE 1. *Continued*

Church Calendar for 1629-30

Date	Sunday	Feast	Date	Sunday	Feast
Nov. 29	1st A		May 23	Trinity	
30		St. Andrew	30	1st T	
Dec. 6	2nd A		June 6	2nd T	
13	3rd A		13	3rd T	
20	4th A		20	4th T	
25		Christmas	24		St. John the
27	1st X	St. John the			Baptist
		Evangelist	27	5th T	
Jan. 1		Circumcision	July 4	6th T	
3	2nd X		11	7th T	
6		Epiphany	18	8th T	
10	1st Ep		25	9th T	
17	2nd Ep		Aug. 1	10th T	
24	7th	Septuagesima	6		Transfiguration
31	6th	Sexagesima	8	11th T	
Feb. 7	5th	Quinquagesima	15	12th T	
14	1st L	Lent	22	13th T	
21	2nd L		29	14th T	
28	3rd L		Sept. 5	15th T	
Mar. 7	4th L		12	16th T	
14	5th L		19	17th T	
21	6th L	Palm Sunday	26	18th T	
25		Annunciation	Oct. 3	19th T	
28	Easter		10	20th T	
Apr. 4	1st E	.	17	21st T	
11	2nd E		24	22nd T	
18	3rd E		31	23rd T	
25	4th E		Nov. 1		All Saints
May 2	5th E		7	24th T	
6		Ascension	14	25th T	
9	after Asc.		21	26th T	
16	Whitsun	Pentecost	28	1st A	

discusses Milton's "new music" and Saint Clement's idea of the "New Song" and the harmony of the Word as the source of a unity of higher order.

22. Cf. Barker's analysis of the imagery, cited in note 4, and Patrides's comment, "The Orders of the Angels," *Premises and Motifs*, pp. 25-26, referenced in note 15, that Milton alludes to the celestial hierarchy and rejects it later.

23. See John Calvin, *Institutes of the Christian Religion*, 2 vols., I. i, 16.2 trans. Ford Lewis Battles, ed. John T. McNeill (Philadelphia, 1960), pp. 198-99, on divine providence's governance of the sun's rising and setting. Milton comically disarms the sun's pagan significance and shows its control by the greater Sun.

24. See Herschel Baker, *The Race of Time: Three Lectures on Renaissance Historiography* (Toronto, 1967), pp. 52-70.

TABLE 2. CHRISTMAS LITURGICAL READINGS, 1629–30

| Calendar Day | Morning Prayer Lessons | Introit | Communion Service | | | Evening Prayer Lessons |
			Collect	Epistle	Gospel	
1st Advent	Isa. i	Ps. i	2nd Coming	Rom. xiii	Matt. xxi	Isa. ii
2nd Advent	Isa. v	Ps. cxx	Use of scripture, hope	Rom. xv	Luke xxi	Isa. xxiv
3rd Advent	Isa. xxv	Ps. iv	1st Coming 2nd Coming	1 Cor. iv	Matt. xi	Isa. xxvi
4th Advent	Isa. xxx	Ps. v	Running race	Phil. iv	John i	Isa. xxxii
Christmas	Isa. ix	Ps. xcviii, viii	Renewal	Heb. i	John i	Isa. vii Titus iii
1st Sun. after Christmas	Isa. xxxvii	Ps. cxxi	Renewal	Gal. iv	Matt. i	Isa. xxxviii
Circumcision	Gen. xvii	Ps. cxxii	Obedience to the Law	Rom. iv	Luke ii	Deut. x Col. ii
2nd Sun. after Christmas	Isa. xli					Isa. xliii
Epiphany	Isa. lx	Ps. xcvi	Leading of star	Eph. iii	Matt. ii	Isa. xlix John ii
1st Sun. after Epiphany	Isa. xliv	Ps. xiii	Knowledge, grace, power	Rom. xii	Luke ii	Isa. xlvi
2nd Sun. after Epiphany	Isa. li	Ps. xiv	Peace	Rom. xii	John ii	Isa. liii

25. Roger Bacon, *Opus Majus*, trans. R. B. Burke (Philadelphia, 1928), pp. 238–39, illustrates the infusion of grace by the multiplication of light. The best history of seventeenth-century optics is Stephen M. Straker, "Kepler's Optics: A Study in the Development of Seventeenth-Century Natural Philosophy" (Ph.D. diss., Indiana University, 1970).

26. Maren-Sofie Røstvig, *The Hidden Sense* (Universitatsforlaget, 1963), pp. 44–58, interprets the numbers and proportions of the ode allegorically; see Christopher Butler's refutation, *Number Symbolism* (London, 1970), pp. 140–43.

27. This division corrects Barker's division into stanzaic sections of eight, nine, and nine; Rajan's division into three sections of eight, eight, and eleven stanzas; Røstvig's division into three sections of nine stanzas each; and Adams's division into two sections. The idea that stanza 27 is a coda is Rajan's. Cf. Patrides, "Approaches to Numerology," *Premises and Motifs*, pp. 64–82, cited in note 15. Milton's play with the proportions of various knowledges by analogy and with the ordering of time by imitation may put numerological analysis in the intelligible context of poetic form and structure.

28. Meier, "Sectarian Discord," describes Milton's use of "middle time" strictly limited by the boundary of Judgment Day, suggesting another avenue toward understanding the Lenten character of the middle of a poem on Christmas.

29. On the inexpressibility topos see Ernst R. Curtius, *European Literature and the Latin Middle Ages*, trans. Willard Trask (New York, 1953), pp. 159–62. Adams, "Miltonic Metaphor and Ramist 'Invention'," documents the poetic "whole" of the ode by examining Milton's use of four Ramistic tropes (p. 89) and looks at some metonymies and the topic of subject and adjuncts (pp. 93–94). I think, however, that Milton does not merge one trope into another but draws liberally on many figures useful for the expression of subject and adjuncts; the language of the Nativity ode is more uniformly metonymic, in this respect, than metaphoric in Adams's sense, and Milton's metonymies argue an even greater poetic unity than Adams suggests.

30. John Milton, *The Art of Logic*, I, xi, in *The Works of John Milton*, 18 vols., ed. Frank Allen Patterson et al. (New York, 1931–38), vol. XI, pp. 93–95.

31. The *peristasis* of a person is elaborated in the proem — name, parentage, nation, country, age, education, nature of mind; *peristasis* of a thing according to its circumstances — cause, place, time, occasion — is elaborated in the hymn proper in order to amplify the event of the Incarnation rather than the person of the Word made flesh. Sister Miriam Joseph, *Rhetoric*, p. 319, quotes Peacham on *peristasis* to the effect that one must beware of "long and tedious stay" in the amplification and avoid making the speech barren; this warning may throw some light on Milton's curious reference to his hymn as "our tedious Song."

32. Cf. Saint Augustine, *On Christian Doctrine* II, 31, on the idea that the sciences of disputation and number hold sway in the institution of reason, and *De Trinitate* XI, in which the trinity of memory, thought and vision, and voluntary attention is paralleled to measure, number, and weight (XI, xi, 18).

33. Marjorie Nicolson, *John Milton, a Reader's Guide to His Poetry* (New York, 1963), p. vi.

34. *Commentariorum de religione Christiana, libri quatuor . . . eiusdem vita à Theophilo Banosius* (Frankfurt, 1576). Banosius praises Ramus's polymathy since Ramus lectured on mathematics, studied all the liberal arts, pursued the arts of invention and preaching with Sturm in Germany, and admired the architecture, optics, painting, and mechanical craftsmanship of the automata and the armillary spheres of Nuremberg (sig. b.4^r–i.4^v). Ramus's analogy establishes links among creation, the word of God, and the soul. As in other writings of the Renaissance, the "architect" often does the work of an

engineer or "clerk of the works," and "architecture" signifies a moving invention as often as it does a static construction in Ramus's mind.

35. Saint Augustine, *De Trinitate* XIV, ix, in *Augustine: Later Works*, trans. John Burnaby (Philadelphia, 1955), p. 113; cf. Milton in *The Reason of Church Government*, on "true worship," Book II in *The Student's Milton*, ed. Frank Allen Paterson (New York, 1930), p. 522.

36. *The Sermons of John Donne*, ed. Evelyn Simpson and George R. Potter (Berkeley and Los Angeles, 1958), IX, no. 5, lines 4–18, p. 131. The editors conjecture that this sermon was preached on Christmas Day at St. Paul's in 1629, and it is not completely unlikely that Milton may actually have heard it. On the influence of another Donne sermon, see William McQueen, "Prevent the Sun: Milton, Donne, and the Book of Wisdom," *Milton Newsletter* II, 63–64.

37. Cf. Michael Lieb's view of such "spiritual architecture" in *The Dialectics of Creation: Patterns of Birth and Regeneration in "Paradise Lost"* (Amherst, Mass., 1970), pp. 5–7.

38. Cf. Werner Jaeger's notion of analogy, in *Paideia: The Ideals of Greek Culture*, 3 vols., 2nd ed., trans. Gilbert Highet (New York, 1939–45), I, xx–xxi, that produces "architectonic" qualities in a poem not because the poem imitates the structural values of architecture but because there are analogous structural standards inherent in language to begin with.

THE FATAL VOYAGE OF EDWARD KING, MILTON'S LYCIDAS

J. Karl Franson

M ILTON'S ELEGY on the death of Edward King has received abundant praise, one scholar calling it "the most perfect poem of its length in the English language."[1] Despite its fame, however, *Lycidas* depicts a catastrophe shrouded in obscurity. While enroute to visit friends and relations in Ireland, King drowned when his ship struck a rock and sank somewhere off the coast of North Wales. The disaster caused considerable stir at Cambridge, where King was in his eleventh year. A number of his associates contributed to a memorial volume, *Justa Edovardo King naufrago* (1638), comprised of panegyrics in Latin, Greek, and English, and concluding with *Lycidas*. Yet even the contributors, Edward's brother Henry among them, apparently knew little about the disaster except that it occurred somewhere between Chester and Dublin and that King's body was never recovered.[2]

The only ostensibly authoritative account, and that on which commentary about King's death is based, is the anonymous Latin prose panegyric that opens the volume, entitled "P.M.S.," which must have been written late because few of the elegists appear to have read it.[3] This account contains information only a survivor of the shipwreck could have known, leading us to assume that other significant details were available at the time. Yet I have been unable to locate any reference to the disaster in correspondence by the elegists or by members of King's immediate family, nor has the shipwreck been described by any chronicler of English sea disasters. We would expect the vessel to be noticed in the British Exchequer port books, but unfortunately these records for the area of King's embarkation, Chester and its outports, are missing for 1637.[4] No inquiry appears to have been made into the disaster, nor has any new information surfaced, leaving King's death as mysterious as Milton and others claim it was.

Because so little is known about the voyage, can a reconstruction be made with any confidence? I believe it can. The "P.M.S." indicates that on 10 August 1637 while enroute to Ireland, King's ship "struck on a rock and was stove in by the shock" while sailing "not far from the

British shore." King fell to his knees in prayer "while the other passengers were busy in vain about their mortal lives" and sank with the vessel.[5] The latter detail must have been supplied by someone on board or perhaps on a nearby vessel who observed King kneeling in prayer, leading us to believe that someone survived to report the disaster. Unfortunately most of the fundamental details are missing from this account, such as the name of the ship and its master, the identities of those who perished and those who survived, the time and place of the ship's embarkation and its subsequent foundering, and the possible roles played by foul weather or pirates.

Several commentators have speculated about the catastrophe, but without evidence. William Hogg, for example, claimed in 1694 that "Some escaped in [a] Boat, and great endeavours were used in that great consternation to get [King] into the Boat, which did not prevail"; at least three scholars subsequently repeat this description as fact. A more recent version by Robert Graves suggests that crew and passengers floated ashore on empty casks, King remaining on board because he could not swim nor grab a cask for himself. This too is carried into later commentary.[6] Most educated guesswork about the voyage, however, has focused on presumed locations of the wreck. Generally Milton scholars writing about the disaster have been cautious not to deviate from the "P.M.S." account, that it occurred "not far from the British shore." This would place it on the Irish Sea somewhere between the mouth of the River Dee and Holyhead, the latter being the major overnight anchorage for sea traffic between North Wales and Ireland (see fig. 1).[7] David Masson appears to have understood these parameters of King's voyage (*PW*, p. 425), but Merritt Y. Hughes, relying on an ambiguous geographical allusion in *Lycidas*, proposes Bardsey Island as a possible site of the shipwreck, which would place King's vessel considerably off course.[8] Likewise untenable and unsubstantiated is the claim made in 1889 by Philip Sulley, also repeated in later commentary, that King's vessel foundered inside the Dee estuary off present-day Parkgate. This is unlikely from a nautical perspective, as I explain later, and fails to correlate with the "P.M.S." According to Geoffrey W. Place, an amateur historian living in Parkgate, "there seems to be no evidence to connect Edward King to Parkgate, or his death to its locality."[9]

Although we may never document many details of King's voyage, I wish to demonstrate that a relatively certain account can be formulated. As a result of recent economic and social studies, reliable information concerning seventeenth-century travel between Chester and Dublin has become available. In addition, modern nautical charts of the

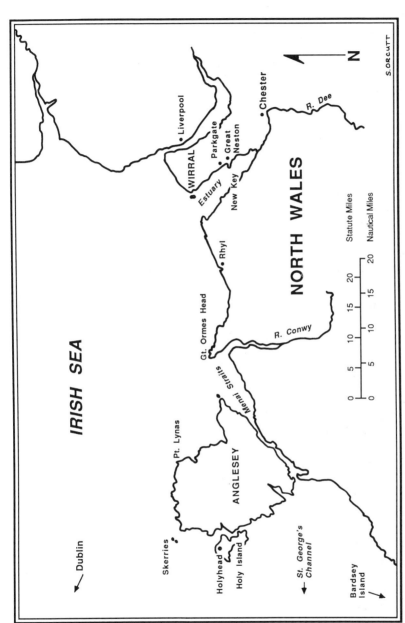

Fig. 1. The area of King's voyage.

IRISH SEA

NORTH WALES

Dublin

Skerries

Pt. Lynas

Holyhead

Holy Island

ANGLESEY

Menai Straits

St. George's
Channel

Bardsey
Island

Gt. Ormes Head

Rhyl

R. Conwy

Estuary

New Key

WIRRAL

Parkgate

Great
Neston

Liverpool

Chester

R. Dee

Statute Miles

Nautical Miles

0   5   10   15   20

0   5   10   15   20

N

S. ORCUTT

Stacey H. Orcutt

North Wales coast provide data on all hazardous offshore rocks, and fortunately for the purposes of this inquiry, only a very few of these correspond with the circumstances depicted in the "P.M.S.," thus narrowing the search for the probable site. Finally, twentieth-century data on tidal streams enable us to estimate with reasonable accuracy King's progress down the Dee to his eventual doom.

On Sunday, 30 July, immediately prior to his departure, King penned a will at Cambridge.[10] Thereafter, it seems probable he spent the following day making final preparations for the 180-mile journey to Chester, departing on the morning of 1 August (Tuesday). He undertook the journey during the Long Vacation at the University, which extended from 7 July to 9 October.[11] Why he did not leave Cambridge until August is unclear, but his eventual departure apparently was dictated by a navigational consideration: 10 August, the day of his death and presumably his embarkation, was the date of a "spring" tide, one of the two highest tides of the month.[12] Regarding King's overland excursion to Chester, the only means of travel available to him was horseback, public coaches being unavailable across the Midlands until the 1650s.[13] Because road conditions frequently were deplorable, King most likely chose major highways whenever possible.[14] Traveling by post-horse, he could reach Chester in four to six days, as the average distance traveled by this means was thirty to forty miles a day (Parkes, p. 62). A study of several seventeenth-century road maps and distance charts leads me to believe he traveled directly west to Northampton, northwest on Watling Street to Coventry, then to Lichfield and Chester.[15] By all accounts King was a devout Anglican and would avoid Sabbath travel, which was frowned upon, so we would expect him to spend the weekend of 6–7 August in devotions and rest, most likely at the cathedral city of Lichfield where his father had died only six months before and where his family had friends.[16] Probably he arrived at Chester a day or two before boarding ship, it being "no easy task to leave England" (Parkes, p. 122). Travel arrangements included obtaining a permit to leave the country (Parkes, p. 122); booking passage on a merchant, mail, or military vessel, as no ships carried only passengers; purchasing provisions for the voyage of 120 nautical miles (one nautical mile equals 1.15 statute miles); and eventually traveling downriver ten or more miles to a Chester outport where seagoing ships anchored.

After completing the arduous, week-long journey from Cambridge and the many preparations for passage to Ireland, King appears to have embarked down the Dee early Thursday morning, 10 August. To reconstruct his voyage, we must establish the following: his most likely point of embarkation, his probable route along the North Wales coast, the vessel's approximate size, normal wind conditions for mid-August, the expected tidal action along the route, and the likely time of embarkation. These estimates will enable us to predict the speed of the vessel as it progressed toward Holyhead, the time it passed each hazardous offshore rock, and the depth of each rock at the time the vessel presumably passed over it.

King's probable point of embarkation can be identified with confidence. It appears certain he did not board a seagoing vessel at Chester itself, despite John Pullen's statement in *Justa* that it was "at this treacherous port that [King] first boarded a boat" and Milton's assertion in the headnote to the second edition of *Lycidas* that King "drown'd in his Passage from *Chester* on the *Irish* Seas."[17] Whether Pullen or Milton refers to the city itself or the broader area of its outports is unclear; Geoffrey Place notes that "it is never certain what travellers meant when they said they sailed from Chester. The whole of the Dee estuary [5 × 15 miles] was known as 'Chester Water.'"[18] The Port of Chester, in fact, extended from mid-central Wales to the River Duddon near the Scottish border. The modest harbor below Chester's Roman walls was no longer used by seagoing ships in King's day. Historians of inland navigation agree that by 1600, if not long before, the River Dee at Chester had become so choked with sand that only small craft were using its harbor, larger vessels anchoring downriver where the channel was deeper. Silting had begun in the fifteenth century after construction of a causeway to provide power for the city's woolen mills.[19] Most of the city's outports were on the Wirral Peninsula, or eastern shore of the Dee, which extended from Shotwick, four miles below Chester, to Hilbre Island at the mouth of the river (see fig. 2).

References to Chester by Pullen and Milton render unlikely an embarkation from Liverpool or Holyhead. Concerning the latter, travelers occasionally took a horse to Holyhead to avoid the dangerous north shore of Anglesey and to offset delays caused by unfavorable winds, as Handel did by coach a century later enroute to Dublin for the first performance of his *Messiah*.[20] A few sailed from the Dee to Anglesey's east shore, then crossed the island to Holyhead. But overland routes in North Wales were decidedly unpopular, presenting travelers many hazards and frustrations in place of those they sought to avoid.[21] Moreover, King did not have sufficient time between 1 and 9 August to ride an additional eighty-five miles to Holyhead; nor would he have encountered any offshore rocks after leaving that anchorage unless his ship were blown immediately off course onto the conspicuous Skerries, which seems quite unlikely.

As it appears certain King embarked down the River Dee, let us consider the seagoing traffic in the estuary. During this period, every settlement below Chester witnessed large vessels anchoring offshore at one time or another, depending on the shifting channel. In *Justa* Pullen accurately portrays the waterway as a busy one, with "numerous ships coming and going."[22] Many of these vessels, according to W. B. Stephens, were Irish owned and manned. The year 1639 was the busiest in the estuary's history, writes Woodward, with an astonishing 709 arrivals or departures of seagoing ships, the majority between June and September.[23] The summer of King's voyage was also busy, an average of perhaps ten to twelve seagoing vessels arriving or departing on each day of favorable weather. Additionally, mail-packet ships shuttled regularly across the channel, small fishing craft and slate trade vessels sailed in and out of the estuary in large numbers, and an occasional military vessel entered as well.[24]

Identifying King's probable point of embarkation on this busy waterway depends on our guessing the kind of ship he chose and which outport was busiest with these ships. It seems probable he had traveled to Ireland often, as many of his immediate family were in residence there.[25] Consequently, we can be quite positive he chose a mail-packet, the larger of which had cabins in the stern (Parkes, p. 111); in this regard, it might be noted that W. Hall, an *Obsequies* elegist, mentions "the fatall barks dark cabbin" (p. 12, line 35), though his account may be largely imaginary. Sensible passengers avoided merchant vessels whenever possible, as they generally were filthy and provided no comforts.[26] Naval vessels also accepted passengers, although a special permit was required (Parkes, p. 113), but we must presume that if King went to his death aboard such a ship, the fact would have been noted.

The major Chester outports along the east bank of the estuary, from south to north, were Shotwick, Burton, Great Neston, Hastewall, Caldey, Dawpool, and Hilbre. Flint, the chief outport on the west bank, was essentially a coal and livestock port.[27] The most frequented outport for mail-packets and passenger trade, according to numerous authorities, was the New Key, or Quay, at Great Neston (today called Neston), which jutted into the estuary ten miles below Chester (see fig. 2). This quay was built between 1557 and 1604 in an effort to strengthen Chester's weakening position as a center of commerce, caused largely by the silting of the Dee. During most of the seventeenth century, the New Key functioned as the major Chester outport for all but the largest vessels engaged in continental trades and transatlantic voyages that anchored at the river's mouth. Not until late in the century did the New Key begin

Fig. 2. The Wirral Peninsula, showing the New Key at Great Neston. Illustration from John Speed, *Theatre* (1611), rpt. in *The Romance of Wirral*, comp. Alice G. Caton (Liverpool: Philip, 1913), endpaper.

to decline as silting began to prevent seagoing ships from reaching it. It seems probable, therefore, that King embarked from this location.[28] After traveling to the New Key from Chester on horseback or aboard a small river craft, King would have made final arrangements for the voyage at the brick quay house a mile below Great Neston (for embarkation arrangements, see Parkes, p. 112). Today the river channel lies several miles west of the site across a salt marsh, the stone quay has long since disappeared (the stones having been sold about 1790), and the quay

house, still standing in the 1920s, has collapsed.[29] When I visited the
area in 1981, a well-marked footpath, commencing at Neston's parish
church, led gently downhill through lanes and fields to the "Old Quay."
At the lonely site, frequented only by dairy cattle, a pile of bricks and
a few scattered stone blocks were all that remained.[30]

I have noted previously that Parkgate has been proposed as the site
of King's embarkation, as well as his foundering, but in 1637 Parkgate
was an isolated, uninhabited spot on the estuary reached from the New
Key by walking a mile along the open shore. No buildings appeared at
the location until about 1700 when it began to compete with the New
Key as an anchorage. Although Parkgate eventually became a fashion-
able resort, no quay was ever built at the site, and we can imagine it
as King's point of embarkation only if the New Key were too overcrowded
to accommodate the regular mail-packet on which he presumably sailed.[31]

Before attempting a reconstruction of King's voyage down the estuary and onto the Irish Sea, I should like to consider the hazards of sea
travel in this region. During the century all extended travel was fraught
with risk. Relatively few Englishmen (and fewer women) traveled at all,
so great were the dangers and discomforts.[32] Sailing along the North Wales
coast was known to be especially perilous: several *Justa* elegists draw attention to this, as does a shipmaster in 1652, who calls the route a "dangerous passage between the kingdoms."[33] Ivor W. Jones observes that
"the North Wales coast proved to be one of the worst hazards of the Atlantic crossing" (p. 20), chiefly because of the "baffling combination of
havens and hazards" along Anglesey's north shore (p. 92). One of the
reasons the area is unsafe for sea travel, according to D. W. Waters, is
the powerful tidal action scouring the shallow seabed, which renders the
waters opaque, obscuring submerged rocks, reefs, and sandbars; the Medi-
terranean, in contrast, exhibits almost no tidal action, resulting in clear
waters and safer navigation.[34] Additional factors include the strong tides,
which create tidal rips or races — areas of turbulence around promontories, offshore rocks, reefs, and sandbars caused by the meeting of op-
posing tides. The first forty-five nautical miles of King's route contain
no such areas of turbulence, but the final fourteen nautical miles, from
Point Lynas to Holyhead, contain over thirty, rendering Anglesey's northern shore a navigational nightmare for any shipmaster approaching the
coast nearer than five or six miles.[35] Rendering navigation even more
uncertain in this area is an August storm track lying within twenty nautical miles of the route, increasing the probability that King's vessel foundered during a storm as suggested by over a third of the *Justa/Obsequies*
contributors.[36]

Compounding these hazards was the absence of sea charts. While it is true that pilot tables called "rutters" were available to provide the literate mariner navigational guidelines, in the earlier seventeenth century they were notoriously unreliable. Not until 1644 did a detailed atlas of the North Wales coast appear, yet it too was inaccurate. Only at the end of the century did a reliable coastal survey become available.[37] Other dangers during the century included the absence of lighthouses and rescue stations, the earliest being built in 1716 and 1828, respectively.[38] King's vessel may have carried a small utility craft, or towed a "long boat" for transporting cargo and passengers ashore, either of which may have functioned as an emergency lifeboat. But these craft held only a few persons, and they were not designed, as modern lifeboats are, to navigate in the heavy seas often present at a ship's foundering, nor in the surf.[39] Even the ships themselves often presented hazards. Because no regulations governed their seaworthiness, many were unsafe: leaky seams in many a ship kept the crew at the pumps rather than on deck, and lack of regulation led to overcrowding and undermanning, thus increasing the likelihood of catastrophe should anything go wrong (Marriott, p. 25).

As if these hazards were not enough, the treacherous coast of North Wales also was remote, wild, and lawless. Travelers by sea and land found the Welsh peasants primitive and hostile. To shipwreck victims they were often vicious. King may have washed ashore, perhaps still alive, but the Welsh customarily offered no assistance to shipwreck victims, even attacking them for their belongings, and gave them no burial — barbarisms not limited to the Welsh coast and condemned in Milton's own "Commonplace Book."[40] A more fearsome threat than the Welsh, however, were pirates. In the 1630s the Irish Sea was a haven for piracy. Not until the Civil War (1642–46) was the area cleared of pirate ships and made safe (in this respect) for commerce (Jones, p. 12). The marauding ships came from Scotland and France, others from North Africa and Turkey seeking white slaves in addition to booty.[41] A sample report by Sir Thomas Button, admiral on the Irish Sea, tells of 150 white travelers seized off North Wales during 1631 and carried to North Africa as slaves (Jones, pp. 11–12). Small wonder that several of the *Justa/Obsequies* elegists refer to this terrorizing activity, implying that King's ship may have been forced onto the fatal rock by pirates.[42] Considering all these dangers, we must conclude that in 1637 the Dee-to-Dublin route was inviting only to the courageous or the reckless voyager. King's depositing a will prior to his departure probably was common practice among long-distance travelers, particularly those journeying through so hazardous a region.

Modern nautical charts (see note 35) are indispensable in determining the probable location of King's death. Besides indicating dangerous promontories, offshore rocks, reefs, and sandbars, they provide depth notations essential to an evaluation of the nautical dangers King's ship would have encountered. Common sense suggests that sailing vessels kept well offshore to avoid these navigational hazards, including a "lee shore" (wind from sea to land) that might carry them to disaster; should favorable winds die, a ship might be carried helplessly onto rocks by the tide, as was the *Alert* in 1823, which drifted onto West Mouse off north Anglesey with a loss of 140 lives (Jones, pp. 96–97). The idea that early mariners clung to the coastline appears to be largely myth: during a voyage depicted in Sir Francis Kynaston's long poem *Leoline and Sydanis* (1642), a ship sailing from the Dee to Ireland passes Anglesey's "solitary coast beyond sight of land."[43]

King's vessel appears to have navigated the estuary safely despite the few offshore rocks and islands near the east bank at the river's mouth. Jones reports the existence of "a thousand [known] wrecks along the coast of North Wales," but few inside the estuary, implying the river was not especially dangerous;[44] in addition, it will be remembered, the "P.M.S." places the vessel on the Irish Sea at its foundering. King would emerge from the estuary through the Welsh Channel, then sail through what is now called the "Inner Passage" three miles off Rhyl (see fig. 3). Proceeding five to seven miles offshore past Great Ormes Head and the mouth of the Menai Straits, the shipmaster would steer for Point Lynas on Anglesey's northeast coast, then sail along the island's north shore, finally turning south past Carmel Head to harbor at Holyhead Bay. The only alternate route lies through the Menai Straits between island and mainland, but because this passage was used primarily by small coastal vessels engaged in slate trade and was known to be particularly dangerous to larger vessels, King's ship most likely avoided it.[45]

If we are to locate the most probable site of King's death, we must reconstruct the ship's course, hour by hour, along the route just outlined. The ship's speed would be determined by its size, wind conditions, and river and tidal currents. Regarding size, it should be noted that Henry King refers to his brother's boat as "small," although whether he actually knew its size is unclear (*Obsequies*, p. 3, line 100). We know that merchant and mail-packet ships operating from the Dee in the 1630s were, indeed, relatively small, averaging only twenty to thirty tons "burden" (or cargo capacity). Such ships would have a waterline length of thirty to fifty feet and a "draft" (depth below waterline when loaded) of only five to six feet.[46] The maximum speed in nautical miles per hour (or knots)

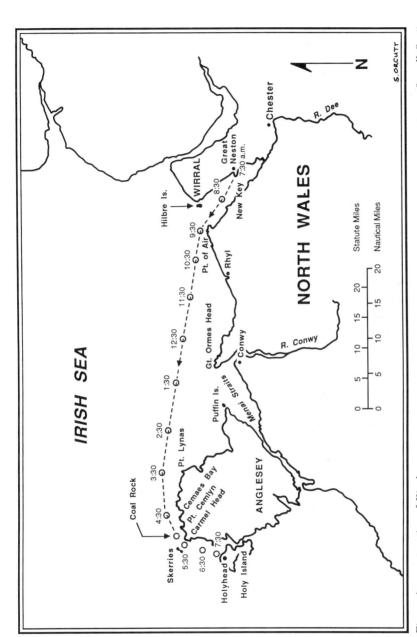

Fig. 3. A reconstruction of King's voyage.

Stacey H. Orcutt

of a sailing vessel in still water, called the "hull speed," is approximately the square root of its length at waterline (*Offshore*, p. 131). Assuming King's vessel were of average size for this period with a waterline length of forty feet, its hull speed would be 6.3 knots, its realistic speed in still water perhaps four knots. This general speed estimate is corroborated by the findings of D. W. Waters, who states that "the ordinary sailing ship [in the seventeenth century] seldom attained a speed of more than 4 to 6 knots, 4 knots, say, on average."[47] Waters's figures are "over-the-bottom" speeds, which include the effects of tidal streams. If, for instance, King's ship were capable of four knots in still water, in a tidal stream of 1.5 knots it would reach an over-the-bottom speed of 5.5 knots, providing its direction were the same as that of the stream.

With regard to wind conditions the ship is likely to have encountered, the prevailing winds over most of the North Atlantic above 40° north latitude are generally from the west.[48] Travelers bound for Ireland, as a consequence, were often delayed awaiting favorable winds, although apparently King was not. August easterlies (winds from the east) average eight to twelve miles per hour in this area, westerlies thirteen to eighteen miles per hour (*Pilot Chart*), thus rendering a voyage to Ireland slower than a return. For this reason, vessels sailing west might be expected to average four to five knots, those sailing east six to seven knots.

Even though wind conditions doubtless played a vital role in King's voyage, he appears to have planned the embarkation, as noted earlier, to coincide with the spring tide of 10 August, which occurred at the New Key about 11:20 A.M.[49] He may have obtained the date of this important high tide from an almanac or computed it himself using a formula widely employed by mariners.[50] Spring tides brought the deepest waters and strongest tidal streams to the estuary, hence increasing the likelihood of departure and subsequent arrival at Holyhead before nightfall.

We must now focus attention on King's probable time of embarkation. Because Holyhead, his presumed overnight anchorage, would be enveloped in darkness about 8:30 P.M. on 10 August, a departure at high water, or 11:20 A.M., would allow only nine hours for this portion of the voyage and require an improbable speed of seven knots. It appears likely, therefore, that King's shipmaster embarked much earlier, taking advantage of the river current to carry the ship to the Irish Sea by the time the tide turned west to help draw it toward Anglesey. Departing at 7:30 A.M. and sailing at an average speed of 4.8 knots would allow the shipmaster to reach Holyhead by sunset at 7:30 P.M., leaving sufficient time for passengers to disembark before nightfall. Even if he were bound nonstop for Dublin, King's mariner probably would follow this schedule, although his route would be farther offshore and the last half of the voyage conducted in the dark. Sailing at night was avoided whenever possible, however, as it greatly increased the navigational risk.

The hypothetical voyage described below and portrayed in figure 3 is based upon estimates made to this point: a vessel of forty feet waterline length with a draft of six feet and a hull speed of five knots; strong easterly winds and a spring tide; embarkation from the New Key on 10 August at 7:30 A.M.; and Holyhead the intended overnight anchorage. As recorded in the notes, I have taken into account the time difference between Neston and Holyhead with respect to high water and low water. Finally, although I have estimated with care the continuously changing effects of river and tidal streams on King's vessel, I have attempted no mathematical precision regarding the ship's speed, there being too few facts concerning the voyage to justify any exactitude.[51]

Casting off from the New Key about 7:30 A.M., King's captain would reach the sea in about two hours.[52] During the following six hours, his vessel would be expected to hold a steady course for Point Lynas of about 280°, arriving off this promontory about 3:30 in the afternoon.[53] No hazardous locations would be encountered during this portion of the voyage unless the ship were forced inshore or lost in a fog, circumstances which might cause it to run aground on a promontory, islet, or island. But we can eliminate these hazards with confidence on the assumption that if King's ship wrecked on such a spot, passengers and crew would have found at least temporary refuge. The "P.M.S." implies, to the contrary, that the fatal rock was not a promontory or island, and that no refuge was at hand. As for offshore rocks, it is true that two lie at the mouth of the River Conwy, but both are more than five miles south of King's route and would be covered by seven feet and eight feet of water respectively when King's ship presumably sailed through the area, thus posing no danger to a ship of six feet draft.[54]

The most perilous portion of King's journey to Holyhead is the final fourteen nautical miles along Anglesey's northern coast. This shoreline is replete with dangers — not only points of land, islets, and islands, but many offshore rocks, reefs, sandbars, and areas of tidal turbulence.[55] King's master doubtless timed his embarkation from Great Neston to enable his vessel to round Carmel Head before the tide ran strongly against it. Three or four hours after low water in this area, spring tides run northeast and east at an astonishing five knots, even higher in the immediate vicinity of Carmel Head (*Sailing Dir.*, p. 276). A vessel sailing west, capable of five knots hull speed and confronted by such a current, would make no progress and be forced to anchor overnight in one of the desolate and dangerous bays along the coast. Following the schedule I am proposing, the vessel would pass Carmel Head before encountering the worst of these tidal extremes: at Point Lynas by 3:30 P.M., it would be opposite Cemaes Bay shortly after low water, occurring in this vicinity about 4:15 P.M., and with favorable winds would reach Carmel Head by 5:30, where it would encounter the beginnings of tidal turbulence and a tidal stream of 2.2 knots against it. About sunset the ship would enter the safety of Holyhead Bay.[56]

Within the final fourteen-mile section of the ship's route lies an area of extreme navigational danger, the four-mile zone between Point Cemlyn and Carmel Head. Eight offshore rocks await the unsuspecting seaman in this zone, and two more lie beyond Carmel Head in the approach to Holyhead Bay.[57] Given sufficient sailing time and satisfactory winds, the sensible mariner would avoid this area by sailing beyond the Skerries before steering south for Holyhead. Presumably because time was short or winds were unfavorable for this detour, King's master apparently sailed directly through this zone, and at a time when the water was low, the tide moving against him, the sea somewhat turbulent in many locations, and if the weather were clear, the sun in his face. Not surprising, then, to find a *Justa* elegist railing at that "wretched pilot of the boat, by whose crime a youth of great hope, my pupil, perished in a rude inglorious death."[58]

Fortunately most of the ten offshore rocks noted above would be deeply enough submerged at low water to pose no danger to King's relatively shallow vessel, even though the tidal rapids they create might cause navigational difficulty: Carmel Rocks, for instance, "are marked by heavy tide rips, except for a short time at slack water" (*Sailing Dir.*, p. 276). Middle Rock, the deepest of these, would be under about thirty-two feet of water when King presumably passed through; the most shallow, excluding the final two rocks to be noticed shortly, is Clipera Rocks, under 8.5 feet of water. Only two offshore rocks in this zone would pose any danger to King's ship during a late afternoon passage on 10 August: East Platters and Coal Rock. Portions of the Platters, a reef about half a mile southeast of the Skerries, dry to a height of 4.6 feet at low water (or four feet, *Sailing Dir.*, p. 281), thus leaving them readily visible in fair weather. About 5:30 P.M., when King probably sailed through this passage, portions of the Platters would be exposed to a height of 1.5 feet. By 6:00 P.M. they would be wholly submerged and hence more treacherous; but if King's ship were sailing over them at this time, it would be too far behind schedule, given tidal conditions, to reach Holyhead before nightfall. Consequently it seems reasonable to assume that King's ship rounded Carmel Head at a time when the Platters were visible, at least at close range. We would expect King's master to be watching for them through this area, since they can be located readily by their close proximity to the always visible Skerries. Finally, *Justa* contributors Pullen and John Pearson describe the fatal rock as "hidden," suggesting a submerged rather than a protruding hazard.[59] These considerations, taken together, appear to diminish considerably the likelihood that King foundered on the Platters.

Excluding the East Platters as a likely location for the disaster leaves but a single offshore rock on King's route capable of "stoving in" his vessel during the late afternoon on the fateful day — Coal Rock. This hazard lies nearly two miles north-northeast off Carmel Head near the end of a rocky bank and directly on the approach to the passage between Carmel Head and the Skerries.[60] A formidable array of six tidal rips with Coal Rock at its center forms a crescent facing east, the direction of King's approach, like open jaws awaiting any unsuspecting craft. At low water (which occurred at 4:17 P.M. on this date), Coal Rock is "awash,"[61] and by 4:50 P.M., when I estimate King to have sailed here, the rock would be submerged at a depth of 1.5 feet, obscured in the opaque Atlantic even at close range in fair weather, and quite capable of sinking King's vessel. Coal Rock would pose a serious threat, in fact, to any vessel of six feet or more draft for about four and a half hours on this August afternoon, or from 2:00 to 6:30 P.M.[62] Its being two miles offshore ensures that unless another vessel were immediately at hand to pick up survivors, or the ship carried or towed a light craft, no shipwreck victims would survive. Thus Hogg probably was right in guessing that "some escaped in [a] Boat," since someone survived and reported the mishap. A small craft with survivors might be rowed to the safety of Cemlyn Bay provided the sea was not rough, but victims in the water or floating on ballast would be carried east by the strong tidal stream farther and farther from land, and eventually through the North Channel to the Hebrides as Milton envisions happening to King's body. A more likely location for the catastrophe is difficult to imagine.

To sum up, it is my estimation that Edward King drowned when his ship collided with Coal Rock two miles off the northwest coast of Anglesey at about 4:50 P.M. on 10 August 1637 while sailing southwest at a speed of 3.7 knots toward an overnight anchorage at Holyhead Bay. If we accept the "P.M.S." account of this tragedy, the only seemingly reliable one available, and assume that King took passage on an average-sized vessel of the period and region, then sailed the common route to Dublin under favorable winds, Coal Rock is the only highly probable site for the disaster.

University of Maine at Farmington

NOTES

I wish to thank the following for their assistance and encouragement: Gordon Campbell (University of Leicester), Frank F. Doran and Shirley A. Martin (University of Maine at Farmington), John T. Shawcross (University of Kentucky), Donald M. Woodward (University of Hull), Lester R. Dickey, Roger M. Fransson, Edward Le Comte, Kathy McLaughlin, Geoffrey W. Place, my wife Jeanine, and my own university for making possible a visit to Cambridge, Chester, and the Wirral Peninsula.

1. J. B. Leishman, *Milton's Minor Poems*, ed. Geoffrey Tillotson (1969; rpt. Pittsburgh: University of Pittsburgh Press, 1969), p. 271.

2. This slim volume, published at Cambridge by Thomas Buck and Roger Daniel, has two parts. The first, *Justa Edovardo King naufrago . . .* , contains a Latin prose panegyric entitled "P.M.S.," an introductory encomium in Latin, and nineteen Latin elegies interspersed with three elegies in Greek. The second, *Obsequies to the memorie of Mr Edward King . . .* , contains eleven elegies in English, and two poems of consolation to Edward's sister Margaret, also in English. The volume, cited in this study as *Justa/Obsequies*, has been thrice reprinted, most recently in a useful facsimile edition by Edward Le Comte, the first with translations and notes (Norwood, Pa.: Norwood, 1978). I refer to this edition in the following pages and here record my debt to it. The majority of the twenty-three contributors whose identities are known were young men at Cambridge ranging in age from fifteen to twenty-four (Le Comte, "Introduction," *Justa/Obsequies*, p. v). Milton, who had completed a master's degree at Cambridge five years before, was studying at Hammersmith. Information about the contributors may be found in Le Comte's introduction and notes, and in Ernest C. Mossner's introduction to *Justa Edovardo King: Reproduced* [in facsimile] *from the Original Edition, 1638, with an Introduction* (New York: Columbia University Press [for the Facsimile Text Society], 1939), pp. xi–xiv.

3. The poetic accounts vary so widely we cannot believe that the authors, as a group, were in possession of the facts. Milton, for instance, describes the day as calm, but nearly half the contributors claim it was stormy. "Either the elegists were not equally acquainted with the facts," writes George Williamson, or else they "were unequally bound by them" ("The Obsequies for Edward King," in his *Seventeenth Century Contexts* [London: Faber, 1960], p. 134). It appears likely, however, that certain contributors, including Milton, "took into account the poems of others, to which they clearly had access" (Michael Lloyd, "Justa Edouardo King," *N&Q*, new series V [1958], 432). See also Leishman, *Milton's Minor Poems*, p. 249; Joseph Anthony Wittreich, Jr., *Visionary Poetics: Milton's Tradition and His Legacy* (San Marino, Calif.: Huntington Library, 1979), pp. 89–97, 127; and Joseph Wittreich, "From Pastoral to Prophecy: the Genres of *Lycidas,*" *Milton Studies*, vol. XIII, ed. James D. Simmonds (Pittsburgh: University of Pittsburgh Press, 1979), p. 73.

The author of the "P.M.S." remains unidentified, but the clumsiness of the writing indicates the person was not a competent Latinist. The following discuss this brief piece: David Masson, *The Life of John Milton* . . . (1881; rpt. Gloucester, Mass.: Smith, 1965), vol. I, p. 651; Mossner, *Justa*, p. vi; William R. Parker, *Milton: A Biography* (Oxford: Clarendon Press, 1968), vol. II, p. 811n69; Leishman, *Milton's Minor Poems*, pp. 247–55; Le Comte, "Translations and Notes," in *Justa/Obsequies*, p. 60n20; James Dale, "Justa Edovardo King," in *A Milton Encyclopedia*, ed. William B. Hunter, Jr. et al. (Lewisburg, Pa.: Bucknell University Press, 1978), vol. IV, p. 176.

For dialogue about the puzzling "P.M.S." title, see Edward Le Comte, "Milton *versus* Time," in his *Milton's Unchanging Mind: Three Essays* (Port Washington, N.Y.: Kennikat, 1973), p. 62n106; Edward Le Comte, "'P.M.S.' in the Edward King Preface," *MQ* XVI (1982), 83; Gordon Campbell, "'P.M.S.' and the Contributors to *Justa Edouardo King*," *MQ* XVII (1983), 58–59; Edward Le Comte, "More on 'P.M.S.,'" *MQ* XVIII (1984), 135; Jeremy Maule, "'P.M.S.' as Obituary Abbreviation," *MQ* XVIII (1984), 135–36; and G. W. Pigman III, *Grief and the English Renaissance Elegy* (Cambridge: Cambridge University Press, 1985), p. 147n20.

4. Exchequer port books, presently housed at the Public Record Office, London, contain information about sea traffic such as ship names, cargo, and cargo capacities. Seldom do they refer to passengers. If King's vessel were Irish owned and manned, which is quite possible, we would hope to find it mentioned in Irish port books, but unfortunately these Irish records for 1637 are also missing.

5. The passage reads as follows: "*haud procul a littore Britannico, navi in scopulum allisa, et rimis ex ictu fatiscente, dum alii vectores vitae mortalis frustra satagerent, immortalem anhelans, in genua provolutus oransque, una cum navigio ab aquis absorptus, animam deo reddidit; IIII. eid. sextileis; anno salutis MDCXXXVII; aetatis XXV*" ("P.M.S.," in *Justa*, sig. A2ʳ). All seventeenth-century dates are given in Old Style; 10 August 1937 is equivalent to our present 20 August.

6. William Hogg, "To the Reader," *Paraphrasis Latina, in Duo Poemata* . . . (London: For the Author, 1694) sig. Bʳ. Gordon Campbell (presently preparing a revised edition of Parker's biography of Milton) believes as I do that Hogg is merely guessing without evidence that a boat was at hand (letter to the author, 11 December 1983). The notion is repeated in the following: *The Poetical Works of John Milton*, ed. David Masson (New York: Crowell, 1892), p. 425, hereafter *PW*; James B. Mullinger, "Edward King," in *The Dictionary of National Biography*, 1964–65, hereafter *DNB*; and Don M. Wolfe, *Milton and His England* (Princeton: Princeton University Press, 1971), item 26. Robert Graves, "The Ghost of Milton," in his *Common Asphodel: Collected Essays on Poetry, 1922–1949* (1949; rpt. New York: Haskell, 1970), p. 322n2; repeated by Michael Stapleton, *The Cambridge Guide to English Literature* (Cambridge: Cambridge University Press, 1983), p. 542.

7. Regarding Holyhead as a key anchorage on the Dee-to-Dublin route, see Ivor W. Jones, *Shipwrecks of North Wales* (Newton Abbot, Devon.: David, 1973), p. 70. I am indebted to Jones for many insights into sea travel off North Wales.

8. Bardsey Island lies thirty-five nautical miles south of the route between Chester and Dublin — a half-day's journey. For Hughes's references to the island, see *John Milton: Complete Poems and Major Prose*, ed. Merritt Y. Hughes (Indianapolis: Odyssey, 1957), pp. 116, 121n (to lines 50–55).

9. Philip Sulley (who has King traveling, however, *from* Ireland), *The Hundred of Wirral* (Birkenhead, Chesh.: Haram, 1889), p. 190. This is repeated in the following: *Cheshire: the Romantic North-West*, ed. Arthur Mee (London: Hodder, 1938), p. 132; Michael Hardwick, *A Literary Atlas & Gazetteer of the British Isles* (Detroit: Gale, 1973), p. 95; and *The Oxford Literary Guide to the British Isles*, comp. and ed. Dorothy Eagle

and Hilary Carnell (Oxford: Clarendon Press, 1977), p. 276, originally stating "it was off [Parkgate] that Milton's friend . . . was drowned," but revised in 1978 (at the suggestion of Geoffrey Place) to read "after leaving [Parkgate] Milton's friend . . . was drowned." The statement by Geoffrey Place in the text comes from a letter to Dorothy Eagle, September 1977 (a copy of which she kindly forwarded to me).

10. King's will is at the Cambridge University archives. Its first and major paragraph, dated 30 July, surely was penned by King, as the handwriting closely resembles the entries in Christ's College admissions book known to have been made by King in 1633–34 while he was praelector. The second paragraph, dated 1 August, appears to be a codicil; although signed "Edward King," this addition, not in his hand, seems to have been penned by his brother Henry King, who also witnessed the document. In addition to examining xerographic copies of the will and associated probate records, I have had the benefit of observations about King's handwriting by Henry G. Button, Honorary Archivist, Christ's College (letter to the author, 7 April 1989).

Subsequent probate records of King's effects are also available at Cambridge. A transcription of the will was entered, as was customary, in the records of the Prerogative Court of Canterbury. The only published study of the will is by David H. Stevens, "The Will of Edward King," in his *Milton Papers* (Chicago: Chicago University Press, 1927), pp. 35–38; Stevens provides a transcription of both portions, but with minor inaccuracies. Unfortunately he does not mention the earlier date, the differences in handwriting, or the existence of probate records.

11. These dates have been supplied by Dorothy M. Owen, Keeper of the Archives, The University Library, Cambridge (letter to the author, 26 September 1985).

12. Spring tides (*spring,* German for *full* or *flood*) occur at or immediately following each new and full moon. The fact that 10 August 1637 (Old Style) was the date of a spring tide has been kindly provided by Commander N. C. Glen, Superintendent of the Tidal Branch, Hydrographic Dept., U.K. Ministry of Defense (letter to the author, 30 March 1984). Corroboration of the date as that of a new moon can be found in Herman H. Goldstine, *New and Full Moons: 1001 B.C. to 1651* (New York: American Philosophical Society, 1973), p. 220.

13. Joan Parkes, *Travel in England in the Seventeenth Century* (1925; rpt. Oxford: Clarendon Press, 1968), pp. 81–84.

14. Virtually all authorities agree that England's major roads during this period were abominable, owing largely to increased commerce, while many secondary roads were no more than unmarked trails. Among many studies, the following might be singled out: Parkes, *Travel in England,* pp. 206–18; Virginia A. LaMar, *Travel and Roads in England* (Washington, D.C.: Folger Shakespeare Library, 1960), pp. 1, 7–10, 19; and Esther Moir, *The Discovery of Britain: the English Tourists 1540 to 1840* (London: Routledge, 1964), pp. 6–10.

15. If King traveled twenty-five to thirty miles a day along this route, which seems reasonable for a long journey, his itinerary would likely approximate the following (distances are given in modern statute miles):

August 1 (T)	Kimbolton	31 miles
2 (W)	Northampton	27
3 (Th)	Coventry	28
4 (F)	Lichfield	27
5 (Sat)	(no travel)	
6 (Sun)	(no travel)	
7 (M)	Newcastle	33
8 (T)	Chester	30

Those wishing further information on traveling English roads during this period might wish to consider the following. Distance tables of selected main roads, given in Old English miles, are presented by Raphael Holinshed, *Chronicles: England, Scotland, and Ireland* (1577; rpt. New York: AMS, 1965), vol. I, pp. 414–21; more complete distance tables, also in Old English miles, are to be found in John Norden, *England; An Intended Guyde for English Travailers* (1625; rpt. Amsterdam: Theatrum Orbis Terrarum, 1979). The first English road atlas, John Ogilby's *Britannia* (1675; rpt. Amsterdam: Theatrum Orbis Terrarum, 1970), is comprised of accurate strip maps with distances in modern statute miles; it also contains a useful chart by J. B. Harley, p. xxi, for converting Old English miles, which varied by location, to modern statute miles. Also helpful in determining overland routes is John Ogilby and William Morgan's "Road Map of 1689," reprinted in Parkes, *Travel in England*, endpaper.

16. On Sabbath travel, see LaMar, *Travel and Roads*, p. 4, and *How They Lived: An Anthology of Original Accounts Written Between 1485 and 1700*, comp. Molly Harrison and O. M. Royston (1963; rpt. Oxford: Blackwell, 1965), vol. II, pp. 148–51.

Edward's father, Sir John King, spent most of his adult life in Ireland as a government administrator. He was a widower at his death on 4 January 1637 and was buried on 30 March at the family estate at Boyle, County Roscommon, Ireland. Sir John's wife, Catherine Drury, died in 1617, and he did not remarry. Edward's sister Margaret had also lived at Lichfield, and her acquaintance with John Hayward, chancellor of the cathedral, prompted his two contributions to *Justa/Obsequies*. Additional information about the King family can be found in Gordon Goodwin, "Sir John King" and "Sir Robert King," *DNB*; Mullinger, "Edward King," *DNB*; and in Family Group Records of Sir John King and Catherine Drury at the archives, Family History Library, The Church of Jesus Christ of Latter-day Saints, Salt Lake City, Utah. Information about John Hayward can be found in John LeNeve, *Fasti Ecclesiae Anglicanae, 1541–1857* (London: University of London Press, 1969), p. 585, and Thomas Harwood, *The History and Antiquities of the Church and City of Lichfield* (London: Cadell, 1806), p. 199.

17. Pullen, in *Justa*, p. 11 (lines 24, 28), trans. p. 15; John Milton, *Poems of Mr. John Milton* (1645; facs. ed., Menston, York.: Scolar, 1973), p. 57.

18. Place, letter to the author, 19 August 1981.

19. The geographical extent of the Port of Chester is given by Joan Beck, *Tudor Cheshire* (Chester: Cheshire Community Council, 1969), p. 9. Edna Rideout, "The Chester Companies and the Old Quay," in *Transactions of the Historic Society of Lancashire and Cheshire* LXXIX (1928), 141, hereafter *THSLC*, estimates that by the end of the fifteenth century larger vessels were anchoring no closer than twelve miles from Chester. Among many who concur that Chester was not regularly used in the earlier seventeenth century as an anchorage for larger vessels are T. S. Willan, *River Navigation in England 1600–1750* (1936; rpt. London, Cass, 1964), p. 19; D. M. Woodward, *The Trade of Elizabethan Chester*, Occasional Papers in Economic and Social History, no. 4 (Hull, York.: University of Hull, 1970), p. 3; and Gwyneth M. Haynes-Thomas, "The Port of Chester," *Transactions of the Lancashire and Cheshire Antiquarian Society* LIX (1947), 35.

20. Geoffrey Place, *This Is Parkgate: Its Buildings and Their Story* (n.p.: Parkgate and District Society, 1979), p. 27.

21. For an account of an August 1626 journey of this sort, see *The Cheshire Sheaf*, 3rd series, XV (1918), 7, item 3502, which cites the "College Diary," Trinity College, Dublin. The overland route from Chester to Holyhead, often no more than an unmarked path, disappeared altogether on the tidal flats between the mainland and Beaumaris (see Ogilby, *Britannia* plate 24, following p. 46). Frank Marriott, "To Dublin—from the Dee," *Cheshire Life* (September 1952), p. 25, writes that "almost all preferred the long

sea voyage [to] the terrifying track across the coastal mountains of North Wales, and the bad road over the Isle of Anglesey."

22. Pullen, in *Justa*, p. 11 (lines 26–27), trans. p. 15.

23. W. B. Stephens, "The Overseas Trade of Chester in the Early Seventeenth Century," *THSLC* CXX (1968), 23, 34; and D. M. Woodward, "The Overseas Trade of Chester, 1600–1650," *THSLC* CXXII (1970), 28–36. Woodward identifies coal as the primary export to Ireland, cattle and sheep the major imports.

24. Parkes, *Travel in England*, p. 111; Rupert H. Morris, *Chester in the Plantagenet and Tudor Reigns* (Chester: For the Author, n.d.), pp. 472, 573–74.

25. From the "P.M.S." we learn that Edward's eldest brother, Sir Robert King, and two of his sisters, "Anne, wife of G. Caulfield, Baron Charlemont" and "Margaret, wife of Lord G. Loder, Chief Justice of Ireland," were among those he wished to visit in Ireland. His brother Henry was at Cambridge but did not accompany him on the journey to Ireland. The whereabouts of his brothers John, Roger (who had matriculated with him at Cambridge in 1626), Adam, and his sister Dorothy are unknown. In 1637 perhaps not all were living.

26. Parkes, *Travel in England*, pp. 111–13; Donald Woodward, "Ships, Masters and Shipowners of the Wirral 1550–1650," *Mariners' Mirror* LXIII (1977), 237.

27. Woodward, "Ships, Masters," 233; Woodward, "Overseas Trade," 34.

28. S. A. Pargeter asserts that "the New Quay near to Great Neston was the outport . . . and hence the main embarkation point for Ireland" during the earlier part of the seventeenth century (writing for the Assistant Director of Resources, Libraries and Museums Dept., Cheshire County Council, letter to the author, 26 February 1981). Geoffrey Place draws attention to a letter in the Cheshire Record Office by Charles I, dated 16 August 1642, that refers to Neston as a major port for Irish commerce (letter to the author). Among many published accounts of Neston's navigational importance during this period, the following are representative: Rideout, who presents the fullest account, "Chester Companies," 141–57; Edna Rideout, "Account Book of the New Haven, Chester, 1567–8," *THSLC* LXXIX (1928), 86–128; Morris, *Chester*, pp. 460–62, 471; Woodward, *Trade*, pp. 2–3; F. V. Emery, "England *circa* 1600," in *A New Historical Geography of England*, ed. H. C. Darby (Cambridge: Cambridge University Press, 1973), p. 298; and Robert N. Dore, *Cheshire* (London: Batsford, 1977), p. 44. Reports of passenger travel to and from the New Key during this period can be found reprinted in the following issues of *The Cheshire Sheaf*, 3rd series XV (1918), 7, item 3502; XIX (1922), 56, item 4601; XXXIV (1939), 62, item 7621, and 68, item 7631; XXXIX (1944), 89, item 8455; and LX (1965), 20, item 11307.

29. Rideout, "Chester Companies," which includes photographs of the quay house. From this study we learn that about 1670–80, as the future of the New Key became threatened, the quay house was converted to an inn called the "Key Hous." About 1850 one room of the inn was known as "The Smuggler's Hole [because] subterranean passages ran [a mile] from it up to Doctor's Meadow somewhere near the present Carnegie Library in Neston" (158).

30. A long sandstone structure lying immediately north of the quay house site, thought by Dore, *Cheshire*, p. 44, to be part of the quay, is a sea wall built during the last century (Place, letter to the author).

31. Parkgate first appeared on a map in 1689, but not until about 1730 was it seriously challenging the New Key as an anchorage for large ships (Rideout, "Chester Companies," 151–52). Place writes that "it is quite possible Edward King sailed from [the New Key]. . . . We can certainly rule out Parkgate, for which there are [only] a few scattered

references as an anchorage from 1611" (letter to the author). Donald M. Woodward voices the same opinion: "I would imagine that Parkgate was *not* the point of departure in the 1630's" (letter to the author, 22 June 1981). Further confirmation that Parkgate was not a regularly used outport in King's day can be found in the following: T. S. Willan, "Chester and the Navigation of the Dee, 1600–1750," *Journal of the Chester and North Wales Architectural, Archaeological and Historical Society*, new series XXXII (1938), 66; and *The Cheshire Sheaf*, 3rd series I (1896), 46–47; XII (1915), 91, item 2985; XIX (1922), 95, item 4690; XXXIII (1938), 29, item 7336.

32. LaMar, *Travel and Roads*, p. 1; Moir, *Discovery*, pp. xv, 4.

33. The elegists are Pullen, *Justa*, p. 11 (line 28), trans. p. 15; Coke (perhaps Francis Cooke or Coke, according to Le Comte, *Justa/Obsequies* facs. ed., "Trans. and Notes," p. 63), *Justa*, p. 20 (line 33), trans. p. 29; and Christopher Bainbrigge, *Justa*, p. 34 (lines 28–32), trans. p. 53. The shipmaster is Capt. Edv. Billingsley, letter reprinted in *The Cheshire Sheaf*, 1st series II (1880–82), 35, item 1052.

34. D. W. Waters, "Science and the Techniques of Navigation in the Renaissance," *Art, Science, and History in the Renaissance*, ed. Charles S. Singleton (Baltimore: Johns Hopkins University Press, 1970), p. 191.

35. In the present study, nautical data comes from the following charts unless otherwise noted: *North Wales: Holyhead to Great Ormes Head*, chart 36122; *England and Wales: Great Ormes Head to Liverpool*, chart 36123; and *Nautical Chart Symbols and Abbreviations*, 7th ed., chart 1. These charts were published at Washington, D.C., by the U.S. Department of Defense, Defense Mapping Agency (Hydrographic/Topographic Center), 1979.

36. *Pilot Chart of the North Atlantic Ocean*, August 1976 (Washington, D.C.: U.S. Department of Defense, Defense Mapping Agency [Hydrographic Center]). Of the nearly thirty contributors to *Justa/Obsequies*, twelve refer to a storm as a major factor in King's shipwreck.

37. For accounts of sea charts during this period, see D. W. Waters, *The Art of Navigation in England in Elizabethan and Early Stuart Times* (New Haven: Yale University Press, 1958), pp. 11–14; D. W. Waters, *The Rutters of the Sea: The Sailing Directions of Pierre Garcie: A Study of the First English and French Printed Sailing Directions, with Facsimile Reproductions* (New Haven: Yale University Press, 1967), *passim*; Waters, "Science and the Techniques," 189–233; and Michel Mollat du Jourdin, Monique de La Roncière et al., *Sea Charts of the Early Explorers 13th to 17th Century*, trans. L. le R. Dethan (New York: Thames, 1984), plate 79 and pp. 255–56. Attention is drawn to rutter inaccuracy and to the 1693 coastal survey by T. S. Willan, *The English Coasting Trade: 1600–1750* (Manchester: Manchester University Press, 1938), p. 21. The 1644 atlas is described by Olwen C. Evans, *Marine Plans and Charts of Wales* (London: Map Collectors' Circle, 1969 [publication 54]), p. 21.

38. According to Jones, *Shipwrecks*, pp. 15, 97, the first lighthouse in North Wales was established on the Skerries, a group of tiny islands seven nautical miles north of Holyhead, and the first lifeboat station at Cemlyn, near Point Cemlyn. Further information may be found in Major A. J. Dawson, *Britain's Life-Boats: The Story of a Century of Heroic Service* (London: Hodder, 1923), pp. 19, 259–68.

39. Nöel T. Methley, *The Life-Boat and Its Story* (London: Sidgwick, 1912), p. 2; Dawson, *Britain's Life-Boats*, pp. 10–11; and William A. Baker, *Sloops & Shallops* (Barre, Mass.: Barre, 1966), pp. 8–12.

40. Welsh barbarisms are described by Jones, *Shipwrecks*, pp. 12, 25, 56. For Milton's statement, see Ruth Mohl's ed. of his "Commonplace Book," in *Complete Prose*

Works of John Milton, ed. Don M. Wolfe et al. (New Haven: Yale University Press, 1953), vol. I, pp. 507–8.

41. Willan, *English Coasting Trade*, pp. 24–30; see also Parkes, *Travel in England*, pp. 119–20; Morris, *Chester*, pp. 476–78; Jones, *Shipwrecks*, pp. 11–12, 52, 70, 73; and Henry Parry, *Wreck and Rescue on the Coast of Wales* (Truro, Corn.: Barton, 1969), vol. I, p. 9. The major piracy centers during the first half of the century were Dunkirk and Algiers, according to Willan, *English Coasting Trade*, p. 29. On this point, see also John K. Laughton, "Sir Thomas Button," *DNB*.

42. Contributors who refer to pirates, although none claim that King's ship was actually attacked, are Nicholas Felton, *Justa*, p. 7 (line 225), trans. p. 11; Pullen, *Justa*, p. 11 (line 14), trans. p. 15, who specifies black pirates; and Henry King, *Obsequies*, p. 3 (line 96).

43. The major portion of the voyage is described in stanza 109:

> The sea-bred steeds so swiftly cut the main,
> As that the sight of every land was lost,
> But a glass being turn'd, they see again
> The island Mona's solitary coast,
> Who of her learnèd Bards may justly boast
> In music, and in prophecies deep skill'd,
> Who with sweet Englens all the world had fill'd.

I am indebted to Gordon Campbell and Jeremy Maule for pointing out this passage, which comes from *Minor Poets of the Caroline Period*, ed. George Saintsbury (1906; rpt. Oxford, Clarendon Press, 1968), vol. II, pp. 88–89; stanza 108 describes the voyage down the Dee, stanza 110 the early morning arrival off the coast of Ireland.

Regarding the avoidance of coastlines, Thor Heyerdahl, *Fatu-Hiva: Back to Nature* (New York: Doubleday, 1974), p. 147, writes, "I had always heard . . . that primitive people could travel at sea only by hugging the coasts of continents and islands. Experience showed me that nowhere is the danger of ocean navigation in a small boat less than at the farthest possible distance from any treacherous coast."

44. Jones, *Shipwrecks*, p. 22; see maps on pp. 13, 29, 43, 59, etc.

45. Commerce through the Menai Straits is described by Parry, *Wreck and Rescue*, I, 9–10. Navigational dangers are noted by Jones, *Shipwrecks*, p. 113, who writes of the passage that it "has always been a treacherous barrier . . . with an unenviable record of disaster."

46. "Merchantmen [in the seventeenth century] were usually quite small," report Ramola and R. C. Anderson, *The Sailing Ship: Six Thousand Years of History* (New York: Bonanza, 1963), p. 143. Donald Woodward believes that "most vessels in the trade[s] were small, even by contemporary standards" ("Sixteenth-Century Shipping: The Charter-Party of the *Grace* of Neston, 1572," *Journal of Irish Economic and Social History* V [1978], 64). He also notes, "Ships, Masters," 234–35, that seagoing vessels on this route during the period 1550–1650 averaged fifteen to forty tons burden, those under ten tons not venturing across the channel; and in "Overseas Trade," 36, Woodward points out that in 1634 vessels averaged twenty tons. Stephens, "Overseas Trade," 34, gives twenty-five tons as the average size of vessels sailing from Chester ports in 1618.

Information about the lengths of seagoing vessels during the period is scanty. Roger C. Anderson, "Ships," *Encyclopaedia Britannica*, 1968 ed., section 1, reports that London-based ships engaging in continental trade during this century were about sixty feet long at the keel, thus approximately forty-five feet at waterline. Sir Francis Drake's *Golden*

Hind, a small three-masted ship, was about sixty feet from stem to stern, or about forty-eight feet at waterline (Douglas Phillips-Birt, *The Love of Sailing* [London: Octopus, 1976], p. 11). Vessels smaller than about thirty feet at waterline probably did not venture regularly onto the open sea (see, e.g., photographs and scale drawings in *Offshore: Cruising, Navigation, Racing* [New York: Time-Life, 1976]).

For this draft estimate of King's vessel, I am indebted to my colleague, Frank F. Doran (an amateur sailor), and to ship diagrams and models pictured in *Offshore*, particularly of the ship *Nina*, pp. 132–33 (which has a draft of nine feet, three inches) and those illustrated in Dorothy Hartley, *Lost Country Life* (New York: Pantheon, 1979), especially the model of the Renaissance *hoy* (fig. 54).

47. Waters, *Rutters*, p. 422. Additional confirmation of these estimated speeds may be obtained by considering the 1626 voyage from Neston to Point Lynas, on Anglesey's northeast shore, that was accomplished in a day (see note 21). Although we do not know the ship's departure or arrival times, we know that high water occurred at 8:30 A.M., according to Commander N. C. Glen (letter to the author, 19 June 1984), a logical time for departure if winds were favorable. Nightfall occurred about 8:30 P.M. Consequently, if this voyage of forty-five nautical miles took place during daylight hours, the slowest average speed at which it could have been made is 3.75 knots. These and subsequent times are given in Greenwich Mean Time.

48. The New Key is at 53° 18′ north latitude. The *Pilot Chart* for August 1976 indicates that prevailing winds during August off North Wales are favorable for sailing to Ireland only twenty percent of the observed time.

49. N. C. Glen, letter to the author, 30 March 1984; for information about the relationship between times of moon phases and spring/neap tides (the latter at the moon's quarters), see Hewitt Schlereth, *Commonsense Coastal Navigation* (New York: Norton, 1982), pp. 98–106.

50. Waters, *Art of Navigation*, p. 18, reports that seventeenth century almanacs give dates of lunar phases, and many provide "tide tables . . . for various stretches of the English or Channel coast, and very often rules for finding the daily times of high water." Elsewhere he explains how these elementary calculations are made (*Rutters*, p. 426). Spring tides were especially vital to the Dee estuary. The "mean tidal range," or average difference between high water and low water, is surprisingly small at this location in comparison to that of other British ports, measuring only 7.6 feet, whereas the average on the British coast is about fifteen feet; at spring and neap tides the range in the estuary is 9.8 feet, thus providing at high tide an additional two feet of water (Schlereth, *Commonsense*, pp. 147–48).

51. Because there exists a differential of fifty-six minutes between the first high water at the New Key at Neston on 10 August 1637 at 11:20 A.M. and the first high water at Holyhead sixty nautical miles distant at 10:24 A.M., it is evident that tidal times along the route between these locations vary approximately a minute for each mile. High water appears earlier at Holyhead, low water later. Hence when high water occurs at Holyhead at 10:24 A.M., for example, it occurs at Point Lynas, twenty nautical miles east of Holyhead, about twenty minutes later, or about 10:44 A.M. To compute the speed of King's vessel, hour by hour, I have adjusted the hull speed of five knots according to the strength and direction of river and tidal currents. Vectoring would add precision to these calculations, but is unjustified here.

52. My estimate of King's progress in the estuary itself is largely guesswork, as nautical charts upon which I have relied provide no information on the speed of river currents. I have estimated the current of the Dee to be about two knots. Four hours before high

water, when I am suggesting King's ship embarked, the tidal stream immediately beyond the mouth of the river would be 1.3 knots *against* the vessel (or in a southeast direction of 101°, 360° being north, 90° east, 270° west). Inside the estuary the stream would be somewhat stronger because of constriction of the channel, probably 1.8 to two knots. A combination of these two currents, consequently, would result in little overall effect on the vessel's hull speed of five knots during the first hour of its voyage. During the second hour, the effect would also be negligible, the tidal current beyond the estuary being 1.4 knots at 104°. King's ship would gain, therefore, about ten nautical miles by 9:30 A.M., placing it opposite Point of Air.

53. From 9:30 to 10:30 A.M., the tidal current is .8 knot at 90°; therefore, the average speed would be 4.2 knots and the distance traveled, 4.2 nautical miles. From 10:30 to 11:30, tide .3 knot at 77°, estimated tidal drag .2 knot, average speed and distance, 4.8. From 11:30 to 12:30, tide .6 knot at 280°, average speed and distance, 5.6. From 12:30 to 1:30, tide 1.1 knots at 277°, average speed and distance, 6.1. From 1:30 to 2:30, tide 1.5 knots at 280°, average speed and distance, 6.5. From 2:30 to 3:30, tide 1.4 knots at 283°, average speed and distance, 6.4. At this juncture in the voyage, to compensate for travel west I have added one hour to the computations, making five hours after high water rather than four.

This itinerary would place the ship opposite Point Lynas, forty-four nautical miles distant, after eight hours of sailing at an average over-the-bottom speed of 5.5 knots.

54. The first of these, presently called Bwrlingau Rock, lies on the outer edge of the Conwy estuary two miles offshore and has a "drying height" of eight feet at low water. Because the mean tidal range during a spring tide in this vicinity is 21.9 feet (Schlereth, *Commonsense*, p. 147) and because the vessel most likely sailed through this general area about two to three hours after high water on this particular day, or about 2:00–3:00 P.M., it is possible to estimate that approximately seven feet of water covered the rock at that time. The second rock, which is unnamed, lies .7 mile southwest of Bwrlingau and has a drying height of six feet, thus was covered by about eight feet of water at the time noted above.

55. In addition to visual details of this treacherous coast provided by nautical charts, written descriptions can be found in Jones, *Shipwrecks*, pp. 92–100, and in *Sailing Directions (Enroute) for Ireland and the West Coast of England* (U.S. Defense Mapping Agency, Hydrographic/Topographic Center, 1976 [publication 142]).

56. From 3:30 to 4:30 P.M., six hours after high water, the tidal current is .6 kn at 320°; the average speed would be 5.6 knots and distance traveled, 5.6 nautical miles. From 4:30 to 5:30, six hours before low water, tide .5 knot at 66°, average speed and distance, 4.5. From 5:50 to 6:30, tide 2.2 knots at 89°, average speed and distance, 2.8. From 6:30 to 7:30, tide 3.4 knots at 95°, average speed and distance, 1.6.

This schedule would place the vessel at Holyhead, fifty-eight nautical miles distant, after twelve hours of sailing at an average speed of 4.8 knots.

57. The modern names of these offshore rocks, from east to west in the order King's ship would encounter them, are as follows: Archdeacon Rock, Coal Rock, Ethel Rock, Passage Rock, Middle Rock, East Platters, North Carmel Rock, Carmel Rocks, Bolivar Rock, and Clipera Rocks.

58. Thomas Farnaby, King's former London schoolmaster and renowned classical scholar (*Justa*, p. 25 [lines 10–12], trans. p. 41). Pullen, *Justa*, p. 12 (line 45), trans. p. 16, also attacks the captain, calling him "wicked."

59. Pullen (whose adjective is *latenti*), in *Justa*, p. 11 (line 33), trans. p. 15; Pearson (*latentia*), in *Justa*, p. 14 (line 5), trans. p. 19.

60. Coal Rock is located at approximately 53° 26' north latitude and 4° 32' west longitude on modern nautical charts. On Speed's map of 1611, it is located at 54° 20' north latitude and 15° 25' east longitude. In 1976 the position of Coal Rock was indicated by "two range beacons, that stand on the NE side of Penbrynyreglwys [above Carmel Head], in range with the beacon on West Mouse. . . . A black conical buoy, equipped with a black conical top and marked 'Coal Rock,' is moored near the NW edge of the bank on which Coal Rock lies" (*Sailing Dir.*, p. 281).

61. This condition of Coal Rock at low water is given in symbol form in Nautical Chart 36122 (the notation is explained in *Nautical Chart Symbols*, p. 13) and in *Sailing Dir.*, p. 281.

62. Coal Rock would be covered by less than six feet of water for approximately two hours and twenty minutes before and after low water.

TO SMITE ONCE AND YET ONCE MORE: THE TRANSACTION OF MILTON'S *LYCIDAS*

Elizabeth Hanson

ALMOST EVERY CRITIC who has confronted *Lycidas* agrees that Milton's purpose in writing the poem was to bring something to an end, although critical opinion varies as to whether that "something" is limited to the swain's mourning, or extends to a larger concern, such as the poet's youthful apprenticeship, or even the whole tradition of pastoral elegy. It is therefore ironic that despite this critical concurrence the poem has generated apparently endless debate over the nature of Milton's goal and the route he has chosen to achieve it. M. H. Abrams, in his famous essay on the poem, confessed to finding this proliferation of interpretations of the poem "embarrassing."[1] What discomforted Abrams was not the fact that the existence of numerous readings of *Lycidas* meant that none could claim to say what the poem finally meant, but rather that each reading claimed to do just that, a claim which the production of new readings mocked. In the years since Abrams put forth the embarrassing case of the "Five Types of *Lycidas*," his anxieties have been answered by the widespread embrace of the indeterminacy of meaning, and consequently the endlessness of interpretation, as a condition of reading poetry. It is all the more striking, therefore, that astute but conflicting recent readings of the poem have continued to share a rhetoric of final mastery. Thus, for example, Stanley Fish writes of "a poem that is finally and triumphantly, anonymous." G. W. Pigman concludes that "Milton has questioned the efficacy of pastoral . . . but rather than abandoning it despondently, Milton transcends it." And Peter Sacks writes, "Milton has calmly assumed that power himself: *he* makes the uncouth swain rise, and he himself has risen, as though he were another sun."[2] Not only do these critics continue to claim to say what the poem finally means, but, more importantly, they insist on finality as part of its meaning, a finality which manifests itself in the poem leaving behind the conditions which produce it. Abrams chose *Lycidas* to pose the problem of interpretative authority because it was "convenient": relatively short, frequently explicated, and "universally esteemed"; his concern is criticism rather than this particular poem (p. 216). But the repetitive celebrations of the poem's triumphant finality suggest a peculiar continuity between the problem Abrams saw in the practice of criticism, the embarrassing reopening that occurs every time someone tries to produce an ending, and the problem Milton negotiated in *Lycidas*.

This essay will argue that *Lycidas* is itself embarrassing in the sense that Abrams finds the criticism of it to be: not because (like all great poems) it is richly ambiguous and therefore susceptible of varying, even endless, interpretation but because the nature of its ambiguity challenges the poem's own claims to offer a final and sustaining consolation. Where, as in *Lycidas*, the project of a poem is to provide assurances of abiding presence in the face of earthly waste and loss, and of final rest in the face of unrewarded "uncessant care," unresolvable ambiguity takes on an especially problematical significance. What emerges in *Lycidas*, I wish to argue, is not so much the instability of linguistic meaning as it is a profound and unresolvable ambivalence in Milton's poetics which exploits the ambiguities of language to make itself known. If critics have felt the need to proclaim again and again the poem's final triumph, it is because the poem denies its own ecstatically proclaimed end to the pain and anxiety which propel it.

The ambiguities responsible for the proliferation of so many "types" of *Lycidas* are not the local puzzles such as the meaning of "the two-handed engine" or the identity of "the Pilot of the Galilean lake." To a surprising degree, they revolve around a single, overarching issue: agency. Is the speaker doing something or is something being done to him? What does he do or what is done to him? Does his role change in the course of the poem? Who is speaking at several critical junctures? Whose voice contains whose? Lying behind each of these questions is a still more profound question: what does it mean to act? Recent discussions of elegy in terms of Freud's notion of "the work of mourning" have helped to make explicit what was already implicit in earlier readings, that the poem is somehow an action as well as an artifact.[3] But the nature of the action performed by the poem remains problematic. Accounts of the work of mourning stress that mourning is actually a *transaction*, that the mourner's loss becomes the precondition for a compensation. That compensation may be, reflexively, the ability to perform the acts which his loss requires of him; in any case, the successful completion of mourning comes when the mourner is able to recognize his compensation for his loss.[4]

Milton's elegy sets out to procure for the uncouth swain and his sympathetic audience a consolation for the premature death of Lycidas and the instability of earthly happiness that it discloses. To interpret the poem is to establish the exact nature of this transaction, the nature of the consolation, its cost to the poet, and the identity of the parties to the deal. Questions of agency in the poem are thus closely tied to questions of the poem's economy, and the former are frequently framed in terms of the latter. Indeed, many readings of the poem may be crudely summarized in terms of a quid pro quo. To take but two examples: The poet loses his autonomous poetic voice, but gains a place in the choir which sings the "unexpressive nuptiall Song" (Fish); the poet loses Lycidas's companionship, but gains his autonomous poetic voice (Sacks). The ability of voice to occupy the position of cost in one version of the transaction, and compensation in another, suggests that, for reasons still to be explored, the transaction is not a resolution of the poet's distress, but its origin.

Although the concept of elegiac consolation, with its interplay between loss and gain, invites discussion in economic terms, for the consolation to be spiritually satisfying to Milton the poem must efface the traces of the transaction it negotiates. Freud insists on the impossibility of that effacement, arguing that "no matter what fills the gap (left by loss) even if it be filled completely, it nevertheless remains something else."[5] But that difference between the lost object and the compensation, which serves as an eternal reminder of the transaction of mourning, is precisely what Christian consolation denies.[6] Christ's death is the dear price paid for man's eternal life, but it is a price immediately refunded in Christ's own resurrection. The transaction implied by Christ's sacrifice disappears into a paradoxical combination of pure gain and no change at all. The consolation in *Lycidas* seems similarly to transcend the transaction of mourning by ultimately denying the loss for which it offers consolation: "Weep no more, woful Shepherds, weep no more, / For *Lycidas* your sorrow is not dead" (165–66).[7] The poet acknowledges the exchange involved in Lycidas's resurrection, but in the same moment sets it aside, placing Lycidas in a pastoral heaven which contains and surpasses everything he has lost:

> So *Lycidas* sunk low, but mounted high,
> Through the dear might of him that walk'd the waves
> Where other groves, and other streams along,
> With *Nectar* pure his oozy Lock's he laves,
> And hears the unexpressive nuptiall Song,
> In the blest Kingdoms meek of joy and love.   (176–81)

The cost of sinking low is wiped out in the ecstasy of mounting high. The singer, himself released by the vision of Lycidas in eternal bliss, does not give up something to get something; he recognizes the way things have always been, that the "heavy change" was more apparent than real.

If the consolation *Lycidas* offers is to be adequate in Milton's own terms it must transcend the elegiac economy of loss and compensation. This strategy of reconceiving sacrifice so that its economy disappears is exemplified in a passage Fish cites from *An Apology*, in which Milton consoles himself for the interruption to his contemplation of divine truths by the demands of political controversy. Milton writes, "I conceaved myself to be not now as mine own person, but as a member incorporate into that truth whereof I was perswaded." Fish notes that Milton's sense of personal cost disappears as he redefines himself as a "member incorporate" acting on behalf of the truth.[8] The passage also reveals, then, that awareness of cost is tied to a sense of individual autonomy, the separateness of self that enables and requires a transactional relationship to the world. But what is striking about Milton's attempt here to efface the individual will, and with it a sense of personal cost, is the eruption of that will in the words "I conceaved myself." In the very act of recognizing his incorporation in the truth, Milton divides himself from it in an assertion of autogenesis. The subversive significance of these words breaks the sentence into two conflicting meanings and the self-generating act they describe tears the "I" from the body of which it is a "member incorporate."

The double effect of Milton's words, simultaneously severing him from and incorporating him into the truth, suggests a paradoxical relationship between self-conception and the unity of the truth. The recognition of the truth, which is also the moment of self-conception, results in a wound to the truth and therefore in a wound to the self conceived as a member incorporate. Ineffaceable cost is incurred within the very recognition that redefines sacrifice as pure gain. In *An Apology*, Milton suggests that to use his voice itself feels like a painful separation from truth until he conceives himself as a member incorporate, a recognition that both effaces and reasserts his separation. In *Lycidas*, painful separation is presented as the occasion which compels the poet to use his voice. In so doing, as we shall see, the poet conceives himself; his voice recreates the separation, even as it produces a vision of transcendant restoration.

The opening words of *Lycidas* declare themselves to be a reopening, testifying to the poet's need to negotiate again the transaction of elegy:

Yet once more, O ye Laurels, and once more
Ye Myrtles brown, with Ivy never-sear,
I com to pluck your Berries harsh and crude,
And with forc'd fingers rude
Shatter your leaves before the mellowing year.　　　(1–5)

The poem originates, then, not merely in loss, but in the past failure of the poet's voice to produce a final, abiding consolation. The laurels, myrtle, and ivy are, of course, traditional symbols of poetic achievement, but they have also been glossed as the traditional materials of funeral garlands.[9] Their capacity to perform this dual function suggests that the transactions of poetic creation and of mourning are inextricably bound up with each other, and not simply coincidental on this occasion. The appearance of these plants as symbols of poetry, though conventional, is striking here; it is the poetic task imposed by Lycidas's death, rather than the death itself, that seems uppermost in the poet's thoughts. This concern points to the poet's ambivalence toward the death of Lycidas; it occasions mourning but it compels poetic achievement. He describes the event as a "sad occasion dear," implying that it is precious as well as painful. The poet is, moreover, not only a reluctant, passive beneficiary of Lycidas's death; in the atmosphere of violence in the opening lines he is implicated as an active participant as well, as a link in a chain of violations. The poet must shatter the leaves of the poetic plants, presumably because the life of Lycidas has been shattered, and with it his own youthful idyll. Yet the power of the poem's opening lies not in the sorrow the poet expresses but in the rough force of the act he perpetrates. The cause of his actions is revealed only in the eighth line, after the shock of his rending of the sacred vegetation has registered. In the sequence of the poem, the violent beginning of the song precedes the death it bewails. The poet did not kill Lycidas, yet somehow his poetry is complicit in the event it bewails.

The speaker's own victimization is, of course, declared in the very words that implicate him. His fingers are "forc'd" by "bitter constraint." But what is striking about the adjectives in these lines is that they seem to modify both subject and object at once. The poet's fingers are "forc'd," as are the shattered leaves and berries. His immature fingers are "rude," as is the assault upon the (also rude) berries. The berries are "harsh and crude," but so is the poet's treatment of them. Both the poet and the plants suffer "bitter constraint." The multiple affiliations of these adjectives reveal an identification between the poet and the plants. But this identification is complicated by the poet's complicity in the violation of the plants, for he and they are not merely victims alike of a violence located in the conditions of life in this world. Rather, the speaker is simultaneously the violator of the natural world and a victim of that violation. It is worth noting that the revisions in the Trinity manuscript, which show Milton's interpolation of the line "And with forc'd fingers rude" and replacement of "crop" with "shatter," enhance not only the violence in this passage but the ambiguity of its agency. Poetic energy and violent death enter *Lycidas* "as two twins cleaving together leap into the world," and cannot be separated in the poet's experience.

In the lines that follow, as the speaker defines his poetic task, his own victimization is expressed as an identification with the dead Lycidas. He mourns:

> For *Lycidas* is dead, dead ere his prime
> Young *Lycidas*, and hath not left his peer:
> Who would not sing for *Lycidas?* He well knew
> Himself to sing, and build the lofty rhyme.   (8–11)

The primary meaning of the complaint, that Lycidas "hath not left his peer," is clear: Lycidas is dead and there is no equal to him left on earth. But like several other crucial phrases in this poem, and the passage from *An Apology* examined above, this phrase disconcertingly asserts another meaning flatly contradicting the primary one. The peer of Lycidas is the poet, who now sings an elegy for Lycidas, just as Lycidas used to "sing and build the lofty rhyme." The poet's peerhood is reinforced a few lines later in the reminiscence: "For we were nurst upon the self-same hill, / Fed the same flock, by fountain, shade, and rill" (23–24). Thus, that Lycidas "hath not left his peer" also implies that he is not gone, that he remains with the poet as part of himself. The double meaning, produced by the peculiar syntax of "he well knew / Himself to sing" underscores this implication. Lycidas not only knew how to sing, but sang himself: the song of the now silenced Lycidas is identified with the poet's song about him. And in singing of Lycidas, the speaker is also singing himself — creating himself in his song. The denial of loss that emerges from within the poet's lament for his irreplaceable friend might be seen as a spurious comfort, typical of an early stage in the mourning process. What I wish to stress here, however, is the unstable and ambivalent relationship between the poet and the dead Lycidas which the contradictory meanings of this line disclose. In lamenting his loss, the poet asserts that Lycidas far surpassed him as a poet. In denying his loss, the poet also implies that he rivals Lycidas and is, in fact, doing so in singing for Lycidas. The poet's singing thus displaces the peer whom it bewails at the same time it identifies the poet with his dead and surpassed peer.

As he starts his song, the identification between the living poet and the dead Lycidas emerges more forcefully; the poet imagines himself dead and another poet singing an elegy for him:

> Hence with denial vain, and coy excuse,
> So may som gentle Muse
> With lucky words favour my destin'd Urn,
> And as he passes turn,
> And bid fair peace be to my sable shrowd.   (18–22)

In the double meaning of "So" ("just as," — "in order that"), comparison shades into incantation. The poet's song will produce the gentle muse who will sing for him and be a replica of his present self. In this imaginative act the poet divides himself, becoming a dead artifact ("destin'd Urn") and a live voice ("lucky words"). By this means the poet projects his voice beyond the present, but at the price of his own death.

At the moment of division there occurs a surprising use of the masculine pronoun. The reader anticipates that the muse will be female, both from custom and because the paragraph commences, "Begin then, Sisters of the sacred well." "Hence with denial vain and coy excuse" seems to accentuate their femininity, although it is unclear whether the line is addressed to the muses or the poet's self, an ambiguity which momentarily feminizes the poet. As the poet divides himself, thereby generating the lucky words which will survive his death, he displaces the female muses with a male muse, expunging the feminine from his poetic. The masculinity and immortality of the poet's voice are simultaneously asserted in an act which imaginatively costs him his life.

As the poet proceeds with memories of his youthful idyll, however, it becomes apparent that the feminine was already absent from the pastoral idyll which preceded the heavy change wrought by Lycidas's death. In that world, where the poet and Lycidas "together both" battened their flocks and played on the oaten flute under the paternal benevolence of "old Damoetas," it appears that male friendship proceeded undisturbed by female intrusion. Their "Rural ditties," to which "Rough *Satyrs* danced, and *Fauns,* with cloven heel," attracted no nymphs. This innocent life of masculine jollity is recharacterized a few lines later as one of poetic labor which depends on the exclusion of the already absent nymphs:

> Alas! What boots it with uncessant care
> To tend the homely slighted Shepherds trade,
> And strictly meditate the thankles Muse,

> Were it not better don as others use,
> To sport with *Amaryllis* in the shade,
> Or with the tangles of *Neœra's* hair?   (64–69)

The moment in which the muse turns and becomes male, as the poet divides himself into living voice and dead artifact, thus merely reenacts what has already occurred in previous poetic transactions. The "heavy change" that compels the poet to sing is in this sense no change at all. It simply makes manifest an economy of poetic production latent in the youthful idyll of the two shepherds.

As the poet turns to address the absent Lycidas in the passage beginning, "O the heavy change, now thou art gone," he echoes Ovid's apostrophe to the dead Orpheus,

> Te maestae volucres, Orpheu, te turba ferarum
> te rigidi silices, te carmina saepe secutae
> fleverunt silvae.   (*Metamorphosis*, XI, 44–46)[10]

in his lament,

> Thee Shepherd, thee the Woods and desert Caves,
> With wild Thyme and the gadding Vine o'regrown,
> And all their echoes mourn.   (39–41)

Following the reminiscence of the shepherds, "together both," this direct address to the dead brings home with poignant force the fact of his absence at the same time that it identifies him with the most powerful of all poets. His absence is underscored by the way in which the vocal plenitude of mourning nature suggested in Ovid's lines is entertained only to be undermined in "And all their echoes mourn." The effect of this line is not only to expose a pastoral, pathetic fallacy but to deny the voices in the landscape connection to any originating subject. The lines themselves are the echo of another long dead poet and their allusiveness elides the poet, making him an echo chamber like the caves and woods. Indeed, the description of Lycidas's death as a "loss to Shepherd's ear" presents the poet as the passive receptacle of voice and Lycidas the lost origin of that voice.

The passage suppresses the presence of the poet in the landscape as a voice, a voice that disturbingly asserts itself at the beginning of the passage in the lament "Now thou art gon and never must return!" which sounds oddly like a command to prevent an unwanted return. It is the poet's own voice, lamenting the dead Lycidas, that fills the aural void left by the death of Lycidas the Orphic poet. In this sense, the death of Lycidas is an advantage to the poet, clearing a space for his own voice.

This suppressed aggression emerges in the simile comparing Lycidas's death to other natural events:

> As killing as the Canker to the Rose,
> or Taint-worm to the weanling Herds that graze,
> Or Frost to Flowers, that their gay wardrop wear,
> When first the White thorn blows;
> Such *Lycidas*, thy loss to Shepherd's ear. (45–49)

In the natural world the poet describes, one element thrives upon the premature destruction of another. The analogy the poet draws between these acts of parasitism and "thy loss to Shepherd's ear," however, deflects the meaning of these exempla, placing in the position of victim the poet's ear, rather than, as we would expect, the prematurely dead Lycidas, and in the position of the destroyer the death of Lycidas. In the reflexive turn of the simile the difference between the poet's roles as aggressive vocal presence and as empty ear collapses. After all, the poet's voice cannot be heard unless poets die. The poet's own vocal presence depends on the incapacity of his voice to make the absent present.

The poet's oppressive sense of the implication of his own voice in death reaches its climax in the image of the "goary visage" of Orpheus floating down the Hebrus.[11] The dead Orpheus, whose severed head continued to sing as it floated down the Hebrus, afforded a rich symbol to a Christian elegist like Milton, because of his dual nature, as supremely powerful poet whose song reflected the divine harmony of the universe, and Christlike sacrificial victim. Although glossed as a type of Christ by Renaissance mythographers, Orpheus nevertheless called attention to the limits of poetic transcendence: while Christ died in order live again, Orpheus's death was permanent.[12] It was only his song that was resurrected.

The significance of the myth to the problematic connections between autonomy, death, and poetic power that Milton explores in *Lycidas* lies not only in the tragic economy of sacrifice the myth insists on, but in the way in which sacrifice is gendered. As Ovid tells the story, following the failed rescue of Euridice, Orpheus separated himself from the society of women, seeking homosexual comforts. It was then that he was able to tame beasts and move stones with his song. But the women whom he had spurned returned, enraged by his neglect of them. Half-naked, slapping their breasts and thighs, they fell upon him, assaulting him by, among other means, stabbing him with sharpened boughs of laurel. When they had dismembered Orpheus, the river Hebrus caught his head and his lyre, which began to sing and play as they were carried to Lesbos, where Apollo rescued them. In this version of the myth, Orpheus sepa-

rates himself from women after the act of weakness engendered by his
love for Euridice, and produces a poetry so powerful that he controls
the natural world with it — as the mythographers would have it, he par-
ticipates in the divine harmonies of the cosmos. The destruction that
follows constitutes at one level a heavy change: corporeal feminine fury
destroys the order established by Orpheus's masterful masculine poetic
voice. But at another level it recapitulates what has already occurred:
the women from whom Orpheus has severed himself return and tear him
apart. This dismemberment, in turn, reproduces his song and immor-
talizes the autonomous voice. As the maenads' choice of weapon makes
clear, it is Orpheus's own poetic mastery that produces his destruction.

   The place where Lycidas died, characterized by female absence and
male poetic power, once great but now dead, ironically reprises the ethos
of male chastity which prevailed during the poet's youthful idyll, and
which enabled Orpheus's poetry:

> Where were ye Nymphs when the remorseless deep
> Clos'd o're the head of your lov'd *Lycidas?*
> For neither were ye playing on the steep,
> Where your old *Bards*, the famous *Druids*, ly,
> Nor on the shaggy top of *Mona* high,
> Nor yet where *Deva* spreads her wisard stream.   (50–55)

The nurturing bond between the nymphs and bards that this passage
seems to allow is also negated in the image of the nymphs as negligent
and playful keepers of a cemetery for once mighty poets. In their lively
frivolity they mock the tragic struggle of great (male) poets, even as their
choice of playground undermines the tragedy. The poet sweeps them
aside, asserting their irrelevance. This dismissal of the feminine, recalling the displacement of the "sisters of the sacred well" and anticipating
the resistance to Amaryllis and Neœra, precipitates the vision of the severed head of Orpheus cast into the Hebrus by the maddened Thracian
maenads:

> Ay me, I fondly dream!
> Had ye bin there — for what could that have don?
> What could the Muse her self that *Orpheus* bore,
> The Muse her self, for her inchanting son
> Whom Universal nature did lament,
> When by the rout that made the hideous roar,
> His goary visage down the stream was sent,
> Down the swift *Hebrus* to the *Lesbian* shore.   (56–63)

Milton's poem enacts what Ovid narrates: the negligent nymphs and ineffectual muse that the poet dismisses return in "the rout that made the hideous roar," and tear the great first poet apart.

The same "wild Rout that tore the *Thracian* Bard," of course, reappears in the invocation to Book VII of *Paradise Lost* when Milton prepares to sing of God's creation of the world, and that later maenadic eruption may serve as a gloss on the one here. It occurs at the end of Milton's exploration of the anxiety attendant on his poetic ambition, in which he acknowledges "Into the Heav'n of Heav'ns I have presum'd, / An Earthly Guest" (13–14), and fears lest, like Bellerophon, he will "fall / Erroneous there to wander and forlorn" (19–20).[13] This passage confronts the problem we witnessed in Milton's earlier declaration, "I conceaved myself to be not now as my own person, but as a member incorporate into that truth whereof I was perswaded"; through his voice Milton enters into the truth, only to fear that this merger is presumption for which he will be cast out and left "forlorn." Milton owns the possible presumption of his powerful singing in order to contain it, before beginning his depiction of God in the act of creating the world. That the invocation concludes with the rending of Orpheus suggests that the poet's work remains perilous despite this strategy. But the death of Orpheus is a result, not of paternal wrath, but, as in *Lycidas*, of maternal failure; he laments, "Nor could the Muse defend / Her Son" (37–38). Milton submits himself to the protection of his abstract, and therefore defeminized, muse, Urania (he invokes "the meaning, not the name"), whom he has already explicitly identified with paternal authority, telling her "thou . . . didst play / In presence of the th'Almighty Father, pleas'd / With thy Celestial Song" (9–11). And he invokes her aid by distinguishing her from the maternal muse, whom he dismisses yet once more: "So fail not thou, who thee implores: / For thou art Heav'nly, shee an empty dream" (39–40). Milton guards himself from Orpheus's fate by allying himself through Urania with "th'Almighty Father" and by negating the maternal muse who is, of course, Calliope, the muse of epic poetry. But this resolution of the fears that attend his project is at best precarious for, as Orpheus's fate makes clear, it is just such exclusion that provokes the rage of the maenads.

The invocation to Book VII reveals that the anxiety over feminine weakness/ferocity which Milton's treatment of the Orpheus myth discloses, in both *Lycidas* and *Paradise Lost*, is an expression of a deeper anxiety about the poet's relation to the authority of the Almighty Father. As the poet sings, he fears that his powerful voice challenges or rivals the governing voice of the Father, with whom he identifies, from whom his own voice acquires its authority, and without whom the poet is "forlorn." Orpheus embodies the poet as governor; the ferocious maenads exceed or challenge Orpheus's control. They are both destroyers of poetry and transgressors against masculine authority, and therefore Milton's enemies.[14] But the contexts in which Milton invokes the Orpheus image suggest that he fears that he too is such a transgressor. The terrible feminine strength of the maenads is a displacement of the power of the poet whose voice subverts the authority of the Almighty Father even as it asserts it. In *Lycidas*, the poet's anxiety about the transgressive power of his voice manifests itself from the beginning of the poem in the image of the poet's fingers rending the foliage and emerges in the subtext of rivalry in the passage that precedes the Orpheus image. The image of the murdered Orpheus attempts a resolution of the contradictions of the poet's work. Milton's revision of "divine head" to "goary visage" in the Trinity manuscript shows an effort to stress Orpheus's death and play down the triumphant aspect of the myth. Yet the triumph of Orpheus is dimly disclosed in the conclusion of the passage, "His goary visage down the stream was sent." With the use of the strongly purposive verb "sent," the poet makes the maenads the agents of this triumph and hints that their awful power is also his own.

In the passage that follows, the poet questions the choice of a poetic career in light of the realizations the death of Lycidas has forced upon him. His complaint, "Alas what boots it with uncessant care / To tend the homely slighted Shepherds trade," as we have seen, is a recharacterization of the poet's situation before the heavy change of Lycidas's death. What was earlier presented as a prelapsarian condition in which there was one sex and all its members danced for joy is here described as a state of sexual abstinence and labor. This recharacterization serves to inscribe the earlier idyll within the myth of Orpheus and therefore implicates it in the destruction which follows. In his complaint about the bootless poetic life, the poet seeks to evade the economy of sacrifice which the death of Lycidas has disclosed to him and to imagine a scenario in which the poet gets to live to enjoy the fruits of his labors:

> *Fame* is the spur that the clear spirit doth raise
> (That last infirmity of Noble mind)
> To scorn delights, and live laborious dayes;
> But the fair Guerdon when we hope to find,
> And think to burst out into sudden blaze,
> Comes the blind *Fury* with th' abhorred shears,
> And slits the thin spun life.   (70–76)

Inadvertently, however, this complaint actually insists on the inescapability of the economy of sacrifice. The "fair Guerdon" the poet strives to gain by scorning delights is fame (and not, for example, the favors of Amaryllis); fame has no need of the poet's "thin spun life" once it has been engendered and, indeed, supersedes it. In fact, the timing of Atropos's action, just as "the fair Guerdon when we hope to find," implies that the poet's death is a necessary precondition to the achievement of fame. And the suggestion of self-immolation in "burst out into sudden blaze" reveals that the poet's triumph cannot be imagined without also imagining his destruction.

The consolation Phoebus offers is to assure the poet that this relation between poetic triumph and death is in fact inevitable: "Fame is no plant that grows on mortal soil." Fame, he assures the poet, "lives and spreds aloft by those pure eyes, / And perfet witnes of all-judging *Jove*" (81–82). In reminding the poet of the immortality of poetic fame, Phoebus seems to correct the poet's understanding of the meaning of poetic creation, to answer pastoral lament with the strain of a higher mood.[15] And, in so doing, he provides the part of the myth of Orpheus which the poet's own account submerged; the meed of death is the resurrection of the song. Indeed, his interjection enacts the Orphic principle that the triumphant voice emerges from the dismemberment of the poet: at "slits the thin spun life," Phoebus breaks the poet's lament and releases poetry from the poet with the words "But not the praise." The eternal life that Phoebus promises is not for the poet but for his work. But, as the poet has shown, acts of exclusion, sacrifice, and division which attend poetic creation are not so much transcended as valorized by Phoebus's consolation. His interruption does not introduce a new strain, but rehearses the transaction which seems always to have already been negotiated in the poem. The division Phoebus's voice proclaims (and effects) between the thin-spun life and the praise recapitulates the poet's imagined division of himself into a "destin'd urn" and "lucky words" at the commencement of his song. And the end he promises, evaluation by "those pure eyes / And perfet witness of all-judging *Jove*," recalls the youthful idyll when rural ditties were performed before the paternal audience of old Damoetas — the experience the poet recharacterizes as sacrifice, as scorning delight and living laborious days.

Phoebus's interjection is an attempt to put a stop to the poet's lament by invoking a divine masculine voice which "pronounces lastly on each deed" and thereby ends the repeated negotiations of the poetic transaction. The interrupting strain of a higher mood is a version of that terminating voice, as is the voice of the poet which will ultimately proclaim

Lycidas genius of the shore and inhabitant of heaven. But, as we have seen, that voice is already implicated in the transactions it would terminate, as a compensation eternally reproducing cost. This contradiction requires that the poet renegotiate the transaction of poetic creation, and so the poet's lamenting "oat proceeds."

Compared to Phoebus's promise of a heavenly meed, the cause of the accident that drowned Edward King appears an irrelevant, even bathetic concern. In his resumption of pastoral lament the poet jarringly reintroduces into the poem what the higher mood has (nearly) transcended: the dead body that is the purchase price of fame. The scene where "Sleek *Panope* with all her sisters play'd" while Lycidas drowned (conflating the earlier negligent absence of the nymphs with the savage presence of the maenads) pulls us back to the threshold of the poet's vision of the dead Orpheus. In the cheaply supernatural explanation for the accident which the poet concocts in the absence of a natural one, "It was that fatall and perfidious Bark / Built in th'eclipse, and rigg'd with curses dark, / That sunk so low that sacred head of thine" (100–102), the poet reinterprets Phoebus's promise; the powerful speech that "pronounces lastly on each deed" becomes "curses dark" when considered from the point of view of cost. The bathos of this explanation arises from its subversion of the hierarchical ordering of experience on which Phoebus's consolation depends. Phoebus acknowledges natural death but promises a heavenly immortality. In his improbable explanation of the accident, the poet collapses the natural into the supernatural, placing all experience on the same level. In so doing he implies a kinship between "all judging Jove" and the "blind Fury" who, with her "abhorred shears," is first cousin to the maenad. Jove's surrogate Phoebus is also subtly implicated as a destroyer in the comparison of Camus's bonnet "inwrought with figures dim" to "that sanguine flower inscrib'd with woe," the hyacinth. That flower, inscribed with the word "alas" to commemorate Phoebus's killing of his beloved, is a text which has superseded a youth through the destructive power of the god. This mythological subtext makes Camus's question, "Ah who hath reft . . . my dearest pledge?" rather more pointed.

In the speech of the "the Pilot of the *Galilean* lake," the pastoral lament for the death of Lycidas is once more broken by a strain of higher mood, promising a final judgment. Here, however, the destructiveness of the voice is made explicit:

> Last came, and last did go,
> The Pilot of the *Galilean* lake,
> Two massy Keyes he bore of metals twain.

> (The Golden opes, the Iron shuts amain)
> He shook his Miter'd locks, and stern bespake,
> How well could I have spar'd for thee, young swain,
> Anow of such as for their bellies sake,
> Creep and intrude, and climb into the fold?
> . . . .
> But that two-handed engine at the door,
> Stands ready to smite once, and smite no more.   (108–15, 130–31)

The rage of this figure (whoever he is) is directed at the corrupted clergy and the Catholic church, concerns which seem to lie outside the poem altogether, and this sudden shift in focus is responsible for the charge of disunity that has repeatedly been brought against the poem. Insofar as this voice ruptures the poem by projecting its anger outward it also seems to escape the relentless cyclic economy I have been tracing. But this fury is in fact framed as an attack on the whole pastoral of otium — the immediate effect of this voice is to shrink Alpheus's streams and drive away the "*Sicilian* muse" — of which Lycidas and the poet are a part. The smiting force of the two-handed engine is aimed at bad shepherds who are implicitly opposed to good ones like Lycidas:

> And when they list, their lean and flashy songs
> Grate on their scrannel Pipes of wretched straw,
> The hungry Sheep look up, and are not fed,
> But swoln with wind, and the rank mist they draw,
> Rot inwardly, and foul contagion spread.   (123–27)

This is a disenchanted revision of the youthful idyll of the poet and Lycidas when they

> drove a field and both together heard
> What time the Gray-fly winds her sultry horn,
> Batt'ning our flocks with the fresh dews of night,
> . . . .
> Meanwhile the Rural ditties were not mute,
> Temper'd to th'Oaten Flute.   (27–33)

The Pilot's speech forces the pastoral idyll to bear two contradictory meanings: the spiritual wholesomeness that will triumph and the selfish corruption that will be vanquished. The destruction of Lycidas, which provokes the rage of the Pilot of the Galilean Lake, thus also anticipates the act of vengeance he prophesies. And this disturbing possibility casts doubt upon the promise that the two-handed engine will be able to "smite once and smite no more."

What makes the pilot's interruption so disconcerting is that it shifts from the classical pastoral of otium to the Christian pastoral of care, without signalling the shift. The tenor changes wholly while the vehicle remains the same. The effect of the Pilot's speech is thus to divide the poem's pastoral voice against itself. It has long been recognized that *Lycidas* possesses a tripartite structure: the poet's lament is thrice broken by versions of the terminating voice that promises an end to the earthly conditions it bemoans. This promise is followed on each occasion but the last by the resumption of the pastoral lament, the subject of which is the fate of the person of Lycidas. This structure is generally seen as a manifestation of the poem's antipastoralism, the "attack," as Balachandra Rajan styles it, "mounted by the higher mood against the pastoral form," which exposes the fragility and inadequacy of pastoral in the face of violent death.[16] Such an approach makes the poem's violence secondary, an expression of the poet's rage at the death of Edward King. But in the opening lines of the poem, in which the poet is both perpetrator and victim of violence, what I have called lamenting and terminating voices originate in each other. The pattern of interruption and resumption shows us that if the terminating voice strives to end the pastoral lament, its violence renews it. The violence in which the poem originates is the attack of the poet's own voice on the poet, and the reflexiveness of the attack is underlined by the pastoral terms in which the terminating voice speaks.

The poet responds to the Pilot's threatened sacrifice of the classical pastoral world by resuming his lament for the person of Lycidas:

> Return *Alpheus*, the dread voice is past,
> That shrunk thy streams; Return *Sicilian* Muse,
> And call the Vales, and bid them hither cast
> Their Bels, and Flourets of a thousand hues.
> Ye valleys low where the milde whispers use,
> Of shades and wanton winds, and gushing brooks,
> On whose fresh lap the swart Star sparely looks
> Throw hither all your quaint enameld eyes,
> . . . .
> To strew the Laureat Herse where *Lycid* lies.   (133–51)

The poignancy of this tribute of flowers is enhanced by the correspondence between the frailty of human life and of the flowers menaced by "the swart Star," whose withering effect on the materials of pastoral is like that of the "dread voice."

The poet entertains this "false surmise" only to slit its thin-spun beauty with an admission of the actual fate of Lycidas. The vision of Lycidas's corpse consumed by the sea recalls the fate of Orpheus torn apart and carried far away by the stream:

> Ay me! Whilst thee the shores, and sounding Seas
> Wash far away, where ere thy bones are hurld,
> Whether beyond the stormy *Hebrides,*
> Where thou perhaps under the whelming tide
> Visit'st the bottom of the monstrous world;
> Or whether thou to our moist vows deny'd,
> Sleep'st by the fable of *Bellerus* old,
> Where the great vision of the guarded Mount
> Looks toward *Namancos* and *Bayona's* hold;
> Look homeward Angel now, and melt with ruth,
> And, O ye *Dolphins,* waft the haples youth. (154–64)

In relinquishing the false surmise that the mourners possess the body of Lycidas, the poet acquiesces in the sacrificial economy against which he has protested in his lamentations. In so doing he reenacts the event we have already seen alluded to in the Orpheus passage and performed by Phoebus's interruption: the death of a poet releases an immortal voice. The person of Lycidas, which the poet has repeatedly invoked, the residue, as it were, which the terminating voices cannot recuperate, is hurled out of the poem, and the poet's voice abruptly shifts to a higher strain:

> Weep no more, woful Shepherds weep no more,
> For *Lycidas* your sorrow is not dead,
> Sunk though he be beneath the watry floar,
> So sinks the day-star in the Ocean bed,
> And yet anon repairs his drooping head,
> And tricks his beams, and with new spangled Ore,
> Flames in the forehead of the morning sky:
> So *Lycidas,* sunk low, but mounted high,
> Through the dear might of him that walk'd the waves. (165–73)

The controversy surrounding the attribution of these lines — the visionary poet, Michael, Lycidas, and anonymous have all been suggested — reveals that the voice which speaks them is, in fact, detached from an owning subject.[17] This is not to say that the voice is impersonal (i.e., to add "nobody" to the list), but rather to stress the means by which it is produced: the severing of the voice from the person of the poet. It makes no difference that it is Lycidas and not the poet who is sacrificed here, for as we have seen from the beginning, the poet has recognized the death which called forth his voice as his own.

That there are no apparent grounds for the poet's assertion of Lycidas's resurrection only enhances its power. It is a command rather than a recognition, an act of poetic power which Sacks is surely correct in describing as an assumption by the poet's voice of "the dear might of him that walk'd the waves."[18] But the triumphant voice which decrees that "Henceforth thou art the Genius of the shore" and places Lycidas in "the blest Kingdoms meek of joy and love" is not a new voice. We heard intimations of it in the command disguised as a complaint, "Now thou are gon and never must return," at the beginning of the poet's lament. There, it will be recalled, the overtones of rivalry bespoke not the poet's victory but his implication in the Orphic economy in which the dead poet's triumphant successor is his own voice. Here the poet's fiat discloses a far more subtle and daring rivalry in which triumph and loss are likewise intertwined. Although he speaks with great assurance, the structure of the consolation the poet provides reveals that he is not transcending but precariously controlling a contradiction. Lycidas's heavenly meed is a blissful passivity. He is elevated to a place where all losses are restored,

> Where other groves, and other streams along,
> With *Nectar* pure his oozy Lock's he laves,
> And hears the unexpressive nuptiall Song,
> In the blest Kingdoms meek of joy and love.
> There entertain him all the Saints above,
> In solemn troops and sweet Societies
> That sing and singing in their glory move,
> And wipe the tears for ever from his eyes.   (174–81)

Like the lamenting poet who heard the echoes of his own voice and the voices of the higher mood, Lycidas is here presented as an ear. The poet is, however, indubitably a tongue. While Lycidas hears the "unexpressive nuptiall Song," the poet is hard at work fashioning the pronouncements that put him there. The poet's vision of Lycidas's new life as a member incorporate of the kingdom of heaven depends on his own exclusion from it.

In the startling shift from the first to the third person at the poem's close, the poet's voice demonstrates the extent of its powers. The voice does not come from the poet, but authors him. The singer whose "forc'd fingers rude" violently initiated the poem is now presented as a fiction of his own song. The coda, then, enacts the feat Milton hints at in *An Apology* when he declares "I conceaved myself to be not as mine own person." This act of self-conception which marks the poet's final triumph is, however, a repetition of the act with which the poet's lament began, the poet's imagined division of himself in order to engender the muse who will sing for him when he is dead. The declaration that ends the poet's lamentation, "For *Lycidas,* your sorrow is not dead," speaks the contradiction in Milton's situation: if Lycidas's bliss is without end, so is the poet's sorrow. In healing the wound created by the death of Lycidas, he casts himself out from the sweet societies to which Lycidas now belongs. The final line of the poem, "To morrow to fresh Woods, and Pastures new," thus paradoxically testifies both to the poet's triumph and to his need to sing his song yet once more.

Queen's University

NOTES

1. M. H. Abrams, "Five Types of *Lycidas,*" in *Milton's Lycidas: The Tradition and the Poem,* ed. C. A. Patrides (Columbia, Mo., 1983), p. 217.

2. Stanley Fish, "*Lycidas:* A Poem Finally Anonymous," in *Milton's Lycidas,* p. 339; G. W. Pigman, *Grief and the English Renaissance Elegy* (Cambridge, 1985), p. 124; Peter Sacks, *The English Elegy* (Baltimore, 1985), p. 116.

3. Both Sacks, *The English Elegy,* and Pigman, *Grief,* offer introductory chapters which situate the elegy in relation to "the work of mourning." Marcia Landy, "Language and Mourning in *Lycidas,*" *American Imago* XXX (1973), pp. 294–312, also treats the poem in terms of the mourning process, and similarly sees the poem as the resolution of conflict that permits the poet to leave his grief behind.

4. See Sacks, *The English Elegy,* pp. 1–37, for a detailed account of this idea.

5. Sigmund Freud, *Letters,* trans. Tania Stern and James Stern, ed. Ernst Freud, (New York, 1960), cited in Sacks, *The English Elegy,* p. 7.

6. Pigman, *Grief,* discusses in detail the Christian resistance to mourning on the grounds that it showed a lack of faith in the Resurrection, and places the English Renaissance elegy in the context of an evolution in the sixteenth century away from the Christian denial of the transaction of mourning and toward what might anachronistically be called Freudian acceptance of it. Pigman sees in *Lycidas* the end of this process, the harmonious acceptance of grief and loss within the context of Christian belief. His attempt to place the experience of mourning in historical context is a necessary corrective to Sacks's ahistorical psychoanalytic reading of elegy, and accurately describes the conflict in Milton's poem. I disagree, however, with his assertion that the poem reconciles Christian faith with the transaction of mourning. Rather, the claim that *Lycidas* marks the end of such a conflict seems to me symptomatic of the anxiety the poem produces, in the ways which the introduction to this paper discusses. Moreover, whatever the change in attitudes toward mourning in the century leading up to *Lycidas,* it is important to assert a difference that discussions of elegy in the context of the work of mourning tend to elide: *Lycidas* is not an act of mourning, but a troping of mourning. Milton's task in *Lycidas* is to work out the relation to God, not of his mourning but of his poetry, and death emerges as one of the terms of that relation, not as an external event.

7. All quotations from *Lycidas* are from Patrides's editions cited above in note 1.

8. Fish, "Lycidas," p. 325.

9. Charlotte F. Otten, "Garlanding the Dead": The Epicedial Garland in *Lycidas*," in *Milton Studies*, vol. XVI, ed. James D. Simmonds (Pittsburgh, 1982), pp. 141–51.

10. ("The mourning birds wept for thee, O, the throng of beasts, the flinty rocks, and trees which had so often gathered to thy songs. Yes the trees shed their leaves as if so tearing their hair in grief for thee.") Ovid, *Metamorphoses*, trans. Frank Justus Miller (London, 1916).

11. The Orpheus allusion has been amply glossed. Several points are relevant here. Caroline Mayerson, "The Orpheus Image in *Lycidas*," in Patrides, *Milton's Lycidas*, p. 120, points out that in his poetry Milton "identifies with Orpheus at the moment of his destruction," rather than with Orpheus the civilizer, who tamed beasts and moved stones, and was invoked in claims for poetry as the first form of government. Kenneth Gros Louis, "The Triumph and the Death of Orpheus," *SEL* IX (1969) pp. 63–80, argues that Orpheus the singer and civilizer was typically invoked in the sixteenth century (examples include both Sidney's *Apology for Poetry* and Puttenham's *The Arte of English Poesie*), while in the seventeenth century the dismembered Orpheus was used to express a sense of the poet's isolation in a world hostile to poetry. Milton's use of the myth in *Lycidas* is thus consistent with his contemporaries, not unique as Mayerson had suggested. No one, to my knowledge, has mentioned the relevance of the sexual aspect of the myth to Milton's poem.

12. For Orpheus as a type of Christ, see Clifford Davidson, "The Young Milton, Orpheus and Poetry," *English Studies* LIX (1978), p. 28.

13. Quotations from *Paradise Lost* are from *John Milton: The Complete Poems and Major Prose*, ed. Merrit Y. Hughes (Indianapolis, 1957).

14. Richard Halpern, "Puritanism and Maenadism in *A Mask*," in *Rewriting the Renaissance*, ed. Margaret Ferguson, Maureen Quilligan, and Nancy Vickers (Chicago, 1986), pp. 88–105, offers an account of maenadism which is particularly interesting in light of my reading of Milton's use of the Orpheus myth. Characterized by a fierce chastity, the eating of raw meat, and wearing of skins to symbolize a rejection of the female tasks of cooking, weaving, and spinning, maenadism was a means by which Attic women "temporarily evaded the patriarchal structures of both *polis* and *oikos*." "As its votaries are wives and household slaves" maenadism "ruptured [structures of patriarchal authority] from within." Halpern sees the figure of the maenad as a menace to the male poet, a relation which becomes explicit in the invocation to Book VII. But, I would argue, the fierce chastity of the maenad reveals that she is at a deeper level the double of the Orphic poet. This doubling suggests that she embodies a contradiction within the structure of patriarchal authority, rather than simply an opponent in its bosom.

15. Balachandra Rajan, "*Lycidas*: The Shattering of the Leaves," in Patrides, *Milton's Lycidas*, p. 270.

16. Ibid., p. 271.

17. See, respectively, Abrams, "Five Types of *Lycidas*," p. 233; William Madsen, *From Shadowy Types to Truth*, (New York: 1963); Pigman, *Grief*, p. 117, and Fish, "Lycidas", p. 33.

18. Sacks, *The English Elegy*, p. 116. Sacks does not seem to allow the possibility that this appropriation qualifies the Christian poet's triumph.

DAMNATION IN A ROMAN DRESS:
CATILINE, *CATILINE*, AND *PARADISE LOST*

Robert Wiltenburg

R EADERS AND SCHOLARS of *Paradise Lost* have never ceased to
wonder, along with the first Miltonist, Andrew Marvell, "Where
couldst thou words of such a compass find? / Whence furnish such a vast
expense of mind?"[1] These questions retain their force not only because
Milton is the most learned and synthetic of poets, but also because, as
one critic has remarked, nothing more plainly shows Milton's "literary
genius" than the "discrimination" with which he "took precisely what
he needed, separating it with a wonderful instinct and insight from a
mass of other suggestions and effects."[2] In our accounting of the sources
of the poem, Ben Jonson, despite his acknowledged presence in Milton's
early poetry, has never counted for much.[3] My purpose here is to assess
the importance of the Catilinarian conspiracy as an element in the for-
mation of the poem, and to suggest that, while Milton is of course drawing directly upon the classical sources (principally Sallust and Cicero),
he is also responding to Ben Jonson's earlier synthesis of those sources
in his tragedy of *Catiline*.

The significance of Cicero in Renaissance literary culture is well
known. The schools held him up as a model prose stylist; his own works
and those attributed to him provided a theory and practice of the ideal
orator (often merging in the Renaissance mind with the ideal poet), a
philosopher-orator whose insight, learning, and skill with words could,
and should, be put to the highest uses of politics and culture. His claims
for this ideal orator suggest some of the most inspiring commonplaces
of humanist education. Thus the orator must take "all knowledge for his
province,"[4] must gain "profound insight into the characters of men, and
the whole range of human nature, and those motives whereby our souls
are spurred on or turned back" (I, xii, 53), that he may become the master of decorum, able to play a central role in the governing of civilized
life, whether it be to "arouse a listless nation" or to "curb its unbridled
impetuousity," to bring the "deceitful . . . to destruction" or "the righ-
teous to deliverance," to encourage the virtuous, reclaim the vicious, cen-
sure the wicked, or praise the worthy (II, ix, 35). Altogether, he will "by

89

his eloquence, either arouse or calm, within the souls of men, whatever passion the circumstances and occasion may demand" (I, xlvi, 202). Cicero's own life stood as witness that much of this high promise could be realized. As Plutarch said, "this man beyond all others showed the Romans how great a charm eloquence adds to the right, and that justice is invincible if it is correctly put in words."[5]

He was of particular interest to Milton, both for a general sense of direction and for many specifics. Surely the young Milton had taken to heart the passage in *De Oratore* in which Cicero, looking to the future, says:

I do not despair of its coming to pass that some day some one, keener in study than we are or ever have been, endowed with ampler leisure and earlier opportunity for learning, and exhibiting closer application and more intensive industry, who shall have given himself up to listening, reading and writing, will stand forth as an orator such as we are seeking, who may rightly be called not merely accomplished but actually eloquent. (I, xxi, 95)

Moreover, there is evidence throughout Milton's work of his deep and persistent interest in Cicero's style, thought, and character. To Milton, "a pure style meant Cicero";[6] he praises his "native *Latinisms*"[7] and quotes, as something that "hath oft come to my minde," Quintilian's saying, that "he hath well profited in Eloquence whom *Cicero* pleases" (CE IV, p. 2). Milton cites and quotes from many of the polemical and philosophical works, for authority and example on points of grammar, logic, Roman law and history, questions of ethics and philosophy — as, for example, the key concept of "right reason" (CE VII, p. 169) — and even occasionally points in theology, such as the idea "that God cannot punish man more, nor make him more miserable, then still by making him more sinnfull," which appears in the divorce pamphlets (CE III, p. 442), and later in *Paradise Lost*, where Satan is "Left . . . at large to his own dark designs, / That with reiterated crimes he might / Heap on himself damnation" (I, 213–15). Not surprisingly, Cicero occupies a prominent place in Milton's plan of education, a scheme intended, in its social dimension, to provide "a compleat and generous Education" fitting a man "to perform justly, skilfully, and magnanimously all the offices both private and publick, of Peace and War" (CE IV, p. 280). As one climax of their studies, students are expected to read at the same time, and presumably with the same attention, "choise Histories, *Heroic Poems*, and *Attic Tragedies* . . . with all the famous Political Orations," to the end that they might be endued "with the spirit and vigor of *Demosthenes* or *Cicero*, *Euripides* or *Sophocles*" (CE IV, p. 285–86).

Yet more striking is Milton's continual identification with Cicero's situation and character. Philip Rollinson has speculated that Milton must have been aware of the "compelling" "kinship" and "curious echoes" between his own life and Cicero's: the rise from modest origins; the doting father and lengthy education; the fierce, learned defense of republican government against its various enemies; the subsequent neglect, banishment, or proscription.[8] What Milton made of such parallels we do not know, but in controversial situations where it is "Milton for the defense," he makes the analogy to Cicero, whose own lifelong preference was for the defense,[9] explicit and fundamental. He describes *Areopagitica*, for example, as not merely the "disburdning of a particular fancie, but the common grievance" of the learned and good who have importuned him to write, even as Cicero had been importuned to write against Verres (CE IV, p. 330). For the gravest task of his career as a controversialist, the several works defending the regicide, he turns again and again to the central episode of Cicero's public career, the confrontation with Catiline. Thus for *Eikonoklastes* he constructs an epigraph, drawn from Sallust, describing the decay and transformation of a lawful kingship that preserves liberty for all into a lawless tyranny of one. He later compa res the arguments made on behalf of Strafford to the pleas of Catiline and of Caesar, who, "hatching Tyranny, injected the same scrupulous demurrs to stop the sentence of death in full and free senate decreed on *Lentulus* and *Cethegus*, two of *Catilines* accomplices" (CE V, p. 157). Similarly, in the *First Defense*, the killing of King Charles is likened to the killing of Catiline (CE VII, p. 337), and Cicero is appealed to as "an excellent man, and publicly entitled the father of his country" who "in many passages" "wonderfully" "extols" (even as Milton now does) the killing of tyrants (CE VII, p. 327). Finally, in the *Second Defense*, as Don M. Wolfe has observed, although "Milton does not draw out a parallel between his *Defensio* and Cicero's four orations *In Catilinam* . . . the comparison is implicit" throughout.[10]

These identifications with Cicero, particularly with Cicero's role in the story of Catiline, are complemented by Milton's deep respect for Sallust, the chief source for that story. That the two were closely linked in his mind is clear from the two letters to De Brass (1657) in which he praises Sallust by adapting Quintilian's praise of Cicero: "a man may know himself no mean proficient in the business of History who enjoys his Sallust" (CE XII, p. 101). Milton indicates in the first letter his pleasure in having persuaded young De Brass that Sallust is indeed the best of the Latin historians, and undertakes to interpret Sallust's remarks in the introductory sections of the *Catilinarian War* "as to the extreme difficulty of writing History, from the obligation that the expressions should be proportional to the deeds." Milton explains that

he who would write of worthy deeds worthily must write with mental endowments and experience of affairs not less than were in the doer of the same, so as to be able with equal mind to comprehend and measure even the greatest of them, and, when he has comprehended them, to relate them distinctly and gravely in pure and chaste speech. That he should do so in ornate style, I do not much care about; for I want a Historian, not an Orator. Nor yet would I have frequent maxims, or criticisms on the transactions, prolixly thrown in, lest, by interrupting the thread of events, the Historian should invade the office of the Political Writer: for, if the Historian, in explicating counsels and narrating facts, follows truth most of all, and not his own fancy or conjecture, he fulfils [sic] his proper duty. (CE XII, pp. 93, 95)

And Milton goes on to praise Sallust's style, characterizing it as the ability

to throw off a great deal in few words: a thing which I think no one can do without the sharpest judgment and a certain temperance at the same time. There are many in whom you will not miss either elegance of style or abundance of information; but for conjunction of brevity with abundance, i.e., for the despatch of much in few words, the chief of the Latins, in my judgment, is Sallust. (CE XII, p. 95)

One can hardly imagine higher Miltonic praise of a prose writer's matter and manner. But what is most remarkable for the present purpose is the caution not to confuse the role of the historian with that of the orator or political writer. This distinction is crucial for the story of Catiline, because Sallust, in his history, and Cicero, in his orations, give us stories which, though differing little in the facts — indeed, it has been suggested that Cicero may be Sallust's chief source of information[11] — differ radically in their significance. In Cicero's four orations against Catiline, we see the orator at work: arousing the listless, fearful Senate to the danger posed by Catiline and the conspiracy, variously appealing to patriotism, self-interest, fear, anger, shame. We see Cicero the consul, the prudent executive, driving Catiline from the Senate and the city, exposing the conspiracy, and apprehending the conspirators still within the walls. But we also see, increasingly, as we proceed from the first oration to the fourth, a self-absorbed Cicero concerned with his own place, honors, and destiny, a Cicero for whom — despite all the intricacies of plot and counterplot, principle and compromise, calculation and timing — the story, the inner logic and larger significance of the events, is almost embarrassingly simple, and might be briefly entitled, "How I saved the state and won eternal glory."

Sallust's story, though not necessarily truer, is a good deal subtler and more complex, being less concerned with the saving of the state than with "the extraordinary nature of the crime and of the danger arising from it."[12] Our name for his work, *Bellum Catilinae (The War of [or with] Catiline)*, does not so nearly express his true subject as the title by which it was more commonly known in the Renaissance: *Coniuratio Catilinae, The Conspiracy of Catiline*. The paradoxical word, *conjuration*, says much in little: how can a conjuration, a swearing of oaths, a binding together in law and obligation, have come to mean a conspiracy, a binding together in violence and despair? How can the same forces, the same virtues that built and sustained Rome now be turned against her? To these questions Sallust proposes no simple answers, but many considerations. The city he finds corrupted by prosperity, and he sees in Catiline the embodied genius of that corruption:

Lucius Catalina, scion of a noble family, had great vigour both of mind and of body, but an evil and depraved nature. . . . His body could endure hunger, cold and want of sleep to an incredible degree; his mind was reckless, cunning, treacherous, capable of any form of pretence or concealment. Covetous of others' possessions, he was prodigal of his own; he was violent in his passions. He possessed a certain amount of eloquence, but little discretion. His disordered mind ever craved the monstrous, incredible, gigantic. (V, 1–5)

And later, having described some of Catiline's particular vices and crimes, including the murder of his stepson, Sallust comments: "In fact, I think that this was his special motive for hastening his plot; for his guilt-stained soul, at odds with gods and men, could find rest neither waking nor sleeping, so cruelly did conscience ravage his overwrought mind" (XV, 3–4).

This description of a strong but dangerously divided personality only begins to suggest the dimensions of Catiline's cultural significance. We must imagine an Achilles incapable of tears, an Odysseus who cares nothing for home, an Aeneas without a destiny who inflicts pain without feeling it himself, a Demosthenes indifferent to the truth and to the public good. What fascinates and appalls in Catiline is precisely this mixture of good and evil growing up together almost inseparably, as even Cicero admitted in another context: "There was very much in him which indicated, not indeed in clear relief, but in outline, a virtuous ideal. He contrived to retain his hold upon many courageous and honest men by a plausible assumption of virtue."[13] This is nowhere more apparent than in the two great speeches given to Catiline, the first inflaming the conspirators, the second at the final battle. The first provides a sharp sample of his character and abilities:

If I had not already tested your courage and loyalty, in vain would a great opportunity have presented itself; high hopes and power would have been placed in my hands to no purpose, nor would I with the aid of cowards or inconstant hearts grasp at uncertainty in place of certainty. But because I have learned in many and great emergencies that you are brave and faithful to me, my mind has had the courage to set on foot a mighty and glorious enterprise, and also because I perceive that you and I hold the same view of what is good and evil; for agreement in likes and dislikes — this, and this only, is what constitutes true friendship. As for the designs which I have formed, they have already been explained to you all individually. But my resolution is fired more and more every day, when I consider under what conditions we shall live if we do not take steps to emancipate ourselves. For ever since the state fell under the jurisdiction and sway of a few powerful men, it is always to them that kings and potentates are tributary and peoples and nations pay taxes. All the rest of us, good and bad, nobles and commons alike, have made up the mob, without influence, without weight, and subservient to those to whom in a free state we should be an object of fear. Because of this, all influence, power, rank, and wealth are in their hands, or wherever they wish them to be; to us they have left danger, defeat, prosecutions, and poverty. How long, pray, will you endure this, brave hearts? Is it not better to die valiantly, than ignominiously to lose our wretched and dishonoured lives after being the sport of others' insolence? Assuredly (I swear it by the faith of gods and men!) victory is within our grasp. We are in the prime of life, we are stout of heart; to them, on the contrary, years and riches have brought utter dotage. We need only to strike; the rest will take care of itself. Pray, what man with the spirit of a man can endure that our tyrants should abound in riches, to squander in building upon the sea and in levelling mountains, while we lack the means to buy the bare necessities of life? That they should join their palaces by twos or even more, while we have nowhere a hearthstone? They amass paintings, statuary, and chased vases, tear down new structures and erect others, in short misuse and torment their wealth in every way; yet, with the utmost extravagance, they cannot get the upper hand of their riches. But we have destitution at home, debt without, present misery and a still more hopeless future; in short, what have we left, save only the wretched breath of life? Awake then! Lo, here, here before your eyes is the freedom for which you have often longed, and with it riches, honour, and glory; Fortune offers all these things as prizes to the victors. The undertaking itself, the dangers, your need, the splendid spoils of war, speak louder than any words of mine. Use me either as your leader or as a soldier in the ranks; my soul and my body shall be at your service. These very schemes I hope to help you carry out as your consul, unless haply I delude myself and you are content to be slaves rather than to rule. (XX, 2–17)

Here indeed is one, like Comus, winding himself into men's hearts with "reasons not unplausible," a tissue of bad thinking and bad faith, a challenge to discernment as difficult as that posed by Satan in *Paradise Lost*. Thus he has learned of their "courage and faith" through the failure of their first plot; the "mighty and glorious enterprise" will be the assassination of their fellow patricians and the burning of the city to create a general panic; good and evil are reduced to "likes and dislikes," and friendship cunningly redefined as a matter of taste rather than the common pursuit of virtue; the declared aim is "liberty," envisioned as "a free state" in which he and his friends will nonetheless be "objects of fear"; he swears by the same faith of gods and men that the very act of rebellion abrogates; ostensibly outraged by luxury and greed, he tempts his followers with "riches" and "spoils"; he disingenuously offers to be a mere "soldier in the ranks," when he is, of course, the inspirer and manipulator of the whole business; and at the last he reveals the deadly dichotomy hidden beneath the rhetoric of liberty: one must be either slave or tyrant, and his choice is clear: better to reign in ruins than serve in Rome.

Within Sallust's story, there is no adequate counterweight to the rhetoric of Catiline — indeed, many of his criticisms of Roman society are Sallust's also. Sallust does describe Cicero's actions, and he praises the first oration as a signal service to the state, but Cicero is nowhere a speaking character. Aside from the brooding historian himself, we hear only Caesar and Cato debating the appropriate punishment of the conspirators. Sallust tells us that these are the two most admirable men of his time: the one stern, upright, patrician, his integrity unshakeable in any circumstances; the other brave, generous, compassionate, popular. As Syme has observed, "In alliance the two had what was needed to save the Republic" (p. 120). But no alliance occurs, or is possible, for in Sallust's view, "Fortune holds sway everywhere" (VIII, 1) and has turned against Rome, bringing "confusion into all our affairs" (X, 1), a confusion in which "under pretence of the public welfare each in reality was working for his own advancement" (XXXVIII, 3) — even, in one degree or another, Cato, Caesar, and Cicero. This is then a story of the perversion of classical ideals, and Sallust's true subject is not Rome saved but Rome lost, a city and a frame of mind in which elements once held in delicate, laborious, and fruitful tension — such things as strength and goodness, eloquence and wisdom, the uprightness of Cato and the compassion of Caesar — have split apart, turned upon each other, become monstrous, desperate, and destructive. At the end, neither we, nor Sallust, nor the army that has defeated Catiline — in the process indiscriminately slaying enemies, guests, and friends — knows quite what to feel:

But the army of the Roman people gained no joyful nor bloodless victory, for all the most valiant had either fallen in the fight or come off with severe wounds.

Many, too, who had gone from the camp to visit the field or to pillage, on turning over the bodies of the rebels found now a friend, now a guest or kinsman; some
also recognized their personal enemies. Thus the whole army was variously affected with gladness and grief, rejoicing and lamentation. (LXI, 7–9)[14]

A sad story, but of great potential use to Milton. There are obviously many points of resemblance between the character and actions of
Sallust's Catiline and Milton's Satan. Rollinson has summarized the "more
than . . . accidental" similarities between them: each is "depraved, yet
boundlessly energetic and immensely talented, a guilty but restless and
ambitious spirit. . . . A consummate liar, hypocrite, and demagogue
[who] foments and sustains a formidable but unsuccessful coup in secret
meetings, public assemblies, and on the battlefield . . . [and] persists even
against insurmountable odds."[15] The weight of these similarities might
well lead us to regard Catiline, the classic perversion of classical values,
as the most direct and compelling of Satan's literary ancestors, at least
on one side of the family.[16] Yet I think Catilinarian material was useful
to Milton in other ways as well. For if we take into account both Milton's
deep Ciceronian sympathies, and the appropriateness of Sallust's story
of civic virtue lost and heroism perverted to his purpose in *Paradise Lost*,
we must then confront the chief problem Sallust's and Cicero's stories
posed for the Renaissance reader: how are these two versions of the same
events, the orator's and the historian's, the "Fall of Catiline" and the "Victory of Cicero," to be reconciled? Was Rome saved or was it lost? That
these competing interpretations must be reconciled was clear.

Sallust's *Catiline* was by a wide margin the single most reprinted
work of ancient history between 1450 and 1700, averaging more than
one printing per year over those two-and-a-half centuries. It was a staple
text of schools and universities. In England alone, not yet a major center of book publishing, there were separate Latin editions in 1569, 1573,
1601, 1615, and 1639; English translations of the account by Constantius
Felicius, an Italian jurist, as early as 1541, and of Sallust in 1608 and
1629.[17] Its significance in Renaissance thinking is sufficiently indicated
by its place in, for example, Leonardo Bruni's influential *Historiarum
Florentini Populi Libri XII* (1449); Eric Cochrane summarizes Bruni's
view of history as follows:

[Each historical epoch] could thus be evaluated qualitatively by the degree to
which the respective [political] community had achieved the twofold goal of internal tranquillity and individual creativity — by the degree, that is, to which it
enabled all of its citizens, under the protection of just and equitable laws, to
develop their own individual talents to the fullest. At least one community had

approached this goal in the past: the Roman Republic before the conspiracy of Catiline.[18]

It is instructive, for those to whom classical texts usually come in small red and green packages, to examine a folio Sallust of the time. These editions are less interested in Sallust per se than in the Catilinarian conspiracy as the supreme and exemplary crisis of Roman civilization. They supply the reader with Cicero as well as Sallust; they add a variety of speeches, both traditional, such as the speech of Porcius Latro against Catiline and the complementary invectives of Sallust against Cicero and Cicero against Sallust, and others devised by contemporary historians to fill gaps in the narrative or flesh out minor characters; and they subject the text to the most intense interpretive pressure, surrounding it with a commentary addressed to as many points of language, law, history, and ethics as possible.[19]

Such materials demanded dramatic synthesis of the kind attempted by Ben Jonson in his *Catiline* of 1611. His was not the first English play on the subject, nor was its general pattern particularly original. Stephen Gosson's *Catilins Conspiracies* (now lost) had, for example, aimed "to showe the rewarde of traytors in *Catiline*, and the necessary government of learned men, in the person of *Cicero*, which forsees every danger that is likely to happen, and forstalles it continually ere it take effect" (H&S X, p. 117). Jonson's play failed initially on the stage, being found excessively declamatory: it features a climactic three-hundred-line epitome of Cicero's first oration — the point at which the first audience, whether from boredom or some more powerful emotion, revolted. Despite this inauspicious beginning, the play was revived in the 1630s and 1660s, becoming "for a time, a staple item in the repertory,"[20] and was republished even unto the second, third, and fourth quartos in 1635, 1669, and 1674. G. E. Bentley concludes that it was the "most familiar of all the plays of [Shakespeare and Jonson] in the seventeenth century," and, indeed, "not *Hamlet, Lear, Othello,* or *Macbeth,* but *Catiline* was the premier English tragedy in the minds of seventeenth-century writers."[21]

What accounts for this popularity? In part, the perceived importance of the subject; in part, its ready, and flexible, application to contemporary politics (we may recall that Milton even managed to argue that the king was the true rebel); but I think the largest factor was Jonson's genuine achievement in adapting and synthesizing these materials into a complexly imagined double action that does justice both to the seriousness and intractability of the challenge embodied in Catiline — as the Chorus asks at the end of act 1, "Can nothing great, and at the

height / Remaine so long"? — and to the heroism, however qualified, of
Cicero. The piece's failure as a play should not blind us to its success
as a dramatic poem. Jonson gives us no simple story of a "traytor" and
a "learned man," but rather a Catiline sharply stylized and magnified
into a figure of demonic horror, and a Cicero in all his long-winded vanity.
His Catiline is less anything specifically Roman than a corrupt and corrupting force of fallen nature, an outsize Jonsonian narcissist — gigantic,
omnivorous, infantile — who, from his sense of "injured merit," has vowed
Rome's violent, incestuous destruction:

> It is decree'd. Nor shall thy Fate, o *Rome*,
> Resist my vow. Though hills were set on hills,
> And seas met seas, to guard thee; I would through:
> I, plough up rocks, steepe as the *Alpes*, in dust;
> And lave the *Tyrrhene* waters, into clouds;
> But I would reach thy head, thy head, proud citie.
> The ills, that I have done, cannot be safe
> But by attempting greater; and I feele
> A spirit, within me, chides my sluggish hands,
> And sayes, they have been innocent too long.
> Was I a man, bred great, as *Rome* her selfe?
> One, form'd for all her honors, all her glories?
> Equall to all her titles? that could stand
> Close up, with ATLAS; and sustaine her name
> As strong, as he doth heav'n? And, was I,
> Of all her brood, mark'd out for the repulse
> By her no voice, when I stood *Candidate*,
> To be commander in the *Pontick* warre?
> I will, hereafter, call her step-dame, ever.
> If shee can loose her nature, I can loose
> My pietie; and in her stony entrailes
> Dig me a seate: where, I will live, againe,
> The labour of her wombe, and be a burden,
> Weightier then all the prodigies, and monsters,
> That shee hath teem'd with, since shee first knew MARS. (I, 73–97)

This Catiline has all the demonic force (and more) of Sallust's, but none
of the complex shading: here his social criticism, his liberality, and other
shows of virtue are little more than manipulative shams concealing a
nihilist disdain of everything outside himself. As is frequently the case
with Jonson's reworking of Roman writers, ambiguities and velleities of
perception and emotion give way to moral imperatives governing will
and action, as Jonson performs his customary "embattling" of vice and
virtue. Thus Jonson clears up Sallust's doubts concerning Caesar's com-

plicity in the plot and eagerly embraces the lurid report, discounted by Sallust, of the sealing of the conspiracy with an infernal sacrament, the blood of a murdered slave. Catiline speaks:

> Be firme, my hand; not shed a drop: but powre
> Fiercenesse into me, with it, and fell thirst
> Of more, and more, till *Rome* be left as bloud-lesse,
> As ever her feares made her, or the sword.
> And, when I leave to wish this to thee, step-dame,
> Or stop, to effect it, with my powers fainting;
> So may my bloud be drawne, and so drunke up
> As is this slaves.   (I, 491–98)

His acolytes conclude the scene by hailing him as the "oraculous" and "god-like" Catiline.

In addition to giving Catiline a coarser, more horrific, more elemental power, Jonson has recast the whole conspiracy in a native idiom: Cicero had attributed the preservation of the state (and of his own consulship!) to the special providence of Jupiter; Jonson completes the theology by making the conspiracy explicitly "hellish" and "devilish." He has also greatly elaborated the "council in hell," carefully particularizing the conspirators—Lentulus pompous, ambitious, credulous, eager to be "master of Rome"; Cethegus raging, bloody, cruel, eager to destroy Rome; others merely greedy or lascivious—in order to more fully demonstrate Catiline's Mosca-like mastery of the tempter's art, in which a single lie must minister simultaneously to several contradictory hopes and fears.

Jonson's other major interpretive contribution is to give a clear moral pattern to Catiline's whole career. Again this is cast in the idiom of "damnation" as it has been described by Dame Helen Gardner: a combination of "presumption and despair" that leads to the "deforming of a creature in its origin bright and good, by its own willed persistence in acts against its own nature."[22] Jonson represents this progressive deformation by a progressive diminution of Catiline's character and presence in the play: while he confidently dominates the opening, he is continually less effective, less "himself" as the play proceeds, and we actually lose sight of him for a time before the glorious despair of the final battle: "yet let us care / To sell our selves, at such a price, as may / Un-doe the world, to buy us" (V, 416–18). Petreius, commander of the senatorial army, reports it as follows:

> The streights, and needs of CATILINE being such,
> As he must fight, with one of the two armies,
> That then had neere enclos'd him; It pleas'd *Fate*,

To make us th'object of his desperate choise,
. . . .
At this we rous'd, lest one small minutes stay
Had left it to be'enquir'd, what *Rome* was.
And (as we ought) arm'd in the confidence
Of our great cause, in forme of battaile, stood.
Whilst CATILINE came on, not with the face
Of any man, but of a publique ruine:
His count'nance was a civill warre it selfe.
And all his host had standing in their lookes,
The palenesse of the death, that was to come.
. . . .
And now had fierce ENYO, like a flame,
Consum'd all it could reach, and then it selfe;
Had not the fortune of the common-wealth
Come PALLAS-like to every *Roman* thought.
Which CATILINE seeing, and that now his troops
Cover'd that earth, they'had fought on, with their trunkes,
Ambitious of great fame, to crowne his ill,
Collected all his furie, and ran in
(Arm'd with a glorie, high as his despaire)
Into our battaile, like a *Lybian* lyon,
Upon his hunters, scornefull of our weapons,
Carelesse of wounds, plucking downe lives about him,
Till he had circled in himselfe with death:
Then he fell too, t'embrace it where it lay.
And as, in that rebellion 'gainst the gods,
MINERVA holding forth MEDUSA's head,
One of the gyant brethren felt himselfe
Grow marble at the killing sight, and now,
Almost made stone, began t'inquire, what flint,
What rocke it was, that crept through all his limmes,
And, ere he could thinke more, was that he fear'd;
So CATILINE, at the sight of *Rome* in us,
Became his tombe.   (V, 629–85)

This is a cleaner and more complete ending than Sallust's: the evil has been confined, localized with Catiline himself, and he is not only killed, but is also compelled to recognize his moral defeat by the triumphant, astonishing *idea* of Rome.

What Jonson sacrifices in the demonization of Catiline, he more than regains in the humanization of Cicero and in the exploration of the nature of his success. To accomplish these aims, he juxtaposes Cicero's self-congratulation with the critical view of Cicero, represented, for example, by Plutarch, who saw in him one whose "excessive delight in the praise of others and his too passionate desire for glory . . . very often confounded his saner reasonings" ("Cicero," *Lives*, VI, 5), and who "made himself generally odious, not by any base action, but by continually prais- ing and magnifying himself . . . the blemish stuck to him like an in- curable disease" (XXIV, 1,3).[23] The result is often, as Anne Barton has observed, to "bring comedy dangerously close to the centre of the play."[24] More than one reader has felt that Cato's "You talke too much to 'hem, MARCUS" (III, 827) could be applied throughout. At the very end, Cicero, like some Adam Overdo who has not yet learned his lesson of humility, is made to marvel at Petreius's modesty and to conclude, with lame self-importance:

> Thanks to the'immortall gods,
> *Romans*, I now am paid for all my labours,
> My watchings, and my dangers. Here conclude
> Your praises, triumphs, honors, and rewards,
> Decreed to me: only the memorie
> Of this glad day, if I may know it live
> Within your thoughts, shall much affect my conscience,
> Which I must alwayes studie before fame.
> Though both be good, the latter yet is worst,
> And ever is ill got, without the first.   (V, 693–702)

One understands why Sallust did not find Cicero an adequate counter- poise to Catiline: the physician is himself infected with the disease. For all its air of historical exactitude, Jonson's play is an exercise in moral rather than historical realism, a meditation on the eternal, powerful, dark challenge to law, reason, and government within the state and within the soul, and on their preservation through such limited, flawed, yet nonetheless essential civic heroism as men are capable of. For Jonson, Rome is always being lost, but it is also occasionally, provisionally, par- tially being saved — and saved by a slightly foolish hero (to be a man born is to be a fool incurable) who, despite his bumptious self-importance, articulates a humane ideal, using all the reasons and passions that come to hand to persuade himself and others to *act* better than they *are*. This is Jonson's humanism at its most humane: the unquenchable idea of Rome that Catiline has never understood.[25] As ever with Jonson, the resolution of the action is carefully qualified. Evil may undo itself, or be arrested for a moment's laughter, insight, or peace; beyond this, in the plays anyway, Jonson will not go. In the masques, we find good dis- placing evil, but Jonson lacks Milton's supreme capacity (and faith) to show us "evil still *producing* good."

Despite these and other evident differences in scope and intent, I think we should regard Jonson's *Catiline* as a significant source for a significant part of *Paradise Lost*. That Milton knew the play we may be certain. His interest in the Catilinarian material is clear, and the play was prominent not only in itself but also as a focus for the contemporary preoccupation with conspiracy, which, as Stella Revard has argued, stands as an important background to the poem.[26] From the time of the Armada until late in the seventeenth century, the international Catholic conspiracy, kept vivid by the extensive annual commemorations of the Gunpowder Plot, was never far from the English mind.[27] We may also recall that Milton's earliest plans for *Paradise Lost* took the form of tragic drama rather than epic — a form for which Jonson's play, with its Senecan chorus to mark the acts, was an acknowledged model.

Several aspects of characterization and structure in the first half of the poem suggest Jonson's influence. Satan is, like Sallust's Catiline, eloquent and initially sympathetic to the reader, but he is also, like Jonson's, powered by a childish jealousy, rage, and despair, being "fraught / With envy against the Son of God" (V, 661–62). Jonson's portrayal of Catiline as a figure at once demonic and inhuman yet also as intimately familiar as a hurt, rejected child prepares the way for Milton's more subtly oxymoronic Satan. More striking still is the similarity in the presentation of the dynamics of damnation. Dame Helen Gardner found the literary roots of Satan's psychology in such damned characters as Marlowe's Doctor Faustus and Shakespeare's Macbeth. In *Catiline* we have perhaps the best evidence of Milton's debt to the earlier drama, for here we find not only the damned but also the damner (in Cicero) and see the characteristic diminishment and self-destruction of the damned as a product of his interaction with a (nearly) all-knowing and all-controlling providence. Moreover, in perceiving and judging this interaction, the reader's sympathies are similarly divided: Jonson's play juxtaposes the energetic vice of Catiline with the speechifying virtue of Cicero in a way that corresponds to our initial impressions (and misimpressions) of Satan and God.

If Milton's Satan owes something to Catiline, his God, both Father and Son, owes something to Cicero. Barbara Lewalski has pointed to the Ciceronian oration as one of the models underlying the Father's speeches in Book III.[28] But the content as well as the form is Ciceronian. Cicero too, in his first speech against Catiline, has been concerned that "many ignorant men as well as villains would be saying that I acted cruelly and tyrannically if I had punished Catiline" (I, xii, 30);[29] he therefore advises the Senate to "let the wicked depart . . . separate themselves from the good . . . [and] assemble in one place" (I, xiii, 32). The reader of the first two books of the poem has seen a similar assembly of the wicked, heard the "villains" charging God with cruelty and tyranny, and, being still "ignorant," is none too certain of the nature of God's justice.[30] Cicero also presents himself, like the Son, as sacrificial redeemer and firm judge of the state: he "rejoices" that his "consulship has been destined almost by fate for the salvation of the Roman people" (IV, i, 2); and he says: "I offer myself, citizens, as a leader for this war; I accept the hatred of the wicked; what can be healed I will cure in some way or other, the members which must be cut off I will not allow to remain to endanger the state" (II, v, 11). The proper balance of judgment and mercy, claimed by Cicero, we see fully enacted in the Son. In a statement that might also, *mutatis mutandis*, summarize God's situation in the poem — the very necessity of having his ways justified to man — Cicero complains:

O wretched the lot of those who administer the state, and even of those who save it! . . . Men will say . . . [that Catiline was] driven out by the force and threats of a consul . . . there will be those who will wish to think him, not a criminal, but an object of pity and me not a most watchful consul but a most cruel tyrant. It is worth my while, citizens, to endure the storm of this false and unjust hatred, provided only the danger of this awful and wicked war is averted from you. (II, vii, 14–15)

Such are indeed the misinterpretations, by fallen angels and fallen readers, to which divine actions and intentions are subject in the poem. And it is precisely this redemptive aspect of Cicero, his fumbling concern that all should repent, abandon the conspiracy, and be saved (a concern he pursues at considerable risk to his own safety), that is particularly emphasized by Jonson, whose Cato upbraids Cicero for trying to save, rather than simply arrest, his would-be assassins (III, 813–28).

We see then how far Cicero is useful to Milton's *initial* presentation of God in Book III: to the imperfectly instructed reader, whose imaginative experience of the poem has begun in Hell, God's ways, both His justice and His mercy, stand in need of much the same sort of justification as Cicero's to the ignorant, negligent, fearful, self-absorbed senators and citizens of Rome. As both poem and reader progress, however, we are invited to discern the difference between Cicero's situation and God's. When, in Book V, Father and Son consider the threat posed by the nascent rebellion, the Father, his words recalling Cicero's exhortations to the Senate, says:

> Let us advise, and to this hazard draw
> With speed what force is left, and all imploy
> In our defense, lest unawares we lose
> This our high place, our Sanctuary, our Hill.   (V, 729–32)

But here, of course, this busy civic heroism is all a joke, the Father "smiling," "laughing," holding his foes "in derision," as he marks, and enables us to appreciate, the difference between prudence and providence.

Beyond these similarities in characterization, in psychological matrix and dynamics, stands a patterned similarity of structural elements. After brief, introductory settings of scene, we begin, in both play and poem, with the damned figure *solus*, then in conversation with a confidant, then in a larger, carefully differentiated conspiratorial company, which proceeds to debate and resolution concerning the best means to prosecute their rebellion or revenge. We shift next to the defenders of the state, and witness their discussions and decisions taken with regard to the plotters. This is followed, after a pause, by the withdrawing of the rebels outside the city or to the north, their final battle with the forces of Rome or Heaven, and their utter overthrow.[31] Such a summary of the chief points of correspondence does not include all the significant events in Books I–VI (Adam, Eve, and the Garden are rather conspicuously missing), but it does cover most of the events in Hell and in Heaven, particularly those bearing on the action completed by the end of Book VI, the story of Satan's fall.

At the end of that Book, Raphael summarizes the lesson for Adam:

> let it profit thee to have heard
> By terrible Example the reward
> Of disobedience; firm they might have stood,
> Yet fell; remember, and fear to transgress.   (VI, 909–12)

Raphael's straightforward account of the angelic rebellion is, or should be, sufficient for the unfallen Adam. Yet the reader of the first half of the poem needs, and has been given, stronger medicine. With the fall of the rebel angels at the end of Book VI, we return to the place where we had begun, now prepared to know it for the first time. A full understanding of this exemplary story has required a continually counterpointed double action (or rather a double perspective on the same action), similar to, though more sophisticated than, Jonson's. Just as we must synthesize Sallust's and Cicero's stories of the Catilinarian conspiracy, so also must we synthesize the hellish and heavenly views of the angelic rebellion, synthesize the drama (and melodrama) of Books I and II and the recollected narrative of Books V and VI. Only then, having experienced disobedience and its consequences both as actor and spectator, as politician and historian, as Satan and as God, are we prepared to share in two judgments upon Satan, reminiscent, respectively, of Sallust's and Jonson's judgments upon Catiline. The first is Abdiel's puzzled, poignant

contemplation of the haughty Satan, "arm'd in Adamant and Gold," at
the beginning of the War in Heaven:

> O Heav'n! that such resemblance of the Highest
> Should yet remain, where faith and realty
> Remain not; wherefore should not strength and might
> There fail where Virtue fails, or weakest prove
> Where boldest; though to sight unconquerable? (VI, 114–18)

Sallust similarly perceives and laments the tragic disjunction between
strength and virtue, a disjunction he, like Abdiel, may resist but cannot
overcome. That must await the second, perfected judgment of the Son
upon Satan at the very end of the battle, where—like Jonson's Catiline
who at the last beholds in the eyes of the soldiers who have defeated him
the embodied idea of Rome itself—Satan and his crew see God's eternal
judgment on them manifested in the Son and are compelled to an anni-
hilating vision of the truth, compelled to know themselves even as they
are known.[32]

> Full soon
> Among them he arriv'd; in his right hand
> Grasping ten thousand Thunders, which he sent
> Before him, such as in thir Souls infix'd
> Plagues; they astonisht all resistance lost,
> All courage; down thir idle weapons dropp'd;
> . . . .
> Nor less on either side tempestuous fell
> His arrows, from the fourfold-visag'd Four,
> Distinct with eyes, and from the living Wheels,
> Distinct alike with multitude of eyes;
> One Spirit in them rul'd, and every eye
> Glar'd lightning, and shot forth pernicious fire
> Among th'accurst, that wither'd all thir strength,
> And of thir wonted vigor left them drain'd,
> Exhausted, spiritless, afflicted, fall'n. (VI, 834–39, 844–52)

What conclusions does this examination of Milton's use of Catiline,
Cicero, Sallust, and Jonson suggest? Most simply, it substantiates Douglas
Bush's judgment that, for all the many sons of Ben, Milton was his "nearest heir."[33] But it also indicates that Jonson remained for the mature Milton a significant predecessor worth assimilating and revising to fit his
own largest purposes.[34] Both Jonson and Milton are drawn to the story
of Catiline and Cicero because it represents a moment of supreme crisis
for civilized values, a challenge that prompts each to reexamine what

the ultimate defenders and guarantors of man's humanity can be. Can Cicero, the philosopher-orator, be trusted to do the job? For Jonson, sturdy humanist that he is, the answer, despite validating concessions, doubts, and qualifications, must be, "Yes." Who else is there? But for Milton, who had himself, like Cicero, spent so much time, effort, and sight "in liberty's defense" (*Sonnet XXII*), only to see the "good old Cause" fail at last, "half yet remains unsung." The humanist response to the problem of moral and social evil embodied in the story of Catiline and Cicero can play only a part — and, having been drawn upon for our least enlightened ideas of God, and even for Satan's later approach to Eve like "some Orator renown'd / In *Athens* or free *Rome*" (IX, 670–71), rather an equivocal part — in his larger purpose, which is to present a more than ethical and political answer to a more than ethical and political problem, to show us not only paradise lost but the promise of a full spiritual "restoration." For this purpose, as old experience had taught him, more is needed than eloquence or philosophy can provide. As the Son in *Paradise Regained*, having been tempted, among other fruits of human wisdom, with the "resistless eloquence" of "ancient" and "famous Orators" (IV, 267–68), replies to Satan:

> Thir orators thou then extoll'st, as those
> The top of Eloquence, Statists indeed,
> And lovers of thir Country, as may seem;
> But herein to our Prophets far beneath,
> As men divinely taught, and better teaching
> The solid rules of Civil Government
> In thir majestic unaffected style
> Then all the Oratory of *Greece* and *Rome*.
> In them is plainest taught, and easiest learnt,
> What makes a Nation happy, and keeps it so,
> What ruins Kingdoms, and lays Cities flat;
> These only, with our Law, best form a King. (IV, 353–64)

Washington University, St. Louis

NOTES

1. Marvell's poem, "On Paradise Lost," is included in *John Milton: Complete Poems and Major Prose*, ed. Merritt Y. Hughes, (Indianapolis, 1957), pp. 209–10, from which I cite Milton's poetry.

2. F. T. Prince, *The Italian Element in Milton's Verse* (Oxford, 1954), p. viii.

3. John G. Demaray, *Milton's Theatrical Epic: The Invention and Design of "Paradise Lost"* (Cambridge, Mass., 1980), has suggested that Jonson's characteristic anti-masque/masque structure may have influenced the initial presentation of hell before heaven; but the complexity of our responses to both heaven and hell undermines the analogy.

4. Cicero, *De Oratore*, 2 vols., trans. E. W. Sutton, ed. H. Rackham (Cambridge, Mass., 1959), II, i, 5. Translations of classical authors are taken, unless otherwise noted, from the Loeb editions.

5. Plutarch, "Cicero," in *Plutarch's Lives*, trans. Bernadotte Perrin, (Cambridge, Mass., 1971), vol. VII, xiii, 1.

6. George Williamson, *Milton and Others*, 2nd ed. (Chicago, 1970), p. 216.

7. John Milton, *The Works of John Milton*, 18 vols., ed. Frank Allen Patterson, et al., (New York, 1931–38), vol. III, p. 347. Cited hereafter in the text as CE.

8. Philip Rollinson, "Cicero," in *A Milton Encyclopedia*, 9 vols., ed. William B. Hunter, Jr. et al. (Lewisburg, Va., 1978–83), vol. II, pp. 54–55.

9. D. R. Shackleton Bailey, *Cicero* (London, 1971), p. 16.

10. *Complete Prose Works of John Milton*, 8 vols., ed. Don M. Wolfe et al. (New Haven, Conn., 1953–82), vol. IV, p. 581.

11. Ronald Syme, *Sallust* (Berkeley and Los Angeles, 1964), p. 73.

12. *Sallust*, trans. J. C. Rolfe (London, 1921), IV, 4.

13. Cicero, *Pro Caelio* (XII, 14), as translated by C. H. Herford, Percy and Evelyn Simpson in *Ben Jonson* (Oxford, 1925–52), vol. X, p. 120. (This edition is cited hereafter in the text as H&S.) Jonson had marked this passage in his folio Sallust.

14. The Loeb edition mistakenly translates *laetitia* as "sorrow"; I have substituted "gladness."

15. Rollinson, *Milton Encyclopedia*, vol. VII, p. 136.

16. Francis Blessington, *"Paradise Lost" and the Classical Epic* (London, 1979), p. xii, argues that Satan "does not, in general, embody the classical tradition or the old heroism but represents a perversion of the values found in Homer and Virgil." This perhaps overstates the case — surely Milton does wish to reject some elements of the old heroism, either because they are intrinsically inadequate or because they end in their own perversion; still, it is with the perversion that he begins. Blessington does not mention Catiline.

17. See Peter Burke, "A Survey of the Popularity of Ancient Historians, 1450–1700," *History and Theory* V, no. 2 (1966), 135–52, and A. W. Pollard and G. R. Redgrave, *A Short-Title Catalogue of Books Printed in England, Scotland, and Ireland, 1475–1640*, 2 vols. (London, 1976, 1986).

18. Eric Cochrane, *Historians and Historiography in the Italian Renaissance* (Chicago, 1981), p. 8.

19. A typical example is Jonson's folio Sallust (Basel, 1564), described by H&S, vol. X, pp. 117–19.

20. Anne Barton, *Ben Jonson, Dramatist* (Cambridge, 1984), p. 154.

21. Gerald Eades Bentley, *Shakespeare and Jonson: Their Reputations in the Seventeenth Century Compared*, 2 vols. (Chicago, 1945), vol. I, pp. 111, 112.

22. Dame Helen Gardner, "Milton's 'Satan' and the Theme of Damnation in Elizabethan Tragedy," *English Studies* n.s. I (1948), 47.

23. The last clause is from the Langhornes's translation, *Plutarch's Lives* (New York, n.d.), vol. II, p. 157.

24. Barton, *Ben Jonson, Dramatist*, p. 157.

25. See J. S. Lawry, "*Catiline* and 'the Sight of Rome in Us,'" in *Rome in the Renaissance: The City and the Myth*, ed. P. A. Ramsey (Binghamton, N.Y., 1982), pp. 395–407.

26. Stella Purce Revard, *The War in Heaven: "Paradise Lost" and the Tradition of Satan's Rebellion* (Ithaca, N.Y., 1980), chap. 3.

27. Nor from Milton's: see the small squibs "In Proditionem Bombardicam," "In Inventorem Bombardae," and the more ambitious "In Quintem Novembris." Concerning the last, B. N. DeLuna has speculated on its "tacit derivation from Jonson's *Catiline*" in *Jonson's Romish Plot: A Study of "Catiline" and Its Historical Context* (Oxford, 1967), p. 337. This seems to me possible, but not necessary.

28. Barbara Kiefer Lewalski, *"Paradise Lost" and the Rhetoric of Literary Forms* (Princeton, N.J., 1985), p. 120.

29. Cicero, *In Catilinam*, trans. Louis E. Lord, in *The Speeches* (Cambridge, Mass., 1959).

30. Georgia Christopher, *Milton and the Science of the Saints* (Princeton, N.J., 1982), p. 116, remarks that "The 'development' of God's character [in the poem] thus measures the jagged course of the narrator's religious experience, which goes from deep rebellion and hatred through clarity, understanding, admiration, and finally to familial love and intimacy."

31. In the poem, these events are divided between the second (Books I and II) and first (Books V and VI) conspiracies of Satan, but the reader's imaginative experience of them is (or strives to be) continuous.

32. For the relation of these two judgments, that of Abdiel and that of the Son, compare Joseph Summers's comment, in *The Muse's Method: An Introduction to "Paradise Lost"* (Cambridge, Mass., 1962), p. 113, on the significance of the reorganization in the second edition: "Milton seems to have discovered that in the poem which he had written the true centre was not the angelic exemplum of man's ways at their most heroic, but the divine image of God's ways at their most providential."

33. Douglas Bush, *English Literature in the Earlier Seventeenth Century, 1600–1660,* 2nd ed. (Oxford, 1962), p. 114.

34. See Richard Helgerson, *Self-Crowned Laureates: Spenser, Jonson, Milton, and the Literary System* (Berkeley and Los Angeles, 1983); and Judith Scherer Herz, "Epigrams and Sonnets: Milton in the Manner of Jonson," in *Milton Studies*, vol. xx, ed. James D. Simmonds (Pittsburgh, 1984), pp. 29–41, who observes that "Milton saw in Jonson a poet not so much like himself . . . as like one version of himself — the poet-legislator, remaker of society through a re-created language" (p. 39).

MILTON AND GALILEO:
THE ART OF
INTELLECTUAL CANONIZATION

Julia M. Walker

D ISCUSSIONS OF MILTON and Galileo are most often located within either the context of Milton's cosmology (was he presenting a post-Copernican universe in *Paradise Lost* or covering his cosmographical tracks with Ptolemaic and Platonic shadowings?) or the context of Milton's travels (did he really meet Galileo or just the Tuscan's Florentine students?).[1] Although these topics are perhaps scholarly first cousins to the concerns of this study, I wish to focus upon a different aspect of the Milton-Galileo relationship: Milton's valorization of Galileo as a martyr to the cause of intellectual freedom. My emphasis here is upon the — perhaps regrettably trendy — word *valorization;* I will use *martyr* and, later, *patron saint* metaphorically. Recent critical debate has presented Milton's use of the Tuscan's name and associations as problematic at best, negative at worst. Approaching this issue from the intellectual context of the recent International Milton Symposium, I must argue that Milton was profoundly affected by the figure of Galileo, a man who presented the world with a universal truth only to be forced, by political and religious pressure, from both his work and a free, active existence. Milton had in Galileo, therefore, not ony a metaphorical version of the traditional saint's legend from which to learn and to teach, not only the figure of a martyr to venerate (and a martyr *of*, not for, the Catholic establishment), but also an intellectual saint's name and a set of icons to invoke as a source of power and authority for his own endeavors. One obvious starting point in this argument is the passage in *Areopagitica:* "There it was that I found and visited the famous *Galileo* grown old, a prisoner to the Inquisition, for thinking in Astronomy otherwise than the Franciscan and Dominican licencers thought";[2] but I want to press beyond the implications of that specific passage to posit a broader, if more subtle, paradigm composed of invocations of Galileo's life and work in Milton's poetry and prose.

There is, of course, nothing particularly subtle about Milton placing Galileo, by name and profession, as the only contemporary human

in *Paradise Lost* (indeed, Harold Bloom contends that Milton places
Galileo in Book I to compel us "to read as he reads" and to accept "his
time as true time"); neither is great subtlety implicit in the fact, which
Frank B. Young points to, that Milton presents "each of Galileo's most
famous discoveries . . . in one or more passage of the epic," nor in his
use of the "Telescope" and the magical "Airy Microscope" in lines 42 and
57 of *Paradise Regained*, Book IV.[3] But what about *Eikonoklastes*, where
he decenters the sun/king analogy only to replace it with a nonearthly
son/sun image? To what extent can Eve's and then Adam's fatal choices
be attributed to a spiritual geocentrism arising from Raphael's dismissal
(or repression), (or incomplete presentation) of cosmological knowledge?
And how far does a veneration of Galileo go toward explaining Milton's
choice of the muse of astronomy for his epic? Before pursuing the arguments suggested by these questions, however, let us first turn to the most
famous of Milton's references to Galileo, the lines in Book I of *Paradise
Lost* which, by simile, describe Satan's shield:

> the broad circumference
> Hung on his shoulders like the Moon, whose Orb
> Through Optic Glass the *Tuscan* Artist views
> At Ev'ning from the top of *Fesole*,
> Or in *Valdarno*, to descry new lands,
> Rivers or Mountains in her spotty Globe.   (*PL* I, 286–91)[4]

Generally accepted as a straightforward compliment of epic proportions,
these lines have recently been called into question on several accounts,
most especially the implications of the vexed term "Artist" in the context
of *Paradise Lost*.

Acknowledging that it has been and is "difficult to think that Milton's 'Tuscan Artist' can be anything more than a synonym" for Galileo,
Neil Harris questions the "disturbing ambiguities" of the simile in which
the term is found, suggesting that, because the simile "is applied to Satan,"
we must read "Tuscan Artist" as "a Satanic image." He goes on to describe the poetic and geographical associations and features of Fiesole,
Florence, and Vallombrosa, as well as the scientific implications of the
telescope, penultimately concluding that we could leave "Tuscan Artist"
to be "satisfactorily enrolled among the Satanic images" were it not that
this would generate "the strange impression that Milton approved of
Galileo's trial and imprisonment." As a way out of this difficulty, Harris
suggests that we must separate the person of Galileo from his accomplishments, as "Milton glorifies not the scientific importance of Galileo's
discoveries, but the symbolic value of *casus Galilei*."[5]

I must argue for the distancing, rather than the conflation, of the figures of the "Tuscan Artist" and Satan. True, Satan's shield and the moon are equated and do constitute, as Harris points out (p. 13), a common pairing in Renaissance epics. But there is no corresponding textual element of the poetic paradigm for the "Tuscan Artist" who views the moon. Satan is not viewing his own shield, nor are the fallen angels actively observing it. The only person viewing the shield is the poet-narrator. If we wish to slice up and match up parts of the simile, we must say that the moon is to the shield as the Tuscan artist is to ———; the only available candidate for the blank is the "I" of the poet-narrator, Milton. *Valorization* is really too mild a term here. But I am not trying to set up a one-to-one correspondence between Milton and Galileo reaching beyond the confines of this simile. Rather I wish to establish the degree of esteem in which Milton held Galileo, esteem that enabled him to grant Galileo the paradigmatic placement which would equate him, however briefly, with the poet-narrator of *Paradise Lost* — and with an angel.

In Book V, we find the description of Raphael's descent from heaven to Paradise:

> From hence, no cloud, or, to obstruct his sight,
> Star interpos'd, however small he sees,
> Not unconform to other shining Globes,
> Earth and the Gard'n of God, with Cedars crown'd
> Above all Hills. As when by night the Glass
> Of *Galileo*, less assur'd, observes
> Imagin'd Lands and Regions in the Moon.   (257–63)

The "winged Saint" stands at the gate of heaven and sees the cosmos with unobstructed sight, *just as* "the Glass / Of *Galileo*, less assur'd, observes / Imagin'd Lands and Regions in the Moon." Here Galileo through his glass sees with sight "less assur'd" than Raphael, as would any mortal compared to any angel, but with sight *analogous*. In both instances, Book I and Book V, the reference to Galileo is positive, for Galileo is associated with two of the unproblematically good figures in the epic, the poet-narrator and the superteacher, Raphael.[6] The association of Galileo and Raphael, moreover, sets up very neatly and, as I will argue later, very significantly, Raphael's role as cosmographical consultant in Book VIII. Furthermore, we can see that, far from wishing us to separate Galileo the man from Galileo the astronomer, Milton presents Galileo and his art in a part-for-whole equation, even to personifying Galileo's "Glass" as able itself to observe.

Viewing Galileo's work or art as a synecdoche for Galileo himself brings us back to Milton's designation of Galileo as an "artist." Roy Flannagan, in a 1986 review of the MRTS prose concordance, focuses on the words *art* and *artist* and their possibly anachronistic meanings for us. Using the Galileo reference as the *locus classicus,* Flannagan examines the terms by means of the prose concordance and the Oxford concordance to the poetry, concluding from the context of their entries that "Milton was not doing Galileo much of a favor by calling him 'Tuscan Artist'" and that Milton's other uses of the terms are overwhelmingly negative.[7] Taking twenty-eight of the entries for *art* in the prose concordance ("the rest were judged neutral, for lack of context"), he judges twenty-one negative and seven positive, observing that the "same ratio seemed to hold true with the word *arts.*" On the basis of this "very unscientifically" conducted survey, Flannagan concludes flatly: "I have yet to unearth a reference to *art* or *artist* in Milton's prose or poetry which suggests that he ever thought about calling himself, or any other great poet for that matter, an artist, and . . . the word *art* is almost always associated with the Black Arts or the kinds of dissimulation practiced in *PL.*" As Flannagan himself admits, his conclusions are based on evidence culled from a reading of only the lines or partial lines in the two concordances. An examination of the terms *art* and *artist* as they function in context yields quite different evidence. Read in context, we find that of the ninety-three uses of *art* and *artist* in the prose, seventy-six are clearly positive.[8] For the poetry, where one might argue that the use of language is even more discreet, the category of "nonjudgmental" is appropriate for six uses, with eight unambiguously positive and nine clearly negative, leaving "Tuscan Artist" in a class by itself as "questionable." For the canon, then, the score stands eighty-four positive, twenty-six negative, six nonjudgmental, one questionable.

As Flannagan observes, "art" is often associated with evil in *Paradise Lost* — out of the nine negative uses in the poetry, seven appear in the epic — but is almost as frequently positive (five uses) or nonjudgmental (one use) in the poem. In the prose, moreover, the word *art* is used to designate an astounding variety of accomplishments, from carpentry to theology, from divinity to alchemy, from writing epic poetry to driving chariots, thirty-two specific *arts* in all, only four of which (warfare, alchemy/slander, fortune-telling, and superstition) are negative.[9]

Perhaps the best way to judge the value Milton places on the words *art* and *arts* is, as Flannagan suggests, to examine his application of these words to his own high calling. In *Areopagitica,* Milton develops the extended metaphor of books as "useful drugs" and "effective and strong med'cins," concluding that bad writers are those who "have not the art to qualifie and prepare these working mineralls" (II, 521). Following this line of thought, Milton stresses his belief that there are many English writers who do have the mastery of such art: "I cannot set so light by all the invention, the art, the wit, the grave and solid judgment which is in England" (II, 535). He continues to harp on this theme in *The History of Britain* as he laments the fact that most of the early English history "hath by the greater part of judicious Antiquaries bin long rejected for a modern Fable," a situation he means to remedy by telling the tales himself, "be it for nothing else but in favor of our English Poets, and Rhetoricians, who by thir Art will know, how to use them judiciously" (V, 3). Planning, as it were, to provide the raw materials of chronicle ready for use by the artists, "our English Poets, and Rhetoricians," Milton not only reveals his lack of hesitation in associating poets with art, but casts himself in a rather lowly, although useful and necessary, role in the artistic process.

In *The Reason of Church Government* we find Milton designating the works of the Greeks and the Italians as "art," and therefore, by association, his own writings — his *Art of Logic* an obvious example. Discussing the choice of plots and topics, Milton argues that having more plots than Aristotle deemed proper for an epic isn't necessarily bad; setting up a dichotomy between nature and Aristotle, Milton places art in a position of mediation: "whether the rules of *Aristotle* herein are strictly to be kept, or nature to be followed, which in them that know art and use judgement is no transgression, but an inriching of art" (I, p. 813). Speaking more specifically, he gives the example of Tasso offering a choice of topics concerning "the pattern of a Christian *Heroe*" to a "Prince of *Italy*," suggesting that English writers could easily do likewise, for: "if to the instinct of nature and the imboldning of art ought may be trusted, and that there be nothing advers in our climat, or the fate of this age, it haply would be of no rashnesse from an equal diligence and inclination to present the like offer in our own ancient stories" (I, p. 814). Granted, the statement that "ought" may be entrusted to nature and art as they come together in poetry is couched in the subjunctive, but we must recall that this sentence falls in the context of an argument based on the premise that English poets are able to achieve the heights reached by the Italians; viewed in this light, the subjunctive becomes simply a mode of presentation, not an implicit question.

We find a similar discussion in *Of Education* when Milton lays out the proper progress of a course of study, the highest level of which is literary theory, the art of writing: "And now lastly will be the time to read with them [histories, heroic poems, Attic tragedies] those organic arts which enable men to discourse and write perspicuously, elegantly, and according to the fitted stile of lofty, mean, or lowly" (II, p. 401). He praises particularly "that sublime art which in *Aristotles poetics*, in *Horace*, and in the *Italian* commentaries of *Castelvetro*, *Tasso*, *Mazzoni*, and others, teaches what the laws are of a true *Epic* poem, what of a *Dramatic*, and what of a *Lyric*, what decorum is, which is the grand master peece to observe" (II, pp. 404–05). Not only is the phrase "sublime art" associated with the works of great writers, but the term is used to describe the achievements of their art and the artistic process by which they are fashioned. Aristotle's *Poetics* is itself art and is about art, the "sublime art" of writing great literature.

In yet another discussion of the art of great poets, we find Milton making a distinction between a man and the man's work — although not to the end that Neil Harris advances. The discussion, in *An Apology Against a Pamphlet*, centers upon good and bad men who write and how Milton finds himself forced to separate bad men from their good work.

For by the firme setling of these perswasions I became, to my best memory, so much a proficient, that if I found those authors any where speaking unworthy things of themselves; or unchaste of those names which before they had extoll'd, this effect it wrought with me, from that time forward their art I still applauded, but the men I deplor'd; and above them all preferr'd the two famous renowners of *Beatrice* and *Laura* who never write but honour of them to whom they devote their verse, displaying sublime and pure thoughts, without transgression. (I, p. 890)[10]

Having designated the works of Dante, Tasso, Petrarch, and others as "art," Milton not surprisingly speaks of his own writing in the same terms. In *The Reason of Church Government*, Milton summarizes his literary ambitions and methods of achieving them:

There ought no regard be sooner had than to God's glory, by the honor and instruction of my country. For which cause, and not only for that I knew it would be hard to arrive at the second rank among the Latines, I apply'd my selfe to that resolution which *Ariosto* follow'd against the perswasions of *Bembo*, to fix all the industry and art I could unite to the adorning of my native tongue." (I, p. 811)

This is perhaps the most explicit association of his own writing with the term *art* we can find in the prose, but it is not the only example. In *An Apology Against a Pamphlet*, Milton speaks of refuting the critics of *Animadversions*, a task which he claims will be simple, as he will have to do so only on theological grounds — so obvious, to him — and not on artistic grounds: "since the Religion of it is disputed, and not the art" (I, p. 899).

Nor is it only in the prose that we find "art" used to refer to the work of great writers. In Book IV of *Paradise Regained*, Satan invites the Son to look around the world below him, specifically — among other locations — at "*Athens*, the eye of *Greece*, Mother of Arts / And Eloquence" (IV, 240–41). True, these are the words of the Fiend, the Evil One; but less than one hundred lines later the Son uses the same words:

> All our Law and Story strew'd
> With Hymns, our Psalms with artful terms inscrib'd
> Our Hebrew Songs and Harps in *Babylon*,
> That pleas'd so well our Victors' ear, declare
> That rather *Greece* from us these Arts deriv'd. (IV, 334–38)

The "artful" hymns and psalms of the Hebrews, then, were the sources from which Athens learned her arts. In neither reference can we here read "art" as a negative term.

The most telling use of "art" in the poetry, however, is — appropriately enough, for this study — found in *Paradise Lost*. In Book IV the poet-narrator is describing Paradise, the rivers, the lakes, the hills and mountains, the plants, and how all the many streams ran:

> whereof here needs no account,
> But rather to tell how, if Art could tell,
> How from that Sapphire Fount the crisped Brooks,
> Rolling on Orient Pearl and sands of Gold,
> With mazy error under pendant shades
> Ran nectar. (IV, 235–40)

So what is "Art" in line 236? Art is what is trying to "tell." Art is poetry — *this* poetry of *Paradise Lost*. The line recalls for us the passage from *The Reason of Church Government* where Milton vows "to fix all the industry and art I could unite to the adorning of my native tongue" (I, p. 811). Here he fears that even his greatest expenditure of "industry and art" may be inadequate to describe Paradise, and we are given a rare example of Milton's use of the modesty topos of the late sixteenth- and early seventeenth-century poets.

So, far from concluding that Milton would never have used *art* to refer to his own or any other poet's work, we can see that he used the term much as we today would use it in the context of literature. But, although it might indeed be possible to make a case for *art*, *arts*, and *artist* as strongly positive on the basis of the these literary applications of the terms, I suggest rather that, for Milton, the term "art" most often meant "area of expertise."

Galileo's area of expertise was astronomy, and it is as an astronomer that Milton uses Galileo. Just as he twice, in Books I and III, likens the actions of *Paradise Lost*'s poet-narrator to the actions of Galileo, Milton on at least one occasion patterns the artistic endeavors of his left hand after the artistic endeavors of Galileo the astronomer. In *Eikonoklastes*, Milton establishes a heliocentric universe from the broken images of medieval and Renaissance cosmographical icons. In his rebuttal of Charles's *Eikon Basilike*, Milton dismisses effectively these lesser icons of kingship, never doing any of them the honor of a full-scale attack. With the most powerful monarchical icon, that of the king as the sun, however, erasure — mere dismissal — is not enough to banish an image so deeply ingrained in the Renaissance imagination. The analogy of the king as sun, central to the image patterns of Shakespeare's *Richard II*, is a natural choice for Charles, both in his pictorial icon and in his prose. In act 3, scene 2 of Shakespeare's play we find the most extended example of Richard's use of this analogy, the one with which Charles was obviously familiar and upon which he draws heavily: Richard refers to himself as "the searching eye of heaven" having been "hid / Behind the globe" while Bolingbroke uses the darkness for his own purposes until he "Shall see us rising in our throne, the east" (37–53).

This icon is too sharply defined in the imaginations of Renaissance Englishmen, not only from this play but from the wealth of material it draws together, for it to be dismissed merely. Milton must remake the icon, re-image the image, replacing the king with a more powerful persona. The sun, in Milton's post-Copernican day, according to the astronomy of Galileo, was an even more powerful image than in the 1590s, now not "just" the chief planet but the acknowledged center (if not for the Inquisition) of the universe. Saying that the king is *not* the sun will not work; to raise the image would be to raise the imaginative association. So Milton avails himself of the other "sun" association which English offers to poets: sun/son. For Milton, of course, this pun is literally (as well as metaphorically) a godsend, for — although this double meaning did indeed resonate in the earlier sun/king analogy — the Puritan, parliamentary society for whom Milton was writing would view the analogy of Charles with Christ as blasphemy; any residual sympathy generated by the long-standing artistic association of sun/king would not only be canceled out by the Protestant sensibilities of the time, but the suggestion of sun/king/Son would appear so outrageous that Charles would have done Milton's work for him.

To accomplish this transformation, this subversion, Milton uses Charles's own words, but takes them out of intellectual context. Charles invokes the icon of the sun/king just as Richard does; Milton refuses to acknowledge that early Renaissance context and forcefully relocates Charles's words in the Puritan context of his own writing and in the cosmographical context of Galileo's work. Milton does not attempt to accomplish this transformation in one fell swoop; rather, he moves, in the space of six chapters, through a series of image patterns calculated to escalate the sense of outrage that the Puritan reader must feel toward the king.

In chapter 10, Milton quotes Charles's use of the icon and transforms sun/king into sunlight/Reformation:

He bodes *much horror and bad influence after his ecclips.* He speaks his wishes: But they who by weighing prudently things past, forsee things to come, the best Divination, may hope rather all good success and happiness by removing that darkness which the mistie cloud of his prerogative made between us and a peacefull Reformation, which is our true Sun light, and not he, though he would be tak'n for our sun itself. (III, p. 455)

Here Milton makes Charles the clouds obscuring the sunlight of the Reformation, but he does not yet capitalize "sun" to accuse Charles of seeing himself as the "Son."

In chapter 11 Milton moves closer to this conflation by playing with the son/father/mother paradigm inherent in Charles' relation to Parliament:[11]

Yet so farr doth self opinion for fals principles delude and transport him, as to think *the concurrence of his reason* to the Votes of Parlament, not onely Political, but Natural, *and as necessary to the begetting, or bringing forth of any one compleat act of public wisdom as the Suns influence is necessary to all natures productions.* . . . Nay that his reason is as Celestial and life-giving to the Parlament, as the Suns influence is to the Earth: What other notions but these, or such like, could swell up *Caligula* to think himself a God. (III, p. 467)

Throughout this passage Milton plays on the probable gender of Parliament, both in an incestuous "reading" of Charles's words — Parliament, according to Milton, has the generative power, not Charles, and therefore Charles should think of Parliament as his mother, upon whom any "begetting" by Charles would go against the laws of nature — and by setting up an absent "Father" and an earthly "Mother" from which the "Son" (implicitly, according to Milton, that would be Charles) has come. Again Milton has suggested a Christ-figure image which was not present in Charles's words as he wrote them; and again he has stopped just short of stating this: Milton does mention a ruler who would see himself as a god, but it is a pagan ruler and a pagan god.

It is in chapter 15 that we find the direct association of Charles with Christ, and — not insignificantly — the quotes from Charles which are closest to Richard II's sun speech in act 3:

Finally, having layd the fault of these Commotions, not upon his own mis-government, but upon the *ambition of others, the necessity of some mens fortune, and thirst after noveltie,* he bodes himself *much honor and reputation that like the Sun shall rise and recover it self to such a Splendour, as Owles, Batts, and such fatal Birds shall be unable to beare.* Poets indeed use to vapor much after this man-ner. But to bad Kings, who without cause expect future glory from thir actions, it happ'ns as to bad Poets; who sit and starve themselves with a delusive hope to win immortality by thir bad lines. . . . And those black vailes of his own misdeeds he might be sure would ever keep *his face from shining,* til he could *refute evil speaking with wel doing,* which grace he seems here to pray for; and his prayer doubtless as it was prayd, so it was heard. But eev'n his prayer is so ambitious of Prerogative, that it dares ask away the Prerogative of Christ himself, *To become the head stone of the Corner.* (III, p. 502)

Here Milton achieves the complete subversion of Charles's use of the com-monplace of sun/king. Now, according to Milton, Charles is claiming — or, even worse, "dares ask away" — the prerogative of Christ, to be the only Sun/Son. Furthermore, lest Charles's words (which Milton must neces-sarily quote to keep up his pattern of "refutation") raise any memories of Shakespeare's lines spoken by another troubled king, Milton follows the quotation from the *Eikon* with an extended reference to "bad Poets." Shakespeare, as Milton has already said, is a great and famous poet, so if these lines are after the manner of bad poets' vapors, then they could not be from Shakespeare; thus, Charles's context and his strongest au-thority on the use of the icon in this context are vaporized and Charles is left appearing to argue himself simply — and therefore blasphemously — as a Christ figure.

When Milton wrote *Eikonoklastes* in 1649, he could employ with impunity the art of Galileo, decentering the earthly king for the univer-sal Son. Whatever thoughts he might have spared for the Tuscan artist, grown old a prisoner to the Inquisition for thinking in astronomy what Milton also thought, could hardly have been more than impersonal ones of intellectual admiration. But how much more closely he must have em-pathized with Galileo as, writing *Paradise Lost* in the 1660s of the re-established monarchy of Charles's son, he spent his own old age in the obscurity of men who think otherwise than those in power.

For it is, of course, those allusions in *Paradise Lost* which most fascinate us about the Galileo connection, those which are the most in need of rescue from the designation "problematic." In Books III and V,

Milton calls our attention to the way in which Galileo sees — like, but less clearly than, the poet-narrator and Raphael; in Books I and VIII, Milton's references to the Tuscan artist focus on *what* he sees. But in all cases the emphasis is on seeing.[12] Neil Harris, suggesting that the "real revolution achieved by Galileo with his emphasis on trial and experiment was to make men believe their own eyes," links Galileo's seeing to the "conflict of vision, sight, appearance, illusion and belief [that] is the key to the fall of man."[13] Somewhat cryptically, Harris remarks that perhaps "Milton's use of the 'Tuscan artist' is not simply theological or philosophical conservatism, but an acute insight into the directions the modern world, ushered in by Galileo, was taking" (pp. 20–21). Harris doesn't push this line of thinking beyond that sentence, but I think that this is exactly what Milton was doing. By presenting us with the "less assur'd" sight of Galileo, Milton gives us a postlapsarian Raphael, and in Raphael's observations on astronomy in Book VIII we find a prelapsarian Galileo.

Read in this light, the much-debated cosmology of Book VIII — seeming to present both a Ptolemaic and a Copernican universe — makes sense as a synchronic presentation of two Galileos, or two Raphaels, if you will. In the "Argument" of Book VIII we are told that "Adam inquires concerning celestial Motions, and is doubtfully answer'd, and exhorted to search rather things more worthy of knowledge." Critics in search of a pre-Copernican Paradise have been quick to jump on the implications of "doubtfully" and "things more worthy," as well as Raphael's line, "whether Heav'n move or earth, / Imports not," while ignoring the rest of his sentence, "if thou reck'n right" (70–71). Most critics read those last four words as referring only to Adam learning "His Seasons, Hours, or Days, or Months, or Years" (69), and conclude of the larger issue, as does Merritt Hughes (p. 188), that "Raphael's reply to Adam's question is non-committal." To make sense out of all of Raphael's reply, we must read "if thou reck'n right" in a much larger context: "if thou reckon right in all things, on all choices"; in other words, if man and woman remain unfallen.

Adam assumes, wrongly, that the earth is "sedentary" (32); Raphael tells him not to spend his time "on studious thoughts abstruse" (39), but instead upon the sorts of knowledge he needs for day-to-day living, knowledge of the hours of the day and the seasons of the year. If Adam learns to reckon rightly in all these things and in all other earthly concerns, he will have no need of more "abstruse" knowledge. Ah, but if he does not. . . . The "iffyness" of this state of affairs is established by Raphael in his subsequent speech. In the ninety-five lines between "if thou reck'n right" and the injunction to "Solicit not thy thoughts with matters hid" (167) there are no fewer than eight *ifs*. This, then, is why Raphael exposes Adam to the knowledge of Copernicus and Galileo, albeit wrapped in the tissue of the subjunctive; he is the creation of a narrator who knows, as does the reader, that Adam will not content himself with that to which he has been assigned. Adam will go beyond the ontological boundaries set by Raphael, and, when he does, he will need to acquire this knowledge. In Book VIII Raphael is speaking to an Adam who still has "this Paradise / And thy fair *Eve*" (171–72), an Adam who is told to "be lowly wise: / Think only what concerns thee and thy being; / Dream not of other Worlds" (173–75), because he does not need such knowledge in Paradise. After the fall, however, he must go on, having failed to be "lowly wise," and learn — as Michael predicts in Book XII — all the stars by name, "all Nature's works, / Or works of God in Heav'n, Air, Earth, or Sea" (576–79). Because Adam's initial assumptions are not replaced, but are instead deferred, they are therefore available for foregrounding by the serpent in Book IX. Adam's belief (which we must assume he shares with Eve: "Her Husband the Relater she preferr'd / Before the Angel" [52–53]) that the earth remains "sedentary," receiving the "Tribute" of numberless "Stars," "Orbs," and "nobler Bodies," helps set the stage of Book IX, where our first parents decide that they, the center of Paradise, should be denied no tribute it might offer. Now Adam and Eve and their descendants will never see with the clear vision of the "winged Saint" Raphael; but eventually those descendants will learn to see with the "less assur'd" arts and eyes of Galileo. Galileo learns imperfectly, for a fallen world, what Raphael already knows in Book VIII. Here, perhaps, is also the solution to the puzzle of the "spotty Globe" of the Tuscan artist's "Optic Glass" in the Book I passage. Even with the aid of his invention, even seeing more clearly than any person has seen before, Galileo still sees with the "spotty" vision of the fallen world.

Galileo's art, though imperfect, is offered again and again throughout the epic as an example of the best endeavors of fallen man. By name and by the iconic associations of the telescope, Galileo's art becomes — patterned as it is, through similes, on the arts of epic figures — a pattern for human intellectual endeavor. Further evidence that Milton considered the study of astronomy to be an art worthy of veneration is his choice of the muse of astronomy, Urania, as the object of his Book VII invocation. Far from being willing to "agree with Dr. Tillyard that the mystery of his Muse is inscrutable" (Hughes, p. 199), I would argue that she is nothing less than the logical choice for an epic of such cosmic scope.

Noam Flinker links Urania with the Book III designation of the Muse as "Light," comparing the darkness of Milton's blindness to the darkness of night, the time for the muse of astronomy to be active in the aid not only of epic poets, but also of astronomers such as Galileo. Flinker observes that "Urania brings the 'Celestial light' to the narrator at night and this clarifies the spiritual potential of all creation. . . . Night and light are not opposites but rather different aspects of God's creation."[14] This is not to argue that Milton took the idea of muses literally any more than he would have literally considered a contemporary human being a saint, but, as Thomas P. Roche, Jr., citing lines 1–9 of Book VII and quoting "The meaning, not the Name I call," argues: "Milton forces the reader to accept two sets of conventions: the classical Muse Urania and the Holy Spirit of orthodox theology, in neither of which he believed,"[15] But he used both of them. And if he did not *believe* in Galileo as a patron saint, he certainly used him as one.

So why, then, does Milton call Galileo an artist? Well, as we have seen from his uses of *art* and *arts* in the prose, he certainly did not mean "master of fine arts," or he would have said so. He meant "expert," an expert in the art, the intellectual endeavor, of astronomy. Roy Flannagan questions why Milton does not call Galileo a scientist. For the same reason, I would answer, that he does not use the even more accurate term *intellectual;* the words did not exist. Although *intellectual* as an adjective has long been in use (the OED cites 1398), *intellectual* as a noun meaning a person — not a mental faculty — was not used until 1652. In the poetry, Milton uses the word four times, all in *Paradise Lost,* always as an adjective. He uses *intellectual* four times also in the prose, again always as an adjective; in *Doctrine and Discipline of Divorce* we find the word used as a noun, but as a plural, *intellectuals* meaning "faculties," the "intellectuals of quotationists and commonplacers" (*DDD* 4.2.230.7). I would like to argue that by "Artist," in *Paradise Lost,* Book I, Milton meant "intellectual"; but under the semantic circumstances, such an argument would be moot. We can anteriorize connotation, but not intention. The *lack* of what seems to us a more discrete term, however, can do much to allay modern anxiety about *artist.*

Given the vocabulary of his time, *artist* could be used by Milton as we would use either *scientist* or *intellectual.* I infer the designation *patron saint* from the patterns formed by the uses Milton makes of Galileo's name and iconography. Just as Milton, by simile[16] and syntactical parallels, associates Galileo with the poet-narrator and with Raphael, so can we associate his patterns of allusion and invocation with the patterns of hagiography. For John Milton, Galileo was a martyr to the cause of intellectual freedom. Milton's Protestantism did not exclude literal martyrs; Milton's imagination did not exclude metaphoric saints. Operating thus in the imaginative realms of the intellect, Milton conferred upon the Tuscan artist a secular, a poetic, an artistic canonization.

State University of New York, Geneseo

NOTES

This argument was first presented, in paper length, at the Third International Milton Symposium in Vallombrosa and Florence, June 1988. I would like to thank the other members of the much-tried Galileo panel—Professors Judith Scherer Herz, Coburn Freer, and Donald Friedman—for the insights I gained from their excellent papers and comments.

1. See Walter C. Curry, *Milton's Ontology, Cosmogony, and Physics* (Lexington, Ky., 1957); Grant McColley, "The Astronomy of *Paradise Lost*," *SP* XXXIV (1937), 209–47; Kester Svendsen, *Milton and Science* (Cambridge, Mass., 1956); Marjorie Hope Nicolson, "Milton and the Telescope," *ELH* II (1935), 1–32; Lawrence Babb, *The Moral Cosmos of "Paradise Lost,"* (Ann Arbor, Mich., 1970); John Arthos, *Milton and the Italian Cities* (New York, 1968); S. B. Liljegren, "Milton and Galileo," in *Studies in Milton* (Gleerup, 1919); David Masson, *The Life of John Milton* (Peter Smith, 1946).

2. *Complete Prose Works of John Milton*, ed. Don M. Wolfe et al., 8 vols. (New Haven, Conn., 1953–82), vol. II, p. 538. All references to the prose cite this edition.

3. Harold Bloom *A Map of Misreading* (Oxford, 1975), p. 132; see also pp. 130–33 for a more extended discussion of the Galileo reference in Book I. Frank B. Young, "Galileo," in *A Milton Encyclopedia*, ed. William B. Hunter, Jr. et al. (Lewisburg, Pa., 1978), vol. III, p. 120.

4. Quoted from *John Milton: Complete Poems and Major Prose*, ed. Merritt Y. Hughes (New York, 1957), the edition used throughout. For a reading of this reference to Galileo as simile, see Linda Gregerson, "Limbs of Truth: Milton's Use of Simile in *Paradise Lost*," in *Milton Studies*, vol. XIV, ed. James D. Simmonds (Pittsburgh, 1980), p. 144.

5. Neil Harris, "Galileo as Symbol: The 'Tuscan Artist' in *Paradise Lost*," *Annali del'Instituto e Museo di Storia della Scienza di Firenze* X (1985), 3–29.

6. The reference to Galileo in Book III, lines 587–90, is similar to these in content and syntactical presentation. Here Satan appears to the poet-narrator as "a spot like which perhaps / Astronomer in the Sun's lucent Orb / Through his glaz'd Optic Tube yet never saw." As in Book I, the way in which the astronomer sees is compared to the way in which the poet-narrator sees; as in Book V, the degree of sight, his ability to see, is less than that of the epic figure—less, but analogous. In the context of this study, some stress might be placed on Milton's description of Raphael—twice associated with Galileo—as a "winged Saint." Arguing for metaphoric and intellectual canonization, however, I will suggest merely this association.

7. Roy Flannagan, "Art, Artists, Galileo and Concordances," *MQ* XX, no. 3 (1986), 103–05. He prefaces his argument by wondering "what linguistic game Milton was playing" by calling Galileo an "artist" rather than a "scientist." According to the OED, *scien-*

tist was not used to mean "person of science" (or anything else) until 1840; Milton never used it because it did not exist.

8. Undertaking to look up all of the occurrences of *art, arts,* and *artist* in the prose and poetry, I read a few pages of context for each. Dividing the possible usages into four categories — strongly positive (e.g., "that sublime art which in *Aristotle's poetics* . . . teaches what the laws are of a true epic poem" [*Of Education* 2.404.2]), passive positive (e.g., "Liberal Arts" and any positive term associated with "art of _____"), passive negative (e.g., "this art of our Adversary" [*DDD* 4.2.228.18]), and strongly negative (e.g., "they whom only error, casualty, art or plot hath joynd" [*Tetrachordon* 2.662.27]) — I found seventy-six uses to be positive and seventeen to be negative in the prose.

9. Designated as "arts" in the prose we find: architecture, painting, divinity, logic, rhetoric, poetry, theology, policy, teaching, warfare, writing epics, building, cooking, driving chariots, adopting Roman customs, hawking, flying, making a pleasing appearance and manner, music, writing, composing songs and lyrics, caring for the body (physick), alchemy/slander, fortune-telling, carpentry, blacksmithing, weaving, superstition, cavalry maneuvers, writing sermons, making and interpreting law, persuasion. In *Animadversions* we find a more general usage of *art,* as Milton discusses "how able professors of every Art may with ample stipends be honestly provided" (I, 724).

10. "And long it was not after, when I was confirm'd in this opinion, that he would not be frustrate of his hope to write will hereafter in laudable things, ought him selfe to bee a true Poem, that is, a composition, and patterne of the best and honourable things; not presuming sing high praises of heroick men, or famous Cities, unless he have in himselfe the experience and the practice of all which is praise-worthy" (I, 890). The poet must be "a true Poem," the artist must be of the same quality as the art.

11. For this reading of *Eikonoklastes,* chapter 11, I am heavily indebted to Marshall Grossman, "Servile/Sterile/Style: Milton and the Question of Woman," in *Milton and the Idea of Woman,* ed. Julia M. Walker (Champaign, Ill., 1988), pp. 148–68.

12. It would be fascinating to know what Milton made of Galileo's eventual blindness; the fact that he seems unaware of it, however, is one of the strongest arguments against his supposed meeting with the astronomer.

13. "Eve sees and hears the snake speaking to her, allows herself to be convinced of what she sees, and thus abandons a pre-ordained order which she knows to be reason. Satan promises that the fruit of the tree of knowledge will clear her sight." (Harris, "Galileo as Symbol," pp. 20–21.)

14. Noam Flinker, "Courting Urania: The Narrator of *Paradise Lost* Invokes His Muse," in *Milton and the Idea of Woman,* pp. 86–99.

15. Thomas P. Roche, Jr., "Spenser's Muse," an unpublished manuscript. Roche concludes: "I can see in Milton's choice a knowledge of Macrobius and Martianus, the power of whose Urania stops at the eighth sphere, which is the reason that Milton does not even try to compete with Spenser's struggles with Calliope, so diffident about the name but not the meaning of his muse. . . . Convinced that the Holy Spirit did not exist except as a manifestation of God the Father, Milton forces the issue to a semantic crisis, after which there is no place to go but to Byron's comically lofty and empty 'Hail, Muse etcetera.'"

16. As Gregerson, "Limbs of Truth," p. 135, points out: "The figure of speech is a turn of the mind; the simile's ground is epistemonogy. The artist makes both an artifact and an instrument with which to see, like the Tuscan artist's glass."

SATAN AND ARMINIANISM
IN *PARADISE LOST*

Keith W. F. Stavely

As we know, in *Paradise Lost* God himself outlines Milton's Arminian theology, making it applicable to angels as well as human beings:

> So without least impulse or shadow of fate,
> Or aught by me immutably foreseen,
> They trespass, authors to themselves in all
> Both what they judge and what they choose; for so
> I formed them free, and free they must remain,
> Till they enthrall themselves:
>
> . . . .
>
> The first sort by their own suggestion fell,
> Self-tempted, self-depraved: man falls deceived
> By the other first: man therefore shall find grace,
> The other none. (III, 120–25, 129–32)[1]

One might easily skip over what is most striking about the inclusion of Satan in this exposition. Why is the possibility of Satan's finding grace brought up at all? We might have supposed that the continued damnation of the archfiend would be routinely assumed, as it is in the orthodox Christian tradition. However, it is but a short step from assuming that Satan will remain Satan, the very source and spring of evil, to assuming that Satan *must* remain Satan. And this is a step that Milton, ruthlessly consistent in his Arminianism as in all else, refuses to take. His universe is not Calvinistic with respect to Satan and Arminian with respect to everyone else. As Diane McColley states, God's pronouncement concerning Satan's future should be regarded as "prophecy, not decree."[2] The key distinction between foreknowledge and predestination applies to Satan as fully as to Adam and Eve. Satan will persist in his fallenness, God knows, just as he knows that Adam and Eve will fall, but the knowledge does not cause the persistence in the one case any more than it causes the fall in the other. And in the latter half of Book III, this Arminian perspective on Satan's situation is made poetically as well as logically consistent.

125

Before we can appreciate this poetic consistency, however, we must understand how Milton's Arminianism functions throughout *Paradise Lost*. How is the principle that God's creatures are "authors to themselves in all" not just articulated as theological doctrine but also poetically embodied? This question is best approached by a look at the second of the many epic similes in Book I, the famous comparison of Satan's "ponderous shield" to

> the moon, whose orb
> Through optic glass the Tuscan artist views
> At evening from the top of Fesole,
> Or in Valdarno, to descry new lands,
> Rivers or mountains in her spotty globe.   (I, 284, 287–91)

Geoffrey Hartman notes that "the place names serve to anchor this observer, and set him off from the vastness and vagueness of hell, its unnamed and restless geography."[3] But it is not only the place names that make this passage a significant moment in the evolution of what Hartman calls "Milton's counterplot." To this point, nearly three hundred lines in, the poem has been preoccupied with matters of cosmic scale and import: with the broad sweep of sacred history, with Satan's plunge from heaven to hell, with his and Beelzebub's recollections of "the glorious enterprise" of their assault upon the godhead. But now for the first time a glimpse is provided of a specified human situation, specified not only geographically, by the place names, but also culturally, as the phrase "Tuscan artist" evokes the entire tradition of Florentine intellectual enterprise and achievement, and as a particular Tuscan artist, Galileo, is seen continuing and extending that tradition with his astronomical researches.

No particular stretch of the critical imagination is required to grasp that the English artist who believed himself to be pursuing "things unattempted yet in prose or rhyme" (I, 16) is here endorsing the efforts of the Tuscan artist "to descry new lands." In a universe governed by God's will, and in which the demonic will is plausibly claimed to be "unconquerable" (I, 106), there nevertheless remains ample scope, this simile quietly insists, for the creative exercise of the autonomous human will. As depicted here, an artist is someone who devotes his portion of the autonomous human will to the construction of civilization. From his own specified place, up on a mountain top (Fesole) or down in a river valley (Valdarno), he seeks out new places, new mountains and new rivers, using his art to widen horizons and open possibilities.

On the other hand, just as Milton is careful to acknowledge the potential similarity between his own ambitious artistic project and Satan's "ambitious aim" (I, 41) of becoming the equal of God,[4] so he glances here at the possibility that Galileo's project could be morally and spiritually perilous. For the phrase "spotty globe" refers at once to the moon, to the telescope (and, by extension, to the eye looking through the telescope), and perhaps also to *the* globe, the earth. Spots, imperfections, possibly sins may thus be found in the eye of the beholder, in the exciting new object which he beholds, and in the familiar environment from which the entire visionary enterprise is launched.[5] A universe which allows for freedom, creativity, and the descrying of new lands must apparently remain vulnerable to the misuse of freedom and creativity and the contamination of all lands.

Clearly Galileo is a figure who is an author to himself in all, vigorously exerting himself in an open universe and running moral and spiritual risks as he does so. But what is most striking about the simile is its inversion of the Arminian epigram Milton had formulated in *Areopagitica:* If "reason is but choosing," then choosing must in large part be but reasoning and perceiving. In exploring this possibility, *Paradise Lost* comes quite close to modern ideas about the relations between observer and observed, according to which an observer does not merely make contact with a preexisting reality, but rather alters that reality by the act of observation itself, thereby constituting a new reality. Thus, Milton's Tuscan artist is left to make what he will of what he views through his optic glass. Earlier, in the poem's first epic simile, the poem's first human character, the "pilot of some small night-foundered skiff" (I, 204), is shown deciding that the huge dark mass he encounters in his nocturnal voyaging is "some island," rather than a whale. And encompassing each situation are the perceptual conundrums and choices posed for the reader: is the moon, and Galileo's scientific exploration of it, "like" Satan's shield and therefore a trap for the unwary, or is it the window upon liberation and hope the phrase "to descry new lands" makes it out to be? Is the whale, Leviathan, primarily defined by its vehicle to tenor relationship to Satan, or is it that which "God of all his works / Created hugest that swim the ocean stream" (I, 201–02), and therefore perhaps an appropriate refuge for the night-foundered pilot after all? It is questions of this sort that Satan must confront in Book III. He too must face up to the obligations imposed by Arminian perceptual freedom.

After struggling through Chaos and emerging from the Paradise of Fools, Satan immediately begins to remind us of both the pilot and the Tuscan artist:

> long he wandered, till at last a gleam
> Of dawning light turned thitherward in haste
> His travelled steps; far distant he descries,
> Ascending by degrees magnificent
> Up to the wall of heaven a structure high.   (III, 499–503)

The night-foundered pilot had been left in a situation in which "wished morn delays" (I, 208), whereas this satanic voyager in the dark is granted the assistance and blessing of "dawning light." The Tuscan artist had labored and struggled to descry merely the bespotted moon, whereas Satan "descries" with relative ease and clarity a magnificent structure ascending straight up to the wall of heaven.

The suggestion that the archfiend himself is being granted the opportunity to choose repentance and faith is made much more strongly a few lines later, when the "structure high" ascending to heaven is identified:

> The stairs were such as whereon Jacob saw
> Angels ascending and descending, bands
> Of guardians bright, when he from Esau fled
> To Padan-Aram in the field of Luz,
> Dreaming by night under the open sky,
> And waking cried, *This is the gate of heaven.*   (III, 510–15)

Most Protestant commentators were agreed in regarding the "stairs" Jacob sees in a dream vision in Genesis xxviii, 12 as a figure of Christ. For example, the *Annotations* prepared by a committee of divines appointed by the Long Parliament stated that "Christ is that Ladder by which God and man are joyned together; and by whom the Angels minister unto us; all graces by him descend upon us; and we by him ascend into heaven."[6] Or as Afro-American Protestants were later to sing, "We are climbing Jacob's Ladder . . . Soldiers of the Cross."

So, near the beginning of his voyage through the created universe, Satan encounters something likened to an Old Testament event that Milton's readers would have recognized as fraught with the promise of grace and redemption. But grace and redemption for whom? The story of Jacob and Esau, as interpreted by Paul in Romans ix, 9–13, was a central text in Calvinist arguments that grace was available only to the predestined elect, God's declaration to Rebecca when she was pregnant with Esau and Jacob that "the elder [Esau] shall serve the younger [Jacob]" (Gen. xxv, 23) being taken to signify the election of Jacob and his descendants to all eternity and the correspondingly eternal reprobation of Esau and his descendants.[7] Against this "rigorous and cruel" position

Milton explicitly argues in *Christian Doctrine*, insisting that "if the elder boy . . . shall serve the younger . . . the elder is not necessarily decreed reprobate. If the younger is considered worthy of more grace, the elder is not necessarily considered worthy of none."[8]

Yet in the present passage from *Paradise Lost*, it is clearly Jacob, he who is considered worthy of more grace, who is granted the vision of abundant graces descending upon him. It may be that Esau should be considered worthy of some grace, but at the moment he in fact receives no grace at all. He is merely that which is left behind. Jacob flees from Esau into the midst of "bands / Of guardians bright" — flees, we might decide to say with the opening of *Pilgrim's Progress* in mind, from the realm of damnation into that salvation for which he and his seed are destined. A Calvinist reading of the passage is further strengthened when it is noted that Milton twice unequivocally affirmed that Jacob had done nothing wrong when he had obtained by deception the blessing which his aging father, Isaac, had intended to bestow upon Esau. This was "the faithfull Act of that Patriarch," a correcting of "the error of his father who was swayed by his absurd passion for Esau" (YP, III, p. 322; VI, p. 763).

Such a quasi-antinomian view placed Milton in disagreement with most other commentators. The *Annotations* commissioned by the Long Parliament insisted that "though Jacob was assured of the Blessing by Faith, yet he did evil to seek it by lyes."[9] At this point, the question of lying having arisen, we may wish to stop considering vehicle apart from tenor. The staircase which Satan views is "such as" Jacob's ladder. And Jacob's ladder, a foreshadowing of the grace made available to the faithful by Christ's mediation between God and humanity, is what Jacob sees after first gaining by disguise and lies a blessing intended for his brother, and then fleeing from that brother's vow of revenge (Gen. xxvii, 6–29, 41–44). As for the brother, Esau, he is consistently portrayed in the scripture story as "an hardy hunter, a man of the sword."[10] The one brother a liar, the other a warrior. Milton's comparison between this Old Testament sequence and Satan's own story is beginning to seem singularly appropriate, for between them Jacob and Esau encompass the two aspects of Satan's fallenness, of which God has recently put us in mind with his remarks about Satan's "purpose to assay / If [man] by force he can destroy, or worse, / By some false guile pervert" (III, 90–92).

Jacob appears, then, to have fled from Esau, from Satan the warrior, only to be dogged by a persistent resemblance between himself and Satan the father of lies, who is indeed at this very point in the poem heading toward guileful maneuvers of the sort in which Jacob has just been engaged—Satan will very shortly disguise himself in order to deceive Uriel. The analogy with Satan transforms Jacob from the member of the invulnerably regenerate elect, which Milton had seemed to say he was in his incidental prose comments, to the sort of wayward, fallen creature we might expect to find in his epic of original sin.

On the other hand, if Jacob is to be perceived as a sinner here, he is also clearly to be perceived as a sinner who has had the option of grace presented to him and has chosen to accept it. After his dream, he "waking cried, *This is the gate of heaven.*" Milton elides many details in order to convey the Arminian moment of faithful acceptance when Jacob judges and chooses correctly, believing that he had been dreaming the truth of God's mercy. In particular Milton elides Genesis xxviii, 14, in which God promises Jacob that "in thee and in thy Seed shall all the families of the earth be blessed." This text was commonly glossed, by Milton himself among many others, as signifying the "spiritual blessings, flowing from the vertue of the promised Seed Christ Jesus, and from him diffused to all the faithful, of what Family, Nation, or Country soever."[11] Perhaps Milton felt that the sense that God's arms are at this moment outstretched in an embrace of everyone would be more effectively conveyed by emphasis not upon the seed of Jacob but rather upon the fact that this revelation occurred in an unexpected spot, "the field of Luz." He chooses the original place name rather than the name Bethel (House of God) which Jacob would bestow after erecting a shrine in remembrance of the revelation (Gen. xxviii, 18–19). That is, we are to be mindful less of the establishment of tradition and orthodoxy than of its disruption— that, as John Diodati remarked, "God appeareth in this Country of Infidels" rather than in Jacob's "Fathers house, where [Jacob had] thought this gift had been peculiar."[12] Above all, such release from the confines of orthodoxy is conveyed by the magnificent penultimate line of the passage, in which Jacob, "dreaming by night under the open sky," becomes an Everyman representation of all human desire and aspiration.

The evocation of Jacob's ladder constitutes an imaginative realization of the universalism that was implicit in the Arminian principle that God "excludes no man from the way of penitence and eternal salvation, unless that man has continued to reject and despise the offer of grace . . . until it is too late" (YP, VI, p. 194). God excludes no man, but few Arminians would have dared to deny that he does exclude the Devil, and one obvious way to read the present passage is as an ironic foretelling of the defeat of Satan's designs by divine providence, in the unfolding of which the story of Jacob and Esau was to be an early episode.[13] But in this instance Miltonic text powerfully reinterprets scriptural allusion and context, for the similitude Milton has chosen to employ cuts both ways. If Jacob, the past manipulator of the divine promises, is tarred by an imputation of similarity to Satan, Satan is by the same token potentially cleansed by an intimation of his present similarity to the Jacob who chooses to have faith in a symbol of Christ. If the passage depicts an escape from satanic intrigues and rages into the clear air of God's open sky, this is so exhilaratingly accomplished that we feel at least momentarily that all things are possible, and even the archfiend might wake up and cry, "*This is the gate of heaven.*" Most broadly, in terms of the overall design and action of *Paradise Lost*, if Satan is here looking at a type of Christ, the Son of God, then he is looking at what he has already chosen to "reject and despise," that "Messiah king anointed" the sight of whom he "could not bear / Through pride . . . and thought himself impaired" (V, 664-65). In other words, God continues to extend the most crucial spiritual invitation to Satan despite Satan's previous rejecting and despising. This reading of the passage and the one which finds in it a prophecy of Satan's defeat are thus both warranted; the choice between them is precisely the choice Satan is being called upon to make.

Nothing is said directly about how Satan actually does reason and perceive and choose at this point. Taken at face value, the lines "the stairs were then let down, whether to dare / The fiend by easy ascent, or aggravate / His sad exclusion from the doors of bliss" (III, 523-25), might seem to weigh against the idea that grace is being offered to him at all. But this picture of a God bent upon tempting and taunting his antagonist is intrusively Manichaean, suggesting the possibility that Satan is here using his perceptual powers and freedoms for no better purpose than projection.[14] And if such is indeed Satan's response, then it accords well with the Arminian schema we have heard God setting forth. Obscuring Satan's vision of the new lands he might descry are his own festering preconceptions of unending combat. As God had explained, "I formed [all creatures] free, and free they must remain, / Till they enthrall themselves."

Satan may thus have rejected and despised the offer of grace, but it is still not too late for him. Standing on the "lower stair" of what will become Jacob's ladder, he is given another opportunity to descry new lands, despite the fact that he is facing away from heaven. He

> Looks down with wonder at the sudden view
> Of all this world at once. As when a scout
> Through dark and desert ways with peril gone
> All night; at last by break of cheerful dawn

> Obtains the brow of some high-climbing hill,
> Which to his eye discovers unaware
> The goodly prospect of some foreign land
> First-seen, or some renowned metropolis
> With glistering spires and pinnacles adorned,
> Which now the rising sun gilds with his beams.   (III, 542–51)

This "sudden view / Of all this world at once" is implicitly compared to what is described just previously in the poem, God's "choice regard" of "the Promised Land to God so dear," from its northern to its southern boundaries (531–37). That is, a mere "gleam / Of dawning light" has just illuminated a scene analogous to a moment near the beginning of sacred history, and now this "break of cheerful dawn" reveals a landscape comparable to Canaan, the landscape of the middle of sacred history. And as before, there is thus both a reminder of the ways in which Satan will be outwitted by providence, and an offer of redemption and regeneration which, if accepted, would make such divine maneuvers unnecessary. Jacob had escaped from Esau's revenge into God's mercy, and this scout (what Satan in fact is at this point in the poem) could likewise escape from his role as the advance guard of the warrior ethic into a universe in which fresh experiences and relieved, elated discoveries are repeatedly made available. However, predictably but not inevitably, "Such wonder seized, though after heaven seen, / The spirit malign, but much more envy seized, / At sight of all this world beheld so fair" (552–54). Satan's self-enthrallment is now represented both more explicitly and more inwardly. The lineation and syntax have Satan enclosed in seizure, pinioned by his own alienated and tyrannical emotions.

When Satan finally lands on the sun, he is handed his (literally) most golden spiritual opportunity of all:

> Here matter new to gaze the devil met
> Undazzled, far and wide his eye commands,
> For sight no obstacle found there, nor shade,
> But all sunshine, as when his beams at noon
> Culminate from the equator, as they now
> Shot upward still direct, whence no way round
> Shadow from body opaque can fall, and the air,
> No where so clear, sharpened his visual ray
> To objects distant far, whereby he soon
> Saw within ken a glorious angel stand,
> The same whom John saw also in the sun.   (III, 613–23)

An environment that is "all sunshine," comparable to high noon, is obviously an appropriate climax to a sequence of cheerful dawns. So also does a reference to the end of sacred history follow naturally after references to its beginning and middle. Satan sees what John of Patmos was to see and record in the Book of Revelation, "an angel standing in the sun," who "cried with a loud voice, saying to all the fowls that fly in the midst of heaven, come and gather yourselves together unto the supper of the great God" (Rev. xix, 17). The scriptural context is the impending final apocalyptic battle between Christ and the Antichrist. As contemporary commentators explained, this angel is "Christs Herauld," whose mission is "to bid all the fowls to a banquet" of the "many dead carcases" of anti-Christian soldiers that "will be left unburied" after Christ's victory. It will be a feast "which God in his wrath upon his enemies hath prepared." The fact that the angel is standing in the sun was thought to be "a cleer token of the ensuing victory: and that the enemies should be destroyed in the sight of the Sun, as surely as we see the Sun."[15] So providential irony is now directed at Satan even more witheringly than in his earlier metaphoric encounters with Jacob's ladder and the promised land. He confronts an unmistakable omen of his ultimate, gruesome defeat.

But if the irony is the more telling, so also are the additional interpretive possibilities raised by the splendor of Milton's verse the more liberating. Commentators noted that the angel's being positioned in the sun and his crying with a loud voice signified the angel's desire "that he might be heard all the world over, as the Sun is seen," and "that the most remote might hear, and come to take their share." Milton's acquaintance John Diodati explicated the angel's cry as "the voice of the Gospel."[16] These exegetical details resonate with the emphasis in Milton's passage on the absolute clarity and distinctness of the view afforded to Satan, that he was in a place where "sight no obstacle found . . . and the air, / No where so clear, sharpened his visual ray / To objects distant far." Having opened out such vistas of virtually boundless possibility, the poet invites us, it seems, to wrest the Revelation text from its wrathful scriptural context and apprehend it as a straightforward rather than a parodic allusion to "the marriage supper of the Lamb" (Rev. xix, 9) and the Christian eucharistic feast in general. In a realm of pure light, the realm to which and for which Milton prays in the invocation to Book III, this "most remote" of all creatures once again has laid out before him, if he has eyes to see and ears to hear, the stunningly bountiful nature of that God and that viceregent Son of God against whom he has thus far chosen to wage war. The choice is his. He can continue to wage the war, preparing a banquet for vultures at the end of time, or he can abandon the contest and take his place at this radiant table of grace and peace.

But of course Satan is entirely unaware of the obvious potential significance of the experience he is having, that he, a "spirit impure," has been made "glad . . . as now in hope" of reliable guidance whereby he might "direct his wandering flight / To Paradise the happy seat of man, / His journey's end" (III, 630–33). What for the night-foundered pilot would be the gladness and hope engendered by the prospect of a safe journey's end, of salvation, is for Satan merely the start of yet another demonstration of how thoroughly in thrall he is to his own self-aggrandizing schemes. As earlier noted in passing, his reaction to a world where all is entirely open and aboveboard, a world without shade and shadow, is to fabricate shadows of disguise and dissembling, proceeding in furtherance of his mission to deceive the glorious revealed angel, Uriel, about his identity and intent. It seems that there is a direct proportion between the increasing clarity and generosity of the divine offering and the deepening malignancy of the demonic rejecting and despising.

The last remark might seem to savor of the sort of doctrinaire antisatanism which I have suggested is *not* the meaning of the lines about daring the fiend by easy ascent, and which has all too often characterized the rejoinders to the satanist readings of A.J.A. Waldock and others.[17] However, such is not my intention. Indeed, one of the advantages of the view here advanced — that during Satan's voyage through creation God sends him a message to the effect that it is still not too late for him to repent — is that it makes possible a more satisfactory account of the episode that Waldock made the crux of his indictment of Milton on charges of willful literary inorganicism. Waldock complained that the splendidly heroic Satan of the first two books "to all intents and purposes *disappears*" and is replaced thereafter by a different, lesser character altogether. The point where we most distinctly feel a "sense of abruptness" in the transition from the first to the second Satan, said Waldock, is Satan's soliloquy at the beginning of Book IV: "the Satan who now begins to unsay all that the other Satan said, who all of a sudden recognizes his 'Pride and worse Ambition' for what they are, who is softened by remorse . . . who realizes belatedly that the service of God was not hard at all, who knows now that he himself is Hell, who lectures perspicuously on his helpless case and example — this is a Satan that we have not felt before, not even dimly felt. And now that he is put before us we still cannot see the connection."[18]

All these features of the soliloquy become readily comprehensible, however, and the connection comes into view, if we allow for the possibility that what Satan has just experienced of the descrying of new lands

has had an impact on him after all.[19] For Satan to say to the sun that
he hates its beams (IV, 37) is for him to recall the emphasis on light in
general, and sunlight in particular, throughout his just-completed travels. For him to give as a reason for this hatred that the sunbeams "bring
to my remembrance from what state / I fell, how glorious once above
thy sphere" (IV, 38–39), is for him to refer quite directly to the "glorious
angel" whom he has just seen "stand" (rather than fall) in a world that
is "all sunshine." Here is a more expressive response to God's offer of grace
than Satan had achieved (or perhaps than the narrator had revealed)
at the time of the experience itself, emotion recollected in turbulence
rather than tranquility, not an acceptance of the offer certainly, but
something more than a simple rejecting and despising of it nevertheless.
Like any other creature who is fallen but still struggling to make a free
choice, Satan is poised between an attentive focus upon God-given reality and his own past and possible future place in it (like Uriel, he has
been glorious above the sphere of the sun and could be again), and a
self-absorbed pride which blurs such a focus even as it is achieved (he
boasts of having been "once above" the sun, whereas he has just seen
Uriel cheerfully abiding there).

The psychic struggle on which Satan now embarks, to sort out these
options and decide between them, feels as authentic as Adam's similar
struggle in Book X: two steps forward, one back; one forward, two back.
It has all the ingredients of the Arminian moment of choice and truth,
including conviction of sin ("my self am hell" [IV, 75]), and direct confrontation with the possibility of repentance: "O then at last relent: is
there no place / Left for repentance, none for pardon left" (IV, 79–80).
But Satan cannot repent and accept the offer of grace, for "Disdain forbids me, and my dread of shame / Among the spirits beneath" (IV, 82–
83). From Satan's own mouth comes an acknowledgment of what the
narrator had intimated in Book III: his self-enthrallment. It is only after
Satan has thus glimpsed his imprisonment in his own reified emotions,
abstractions, and schemes that he deludes himself with the convenient
fiction that God is a grim Calvinist "punisher" who would never grant
pardon even if Satan should be so untrue to himself as to beg for it:

> For never can true reconcilement grow
> Where wounds of deadly hate have pierced so deep:
> Which would but lead me to a worse relapse
> And heavier fall: so should I purchase dear
> Short intermission bought with double smart.
> This knows my punisher; therefore as far
> From granting he, as I from begging peace.   (IV, 98–104)

Having tried but failed to break free of self-enthrallment, Satan reappropriates the perceptions and values by which he is possessed with intensified vehemence and defiance. He is like a recovered alcoholic who, once he backslides, scorns the very idea of sobriety and mires himself in a worse addiction than before. This is a thoroughly plausible psychological dynamic and prepares quite logically and naturally for Satan's subsequent "degradation."

At the close of the war in heaven in Book VI, later in the poem but earlier in Satan's career as a rebel and sinner, Milton provides a blunter account of the demonic refusal to accept the divine offer of grace. As the Son of God drives the satanic army before him, we are told that

> he meant
> Not to destroy, but root them out of heaven:
> The overthrown he raised, and as a herd
> Of goats or timorous flock together thronged
> Drove them before him thunderstruck.   (VI, 854–58)

The overthrown he raised. Even when the deity has been forced to transform himself into a God of wrath, he continues to make available the choice between the sheep and the goats. And the subsequent language stresses the devils' Arminian free agency, that they choose their own damnation: "headlong themselves they threw / Down from the verge of heaven" (VI, 864–65).

The Arminian free choice of faith was supposed to be the entry into a life of sanctifying works, of the sort Galileo briefly exemplifies in the simile in which he appears in Book I. The passage just noted is Milton's terse recognition that there was also such a thing as an Arminian free choice against faith, and the overall representation of Satan constitutes Milton's further recognition that one might make such a choice and then proceed to invert the prescribed pattern, live by a work ethic devoted not to sanctification but rather to the heaping up of damnation: "If then his providence / Out of our evil seek to bring forth good, / Our labour must be to pervert that end, / And out of good still to find means of evil" (I, 162–65). Satan thus inhabits an Arminian universe not only in the sense that he is free to decide his own spiritual destiny, but also in the sense intended by Christopher Hill when he states that "we are all . . . Arminians now" in the era of the Protestant ethic and the spirit of capitalism.[20] More specifically, the archfiend progresses in the course of the poem from "a rebel against authoritarianism and an indomitable laborer and builder in the wilderness to an imperialist policy maker and insatiably combative technocrat," from "soaring grandiloquence to fast-talking conjurations," and this progress anticipates and encapsulates the pattern of the capitalist centuries that were emerging even as *Paradise Lost* was being written and published.[21]

The analysis of Satan in the book of mine from which these words are quoted is part of that book's larger argument about the overall historical status and relevance of *Paradise Lost*. I maintain that the Puritan epic poem contains a startlingly accurate prophecy of the development of the most distinctly Puritan society and culture, that of New England and the United States. Just as the degradation of Satan looks ahead to the degradation of American society and culture in its capitalist aspect, so the degeneration of the relationship of Adam and Eve by the end of Book IX into a vain contest that appears to have no end mirrors the tensions besetting that same society and culture insofar as it has been unable to resolve its long-standing contradiction between hierarchical and egalitarian norms of social structure and daily experience.[22] This is a view which may be felt to render even more somber the historical vistas of Books XI and XII: the failure of the human race to achieve regeneracy on any significant scale is now seen to encompass the centuries since *Paradise Lost* was written, as well as all those preceding it back to the Fall itself.

But if *Paradise Lost* is filled with an undeceived recognition of fallenness, it is also animated by a determination not to relinquish the sources of life and hope. "The experience of defeat" after the English Revolution did not elicit from Milton a sigh of resignation to tragic necessity.[23] In the case of Adam and Eve, after representing to the fullest extent the depth of their conflict, he nevertheless in Book X leads our first parents through conflict to reconciliation and a livable future.[24]

In Satan's case, there is of course no reconciliation, no repentance, no emergence from the valley of the shadow of death into the broad sunlit uplands of the magnificent universe God has created. But it is of the utmost importance that God never withdraws the possibility of such reconciliation, such repentance, such an emergence. By his portrayal in Book III of God's imperturbable generosity and patience, extended even to the very archetype of sin and evil, Milton testifies more dramatically than by any other means to his refusal to believe that the latest chapter in the long story of human failure meant that reality was designed in such a way as to make human failure a foregone conclusion. If Milton was, as Boyd Berry has stated, a "radical activist," then *Paradise Lost* is the supreme expression of the radicalism of his activism.[25] It represents reality as being constantly and without exception available for reshaping, for good and ill, by the choices and actions of every creaturely agent—demonic, angelic, human; fallen, upright, and struggling between the two. Because Milton is determinedly consistent about the Arminian freedom and openness of the world he has created and bequeathed to us, we can remain open to his closing promise that our world is still all before us, in spite of the many additional chapters of human failure we have ourselves written.

Cambridge, Massachusetts

NOTES

1. The text used is *The Poems of John Milton*, ed. John Carey and Alistair Fowler (London, 1968).

2. Diane Kelsey McColley, *Milton's Eve* (Urbana, Ill., 1983), pp. 189–90.

3. Geoffrey Hartman, "Milton's Counterplot," in *Milton: A Collection of Critical Essays*, ed. Louis L. Martz (Englewood Cliffs, N.J., 1966), p. 103; originally published in *ELH* XXV (1958).

4. See William G. Riggs, *The Christian Poet in "Paradise Lost"* (Berkeley and Los Angeles, 1972), pp. 18–20.

5. In Book III, lines 588–90, when Milton imagines Galileo seeing Satan land on the sun, he compares Satan to a sunspot.

6. *Annotations Upon All the Books of the Old and New Testament* . . . , 2 vols., 3rd ed. (London, 1657), vol. 1, no pagination. The members of the committee were drawn from the Westminster Assembly. See also what is said about Genesis xxviii, 12 in, among others, Martin Luther, *Luther's Commentary on Genesis*, 2 vols. (Grand Rapids, Mich., 1958), vol. I, pp. 131–32; John Calvin, *Commentaries on the First Book of Moses Called Genesis*, 46 vols. of Calvin's biblical commentaries (1843–55; rpt. Grand Rapids, Mich., 1948–63) vol. II, p. 113; John Diodati, *Pious Annotations Upon the Holy Bible*, 3rd ed. (London, 1651), no pagination. John (Jean, Giovanni) Diodati, eminent professor of theology at Geneva and vehement opponent of Arminianism at the Synod of Dort, was the uncle of Charles Diodati, the friend of Milton's youth. Milton called on him, possibly lodged with him, in the course of his Continental travels in 1639.

7. See, e.g., Calvin, *Commentaries on . . . Genesis*, p. 85. All biblical quotations are from the Authorized Version.

8. *Complete Prose Works of John Milton*, 8 vols., ed. Don M. Wolfe et al. (New Haven, 1953–82), vol. VI, p. 197; all further references abbreviated as YP and incorporated into the text.

9. *Annotations*, vol. I, comment on Genesis xxvii, 19. See also Calvin, *Commentaries on . . . Genesis*, pp. 85, 88, 93; Joseph Hall, *Contemplations on the Historical Passages of the Old and New Testament*, 3 vols. (1633; rpt. London, 1831) vol. I, pp. 83–84; *The Dutch Annotations Upon the Whole Bible*, 2 vols., trans. Theodore Haak (London, 1657), vol. 1, no pagination, comment on Genesis xxvii, 19. Only Luther, among the sources I have examined, comes close to agreeing with Milton's unqualified approbation of Jacob's conduct; see *Luther's Commentary*, vol. II, pp. 108–09, 111–12, 116.

10. *Annotations*, vol. 1, comment on Genesis xxvii, 34.

11. Ibid., comment on Genesis xxviii, 14; see also YP, VI, p. 418.

12. Diodati, *Pious Annotations*, comment on Genesis xxviii, 16.

13. Another widely accepted meaning for Jacob's ladder was providence. See, e.g., Calvin, *Commentaries on . . . Genesis*, p. 113; Matthew Poole, *A Commentary on the Holy Bible*, 3 vols. (1683–85; rpt. London, 1962), vol. I, p. 66. In the eighteenth century, the ultimate salvation of all reprobate souls, including devils, would be affirmed in Andrew Michael Ramsay, *The Philosophical Principles of Natural and Revealed Religion*, 2 vols. (Glasgow, 1748), vol. I, pp. 431–32, 436, 491–92; vol. II, p. 325. Ramsay's arguments were used by Thomas Clap, president of Yale, as the climactic point in his summary indictment of the Arminian errors that were creeping into New England; see *A Brief History and Vindication of the Doctrines Received and Established in the Churches of New-England . . .* (New Haven, 1755), pp. 22–23.

14. This is a speculation in which we are led to indulge all the more freely by the speculative note ("whether") which governs the passage; cf. the Carey/Fowler commentary on the lines.

15. *Annotations*, vol. II; *Dutch Annotations*, vol. II.

16. *Annotations*, vol. II; Diodati, *Pious Annotations*.

17. A relatively recent example of this tendency is William Kerrigan's idea that the passage just discussed is not a genuine spiritual invitation to Satan but merely a malign satanic parody of the poet's petition to the "celestial Light" at the beginning of Book III; see *The Prophetic Milton* (Charlottesville, Va., 1974), p. 150. In *"Authors to Themselves": Milton and the Revelation of History* (Cambridge, 1987), p. 66, Marshall Grossman notes only the passage's prophecy of Satan's defeat.

18. A.J.A. Waldock, *"Paradise Lost" and Its Critics* (Cambridge, 1947), pp. 81–82, 85–86.

19. William Empson, *Milton's God* (Norfolk, Conn., 1961), pp. 61–62, touched upon the argument I am about to make when he speculated that Satan is reacting in the soliloquy to his recent experience of "the overwhelming beauty of the created world." See also Grossman, *"Authors to Themselves,"* pp. 71–76.

20. Christopher Hill, *The World Turned Upside Down: Radical Ideas During the English Revolution* (New York, 1972), p. 276.

21. Keith W. F. Stavely, *Puritan Legacies: "Paradise Lost" and the New England Tradition, 1630–1890* (Ithaca, N.Y., 1987), pp. 90–91, 271; for the full argument here summarized, see chapter 3.

22. Ibid., chap. 2.

23. See Christopher Hill, *The Experience of Defeat: Milton and Some Contemporaries* (New York, 1984).

24. Stavely, *Puritan Legacies*, pp. 273–79.

25. Boyd M. Berry, *Process of Speech: Puritan Religious Writing and "Paradise Lost"* (Baltimore, 1976), p. 3.

PARADISE LOST, HISTORY PAINTING, AND EIGHTEENTH-CENTURY ENGLISH NATIONALISM

Stephen C. Behrendt

I N HIS ACCOUNT of eighteenth-century English art, Joseph Burke observes that the success of Thomas Macklin's Poets' Gallery and Bible Gallery, Alderman John Boydell's Shakespeare Gallery, and Robert Bowyer's Historic Gallery during the final dozen years of the eighteenth century demonstrated "that the future of *istoria* [or history painting] lay not on the walls of churches and palaces but in the pages of printed books." Indeed, Burke calls book illustration "the underground channel by which traditions of *istoria* were kept alive" in England when paintings on the grand scale fell from fashion in the latter eighteenth century.[1] Burke's point is especially apropos of the history of illustrations to *Paradise Lost*, the most frequently illustrated English book of the period.[2] By the end of the eighteenth century, and during the early years of the nineteenth, Milton's works were being illustrated by such considerable artists as William Blake, John Martin, and Henry Fuseli, who in 1799 exhibited his own Milton Gallery. Indeed the success of James Gillray's 1792 portrayal of Queen Charlotte, Lord Chancellor Thurlow, and William Pitt the Younger as "Sin, Death, and the Devil" dramatically demonstrates the extent to which a distinctive and broadly familiar iconographic tradition had solidified around Milton's epic. Milton's illustrators played a large part in both the epic's reputation and the ways in which it was read and understood. Even when their influence was as deleterious as their visual interpretations were misguided — as was all too often the case — their work contributed nevertheless to the poem's indisputable popularity among readers of all sorts.

It is instructive to look back at the century and a quarter following Milton's death to gain a better understanding of how his diffuse epic achieved such preeminence among readers, critics, and both verbal and visual artists. Doing so necessarily forces us to consider a number of related questions that, as often as not, lead to still other questions before they begin to yield answers. Which scenes were illustrated, for instance, and why? What was the contemporary estimate of the poem as poem (and also as epic) at various points in the eighteenth century, and how did the poem's changing reputation (and Milton's as well) affect both the subject matter and the treatment of its illustrations? What effects followed, among illustrators, from the heterodox nature of a poem that had set out deliberately and explicitly, as Barbara Kiefer Lewalski has effectively demonstrated, both to incorporate and to exploit a rich diversity of literary modes in a new poem of rich intertextuality?[3] Are there any significant relationships — in terms of both scene selection and visual representation — among book illustration, history painting, and the theatre, that enormously popular art form which, under the aegis of actors like David Garrick and adaptors like George Colman, was revising and transforming — some would say corrupting — original works not just of Milton but of Shakespeare as well? In beginning to think about these and other questions it is, of course, helpful to bear in mind that every age tends to "use" art differently, making it over in large measure to suit the interests, tastes, and moral or political exigencies of the particular age. Hence the history of *Paradise Lost* illustration in the eighteenth century is also a record of the century's changing cultural, spiritual, and political outlook.

In his revisionist study of Milton's presence and persistence in the eighteenth century, Dustin Griffin contends that we ought to regard Milton not as the great artistic *stifler* of the century ("the great Inhibitor," as Harold Bloom calls him in *The Anxiety of Influence*), but rather as the source of a rich vein of increasingly familiar material that might profitably be mined not just by journeymen imitators of questionable talent but also, more importantly, by artists of real ability who could build upon the foundation Milton had laid and who were not afraid to raze his structures in order to renovate them. Rather than crippling the artists who followed him, Griffin argues, Milton "helped to stimulate some of the best poetry of the century."[4] The same might be said about Milton's effect upon visual art, and a consideration of eighteenth-century English history painting can help us draw nearer to informed answers to some of the questions I have just raised.

Like the traditional epic poet, history painters typically set out to fuse in their art a strong narrative line with a high moral purpose. Painters like Benjamin West, for instance, in the latter half of the century, regarded painting generally — and history painting specifically — as "a moral and teaching enterprise" in which verbal and visual art worked in concert both to represent and to shape the substance and ideals of culture. John Barrell calls this the genre in which the artist is most eminently capable of representing humanity according to its true nature and end, which, according to Barrell, is "to be so entirely a citizen that he pursues no interest which is not the interest of the public."[5] Historical painting, especially when it treated classical and biblical themes, was accounted superior to other forms of art "largely because of the elevated teachings to be drawn from it."[6] Sir Joshua Reynolds, first president of the Royal Academy (and West's predecessor in that position), naturally used the weight of his influential position to lend force to the argument which he articulated in his annual discourses, that the essence of history painting (which Reynolds remarks "ought to be called Poetical [Painting], as in reality it is") lay in the "great" (or grand) style, a style characterized by its "great nobleness" and its devotion to rendering its subjects with "as much dignity as the human figure is capable of receiving."[7]

This is, of course, very much the moral and intellectual program set forth earlier in the period by DuFresnoy, Jonathan Richardson, and Shaftesbury, all of whom had—following the fifteenth-century Italian theorist Leon Battista Alberti—located history painting, or *istoria*, at the pinnacle of the visual arts. Alberti had written that in the didactic genre of *istoria* art might parallel poetry if paintings addressed issues of broad aesthetic and ethical dimensions: simply put, history painting was to relate a story from ancient or biblical history "that conveyed an instructive lesson concerning universal moral values."[8] There could be few stories of more universal import than that which Milton relates in *Paradise Lost*, nor could there be more obvious matter upon which eighteenth-century visual artists might set out to engage in artistic collaboration.

So there existed a seemingly natural affinity between the moral and intellectual underpinnings of Milton's epic and those of history painting generally. Moreover, as the tradition of *istoria* had developed on the Continent during the sixteenth and seventeenth centuries, the tide had turned away from the genre's initial emphasis on "documentary," historically realistic depictions and toward landscape settings that were more imaginary than real and costumes that eschewed contemporary dress for stylized renditions of the attire of ancient Greece and Rome. Instead of depicting historical figures in contemporary dress, as some Renaissance artists had done, the later history painter frequently clothed contemporary figures in ancient costume.[9] This tendency helps to account for the fondness among Milton's illustrators for depicting both the heavenly and the satanic legions in antique military costume, although the motif is present in Genesis illustration as early as the Renaissance. This tradition of classical costuming helps explain the sensation that ensued when in 1771 Benjamin West dramatically rejected the convention and portrayed the dying General Wolfe in contemporary military attire, surrounded by other realistically dressed figures (*The Death of General Wolfe*). Had West portrayed Wolfe nude, or dressed in a toga, and surrounded by classically dressed allegorical figures, all might have been well: certainly all would have been conventional. But his decision to employ contemporary costume declared his conviction that the modern age, too, held the potential for greatness that made it akin to—even equal to—the great age of antiquity. That others (like Edward Penny) had likewise treated Wolfe's death in contemporary, documentary fashion was beside the point: West had deliberately and specifically invoked visual motifs and models from the tradition of *istoria* and the world of ideality it implied, for instance by echoing in Wolfe's position Van Dyck's *Deposition*.[10]

Many eighteenth-century theorists, however, particularly after midcentury, had declared that the epic poet's task was in any event not to duplicate the ancient world (and thus merely to imitate Homer and Virgil) but rather to portray the modern world in suitable epic terms. Goldsmith, for instance, advised the modern poet to "boldly follow nature in the dress she wears at present," for, he argued, an accurately delineated modern hero would undoubtedly "fill the scene of an epic poem with more dignity, and interest us more than all the swift-footed Achilles's, or pious Eneas's of antiquity."[11] It was from something of the same conviction, a conviction both aesthetic and political in its deliberate repudiation of European convention, that the American artists in England—West, Copley, and Trumbull—were revolutionizing history painting by incorporating historical accuracy in costume (even if not in actual details of setting and character) in their depictions of recent military events.[12] The situation is very different, however, in the case of *Paradise Lost*, whose subject matter is both impossibly remote and perennially immediate, and it is undoubtedly significant that Milton's epic seems seldom to have been of much interest to American artists, despite its apparently universal moral significance.

The illustrator of *Paradise Lost* easily and naturally skirts the difficulty over costume since his mortal characters are, of course, conveniently nude or nearly so, while his nonmortal characters easily fall heir to the sort of drapery traditionally associated with classical art, in keeping with the elevated subject matter. Moreover, the Edenic landscape is by its very nature subject to the sort of fantastic idealizing that history painting had more and more embraced, as we see in the increasingly lush landscapes in illustrations to *Paradise Lost* by Richard Corbould, Francis Hayman, Richard Westall, and E. F. Burney, pictures that respond also to the stimulus of the pastoral mode that Milton specifically invokes in his descriptions of Eden. The repositioning of the natural environment from unobtrusive backdrop to absolute centrality and relative star status is itself a change we normally associate with Romanticism. Like so many features of that great movement, however, its sources are very much a part of the eighteenth-century visual tradition (including painted stage scenery) that is reflected in *Paradise Lost* illustrations. In like manner, the increasing emphasis upon the physical, sensual beauty of the nude or nearly nude Adam and Eve reflects the corporeal "naturalness" inherent in the concept of the noble savage and the Romantic fondness for nakedness, for the literal and metaphorical rejection and removal of the "clothing" that conceals and obscures the natural body unadorned with anything but its innate beauty.[13]

Paradise Lost served many purposes in the eighteenth century, so that its history is also a record of the century's changing cultural, spiritual, and political outlook. It was esteemed both as a guide to the moral life and as a "history" of humanity's fall from innocence and liberty into the voluntary servitude of vice and filial ingratitude. It was in this sense also a political poem, in that it reflects Milton's view that politics is at heart a moral activity grounded in the essential liberty that affords the individual both the freedom and the responsibility to choose among personal and public alternatives which are inherently moral in nature. The source of this liberty — which is first internal and only secondarily external or public — is virtue. Hence the poem could be — and was — read also as a guide to piety and submission, and to the supposedly appropriate relations between men and women, mortal and deity, subject and heavenly king, complete with a dramatic brief on the rewards and punishments for choosing correctly or incorrectly among the myriad temptations that daily try the souls of individuals. The implied relationship between the moral-spiritual and the temporal-political aspects of Milton's poem stuck a responsive chord with its eighteenth-century readers. Indeed, as Griffin observes, Milton's sympathetic eighteenth-century biographers regularly remarked upon the significant linkage of his positions as representative of and apologist for English liberty and "exemplar of moral integrity."[14]

Finally, *Paradise Lost* was an *English* masterpiece, composed by a poet whose own life had demonstrated his willingness to make extraordinary sacrifices in service to his country and to his God. For an age in which nationalism was an increasingly central feature of English culture, this was a most important point. Milton's life seemed to exemplify the standard of moral goodness required by Cicero and Quintilian, who demanded that the rhetor-statesman possess both an intellectually informed and committed, and a personally experienced, moral goodness, a grounding in the "poetic character" based in virtue and learning which Plato had articulated in the *Republic* and *Laws*.[15] His eighteenth-century countrymen saw in Milton the embodiment of his own claim that

he who would not be frustrate of his hope to write well hereafter in laudable things, ought himself to be a true poem, that is, a composition and pattern of the best and honorablest things — not presuming to sing high praises of heroic men or famous cities, unless he have in himself the experience and practice of all that which is praiseworthy.[16]

These are, of course, almost precisely the qualifications for the history painter as defined by neoclassical theorists. Moreover, Milton had in *The Reason of Church Government* attributed to his own activity a distinctly nationalistic impulse: "to be an interpreter and relater of the best and sagest things among mine own citizens throughout this island in the mother dialect," and thereby to validate the primacy of English as the proper language of modern epic art.[17] Indeed his "Epitaphium Damonis" and "Mansus" indicate that Milton had early on envisioned an epic on subject matter drawn from English history.

Particularly in the very public intellectual and sociopolitical role which was his inevitable inheritance as epic poet, Milton served to focus England's literary self-consciousness, its sense of its relation to the literary past, and its own achievements and ambitions. As a poet writing in his maturity in English Milton had both joined and culminated "the one pure, undefiled source" for English artists whose pride was lodged in their own national artistic past.[18] In this respect Milton played a key part in eighteenth-century England in the impulse which K. R. Minogue attributes to all nationalist cultural activity, the urge to "discover a past which will support the aspiration of the present."[19] Indeed, one of Milton's central functions in the eighteenth century was to serve, along with Shakespeare, as a prototypical representative of what Gerald Newman calls an "abstract National Character, a moral, intellectual and aesthetic personality with supposedly national traits." Newman notes that such a mythic — or mythologized — ideal of character (which interestingly prefigures the mythic figure of Albion conceived by Milton's great Romantic admirer, Blake) serves a unifying and rallying nationalistic function by promoting an image of "a real national community worthy of it."[20]

A particular characteristic of eighteenth-century English nationalism that appears in all the arts — indeed in all aspects of culture — is a new preoccupation with native genius as distinct from foreign models and influences. By midcentury the drive to exorcise all traces of French aesthetic dominance was particularly strong, as the writings of Samuel Johnson, to name only one prominent anti-Gallican, demonstrate. Milton's epic was increasingly regarded in the eighteenth century as a "national treasure," any attack upon which, as even Johnson affirmed, was an affront to the honor of England.[21] Milton is to be distinguished in this respect from Shakespeare, whose importance as a source and stimulus for history painters in the period is also great, but for somewhat different reasons. William Hayley later recalled that Boydell's Shakespeare Gallery had stemmed from what he termed "patriotic" motives and what we now recognize to have been the increasingly nationalistic impulse in English art of the later eighteenth century.[22] The epic genre, however, embodies a firmly established tradition of national and nationalistic significance — of cultural consequence — greater than that of the drama, as the eighteenth century fully appreciated. Moreover, in its masterful eclectic fusion of biblical and classical materials, *Paradise Lost* constituted "the greatest single source for sublime imagery composed in the English language," a point not lost upon Edmund Burke, who in codifying the tough, melodramatic qualities of the sublime in his *Enquiry on the Sublime and the Beautiful* (1757) had drawn freely upon Milton's poem in illustrating his principles, and who had inculcated those principles in his Irish protégé, the history painter and Milton illustrator James Barry.[23]

Milton occupied a peculiar place in the consciousness of the writers who followed him, however, for he seemed at once dramatically immediate and impossibly remote. The age in which Milton had lived his life and composed his works was enormously different from that which followed the Glorious Revolution, and it is one of the curious ironies of literary and cultural history that the Romantic period "stood close to him in imaginative sympathy and was better able than the eighteenth century to value his true poetic quality."[24] Perhaps it was at least in part the galvanizing effect of the French Revolution, which lent an entirely new impetus to English nationalism, while at the same time placing Milton's views of individual and collective political liberty in a new and immediately relevant light, that led to the emergence of a radically different view of Milton as man, as thinker, and as artist in that later period. This view is epitomized in Shelley's declaration in 1819 that "the sacred Milton was, let it ever be remembered, a republican, and a bold inquirer into morals and religion," and in Blake's more pithy claim nearly thirty years earlier that Milton "was a true Poet and of the Devils party without knowing it."[25] It is, then, very significant that when grand-style history painting in England began seriously to decline (for both aesthetic and economic reasons), Milton's reputation as moral historian in the grand style of *istoria* began also to be displaced by the new, Romantic view of Milton as political and intellectual radical, as prophet and patriot. The concomitant interest in Milton the man — the private as well as public individual — is reflected both in biographies like that of William Hayley, published in the 1790s, and in paintings like Fuseli's *Milton Dictating to His Daughter* (1793–96).

In the final quarter of the century many factors — increasing nationalism, the burgeoning effects in the arts of the Burkean sublime, and technological advances in the production of illustrated books — coalesced to produce a rapid expansion in the number and style of illustrations to *Paradise Lost*. Not only did book illustrations proliferate, so did freestanding, separate works of art like the paintings in Fuseli's Milton Gallery. Milton was everywhere, both as man and as poet, and so were critical and cultural misconceptions and misconstructions of his work and its significance. One reason why William Blake apparently considered it essential to "liberate" Milton, by reaffirming the fundamental truth of Milton's vision and at the same time exposing what he regarded as both its inherent errors and the errors of Milton's critics, was that Milton did in fact exert such enormous moral and intellectual influence upon English culture.[26]

It is frequently argued in the twentieth century, as it was in the eighteenth, that the apparent decline of the epic genre resulted from massive cultural changes in the western world generally in the eighteenth century.[27] Cowper's deflation of the genre in *The Task* at the century's end effectively closes a chapter opened by Pope's *Rape of the Lock* at the beginning. But Cowper's poem tells only part of the story, quite obviously, for the epic was in fact being transformed into the new and internalized psychological forms of which *Milton* and *Jerusalem, The Prelude, Don Juan,* and *Prometheus Unbound* are spectacular and diverse examples. In precisely the same fashion, English history painting changed in the 1770s and 1780s, forgoing the classical restraint of Gavin Hamilton, Reynolds, and West for a distinctly more dramatic and dynamic style that involved artist and viewer alike in imaginative, emotive, and strongly psychological activity.[28] Like the other arts, painting was moving toward the combination of emotional, oracular, pastoral, primitive, and intensely subjective elements we associate with Romanticism and the Romantic attempt to reclaim and reanimate a native aesthetic past.[29] This change involved, too, a more particularized treatment of the heroic figure, whose distinctive personal characteristics need no longer be subordinated by the artist to the generalizing iconographic conventions of *istoria*. Blake, for instance, rejected Reynolds' leveling notion that the real subject of history painting is mankind in general: "A History Painter Paints The Hero & not Man in General, but most minutely in Particular."[30] Consequently, not only the traditional hero was seen as fit subject for *istoria* (or heroic art generally) but so were artists and their productions themselves. Hence Blake's *Milton*, like his Milton illustrations (and, to a lesser but nevertheless important extent, like Fuseli's Milton subjects), marks the creative encounter of great artists and great art which reformulates and perpetuates precursor works (and their makers) in the productions of the later artist.

One key to better understanding both the power and the persistence of *Paradise Lost* in the eighteenth century lies in the fact that it is at heart a dramatic work centering upon the greatest moral and intellectual choice in the history of humankind. The abiding concern with such profound choices is apparent from the popularity in eighteenth-century England of variations upon the visual topos of the choice of Hercules, as in Benjamin West's popular painting of the subject (fig. 1) and its equally popular topical antecedent, *Garrick Between Comedy and Tragedy* (fig. 2), in which Joshua Reynolds had deliberately invoked the context of the choice of Hercules, the allusion to which his audience was expected to recognize. It is, therefore, scarcely surprising to find in some depictions of the temptation scene in Book IX echoes of this same visual tradition (fig. 3). Unfortunately, the allusion tends to work to the disadvantage of Eve, whose typically (and increasingly) lovely physical presence provides what the viewer is implicitly encouraged to recognize as the negative counterpart to the significantly invisible God whose presence within Adam's mind and conscience is generally manifested through Adam's obvious physical and emotional distress at this moment of crisis. The dramatic crisis posed by Adam's need to choose between what is physically present and what is present within his soul, so to speak, is itself analogous to the crisis faced by the later eighteenth-century and Romantic theatergoer, who was likewise increasingly asked to participate in the wrenching moral and intellectual dilemmas of protagonists like Karl Moor (in Schiller's *The Robbers*, a play popular in England in translation) or Beatrice Cenci (in Shelley's tragedy of 1819), dilemmas to which traditional, morally conventional "answers" are no longer either clear or sufficient.

In fact, important connections exist among eighteenth-century illustrations of *Paradise Lost* and the way in which both the form and the style of theatrical productions were represented in the visual arts — both on canvas and in the engraved book illustration. Francis Hayman, for instance, whose midcentury illustrations of Milton's poetry became im-

Figure 1. Benjamin West, *The Choice of Hercules* (1764). Courtesy of the Board of Trustees of the Victoria and Albert Museum.

Figure 2. Sir Joshua Reynolds, *Garrick between Comedy and Tragedy* (1760–61). Private collection.

Figure 3. Richard Corbould, "Eve Tempting Adam" (from *Paradise Lost*, Book IX; 1795–96). Stephen C. Behrendt.

mediately popular, was both a history painter and a scene painter for Drury Lane. An artist who fused the British *istoria* tradition of Sir James Thornhill with the elegant French manner of his second master, the illustrator Gravelot, Hayman had been regarded by his contemporaries as the greatest historical painter in England before the arrival of Giovanni Battista Cipriani in 1755.[31] His familiarity with practical matters of staging and gesture (or pathos-formulae, in the manner of LeBrun) is apparent in his works in his conspicuous use of levels and his fondness for the dramatically struck pose that all too easily becomes melodramatic.

The theater had by midcentury become a popular subject for artists drawn to the many dramatic subjects it offered them. While a whole subgenre of play-vignettes and portrayals of popular thespians in various roles quickly evolved, the more subtle influence of the theater upon the visual arts may be observed in the increasing fondness for figure arrangements (including the positioning in crowd scenes) and physical "settings" that parallel contemporary theater practice.[32] The relationship was, of course, symbiotic, with the theater (as always) following developments in the other arts more than actually precipitating them. But its more broadly public nature inevitably lent the theater a significant role in the dissemination and further popularization of developments in both the visual arts and literature, upon both of which it depended for its own sustenance.

The connection between the stage and grand-style art in the tradition of *istoria* was a natural one for the eighteenth century in any event. In his widely read manual of painting, Daniel Webb wrote in 1761 that "history painting is the representation of a momentary drama: we may therefore, in treating of compositions, borrow our ideas from the stage."[33] Eighteenth-century illustrations to *Paradise Lost* increasingly focused upon moments of greatest dramatic potential — the most effectively "stageable" scenes. Coupled with the idiosyncratic unwillingness of Protestant art to portray God directly in human form,[34] this emphasis upon the dramatic moment helps somewhat to explain the curious treatment accorded Book III by its illustrators. Rather than depicting the key act of the entire epic and the epitome of selfless and morally generous choice — the Son's offer to die for humanity — illustrators regularly substituted a sentimental rendering of Uriel's conversation with the disguised Satan, which occurs at the end of Book III. This is a particularly telling instance of the deplorable tendency among illustrators (and those who commissioned them) to depict critically or thematically inappropriate subjects merely because they possessed inherent dramatic or sentimental interest as scenes of action or confrontation. By such devices did illustrators all too frequently misrepresent both the letter and the spirit of Milton's epic, with serious consequences for the manner in which the poem was read and understood by many a reader.

A similar point might be made about the relative absence of the Father from illustrations. Even in Book III, where his presence in the heavenly scene ought to have been both natural and inevitable, he is conspicuously absent, the scene in heaven — on those rare occasions when it was represented at all — being given over to the figure of the Son, generally accompanied by some iconographic reference to the cross. Given the insistent presence of Satan in eighteenth-century illustrations, and the frequently unheroic and even visually unattractive portrayals of the Son, it is little wonder that Satan came to possess among his illustrators many of the heroic attributes of the neoclassical tradition of *istoria*, even when the artist attempted deliberately to invert or undermine the conventional signification of those attributes.

A related curiosity among *Paradise Lost* illustrations in the eighteenth century is the resistance to representing the Crucifixion as a part of Michael's account to Adam of the future, particularly since both the Crucifixion and the Deposition were established subjects (and visual *topoi*) in history painting. Perhaps an explanation may be deduced from the fact that most illustrators chose to illustrate Book XI with some version of the death of Abel or the Deluge, and then turned to Book XII for the Expulsion, thereby keeping both illustrations firmly rooted within the Old Testament — indeed within Genesis. The Deluge was, however, particularly after Poussin's remarkable painting of the subject (1665), popular with artists generally as a prototypical example of the sublime, whose fusion of natural catastrophe with apocalyptic import links the Old and New Testaments.[35] By illustrating Book XI with this great cataclysmic scene and then following it (and ending) with a typically bleak and woeful Raphaelesque Expulsion, however, illustrators misrepresented Milton's poem at the same time that they sensationalized it. Illustrators who suggested the Crucifixion at all typically did so by means of iconographic reference, as for instance by introducing a cross into a scene in which the Son is present.

It was Blake, finally, whose watercolor designs were never actually engraved for use as book illustrations, who introduced to *Paradise Lost* illustration the powerful explicit representation of the Crucifixion and thus refocused attention upon the act of creative self-sacrifice by Milton's "one greater man" in a vision whose iconography both recalls the Fall and prefigures the Last Judgment. Unlike the more traditional history painter and illustrator, Blake sought in his art to fuse epic and prophecy, his purpose being less to recount history than "to bring it to an apotheosis," his intent not simply to record the patterns of the past but to discover and articulate both an imaginative and a "real" means of release from them.[36] What most distinguishes his Milton illustrations is the determination with which Blake explores in the matter of Milton's epic the elements of universal psychodrama, moving—as the Romantic epic does—toward greater interiority and a recognition of the universal moral, political, and imaginative significance of the archetypal themes of power, will, love, and choice upon which Milton's epic turns.

The preference among illustrators for immediately dramatic scenes also helps to explain another facet of *Paradise Lost* illustration to which I have already alluded: the elevation of Satan to exalted, quasi-heroic status. Normally associated almost exclusively with the Romantic period (and mistakenly attributed to artists like Blake and Shelley), this tendency to heroize Satan is very much a part of the eighteenth-century tradition of illustration. Writing to William Hayley in 1794, the troubled painter George Romney signaled the shift in interest which had already taken place respecting Milton's characters when he announced his intention of painting six subjects from Milton: "three where Satan is the hero, and three of Adam and Eve. Perhaps six of each."[37] Both the Son and the Father are conspicuously absent from Romney's plan, despite Hayley's subsequent protestations about Romney's "sincere and cordial reverence for the Gospel" and his claim that the artist planned at length to devote his artistic efforts to religious subjects.[38] Romney's revealing comments suggest the extent to which, particularly in light of the French Revolution, *Paradise Lost* was being read late in the century as a sort of history of the overthrow of tyranny and oppression by forces of energetic political opposition whose figurehead Satan was frequently taken to be.

This sort of topical relevance, especially as it relates to contemporary political events, also figured increasingly in eighteenth-century history painting, even as it did in theater: Addison's *Cato* is perhaps the clearest example of a dramatic political allegory with important and continuing contemporary significance. Already by the 1760s, for instance, Benjamin West had internalized much of what he had found in the paintings of Hamilton, Jean-Baptiste Greuze, and Anton Mengs, evolving in the process a vehicle for his own history paintings which combined classical subject matter and distinctly theatrical staging with demonstrable contemporary political commentary.[39] This interest in didactic historical painting converged most obviously with the burgeoning English nationalism in Bowyer's Historic Gallery of 1789, the paintings from which were subsequently engraved for publication in the multivolume 1806 edition of Hume's history of England published by Bowyer.[40]

Pernicious though he is, Satan generally emerges in illustrations for *Paradise Lost* as unquestionably the most active, dynamic figure of all of Milton's characters, and this lends him a visual interest to which any reader/viewer must instinctively respond. Of course, the topos of the serene Christ figure defeating the contorted Satanic figure has a long lineage in earlier art, in terms of both St. George and the dragon and Michael (or Christ) defeating Satan. The moral, spiritual premise underlying such depictions is that passion is a condition of excess appropriate to Satan but singularly unbefitting angels or deities. Hence even when Blake depicts the Son casting Satan's legions from heaven in a powerfully symbolic design, the Son wears an expression of serenity that contrasts sharply with those of the routed rebels. Much the same may be said of other earlier, more representational renditions of the war in heaven, in which the Son — even when he is placed within the context of considerable activity — frequently strikes twentieth-century eyes as oddly passive.

Milton's illustrators unquestionably exerted considerable influence upon the overall reputation of *Paradise Lost* in the eighteenth century, then, helping to shape and solidify that reputation even as they responded to it. They could give physical form to Milton's characters and events, and could counterbalance the intellectual complexities of his dense verse with the straightforward clarity of dramatic visual images. When executed faithfully, their illustrations could be immensely helpful to the reader/viewer. But all too often illustrators seriously misrepresented the poem, as they did for instance when they consistently substituted for the relatively hopeful note upon which Milton concludes his poem the dark and pessimistic visions of the Expulsion they had derived from Raphael and Masaccio, thus superimposing upon Milton's text a strong iconographic tradition which was part of their own natural heritage as visual artists, despite the fact that it contradicted Milton's text.

Unfortunate errors of this sort notwithstanding, as the eighteenth century progressed Milton's illustrators kept *Paradise Lost* quite literally before the public eye, a reminder that the poem had, according to Thomas Warton in 1785, "acquired the distinction of an English classic," thus demonstrating that England's literature and culture had matured.[41] The later eighteenth century was, as Newman notes, a time of unprecedented activity in the discovery and promotion of everything which might be seen to be a part of the "natural cultural heritage" which was so necessary to the growth of nationalism.[42] As this nationalistic fervor came to permeate art and culture at all levels, the illustration of Milton's epic—like both the reading and the public discussion of it—became part of a national "civic duty." Illustration did indeed help to keep alive, on the reduced scale of the illustrated book, both the didactic tradition of *istoria* and the ideal of a national school of distinctively English art, both verbal and visual, even as contemporary illustrated editions of Shakespeare and of English histories like Rapin's and Hume's were doing. But it was the powerful convergence of the "epic" and the "English" that lent such distinction to *Paradise Lost* for the English reader and critic. Milton's illustrators functioned, in the final analysis, both to popularize and to propagandize the epic, even as in setting out to visualize it they inevitably became its interpreters as well. In the process, they reminded readers and viewers that although the author of the greatest English epic grew daily more distant from their own rapidly changing times, he still spoke compellingly to perennial concerns.

University of Nebraska

NOTES

1. Joseph Burke, *English Art: 1714–1800* (Oxford, 1976), pp. 257, 96. See also Larry Silver, "Step-Sister of the Muses: Painting as Liberal Art and Sister Art," in *Articulate Images: The Sister Arts from Hogarth to Tennyson*, ed. Richard Wendorf (Minneapolis, 1983), pp. 58–59.

2. See Marcia R. Pointon, *Milton and English Art* (Toronto, 1970), p. xxxii, and Ronald Paulson, *Book and Painting: Shakespeare, Milton, and the Bible: Literary Texts and the Emergence of English Painting* (Knoxville, Tenn., 1982).

3. Barbara Kiefer Lewalski, *"Paradise Lost" and the Rhetoric of Literary Forms* (Princeton, N.J., 1985), esp. chap. 1.

4. Dustin Griffin, *Regaining Paradise: Milton and the Eighteenth Century* (Cambridge, 1986), p. ix; Harold Bloom, *The Anxiety of Influence: A Theory of Poetry* (New York, 1973), p. 32.

5. John Barrell, *The Political Theory of Painting from Reynolds to Hazlitt: 'The Body of the Public'* (New Haven, Conn., 1986), p. 18.

6. John Dillenberger, *Benjamin West: The Contest of His Life's Work, with Particular Attention to Paintings with Religious Subject Matter* (San Antonio, Tex., 1977), pp. 11–12.

7. Sir Joshua Reynolds, "Discourse Four" (1771), *Discourses on Art*, ed. Robert R. Wark (London, 1966), pp. 57–58.

8. Ann Uhry Abrams, *The Valiant Hero: Benjamin West and Grand-Style History Painting* (Washington, D.C., 1985), pp. 15–16. Charles Alphonse DuFresnoy's *De Arte Graphica* (1695) was translated into English by Dryden in 1695 and again by William Mason in 1778, for an edition with annotations by Joshua Reynolds. Shaftesbury's "Essay on Paint-

ing[,] Being a Notion of the Historical Draught or Tablature of the Judgment of Hercules" appeared in 1714, and Richardson's *Essay on the Theory of Painting* in 1725.

9. Abrams, *The Valliant Hero*, p. 15.

10. Burke, *English Art*, p. 246.

11. From a review of Kedington's *Critical Dissertations Upon the Iliad*, published in the *Critical Review* (January 1760) and reprinted in *The Complete Works of Oliver Goldsmith*, 5 vols. (Oxford, 1966), vol. 1, p. 217.

12. In his important early article on this phenomenon, Edgar Wind, "The Revolution of History Painting," *Journal of the Warburg Institute*, II (1938–39), 116–27, observed that while the academicians refused to depict ordinary men as heroes, a new generation of historians that included Gibbon, Hume, and Voltaire "refused to believe in heroes who could not be depicted as ordinary men."

13. Nakedness also bore symbolic significance for the antinomian tradition. If clothing was associated with the Fall and with shame and guilt, then to put off one's garments was to reject the old and unregenerate self and to assert the new and regenerate which had in fact been inherent all along but covered and obscured by the Fall. See J. C. F. Harrison, *The Second Coming: Popular Millenarianism, 1780–1850* (New Brunswick, N.J., 1979), p. 18.

14. Griffin, *Regarding Paradise*, p. 22.

15. Lewalski, *The Rhetoric of Literary Forms*, p. 22.

16. "Apology for Smectymnuus," in *John Milton: Complete Poems and Major Prose*, ed. Merritt Y. Hughes (New York, 1957), p. 694.

17. *The Reason of Church Government*, in Hughes, p. 668.

18. Griffin, *Regaining Paradise*, p. 33, and Paulson, *Book and Painting*, p. 5. John Sunderland remarks on this phenomenon in the visual arts in *Painting in Britain: 1525 to 1975* (New York, 1976), pp. 33–34.

19. K. R. Minogue, *Nationalism* (Baltimore, 1970), p. 27.

20. Gerald Newman, *The Rise of English Nationalism: A Cultural History 1740–1830* (New York, 1987), p. 127.

21. See Griffin, *Regaining Paradise*, p. 35.

22. William Hayley, *The Life of George Romney, Esq.* (Chichester, England, 1809), p. 110.

23. William L. Pressly, *The Life and Art of James Barry* (New Haven, Conn., 1981), p. 152; Pointon, *Milton and English Art*, p. 63.

24. James Holly Hanford, *A Milton Handbook*, 4th ed. (New York, 1946), p. 345.

25. *The Complete Poetical Works of Percy Bysshe Shelley*, ed. Thomas Hutchinson, rev. G. W. Matthews (Oxford, 1970), p. 206; preface to *Prometheus Unbound*. *The Complete Poetry and Prose of William Blake*, rev. ed., ed. David V. Erdman (Garden City, N.Y., 1982), p. 35; *The Marriage of Heaven and Hell*, plate 6.

26. See Stephen C. Behrendt, *The Moment of Explosion: Blake and the Illustration of Milton* (Lincoln, Neb., 1983).

27. Griffin, *Regaining Paradise*, p. 50, observes that his own comment to this effect echoes the eighteenth-century views of commentators like Horace Walpole, Thomas Blackwell, Hugh Blair, and Lord Kames.

28. Simon Wilson, *British Art from Holbein to the Present Day* (London, 1979), p. 57.

29. See Newman, *The Rise of English Nationalism*, p. 120, where this shift is viewed as part of the whole phenomenon of the nationalistic search for a distinct cultural identity.

30. Hughes, p. 652; annotations to Reynolds, *Discourses on Art*.

31. See Edward Croft-Murray, *Decorative Painting in England, 1537–1837*, 2 vols. (Feltham, Middlesex, 1970), vol. II, p. 36.

32. See Abrams, *The Valiant Hero*, p. 106.

33. Daniel Webb, *An Inquiry Into the Beauties of Painting . . . and Into the Merits of the Most Celebrated Painters, Ancient and Modern* (London, 1761); cited in Abrams, *The Valiant Hero*, p. 123.

34. Pressly, *James Barry*, p. 113.

35. See Morton Paley, *The Apocalyptic Sublime* (New Haven; Conn., 1986), p. 2, and Nancy L. Pressly, *Revealed Religion: Benjamin West's Commissions for Windsor Castle and Fonthill Abbey* (San Antonio, Tex., 1983), esp. pp. 28–32.

36. See Joseph Anthony Wittreich, *Visionary Poetics: Milton's Tradition and His Legacy* (San Marino, Calif.: 1979), p. 34.

37. Hayley, *George Romney*, p. 212.

38. Ibid., pp. 210–11.

39. Abrams, *The Valiant Hero*, pp. 123, 127.

40. David Hume, *The History of England* (London, 1806).

41. Thomas Warton, *Poems on Several Occasions* (London, 1785), p. 589; Griffin, *Regaining Paradise*, p. 35.

42. Newman, *The Rise of English Nationalism*, p. 112.

AGAINST THE WILES OF THE DEVIL: CARLOTTA PETRINA'S CHRISTOCENTRIC ILLUSTRATIONS OF *PARADISE LOST*

Lloyd F. Dickson

T HOUGH HER ILLUSTRATIONS of *Paradise Lost* have been noted by a number of Milton scholars, little biographical informa-tion is available about Carlotta Petrina, who completed twelve master-ful plates for an edition of the epic published in 1936 by John Henry Nash for the Limited Editions Club of San Francisco. Petrina studied in the late twenties and early thirties in New York at the Art Students League and the Cooper Union Art School. Besides *Paradise Lost*, she illustrated *The Aeneid, South Wind*, and *Henry VI*. During the late for-ties and early fifties, Petrina exhibited at the Salon d'Automne in Paris, the Art Institute of Chicago, and the Pennsylvania Academy of Fine Arts. In 1952, La Finestra in Rome featured her work in a solo exhibition.[1]

Petrina's illustrations demonstrate her thorough knowledge of the epic's biblical traditions and allusions. Her work is more than mere decora-tion; it constitutes a thoroughly christocentric interpretation of the epic, centering on the works of God the Father and his Son, with special focus on Christ's roles as mediator, soldier, and savior. Her unique illustration of Christ's intercession for Adam and Eve in Books X and XI deserves special attention.

In the opening illustration (fig. 1), Petrina portrays Satan as a tre-mendous titan, fearsome but helpless against divine power as he plunges hellward. This is the only illustration in which Petrina focuses on Satan, and it renders no royal honor to the Prince of Demons. Just prior to the expulsion, Milton's Satan enjoys brief glory battling Michael and the heavenly host, but, as Stella Purce Revard states in her excellent study of Satan as an epic hero: "After this brief and splendid moment of angelic duel the war swiftly deteriorates and, what is more signifi-cant, Satan never again rises to be an epic opponent." Revard also notes that "his fall is not glorious. He is driven with his angels in mass, like a herd of goats and timorous flocks."[2] Petrina's reading of Milton agrees with Revard's, and her illustrations never allow Satan a glorious mo-ment: Satan's preeminence here is purely by virtue of his position as the last fallen among the rebel angels, an ironic and ignominious kind of superiority. In the remaining illustrations, Satan appears only twice more.

Naked, bewildered, and shrieking in fright, Petrina's Satan here inspires more humor than awe. He is clearly no hero. His backward fall suggests helplessness and confusion, while the blackness above him suggests dark chaos fixed between heaven and hell. Other Milton illustrators, among them Francis Hayman, William Blake, J.M.W. Turner, and Gustave Doré include reminders of heavenly glory in their portrayals of the fall — radiant angels or bright clouds that accentuate Satan's loss. The only sign of divine presence in Petrina's illustration is a jagged bolt of lightning at upper left that points like a divine finger at Satan and the fateful lake of fire below. Petrina may have patterned her lightning after the bright arrows in Henry Aldrich's 1688 illustration of "Satan Rising from the Flood" that signify the various downward plunges of rebel angels. Francis Hayman and William Blake depict the falling Satan as a valiant soldier, resigned to accept his fate.[3] Hayman's Satan is haughty in his fall: grasping a broken spear in his right hand and making a fist with his left, he shakes his arms at Christ in rage and defiance. Blake's Satan, pensive and determined, looks bravely downward as he falls, while the lesser rebels writhe and scream in fright. Petrina's Satan exhibits no such defiance, bravery, or honor. His outstretched arms and contorted expression reveal his fear of the burning lake.

Petrina makes it clear that Satan loses much of his heavenly beauty even before he falls into the lake. With deeply furrowed brows, beady eyes, and flaring nostrils, Satan's face is savage and brutish. His ear is malformed, and his teeth are decayed. His disheveled wings cannot break the fall, suggesting the damage he sustained in heaven's battle. But Satan is not completely deformed; he retains magnificent musculature and bodily form. Petrina's rebel angels in Books VI and X have battle armor, but here in Book I they are naked as a sign of their shame in defeat.

Petrina conflates Satan's fall and that of the other rebel angels, showing demons on the beach who have already roused themselves and escaped the "Adamantine chains and penal fire" (I, 48).[4] In Milton's text, however, Satan is the first of the spirits to recover from the fall; he rises above the fiery flood to call his legions to order (I, 300). The chronological conflation allows Petrina simultaneously to focus on Satan in midair and to show the agonies of angels strewn about the shore, "confounded though immortal" (I, 53). Two of the angels on the left bank appear to be fighting their way out of the lake of fire. Others, lying or kneeling on the bank, resemble Milton's lofty simile: "Angel Forms, who lay intrans't / Thick

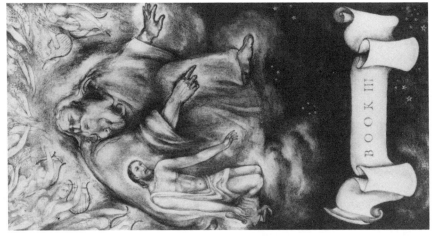

Figure 1

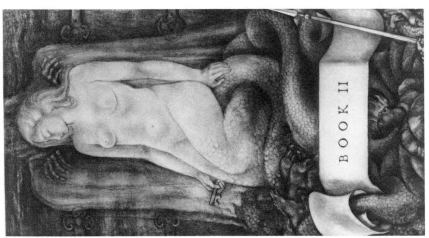

Figure 2

Figure 3

as Autumnal Leaves that strow the Brooks / In Vallombrosa, where th'
Etrurian shades / High overarch't imbow'r" (I, 301–03).

Leaping flames form a background to Petrina's pool of black fire,
effectively illustrating Milton's "darkness visible" (I, 63). Along the left
bank of the dark pool a subtle reflection of the shore, barely visible, suggests the strange hellish "light in darkness." This captivating idea was
not original with Milton. As John Steadman tells us, "That Hellfire sheds
no light was a theological commonplace, well-known to Milton's contemporaries; and various other English writers of his century allude to
it." Among the early church fathers who preached on the qualities of
hell's fire is St. Gregory the Great, who held that hellfire "denies light
for consolation, but provides it for greater suffering."[5]

No doubt Milton knew these contemporary views, but his descriptions of hell most often echo the Old Testament. Milton was well acquainted with the concept of Sheol (the grave), the Hebrew parallel to
the New Testament Greek concept of Hades. Job, in his depths of despair,
described Sheol as "a land of darkness, as darkness itself; and of the shadow
of death, without any order, and where the light is as darkness" (Job x,
22). In Petrina's illustration, this strange fire, flowing "black and deep"
toward the distant flames of the burning lake, also suggests Milton's debt
to the classics:

> Of four infernal Rivers that disgorge
> Into the burning Lake their baleful streams;
> Abhorred Styx the flood of deadly hate,
> Sad Acheron of sorrow, black and deep;
> Cocytus nam'd of lamentation loud
> Heard on the rueful stream; fierce Phlegeton
> Whose waves of torrent fire inflame with rage.   (II, 575–81)

On the far shore of the black river or pool, "doleful shades" appear,
demons who have pulled themselves from the Stygian water. Just below
the banner, other angels lie still half-submerged in dark liquid fire,
senseless from the impact of their fall. Several of the fallen angels in the
foreground appear feminine, in keeping with Milton's reference to "those
male / These feminine" (I, 422–23). One lies prostrate with wings broken
apart, a sign of the full rupture with heavenly purity. Every aspect of
Petrina's illustration communicates the catastrophic nature of the angelic
fall. Even the banner displaying the book number indicates the violence
of the fall, for its edges are serrated, flamelike. The remaining banners,
except in Book XII, are full and unfurling.

Artists who attempt to let the text of Book II guide them face a dif-

Figure 5

Figure 6

Figure 4

ficult challenge in illustrating Milton's somewhat vague personifications of Sin and Death. Petrina fares better than many, especially in her portrayal of Sin (fig. 2). Her illustration is notable for its avoidance of a dramatic moment which Marcia Pointon called "the most popular single scene with later artists": the confrontation between Satan and Death.[6] Petrina probably noted other artists' difficulties with the confrontation. J. Gilray's illustration of the scene falls so far below the grandeur of Milton's text that it appears comic. And one wonders if Gilray did not mean it so, for the conflict is funny: Satan and Death exchange a vociferous barrage of ridiculous insults. Petrina may have wished to avoid confusion and thus chose instead to focus on the ravishing figure of Sin.

Petrina presents Sin as a sensual, seductive woman with flowing hair, a serene and beautiful face, voluptuous breasts, and perfectly formed limbs. Her kneeling posture falsely suggests humility and submission. Sin as a seductress is a common biblical image that Milton drew upon for his personification in Book II. Proverb, chapter vi, verse 23, warns against the seductress, and Proverb, chapter vii suggests that the way a harlot seduces a young man is similar to how sin entices a simple and foolish man, "till a dart strike through his liver as a bird hasteth to the snare, and knoweth not that it is for his life" (23). The great whore of Revelation, chapter xvii, is a symbol of sin, "with whom the kings of the earth have committed fornication" (2). Milton clearly describes Sin's attractive feminine attributes, but his description of the bestial nether parts is vague and particularly troublesome for artists:

> She seem'd a Woman to the waist, and fair,
> But ended foul in many a scaly fold
> Voluminous and vast, a Serpent arm'd
> With mortal sting: about her middle round
> A cry of Hell Hounds never ceasing bark'd
> With Cerebean mouths full loud, and rung
> A hideous peal: yet, when they list, would creep,
> If aught disturb'd thir noise, into her womb.   (II, 650–57)

Metaphorically the serpent connection with sin is obvious, but Milton even makes it natural (in the biological sense), for Sin is the daughter of Satan and shares his evil attributes. The problem of showing where woman ends and serpentine limbs begin has plagued many illustrators. Aldrich's 1688 depiction provides no evidence of transformation: Sin looks merely like a woman seated among a throng of snakes. Petrina deemphasizes the serpentine nature of Sin's nether parts, but very plainly depicts the transformation. The folds of her serpentine members fill the lower

Figure 9

Figure 8

Figure 7

third of the illustration, suggesting the immanent nature of sin. The snaky coils even wrap around the banner. The howling curs, offspring of Sin's rape by Death, do not, as in the text, issue forth from Sin's loins, but stride among the serpentine folds. In her right hand, Sin holds the key to the gates of hell. On either side of Sin, at shoulder and waist heights, hang the massive hinges of hell's gate.

In this illustration Petrina allows Satan a minimal appearance. Entering from the bottom, he rises to the gates from the bowels of hell and gapes upward at Sin in admiration and awe. Satan's position suggests that Petrina has symbolically relegated him: at the feet of Sin, Satan looks more like a subject than a king. Little of Satan's body is visible, but we can see that he holds a large spear in his left hand and grips a large shield in his right, ready for his confrontation with Death.

Milton's Death has inspired depictions ranging from skeletons to ogres. This great variety is understandable, for Milton's description of Death is nebulous:

> The other shape,
> If shape it might be call'd that shape had none
> Distinguishable in member, joint, or limb,
> Or substance might be call'd that shadow seem'd,
> For each seem'd either; black it stood as Night.
> Fierce as ten Furies, terrible as Hell,
> And shook a dreadful Dart; what seem'd his head
> The likeness of a Kingly Crown had on.   (II, 666–73)

Petrina's Death is a semitransparent shade, scarcely discernible. Sin partially hides his head and body, but we can see his crossed arms and bony hands which suggest rapaciousness and insatiable hunger. Petrina simplifies the problem of depicting a formless body by providing Death with an obscuring cloak. Far from being the "King of Terrors" (as Addison nicknamed him), Death crouches behind Sin, inactive. We see none of Death's fierceness or awe-inspiring fury, and his "likeness of a Kingly Crown" is not visible because the top of his head extends beyond the top of the illustration.

Book III is of key importance to Milton's purpose "to assert Eternal Providence / And justify the ways of God to men" (I, 24–25), taking us into the Holy of Holies to witness the Heavenly Council as it develops the divine plan to punish sin, exalt Christ, and redeem mankind through supernatural means. It is both the theological and dramatic center of Milton's epic, focusing on the dialogue between the Father and the Son. Irene Samuel has suggested that the dialogue between Father and Son

Figure 12

Figure 11

Figure 10

may be a kind of cosmic debate about the destiny of mankind.[7] In Samuel's view, Christ's words mark "the distinctive tones of a quite different voice" from the Father. Petrina's illustration suggests such a debate between the Father and the Son.

We recall that the Father initiates the dialogue when he observes Satan "coasting the wall of Heav'n on this side Night" (III, 71) en route to Paradise: "Him God beholding from his prospect high, / Wherein past, present and future he beholds, / Thus to his only Son foreseeing spake" (III, 77–79). Petrina's God has an angry brow and eyes and a severe mouth (fig. 3). With his right hand, the Father points accusingly at the "ingrate" man, soon to fall. Despite his foreknowledge, God burns in anger at the weakness of his children:

> Man will heark'n to his [Satan's] glozing lies,
> And easily transgress the sole Command,
> Sole pledge of his obedience: So will fall
> Hee and his faithless progeny: whose fault?
> Whose but his own? ingrate, he had of mee
> All he could have; I made him just and right,
> Sufficient to have stood, though free to fall
>
> .   .   .   .
>
>   They therefore as to right belong'd,
> So were created, nor can justly accuse
> Thir maker, or thir making, or thir Fate;
> As if Predestination over-rul'd
> Thir will dispos'd by absolute Decree
> Or high foreknowledge; they themselves decreed
> Thir own revolt, not I: if I foreknew,
> Foreknowledge had not influence on thir fault,
> Which had no less prov'd certain unforeknown.
>
>   (III, 93–99, 111–19)

The Father's fierce expression and pointing finger reflect his anger and the pronouncement of sin's catastrophic penalty. Looking at the Father in Petrina's illustration, we can almost hear him say as he points at Adam: "Die hee or Justice must" (III, 210). Like Milton, Petrina draws upon Old Testament tradition in depicting God the Father as judge of the universe. He towers above Christ, and his white hair and beard give him a sage, timeless appearance—this is the God of Abraham, Isaac, and Jacob, the God of the Old Testament.

Christ, in "meek aspect" (III, 266), accomplishes his first intermediary act between God and mankind, compassionately pleading man's case before the Father:

> For should Man finally be lost, should Man
> Thy creature late so lov'd, thy youngest Son
> Fall circumvented thus by fraud, though join'd
> With his own folly? that be from thee far,
> That far be from thee, Father, who art Judge
> Of all things made, and judgest only right.   (III, 150–55)

Petrina shows Christ at the right hand of the Father in the human form common to the Western tradition, clad in tunic with dark mustache and beard. This representation emphasizes Christ's intimate connection with humanity and points toward the incarnation. Since Christ has a halo and the Father does not, he is obviously the focus of the illustration. The contrast between Father and Son points to differences in the Old and New covenants: the Father's severe Mosaic law versus Christ's gospel of love and merciful redemption. Christ's loose garment suggests a towel, such as the one he uses to teach service to his disciples (John xiii, 4; xii–xiv). Christ's kneeling posture also suggests service. Petrina's portrayal of Christ as servant is particularly astute, for Christ's servanthood is closely associated biblically with the incarnation: "Who, being in the form of God, thought it not robbery to be equal with God: But made himself of no reputation, and took upon him the form of a servant, and was made in the likeness of men" (Phil. ii, 6–7). Christ's meek expression, together with the outstretched palms, suggest the meekness with which Christ would face the malefactors prior to his crucifixion. Petrina shows the Son with hands outstretched in a gesture of blessing or healing.

The rich biblical allusion of Milton's text inspired Petrina to present an illustration of Book III that is amazingly like Daniel's prophetic vision of the exalted Son:

And the Ancient of Days [God the Father] did sit, whose garment was white as snow, and the hair of his head like the pure wool;

. . . .

I saw in the night visions, and, behold, one like the Son of Man [Christ] came with clouds of heaven, and came to the Ancient of Days, and they brought him near before him. And there was given him dominion, and glory, and a kingdom, that all people, nations, and languages should serve him: his dominion is an everlasting dominion, which shall not pass away, and his kingdom that which shall not be destroyed. (Dan. vii, 9: ix, 13–14)

Petrina's angels represent "all the Sanctities of Heaven" (III, 60) mentioned in Milton's text, the cherubim and seraphim, who ceaselessly await God's word. Since these spirits carry harps, it appears that Christ's ex-

altation and his appointment as Savior is at hand. Milton's angels react
musically to Christ's divine appointment:

> Then Crown'd again thir gold'n Harps they took,
> Harps ever tun'd that glittering by thir side
> Like Quivers hung, and with Preamble sweet
> Of charming symphony they introduce
> Thir sacred Song, and wake raptures high;
> No voice exempt, no voice but well could join
> Melodious part, such concord is in Heav'n.　　　(III, 365–71)

Several of the angels carry blossoms of the "Immortal Amarant" (III,
353) and wear crowns, trappings used to praise the new-appointed savior
of mankind:

> No sooner had th' Almighty ceas't, but all
> The multitude of Angels with a shout
> Loud as from numbers without number, sweet
> As from blest voices, uttering joy, Heav'n rung
> With Jubilee, and loud Hosannas fill'd
> Th' eternal Regions: lowly reverent
> Towards either Throne they bow, and to the ground
> With solemn adoration down they cast
> Thir Crowns inwove with Amarant and Gold,
> Immortal Amarant, a Flow'r which once
> In Paradise, fast by the Tree of Life
> Began to bloom, but soon for man's offense
> To Heav'n removed where first it grew, there grows
> And flow'rs aloft the Fount of Life.　　　(III, 344–57)

Beneath this joyous scene, stars shine dully in comparison with heaven's
glory. This is the human universe, the "pendant world" of man. Although
the earth is not visible, God's pointing finger signals that it is near.

From Heaven, Petrina descends to the garden of Book IV, where
love and harmony still reign (fig. 4). At center, Adam and Eve embrace
in simple, pure affection. Adam is as handsome and masculine as Eve
is beautiful and feminine. Adam's face is serene and contemplative, while
Eve's expresses tender love and adoration for her mate. Their features
and dark skin suggest their ethnic origins, in keeping with Milton's biblical geography which places the Garden of Eden between the Tigris and
Euphrates Rivers, in present-day Iraq. Flora abound in "wanton growth"
(IV, 629) as Eve suggests. Not yet frightened of man, the animals draw
close to Adam and Eve. The monkey pushes back a branch to look on
the lovers; a bird glides past Adam's right shoulder. This idyllic portrayal

of Eden emphasizes the innocence of the prelapsarian world. Petrina's scene seems a precise rendering of Milton's text:

> Under a tuft of shade that on a green
> Stood whispering soft, by a fresh Fountain side
> They sat them down,
> . . . .
> Nor gentle purpose, nor endearing smiles
> Wanted, nor youthful dalliance as beseems
> Fair couple, linkt in happy nuptial League,
> Alone as they. About them frisking play'd
> All Beasts of th' Earth.   (IV, 325–27, 337–41)

Just to the left of Adam and Eve are "two gentle Fawns" (IV, 404), symbolizing the tender innocence of the setting. One deer drinks from the pleasant waters, while the other's head rests upon its mate. The waters are adorned with lilies. Just behind Adam and Eve are

> All Trees of noblest kind for sight, smell, taste;
> And amid them all stood the Tree of Life,
> High eminent, blooming Ambrosial Fruit
> Of vegetable Gold.   (IV, 217–20)

Adam and Eve know not that Satan, in the form of a cormorant, has already defiled the garden with his presence. He sits among the branches of the Tree of Life and leers at the chaste dalliance of the lovers, "devising Death / To them who liv'd" (IV, 197–98). Again, Petrina portrays the calm before a storm. In Book II, Satan's conflict with Death was physical, but his confrontation with Adam and Eve here is spiritual. Just below the cormorant is a predatory cat that may also signify Satan's presence. We recall Milton's lines:

> Down he alights among the sportful Herd
> Of those fourfooted kinds, himself now one,
> Now other, as thir shape serv'd best his end
> Nearer to view his prey, and unespi'd
> To mark what of thir state he might more learn
> By word or action markt: about them round
> A Lion now he stalks with fiery glare,
> Then as a tiger, who by chance hath spi'd
> In some Purlieu two gentle Fawns at play,
> Straight couches close, then rising changes oft
> His couchant watch, as one who chose his ground
> Whence rushing he might surest seize them both
> Gript in each paw.   (IV, 396–408)

The only creature conspicuous in his absence is the serpent, of whom Milton says, "close the Serpent sly / Insinuating, wove with Gordian twine / His braided train, and of his fatal guile / Gave proof unheeded" (IV, 347–50).

Eve's troubling dream turns Petrina's focus from joyous dalliance to Book V's sober dinner interview with the angel Raphael (fig. 5). The couple's tender smiles and adoring glances are supplanted by an almost sullen, pensive mien. Eve gives little heed to her guest; she seems distracted by a vine. Adam, with an armful of fruit, is gravely attentive. This somber atmosphere seems strangely out of place within Eden. Petrina's scene is the bower, where flowers abound, but animals dare not enter, for "such was thir awe of Man" (IV, 705).

Jane M. Petty has studied extensively Book V's dream theme and finds a kind of "dream concourse" between angel and man: Adam recounts his creation and Eve's (events in Book VII), "divine acts which occurred while he slept"; Raphael in turn tells dreamlike stories of heaven's great war. Raphael's narrative is dreamlike in that he describes vivid scenes from his angelic memory by translating them into language comprehensible to the human mind. Raphael's face bears out this idea: as he looks at Adam and Eve, he gazes off in the manner of one in deep recollection.[8]

Raphael is magnificent in beauty and in size, as the tininess of the fruits in his hand suggests. Raphael's hugeness accentuates his God-given power and the importance of his mission to fulfill "All Justice" (V, 245). Northrop Frye calls Raphael a ministering spirit who instructs by acting as a model for humans.[9] Adam and Eve have little opportunity to see Raphael in action, but the seraph teaches by testifying to his own devotion:

> Myself and all th' Angelic Host that stand
> In sight of God enthron'd, our happy state
> Hold, as you yours, while our obedience holds;
> On other surety none; freely we serve,
> Because we freely love, as in our will
> To love or not; in this we stand or fall.   (V, 535–40)

Raphael's prominent halo suggests a special aegis of holiness placed upon him for the mission of instructing Adam and Eve. His mission is parallel to that given the Holy Spirit: he does not speak his own will, but the will of the Father. Speaking to his disciples, Christ said: "Howbeit when he, the Spirit of truth, is come, he will guide you into all truth; for he shall not speak of himself; but whatsoever he shall hear, that shall he speak; and he will show you things to come. He shall glorify me; for he shall receive of mine, and shall show it unto you" (John xvi, 13–14). Raphael is that "Spirit of truth" guiding Adam and showing "things to come" (temptations and trials) as Michael also does in more detail after the fall. Milton's text suggests that Raphael speaks under divine inspiration by referring to him as "the Godlike Angel" (VII, 110).

The fruits at the center of the illustration symbolize Eden's plenty and the perfection of God's provision. Raphael praises God's bounty in Eden and tells Adam: "For know, whatever was created, needs / To be sustain'd and fed" (V, 414–15). The meal functions as grounds for Adam's instruction, in keeping with Raphael's role as "the sociable spirit" (V, 221). Adam's instruction at the table proceeds with the flow of polite but serious conversation, eventually focusing on the similarities and problems of physical and mental appetites.

In her illustration of Book VI, Petrina portrays for the first time an ongoing physical fray (fig. 6). For Book I she showed Satan after battle, and for Book II she showed Satan prior to battle, but here Petrina shows the precise instant of Christ's magnificent victory in expelling Satan and the rebel angels. Christ's sudden intervention on the third day of celestial battle effects Satan's physical defeat in the heavenly realm much like Christ's resurrection on the third day after the crucifixion effects Satan's spiritual defeat in the earthly realm.

Behind Christ, the heavenly host, armed and on horses, stand in awe of the Son's power. Milton suggests the armor by referring to "Spears, and Helmets throng'd, and Shields" among the angels (VI, 83). The horses come not from the text but from John's vision of the apocalypse: "And I saw heaven opened, and behold a white horse; and he that sat upon him was called Faithful and True, and in righteousness he doth judge and make war. . . . And the armies which were in heaven followed him upon white horses, clothed in fine linen, white and clean" (Rev. xix, 11, 14). Petrina's scene prefigures the final battle at Armageddon and Christ's ultimate victory over Satan.

Although the archangel Michael plays an important part in the battle against Satan, Petrina does not allow him to stand out: Christ alone is worthy of glory. The prime focus on Christ in battle is important because it sets him apart physically and functionally from the other fighters. Stella Purce Revard points out that Christ appears climactically as "more than champion and general" in this heavenly battle: "He is the bodily fulfillment of God's Will."[10] Christ's victory is confirmation to angels and devils alike of God's wisdom in choosing to exalt the Son.

Petrina portrays the Son's awesome fierceness in battle. His face is set like flint against the rebels, with no sign of love or mercy. Christ's

ferocity in battle reinforces his unity with the Father and the accomplishment of the divine will. As he mounts the mighty chariot, Christ declares:

> Scepter and Power, thy giving, I assume
> And gladlier shall resign, when in the end
> Thou shalt be All in All, and I in thee
> For ever, and in mee all whom thou lov'st;
> But who thou hat'st, I hate, and can put on
> Thy terrors, as I put thy mildness on,
> Image of thee in all things.   (VI, 730–36)

Petrina's Christ has indeed "put on terrors." Light pours from his head
and cape, and he stretches forth his mighty arms to thrust the rebels out.
From his outstretched left hand, balls of fire shoot forth into the routed
crew: "and from about him fierce Effusion roll'd / Of smoke and bicker-
ing flame, and sparkles dire" (VI, 765–66). Christ's armor illustrates his
role not only as savior but also as conqueror and vanquisher of Satan.
God the Father describes Christ's armor as he sends the Son to battle:

> Go then thou Mightiest in thy Father's might,
> Ascend my Chariot, guide the rapid Wheels
> That shake Heav'n's basis, bring forth all my War,
> My Bow and Thunder, my Almighty Arms
> Gird on, and Sword upon thy puissant Thigh.   (VI, 710–14)

The main accoutrements of battle are bow and sword, but Petrina
has ignored these weapons in favor of a more conventional Christian image: the armored warrior of God. Drawing from the Pauline tradition,
Petrina shows Christ as the embodiment of spiritual warfare: Ephesians,
chapter vi, verse 11, admonishes saints to "put on the whole armour of
God, that ye may be able to stand against the wiles of the devil," and
chapter vi, verses 14 to 17, catalogs the armor pieces: "Having your loins
girt about with truth, and having on the breastplate of righteousness;
and your feet shod with the preparation of the gospel of peace; above
all, taking the shield of faith, wherewith ye shall be able to quench all
the fiery darts of the wicked. And take the helmet of salvation, and the
sword of the Spirit, which is the word of God." Petrina may also have
had in mind the crusaders of the twelfth century, armored warriors who
sought to seize Jerusalem from unbelievers.

Christ's armor appears to be an ornate Milanese design of the sixteenth century.[11] The breastplate and the burgonet on Christ's head exhibit very precise metalwork. The detailed halo may actually be part
of the armor, for ornate helmets of sixteenth-century northern Italy often
were made with magnificent combs that resembled halos. The halo has

the design of the cross, which converges at Christ's head and suggests Christ's bodily presence on the center of Calvary's cross.

The cross appears also on Christ's breastplate, where it radiates holy light and signifies the special power of the radiant Urim that Milton mentions in his text: "Hee in Celestial Panoply all arm'd / Of radiant Urim, work divinely wrought" (VI, 760–61). Merritt Hughes (p. 341) notes: "The Urim are first mentioned in the Bible as something to be worn in Aaron's high-priestly 'breastplate of judgment' (Exod. xxviii, 30). Their radiance here is part of the symbolism of the spiritual light incarnate in the Son as God's judge and executioner." I would add that the New Testament links Christ and Aaron in their priestly offices, and the presence of the Urim upon Christ's breastplate also refers to his blood atonement as savior of mankind.

The Father's chariot (not Christ's, see VI, 711) is not completely visible in Petrina's illustration, but we can see that angels, spirits of flaming fire, are the wheels of the cart and also go before Christ as ensigns of his holy presence. These angels fit the description given by Milton, who apparently drew upon Ezekiel's Babylonian vision: "Also out of the midst thereof came the likeness of four living creatures. And this was their appearance; they had the likeness of a man. And every one had four faces, and every one had four wings" (Ezek. i, 5–6). Ezekiel's angels each had four different faces, those of a man, an ox, a lion and an eagle (Ezek. i, 10). Milton describes his forerunning angels as the "fourfold-visag'd Four, / Distinct with eyes, and from the living Wheels, / Distinct alike with multitude of eyes" (VI, 845–47), but mentions nothing of the spirit's faces. Petrina shows these spirits with identical faces, each face looking in one of the four directions. Two of these fourfold spirits run before the chariot, and another appears on the side, ablaze and spinning as the chariot's left wheel. Ezekiel also mentions the presence of eyes upon the chariot, which Petrina shows on the rim of the left wheel. The eyes suggest the omniscient or all-seeing nature of God.

Petrina's Christ pauses at the very wall of heaven, "which op'ning wide, / Roll'd inward, and a spacious gap disclos'd / Into the wasteful Deep" (VII, 860–62). Petrina also shows fallen angels at the very bottom of the illustration as if they have already rebounded upon the ground, senseless, with their ineffectual weapons and shields strewn about them. Petrina apparently conflates the scene (eliminating the nine-day fall of the routed angels) to contrast the glory of Christ with the ignominy of the fallen ones. Just to the right of the leading spirits, some of Satan's crew appear to be yet falling headlong toward hell.

Petrina's illustration of Book VII continues the theme of Christ's work, depicting his power in creation (fig. 7). For Book III, she showed Christ as intercessor and savior; for Book VI, as soldier and vanquisher of Satan; now she turns her attention to Christ as creator. The creation immediately follows the fall of Satan and his angels (see VII, 131–38), for upon Christ's victorious return God the Father plans the repair of heaven's decimated population through the creation of a race that may lend him obedience and thus obtain heaven. The Father entrusts Christ with this divine act of creation: "by thee / This I perform, speak thou, and be it done" (VII, 163–64). Milton's emphasis here is on Christ as the Word: "In the beginning was the Word and the Word was with God, and the Word was God. The same was in the beginning with God. All things were made by him; and without him was not any thing made that was made" (John i, 1–3).

Petrina's illustration suggests a simultaneous creative movement through chaos as Christ speaks the universe into existence. Raphael suggests this by telling Adam: "Immediate are the Acts of God, more swift / Than Time or Motion, but to human ears / Cannot without process of speech be told, / So told as earthly notion can receive" (VII, 176–79). Further support for simultaneous creation is Milton's description of newly created, yet fully mature plant life:

> He scarce had said, when the bare Earth, till then
> Desert and bare, unsightly, unadorn'd,
> Brought forth the tender Grass, whose verdure clad
> Her Universal Face with pleasant green,
> Then Herbs of every leaf, that sudden flow'r'd
> Op'ning thir various colors, and made gay
> Her bosom smelling sweet: and these scarce blown,
> Forth flourish'd thick the clust'ring Vine, forth crept
> The smelling Gourd, up stood the corny Reed
> Embattl'd in her field: and th' humble Shrub,
> And Bush with frizzl'd hair implicit: last
> Rose as in Dance the stately Trees, and spread
> Thir branches hung with copious Fruit: or gemm'd
> Thir Blossoms: with high Woods the Hills were crown'd,
> With tufts the valleys and each fountain side,
> With borders long the Rivers.   (VII, 313–28)

Petrina's swirl of creation conflates the traditional six days into one harmonious instant. The very transformation from ethereal vapor to earthly substance occurs in the counterclockwise movement of the swirl: vapor gradually becomes half-formed beasts. We see mammals and plants, but no fowl and sea creatures. Man is at the center of the illustration, a position symbolic of his dominion over the animals: "Not prone / And Brute as other Creatures, but endu'd / With Sanctity of Reason" (VII, 506–08). Arms and legs wrapped tightly, Adam sleeps in a fetal position.

The lesser lights of the stars and a crescent moon appear at lower left, but in the upper right corner Petrina depicts glowing light in a way that resembles a sunrise. Since the ethereal vapors seem to originate from this far horizon, the light may indeed be the "Son" sending forth his powers of creation. The vapors come forth from and return to this distant light.

In Book VIII, Petrina continues illustrating creation (fig. 8), returning to a depiction of God the Father as he forms Eve from Adam's rib. Portrayed much as he appeared for Book III's Heavenly Council, the Father gently opens Adam's side and "under his forming hands a Creature grew, / Manlike, but different sex, so lovely fair" (VIII, 470–71). Petrina shows God in the very act of forming Eve: though her body appears complete, her eyes are dull and empty, suggesting that God has not yet endowed her with the "breath of life," or sentience. This act of creation is portrayed as intimate and tender, whereas the depiction of Christ's creation of the universe seems impersonal, holding little suggestion of the deity's love. Perhaps the tenderness of the Father's creation of Eve, as portrayed by Petrina, can be attributed to Adam's adoring dream narrative of the event, for Adam relates that after speaking to the Creator of his heart's desire for a mate, he, "dazzl'd and spent, sunk down, and sought repair / Of sleep, which instantly fell on me" (VIII, 457–58). God privileges Adam with seeing Eve's creation in a kind of dream vision:

> Mine eyes he clos'd, but op'n left the Cell
> Of Fancy my internal sight, by which
> Abstract as in a trance methought I saw,
> Though sleeping, where I lay, and saw the shape
> Still glorious before whom awake I stood;
> Who stooping op'n'd my left side, and took
> From thence a Rib with cordial spirits warm.   (VIII, 460–66)

God does not retain the angry countenance from Book III's illustration when he contemplated the fall of his "ingrate" creatures; instead, he is now pleased that, in fulfillment of divine will, Adam has requested a helpmate. Adam recounts the good-natured dialogue between himself and the deity: "And the vision bright, / As with a smile more bright'n'd, thus replied" (VIII, 367–68); and again, "Whereto th' Almighty answer'd, not displeased" (VIII, 398). God is still clad in the white robe seen in the earlier illustration, but he drapes it across his left knee to free himself for the delicate work of forming Eve.

It seems significant that Milton places Adam's creation outside the Garden, while Eve is created within Paradise. This subtle geography suggests that Eve, like the other pleasures in Eden, is created for Adam's delight, whereas Adam, as the first created human, is created for God's delight. In an account of his first day on earth, Adam tells how he saw (again in a kind of dream vision) his flight to "the Garden of bliss":

> One came, methought, of shape Divine,
> And said, thy Mansion wants thee, *Adam*, rise,
>
> . . . .
>
> So saying, by the hand he took me rais'd,
> And over Fields and Waters, as in Air
> Smooth sliding without step, last led me up
> A woody Mountain; whose high top was plain.
>
> (VIII, 295–96, 300–03)

This "high top" appears to be the spot in Eden that Petrina chose for her depiction of Eve's creation.

Petrina's illustration of Eve being drawn from Adam's side suggests eternally ordained religious and societal covenants: Eve's creation signifies the nuptial covenant that is to be practiced by all mankind. Literally, Eve and Adam are "one Flesh," for she is created from Adam's rib; symbolically, they are "one Flesh" by wedded union (VIII, 499). Milton reiterates the nuptial injunction from Genesis, chapter ii, verse 24: "Therefore shall a man leave his father and his mother, and shall cleave unto his wife: and they shall be one flesh." The Old Testament considers the nuptial covenant confirmed by Adam and Eve an indispensable part of God's plan for the development of human society.

Adam gives not only the account of Eve's creation and his subsequent marriage to her, but also exposes his weakness for her beauty:

> Here only weak
> Against the charm of Beauty's powerful glance.
> Or Nature fail'd in mee, and left some part
> Not proof enough such Object to sustain,
> Or from my side subducting, took perhaps
> More than enough; at least on her bestow'd
> Too much Ornament, in outward show
> Elaborate, of inward less exact.   (VIII, 532–39)

The dark background of Petrina's illustration of Eve's creation suggests coming sorrows.

Sorrow comes to fruition in book IX as Adam and Eve fall prey to their weaknesses: Eve to the alluring beauty of the tree and the charms of the serpent, Adam to the charms of Eve. Petrina chooses to focus on Eve's particular sorrow (fig. 9), portraying her as a solitary weeper in a forlorn new world of woes. Petrina transforms Eden's geography to communicate the universal devastation caused by original sin and to signify the sorrow Eve feels as a result of it. The garden, heretofore filled with "goodliest trees loaden with fairest fruit" (IV, 147), becomes a barren wasteland. "That new world of light and bliss" (II, 867) grows dark and desolate in response to sin. Barrenness and darkness signify the depth of the wound, which goes beyond merely human ramifications: God's pendant world is forever changed by sin.

Petrina, like Gustave Doré, uses landscape effectively to convey tone and atmosphere. Doré's engravings feature magnificent geographical panoramas that set the mood for each scene and create in the reader expectations as to the course of events, whether good or bad. Doré's illustration for Book VIII shows Raphael ascending to heaven, resplendently bathed in light, but encircling Eden are huge, dark clouds, foreshadowing the sorrows of Book IX. His six plates for Book IX all have suggestive, brooding topography. In his final illustration of Book IX, Doré shows Adam and Eve after both have sinned, clad in withered leaves and standing with frustrated expressions beside an enormous barren tree. Behind this large tree is a forest similarly defoliated, but veiled in darkness.

Although Doré's illustrations may have influenced Petrina's design for Book IX, the text itself suggests that Nature feels sympathy and empathizes with the fallen pair. We recall that when Eve reached forth her hand to pluck the fruit and "feed at once both Body and Mind" (IX, 779), "Earth felt the wound, and Nature from her seat / Sighing through all her Works gave signs of woe, / That all was lost" (IX, 782–84). Even Adam, yet sinless, "the falt-ring measure felt" (IX, 846) when sin leapt into the world. Adam does not know exactly what has occurred, but he worries about his mate. The flowers, best sign of Eden's beauty and perfect peace, also tremble at sin. As Adam meets Eve and hears her sad story, "From his slack hand the Garland wreath'd for *Eve* / Down dropp'd, and all the faded Roses shed" (IX, 892–93). Adam's sin elicits a similar pathetic reaction from nature:

> Earth trembl'd from her entrails, as again
> In pangs, and Nature gave a second groan,
> Sky low'r'd, and muttering Thunder, some sad drops
> Wept at completing of the mortal Sin
> Original.   (X, 1000–04)

Petrina's Eve bows her head in shame and hides her face, wherein lie "the signs / Of foul concupiscence" (IX, 1077–78). She now knows misery, "death's harbinger" (IX, 13). For C. S. Lewis, as for Petrina, Eve is the focus of Eden's guilt because she brings death to the world. Lewis impugns Eve's motive for giving Adam the fruit: "I am not sure that the critics always notice the precise sin which Eve is now committing, but there is no mystery about it. Its name in English is Murder."[12] Eve's misery is even more acute in the light of her earlier boast that she could repulse the tempter and bring him shame should he attempt to seduce her (IX, 378–84).

Petrina's portrayal of Eve calls to mind the scene in Book IX when Satan sees her working along among the flowers which "Hung drooping unsustain'd, them gently she upstays / Gently with Myrtle band, mindless the while, / Herself, though fairest unsupported Flow'r, / From her best prop so far, and storm so nigh" (IX, 430–33). After the sin occurs, Adam compares Eve to the denuded flowers: "How art thou lost, how on a sudden lost, / Defac't, deflow'r'd, and now to Death devote?" (IX, 900–01).

Behind Eve, a gloomy mountain looms, bearing a lone, defoliated tree which appears dead. This is Petrina's rendering of the Tree of Knowledge after it has been ravaged by Eve. In the distant background of the illustration, clouds gather as for a coming storm. Sin has upset Eden's gentle climate. The gathering clouds are outward evidence of the emotional storms within Adam and Eve:

> They sat them down to weep, nor only Tears
> Rain'd at thir Eyes, but high Winds worse within
> Began to rise, high Passions, Anger, Hate,
> Mistrust, Suspicion, Discord, and shook sore
> Thir inward State of Mind, calm region once
> And full of Peace, now toss't and turbulent.   (IX, 1121–26)

Likewise, the outward darkness of Eden also parallels the inward darkness fallen upon Adam and Eve by their forbidden knowledge. After consuming sexual pleasure through new-discovered lust they sleep but soon awake:

> As from unrest, and each the other viewing,
> Soon found thir Eyes how op'n'd, and thir minds
> How dark'n'd; innocence, that as a veil
> Had shadow'd them from knowing ill, was gone,
> Just confidence, and native righteousness,
> And honor from about them, naked left
> To guilty shame.   (IX, 1052–58)

Just in front of Petrina's Eve is a misty collection of moisture on the ground, suggesting Eve's tears or those "sad drops" from the sky. The misty appearance of the moisture brings to mind Satan's subtle return to Eden: "thus wrapt in mist / Of midnight vapor [I] glide obscure" (IX, 158–59). This vaporlike moisture seems to fit well into nature's foreboding darkness. Merritt Hughes finds the satanic mist a key foreshadowing image: "Book IX is keyed for the act of darkness by the opening scenes of Satan's second entry into Eden at midnight and of his quest — 'wrapt in mist / Of midnight' — for the serpent in which he must 'incarnate and imbrute' his essence."[13]

Petrina's illustration for Book X (fig. 10) is a unique interpretation of events because she conflates scenes from Eden and hell, and she presents Christ in an angelic theophany. Her continuing focus is the work of Christ. Here he is divine judge and priest. As judge, he confronts Adam and Eve with their sin and immediately punishes Satan and his hellish fiends with a humiliating delusion. As priest, Christ covers Adam and Eve in his arms and in his redemptive robe. At upper left, Petrina portrays one small corner of Eden, where a holy being overlooks a pit of confused demons. This winged spirit is the theophany of Christ mourning Adam and Eve's tragic sin. Christ has descended at God's request: "But whom send I to judge them? whom but thee / Vicegerent Son, to thee I have transferr'd / All Judgment, whether in Heav'n, or Earth, or Hell" (X, 55–57).

According to Milton's text, this angelic form must be Christ, for immediately after the Fall, "Up into Heav'n from Paradise in haste / Th' Angelic Guards ascended, mute and sad" (X, 17–18), fleeing sin's taint. Christ only was left with Adam and Eve. Milton does not describe the descending Christ in angelic form, but Petrina's rendering draws from Old Testament descriptions of theophanies, whereby Christ appeared as the "Angel of the Lord." The presence of God is called "the angel of the Lord" in theophanies seen by Abraham (Gen. xxii), Hagar (Gen. xvi), Balaam (Num. xxii), Joshua (Judg. ii), and many other Old Testament characters. C. I. Scofield, in his Bible annotations, provides an explanation of this Hebrew phrase: "In the O.T. expression 'the angel of the Lord' (sometimes 'of God') usually implies the presence of Deity in angelic form (Gen. xvi, 1–3; xxi, 17–19; xxii, 11–16; xxxi, 11–13; Ex. iii, 2–4; Jud. ii, 1; vi, 12–16; xiii, 3–22)."[14]

Christ's head is bowed in sorrow, and he embraces Adam and Eve, no longer naked, but now clothed in the lamb skins of redemption. The skins signify the shedding of blood for the remission of sin and foreshadow the crucifixion of Christ as the slain Lamb of God. Christ's intimate em-

brace of Adam and Eve signifies his deep love for mankind and the fullness of his redemption:

> Nor hee thir outward only with the Skins
> Of Beasts, but inward nakedness, much more
> Opprobrious, with his Robe of righteousness,
> Arraying cover'd from his Father's sight.   (X, 219–22)

At center, demons writhe in anger and pain after tasting bitter ashes
instead of succulent fruit from the Tree of Knowledge. Christ sends this
delusion to nullify Satan's pride in despoiling God's children of Paradise.
Petrina's demons are uglier than those she has heretofore shown, illustrating their continual descent from former glory. The armor, which
the demons lacked in the illustration for Book I, recalls the shame of
Satan's defeat in heaven. Satan is nowhere clearly visible in this illustration. Once again, Petrina has refused him a spotlight.

Serpentine limbs writhing in the throng show that Petrina's demons
are in the midst of their hideous transformation. Above them appears
the vision of:

> A Grove hard by, sprung up with this thir change,
> His will who reigns above, to aggravate
> Thir penance, laden with fair Fruit, like that
> Which grew in Paradise, the bait of Eve
> Us'd by the Tempter.   (X, 548–52)

Demons pass boughs of these trees among themselves, believing they are
about to ingest divine knowledge by eating the holy fruit. Through de-
vouring the fruit, the rapacious demons hope to gain greater advantage
in tormenting God. To thwart Satan's plans, God instructs Michael to
protect the trees of Paradise from demonic intruders and would-be tasters:

> guard all passage to the Tree of Life:
> Lest Paradise a receptacle prove
> To Spirits foul, and all my Trees thir prey,
> With whose stol'n Fruit Man once more to delude.   (XI, 122–25)

God protects the Tree of Knowledge from demonic plundering and gives
them instead this phantom fruit. A number of demons seen at the very
bottom of the illustration have already attempted to eat the delusive fruit
and are gnashing their hands and teeth in agony and rage, for when they
closed their mouths they "instead of Fruit / Chew'd bitter ashes" (X,
565–66).

A further suggestion of the serpentine nature of the demons appears in the area behind the imaginary grove. In a sealike expanse, many serpentine creatures raise their heads from the Stygian waters. Petrina appears to borrow demonic description from Book I, in which Satan is described as lifting his head above the waves of the fiery lake like "Leviathan, which God of all his works / Created hugest that swim th' Ocean stream" (I, 201–02). Leviathan, a term linked to Satan in Old Testament passages, has often been described as a type of sea monster or dragon. The prophet Isaiah foretells the destruction of this evil sea monster in the day of judgment: "In that day the Lord with his sore and great and strong sword shall punish leviathan the piercing serpent, even leviathan that crooked serpent; and he shall slay the dragon that is in the sea" (Isa. xxvii, 1).

In Book XI, Petrina continues her christocentric theme by retaining the theophany (fig. 11). Instead of portraying Michael according to Milton's text, Petrina conflates the angelic captain with the "Angel of the Lord" from her previous illustration. This central angelic figure functions both as Michael, in his role as prophetic seer, and as a theophany of Christ, in his role as intercessor. This claim is consistent with Milton's text and with Petrina's use of the theophany in Book X.

Since Petrina's careful attention to Milton's text has been demonstrated numerous times in earlier illustrations, her deviations from the text may be clues to her interpretation of the epic. Petrina's illustration of Book XI shows a very close reading of the text, yet she chooses to ignore Milton's precise description of Michael, who does not appear to Adam in angelic form:

> th' Arch-Angel soon drew nigh,
> Not in his shape Celestial, but as Man
> Clad to meet Man; over his lucid Arms
> A military Vest of purple flow'd;
>   . . . .
> His starry Helm unbuckl'd show'd him prime
> In Manhood where Youth ended; by his side
> As in a glistering *Zodiac* hung the Sword,
> Satan's dire dread, and in his hand the Spear.
>
> (XI, 238–41, 245–48)

Petrina's Michael is missing the sword, helmet, and military vest, and he is not "as Man / Clad to meet Man," that is, in human form. Her conflation of the angel Michael with a theophany endows the illustration with double meaning, and allows Petrina to retain a christocentric focus. Christ's role in Book XI is as "great Intercessor" (XI, 19), interpreting the prayers of Adam and Eve and presenting them to God the Father. In Petrina's illustration, the angelic being accomplishes this intercessory work: with hands uplifted, he presents these repentant "Sighs and Prayers" (XI, 23–24) to heaven.

Petrina illustrates the presence of God and his acceptance of these prayers by the traditional symbol of the Holy Spirit, the dove. The olive branches in the dove's beak suggest peace through God's acceptance of the prayers. The glowing arc in the sky suggests the rainbow, God's sign of the covenant he confirmed with Noah and postlapsarian mankind. In Ezekiel's vision, the rainbow was also a manifestation of God's presence: "As the appearance of the bow that is in the cloud in the day of rain, so was the appearance of the brightness round about. This was the appearance of the likeness of the glory of the Lord" (Ezek. i, 28).

The angelic spirit kneels, and with its enormous wings shields Adam, who bows in repentance and worship. Milton's Eve, whose eyes are drenched with sleep by the angel, lies at the bottom of the hill; she is not visible in Petrina's illustration. After his eyes are cleansed with holy Euphrasy, Adam views "supernal Grace contending / With sinfulness of Men" (XI, 359–60) from this promontory. The hilltop is a natural place for viewing mankind's future world, but height also suggests God's presence. Moses received God's law atop Mount Sinai, and Christ was transfigured atop the Mount of Olives.

Just to the right of the hill, there is an enactment of mankind's first murder. Adam's son Cain, enraged that God has rejected his sacrifice in favor of Abel's, hammers the fatal blow upon his brother. Behind them is the holy altar yet aflame with God's "propitious fire" (XI, 441), which consumed Abel's sacrificial lamb. Petrina rings the entire scene round about with fire, suggesting the passion which seized Cain.

Above this murder scene, there stands a large building which suggests the Tower of Babel, symbol of man's rebellious ecumenism and his renewed desire to be like God. The silhouetted figures just above this building further suggest that it is Babel, for the figures appear to be Nimrod (whose name means "rebel") and his crew:

> Hee with a crew, whom like Ambition joins
> With him or under him to tyrannize,
> Marching from *Eden* towards the West, shall find
> The Plain, wherein a black bituminous gurge
> Boils out from under ground, the mouth of Hell;
> Of Brick, and of that stuff they cast to build
> A City and a Tow'r, whose top may reach to Heav'n. (XII, 38–44)

Near those silhouetted figures is a volcano, spewing forth "bituminous gurge." This is the "mouth of Hell," from which Nimrod and his compeers fetch materials to build Babel. This rowdy crew goes about their violent deeds "with Dart and Jav'lin, Stones and sulphurous Fire" (XI, 658). A close look at the illustration reveals one silhouetted figure with a stone raised above his head as weapon, while other likewise dark figures run about with clubs upraised.

To the left of this scene lie the pyramids of Egypt, illustration of God's forsaking the heathen to form a chosen people, Israel. Those pyramids refer to the story of Joseph, who is often seen as a type of Christ in providing deliverance from famine for the Jews. But a new pharaoh who does not know Joseph seeks "to stop thir overgrowth, as inmate guests / Too numerous; whence of guests he makes them slaves / Inhospitably, and kills thir infant Males" (XII, 166–68). The pyramids also suggest the story of Moses, who delivers the Jews from slavery and is seen as a type of Christ who provides salvation. Milton's text supports this messianic reference by stating that "Moses in figure bears, to introduce / One greater, of whose day he shall foretell, / And all the Prophets in thir Age the times / Of great Messiah shall sing" (XII, 241–44).

Just below the pyramids, Petrina shows three crosses which signify Mount Golgotha and Christ's crucifixion. Raphael briefly narrates the events of the life of the messiah and points out that

> For this he shall live hated, be blasphem'd,
> Seiz'd on by force, judg'd, and to death condemn'd
> A shameful and accurst, nail'd to the Cross
> By his own Nation, slain for bringing Life;
> But to the Cross he nails thy enemies,
> The Law that is against thee, and the sins
> Of all mankind, with him there crucifi'd.   (XII, 411–17)

Below this scene, "Others to a City strong / Lay siege" (XI, 655–56), while armed horsemen take part in the "cruel Tournament" of war (XI, 652). At the foot of the mount, Petrina shows victims dead "By Fire, Flood, Famine, by Intemperance more / In Meats and Drinks, which on the Earth shall bring / Diseases dire" (XI, 472–74).

Petrina's final illustration for *Paradise Lost* (fig. 12) is one of dramatic beauty and symmetry. God's flaming sword, the archangel, and the Tree of Life all share the center of the illustration with the banished Adam and Eve. The angel, the sword, and the tree signify God's dispensations to man: the sword dispenses God's judgment; the angel serves God's sentence and comforts Adam and Eve; the tree symbolizes a future dispensation from God: eternal life.

The sword descends from heaven accompanied by holy fire, intimating that it has been sent by God the Father. As an instrument of justice, the sword parallels God's own magisterial word; it is the embodiment of God's sentence to banish Adam and Eve. The flaming sword is also an instrument of God's justice in John's apocalyptic vision: "And he had in his right hand seven stars: and out of his mouth went a sharp two-edged sword: and his countenance was as the sun shineth in his strength" (Rev. i, 16). Hebrews, chapter iv, verse 12, compares the Scriptures (God's word) with a two-edged sword that is "quick and powerful" and divides asunder the "soul and spirit." In the Scriptures, God's word is often accompanied by fire: the prophets Ezekiel, Daniel, Isaiah, and John received their messages from a God who manifested himself in fire and intense light; Moses was called from a burning bush; the Ten Commandments came down from a storm of lightning; God's word was put into the mouths of the apostles with "tongues of fire" (Acts ii).

In *Paradise Lost,* God's angels minister his will and bring to pass his judgments: Raphael descends to warn Adam and Eve of the temptation in order to "fulfill all justice," and Michael descends to lead Adam, both physically and mentally, away from the blameless perfection of Eden. Though it is his divine charge to dismiss man from Paradise, Michael also provides comfort at God's behest:

> Dismiss them not disconsolate; reveal
> To Adam what shall come in future days,
> As I shall thee enlighten, intermix
> My Cov'nant in the woman's seed renew'd;
> So send them forth, though sorrowing, yet in peace. (XI, 113–17)

"As I shall thee enlighten" indicates God's active guidance in Michael's narration. Just as Raphael expressed words and feelings from God, Michael gives hope to Adam under divine inspiration. Since the angel has served as God's oral amanuensis, Michael's countenance of displeasure and sadness at the banishment of Adam and Eve likely reflects God's own feelings about the event. Despite man's hope for the future, Michael is disturbed because he knows that man's dispossession from Paradise bodes future battles with the adversary.

In the fashion of Isaiah's vision, the nether parts of Michael and the other angels in this illustration are not visible because they are covered with an extra set of wings. Isaiah, chapter vi, verses 2 to 3: "Above [God's throne] stood the seraphim: each one had six wings; with twain he covered his face, and with twain he covered his feet, and with twain he did fly. And one cried unto another, and said, Holy, holy, holy, is the Lord of hosts: the whole earth is full of his glory." The angels in Petrina's illustration also flee the holy flame which proceeds from God. The fire proceeding from the sword radiates in three tiers, each successively brighter than the other. These tiers of flame suggest a thrice holy God.

Although the sword and the angels are instruments of God's present dealings with mankind, the tree refers to man's future state when he shall inherit the new paradise of Christ's kingdom, for the Tree of Life shall then provide man with eternal life. John's vision of Christ's kingdom included the Tree of Life:

And he showed me a pure river of water of life, clear as crystal proceeding out of the throne of God and of the Lamb.

In the midst of the street of it, and on either side of the river, was there the Tree of Life, which bare twelve manner of fruits, and yielded her fruit every month: and the leaves of the tree were for the healing of the nations.

And there shall be no more curse: but the throne of God and of the Lamb shall be in it. (Rev. xxii, 1–3)

The curse of Adam and Eve is eventually removed, and Christ allows man to partake of the Tree of Life and enjoy immortality with him.

Despite the hope which Michael gives to Adam and Eve, Petrina depicts their departure as a greatly sorrowful one. Adam and Eve flee the flaming sword in sadness: Adam attempts to look up at the sword, but shields his eyes from the intense brightness; Eve also covers her face, but looks downward, as if weeping. The positions of their feet, especially Eve's, suggest that they go forth haltingly, with "wand'ring steps and slow" (XII, 648). They are at the very brink of Eden, with the cliffs of Paradise (XII, 637–40) rising dramatically on both sides of them. Petrina's dark cliffs suggest gloomful mourning, fruitlessness, death. All the world before them is dark, while Paradise (directly behind them) remains filled with pure light.

In only two illustrations (for Books I and XII) does Petrina portray a torn banner: It signifies expulsion and irreversible rupture between God and his creatures. For Satan and his crew, the rupture is irreparable, but for man there is promise of reconciliation. This promise of redemption through Christ Petrina makes visible in the redemptive skins that Adam and Eve wear as they depart from Paradise.

University of Southern California

NOTES

Carlotta Petrina's illustrations are reproduced courtesy of the William Andrews Clark Memorial Library, University of California, Los Angeles, and the Limited Editions Club, New York.

1. Carlotta Petrina, also known as Charlotte Kennedy, was listed as an Italian resident at Naples in *Who's Who in American Art* (New York, 1962). A footnote stated that the editors had not received any recent information from the artist.
2. Stella Purce Revard, "Satan as Epic Hero," in *The War in Heaven: "Paradise Lost" and the Tradition of Satan's Rebellion* (Ithaca, N.Y., 1980), pp. 228, 234.
3. Marcia R. Pointon, *Milton & English Art* (Toronto, 1970), p. 47. Hayman's illustrations originally appeared in the 1749 Thomas Newton Edition of *Paradise Lost and Paradise Regained*. Pointon discusses Hayman and his illustrations of Milton's works on pp. 47–57. She notes Blake's illustrations of Milton, which were completed during the period 1800–25, on pp. 135–66.
4. The text of *Paradise Lost* used throughout is *John Milton: Complete Poems and Major Prose*, ed. Merritt H. Hughes (Indianapolis, 1957).
5. John Steadman, *Milton's Biblical and Classical Imagery* (Pittsburgh, 1984), pp. 121, 124.
6. Pointon, *Milton & English Art*, p. 14. Pointon discusses several major illustrations of this confrontation in chapters one and two on pp. 6–7, 14, 48, 53.
7. Irene Samuel, "The Dialogue in Heaven: A Reconsideration of *Paradise Lost* III 1–417," in *Milton: Modern Essays in Criticism*, ed. Arthur E. Barker (London, 1965), p. 235. The essay in this anthology has been reprinted from *PMLA* LXXII (1957), 601–11.
8. Jane M. Petty, "The Voice at Eve's Ear in *Paradise Lost*," *MQ* XIX, no. 2 (May 1985), 43.
9. Northrop Frye, *The Return of Eden* (Toronto, 1965), p. 24.
10. Revard, "Satan as Epic Hero," p. 247. She comments on Milton's independence in depicting Michael as a notably less significant figure in the heavenly battle than did others of the Renaissance tradition.
11. For illustrations and explanations of northern Italian and other European armor designs during the period circa 1066 to 1700, see Claude Blair's *European Armour* (London, 1958).
12. C. S. Lewis, *A Preface to "Paradise Lost,"* (London, 1961), p. 125.
13. Merritt Y. Hughes, *Ten Perspectives on Milton* (New Haven, Conn., 1965), p. 70.
14. *The Scofield Reference Bible*, ed. C. I. Scofield (New York, 1945), p. 1291.

SILENCE AND DARKNESS
IN *PARADISE LOST*

Shirley Sharon-Zisser

T HE LIGHT-DARKNESS IMAGERY in *Paradise Lost* has long
been recognized as an essential component in the epic vehicle designed to imply and justify the ways of God to man. As Merrit Y. Hughes
points out, since Ida Langdon's remark in 1921 that the significance of
light and darkness in the poem "is proved by the many passages containing such words as 'light,' 'lustre,' 'radiant,' 'shining,' 'dark,' 'darkness,'
'gloom' and 'night,'" critics have attempted to define its metaphorical
import in reference to this cluster of images. Thus, to cite but a few examples, Lawrence Babb sees the "lights and darks" in *Paradise Lost* as
"most striking," Walter Clyde Curry terms "light and its composite darkness" the poem's "most ineffable symbol," D. C. Allen suggests that "the
visual imagery of *Paradise Lost* . . . depends . . . on contrasts between
light and darkness," and Jackson I. Cope finds that "Milton's paradoxical symbolic" hinges on images of light, darkness, sight, and blindness.[1]
Indeed, the text seems to invite a close scrutiny of the function of light
and darkness, which appear as characterizing qualities of all regions it
traverses and figure as central symbols in the richest of its metapoetic
and autobiographical statements: the prologue to Book III.

Numerous critics, however, rather than studying these prominent
images closely so as to characterize their exact function in the metaphysics, epistemology, or psychology implied by the poem, have been content to reduce their meaning to the traditional synonymity for good and
evil, originating in the Platonic equation of light with the True and the
Good. At times, this reduction appears as an unquestioned implicit assumption in an illustration of other theses concerning the poem. Thus,
Peter Fisher chooses to elucidate his claim that "Milton tended to adopt
an attitude which approached a dualism of good and evil," by adding
"light and darkness" as their syntactical parallels. And Edward J. Zimmerman assumes the same synonymity when he chooses to title his thesis dealing with the assumption that in Milton's world good ultimately emerges
out of evil, *"Light out of Darkness."*[2]

However, the lure of identifying a connection between Milton and other great minds who came before him, of establishing *Paradise Lost* in the literary or philosophical tradition of Plato, Augustine, or Dante, seems to have misled critics who investigated the images of light and darkness. Thus Curry, in accordance with his assumption that "Milton is apparently unwilling to employ a private and personal symbology in the presentation of his concepts [but] rather attaches himself to established traditions which furnish a terminology become reputable by long use," contends that "light is in many circumstances the traditional and universal symbol representing spiritual goodness, truth or divine beauty; [while] its contrary, darkness, symbolizes spiritual depravity and all manifestations of evil." Similarly, Lawrence Babb suggests that for Milton, as for Plato, light symbolizes righteousness. "The great stage of the narrative," writes Babb, "its upper region gloriously radiant — its lower totally dark — presents a moral idealism through the medium of an intense *chiaroscuro.*"[3] In other words, interpreted in a Platonic context, Milton's light and darkness are conceived as the frontiers delimiting the universe in both the physical and the moral senses.

An interpretation in light of the Augustinian model, however, produces a rather different visual rendering of the Miltonic universe in terms of light and darkness. In this model, as presented by Louis Martz, light symbolizes the indestructible "intellect of man . . . which works toward knowledge," and the higher divine intellect which guides it "even when the mind is not conscious of its presence." Dark, on the other hand, symbolizes the "fallen world of everyday life." Thus, the "darkness visible" of hell is viewed by Martz as a "metaphor by which Milton interprets the actions of the world we know," and the movement from hell, through Chaos in Book II, to heaven in Book III and then to earth in Book IV as implying, on a deeper, more essential level, "a journey backward and inward" from that world "toward the inner Light by which man is enabled to see a Paradise that lies within." In Martz's interpretation, then, Milton's universe is envisioned not as a space stretching between the poles of light and darkness, but as "a picture with a dark border but a bright center" in which the "opening and the closing books present the dark border of the world we know . . . [and] at the center, the voice of the bard . . . perform[s] a journey . . . to discover the springing center of creativity."[4] Yet despite the visual difference, the Platonic and Augustinian interpretations have in common the attempt to trace, and hence necessarily to reduce, Milton's conception to an antecedent "source," as well as the resulting tendency to ignore details that diverge from that alleged source and to interpret the light-darkness imagery as univocal and unambiguous.

Irene Samuel, however, acknowledges the inadequacy of such reduction. "For anyone familiar with the *Commedia* of Dante," writes
Samuel, "Milton's whole use of light and dark is bound to be reminiscent
of the other great Christian poet's comparable system of symbols."[5] Yet,
whereas Dante's ladder of light "constitute[s] an ontological principle
which r[uns] through the whole of reality, from the sensible to the intelligible to God,"[6] and makes for "an elaborately regulated heaven,"
Milton's light-darkness imagery includes a "suggestion of diversity."[7]

Other critics, too, have expressed full recognition of the multivocality
and sophistication with which Milton treated light and darkness. Two
passages, for example, the description of God's skirts as "dark with excessive bright" (III, 380) and the simile in which Satan is likened to an
eclipsed sun, which "Darkened so, yet shone" (I, 599), employ both light
and darkness as qualifiers for a wholly beneficent and, in turn, a wholly
malignant entity, thus precluding their univocal labeling as signifying
good and evil.[8] Furthermore, as Joseph Summers points out, "there is
alternating light and dark in heaven itself and . . . first rate artificial
lighting in Hell." This stylistic phenomenon, concludes Summers, shows
that in *Paradise Lost* "physical and spiritual light and dark may have
a paradoxical relationship" which functions as a reflection of "the complexity of the judgments [the reader is] asked to make."[9] Similarly, Kester
Svendsen suggests that in *Paradise Lost* the "traditional associations of
light with reason and goodness and dark with passion and evil" are only
one side of a "double metaphor" which projects their obverse as well,
so as to make palpable to the reader "the whole frame of choice" which
is "central in the poem."[10]

In other words, Milton's paradoxical conjunctions of light and darkness may be taken as designed to structure a textual analogue to the essential human dilemma of oscillation between good and evil. The contradictory possibilities for interpretation of the light-darkness imagery are
given to readers within the poem, as the options of good and evil are
open to them as part of the metaphysical structure of the universe as
depicted by Milton. The reader thus functions as a value giver to the
fictional world as much as to extratextual "reality." And the reading process itself becomes a reenactment of the moral choice which is the text's
thematic core. By means of the paradox of light and darkness, as Rosalie
Colie explains, the text of *Paradise Lost* cuts "across the conventional
limits between 'art' and 'reality,'" becoming not merely a mirror held
up to a nature in which everything is conceived of as containing or implying its opposite, but a paradoxical reality in itself.[11]

However, the paradox involving light and darkness in *Paradise Lost* is not limited to neatly balanced conjunctions of images from the two poles. A wider and closer view of the poem reveals that on the ostensibly negative side of the light-darkness polarity, there is, on the stylistic level, a repeated association of darkness with silence in numerous images relating to the created world, such as, "Night with her will bring silence" (VII, 106), the reference to night as "the silent hours" (VII, 444), and to the moon's "silent" course (VIII, 163). The incorporation of a third element into the light-darkness imagery cluster multiplies the possibilities for interplay among its constituents and distinguishes it from those presented by Milton's alleged "sources." Consequently, this unique cluster, while evoking associations of antecedent light-darkness symbolisms, resists being reduced to them. The attachment of silence to darkness in many of Milton's images, then, may have been one of the devices for constructing a fictional world which is not susceptible to a breaking down into isolated, traditional categories, but whose components constantly interpermeate each other in their creation of what Rosalie Colie terms the "multiplex . . . simple truth."[12]

Moreover, the association of silence and darkness introduces another tradition into the poem, alongside the Platonic and the Augustinian: that of the *Theologia Negativa*, the conception according to which God is an impossibility containing all opposites and therefore cannot be apprehended through the ordinary linguistic or sensory vehicles of human perception. Most neo-Platonists, explains Edgar Wind, considered the "ultimate truth" to be a supreme mystery which transcends the understanding and must therefore be apprehended through a state of darkness in which the distinctions of logic disappear, or a state of silence for which Pythagoras became the consummate symbol.[13] This tradition, dating back to Proclus's statement that even were we to be completely silent about God, our silence would be too positive, is reverberated in the writings of negative theologians like Philo, Gregory of Nyssa, and Dionysius the Aeropagite, who maintained that the divine essence may be apprehended only in a state of total passivity of the flesh.[14] And in the Renaissance, the same tradition was reformulated in Giordano Bruno's statement that "God is better honored and loved by silence than by words, and better seen by closing the eyes to images than by opening them."[15] Darkness and silence, then, in this conception, characterize the place where God is "because he cannot be known," and into which the soul, in its search for truth, progressively penetrates "until eventually [it] is cut off from all that can be grasped by sense or reason."[16]

This conception, moreover, seems to be echoed in the words of the second invocation, in which the poet may be understood as pointing out that physical blindness provides the occasion to "see and tell / Of things invisible to mortal sight" (III, 54–55). Indeed, this understanding of the passage as proclaiming the spiritual compensations for physical blindness underlies several diversely oriented critical scrutinies. In "a moment of grace," writes A. B. Chambers, "the epic poet . . . of necessity forsakes the body's gate of wisdom," which had been distorted in the Fall, "in order to open an entrance into the soul."[17] Blindness, then, according to Chambers's interpretation, is not merely compensated for, but is itself a necessary gateway for communion with the godhead. Franklin Baruch similarly remarks on this passage that blindness "is made to take on the role not of bodily impairment, but of a precondition for vision embracing the universe itself," but relegates it to a psychological rather than theological context, as the poet's own substitution, or unconscious sublimation for loss of sight.[18] Finally, Herman Rapaport presents the structure of loss and compensation which he finds in the second invocation in a textual as well as a psychological context. Blindness, for Rapaport, signifies symbolical castration. Its acknowledgment in the invocation is hence correlative to the poet's overcoming the fear of castration, which provides him with the "reserves of strength" with which he produces the ultimate compensation for his blindness: a text which surpasses that of his masters.[19]

Moreover, the text as a whole may be seen as involving the reader in a parallel, discursive experience of loss and compensation. In a recent deconstructionist study, Mary Niquist pointed out that the text of *Paradise Lost* itself provides "no internal exegesis" of the Father's Word in Book V, but rather two responses; the first, Satan's, is a distortion and misinterpretation, and the other — Abdiel's — is a reflection of the Father's original text, "preserving the intimate connection between signifier and transcendental signified." Hence, concludes Niquist, "the either-or of subversive and unmediated reading displaces itself in an intertextuality that adheres forever to the written outside of the Word." That is, the reader, according to Niquist, is compelled by the text of *Paradise Lost* itself to search for the meaning of the Word in external "intertexts."[20]

This, however, is not an inevitable conclusion. For, rather than forcing the reader to turn to other texts, the silence accompanying God's Word in *Paradise Lost*, helpfully pointed out by Niquist, may be taken as designed to throw readers back upon themselves, to compel them to construct the meaning of the Word within their own consciousness. The text itself, then, may be seen as structuring an experience of absence, a "universal blank" (III, 48) which the reader fills, and which is both mimetic of the poet's existential experience and creative of one of the two epistemological states in which, according to the *Theologia Negativa*, man can apprehend God. Thus, *Paradise Lost* may be viewed as a poem in which the "theme . . . of the necessity of entering the dark in order to see the light,"[21] suggested in the second invocation, works together with the absent discourse implied in its structure to provide a poetic realization of the epistemological conditions for divine knowledge.

This interpretation, however, while illuminating the role of the negative theology tradition in the poem, cannot be considered exhaustive, as it disregards the no less emphasized role of other traditions of darkness symbolisms. Yet, an attempt to construct an interpretation which allows for the co-existence in the text of the Platonic tradition, which equates darkness with ignorance and evil, and the tradition of negative theology, in which silence and darkness refer to epistemologically positive states — in point of fact the only states in which divine knowledge may be acquired — seems to lead to a contradiction. This ostensible contradiction may be explained (or rather, explained away) as an inevitable result of Milton's extreme erudition, which led him to produce an "eclectic" epic.[22] The extent of Milton's knowledge, it may be argued, is expressed in an exceptionally rich poem, but one, as Lawrence Babb puts it, which "is not consistent with experience and not consistent with itself."[23] Or, without attributing any flaws to the poet, the presence of the two clashing traditions in his text may be seen as a manifestation of the Christian doctrine he was trying to inculcate, in which, as Rosalie Colie points out, contradictions and double meanings are part of a *concordia discors* which reflects the nature of God himself.[24]

However, as I propose to show, an examination of the poem itself reveals that the coexistence in it of the two traditions does not form a contradiction, but is rather part of a complexly structured scheme, in which silence and darkness, as images, dramatic situations, and metaphors, perform several integrative functions. First, as numerous critics have pointed out, Milton solves the stylistic problem of finding the language in which to write about all dimensions of the cosmos, including the supra-human realm of knowledge, by likening spiritual to corporeal forms or "measuring things in Heaven by things on Earth" (VI, 893); that is, by analogies or "accommodations."[25] On the literal level, silence and darkness, as familiar human experiences, help visualize and hence conceptualize the alien regions of heaven, hell, or Chaos.

Furthermore, Milton's scheme is conceptually as well as spatially multidimensional. It follows the neo-Platonic tradition not only in its insistence on the Chain of Being, the "gradual scale sublimed" expounded by Raphael in Book V, but also in the sense that each of its metaphysical, spatial, or "macrocosmic" constituents is "microcosmically" reflected as a state of mind—that is, has psychological as well as epistemological ramifications. On the nonliteral level, therefore, the metaphoric or symbolic significations of silence or darkness as physical qualities in any of the cosmic regions are paralleled in the cognitive and psychological states associated with that region.

These significations, moreover, are often double-valued. For, in Milton's scheme, every positive fact entails an obverse negative: the very creation of an order, as Mary Niquist points out, is "traversed as if endlessly by the enmity of Satan";[26] and similarly, the free obedience God requires of man as "proof sincere / Of true allegiance" (III, 103–04) entails his being "free to fall" (III, 99). Thus, any positive value attributed to silence or darkness in any of the spatial realms of the poem entails a negative aspect, which, in turn, is reflected on all the associated conceptual dimensions.

Finally, this internal principle receives an intertextual reinforcement from the presence in the text of the two conflicting traditions of darkness symbolisms. Each of these single-valued symbolisms by itself, Milton seems to be saying, cannot provide an adequate correlative for the structure of the universe. Yet their combination enables one to emphasize both the negative and the positive aspects of silence and darkness in their various nonliteral significations. However, while partially accepted to this end, both traditions are also criticized; that is, like the constituents of the reality implied by Milton, they are shown to be negative as well as positive. In other words, once incorporated in the text, the two darkness symbolisms enact the ontological principle the text affirms: that every positive existence is double-valued. The double-valued cluster of silence and darkness components in the text, then, while constituting surface complexity, acts also as an Ariadne thread running through all its dimensions and maintaining conceptual order within it.

First, darkness is an attribute of the two realms external to creation and antithetical to heaven and earth: hell and Chaos. In hell, as it is described in Books I and II, there is "No light, but rather darkness visible," which is so thick as to be "palpable." Hell is "gloomy" and "void of light," a "dark opprobrious den." This lack of light, moreover, seems to be metonymic for the lack of any positive content characterizing hell. Hell is a "deep" or "abyss" which is "hollow," that is, empty of any limits or structures. It is a place which is both "wild," lacking any positive order, and "waste," sterile and incapable of movement toward life, which is the establishment of such an order. The civilization of hell, as Joseph E. Duncan notes, "is sterile and insubstantial in its isolationism."[27] This hollowness, in turn, is "boundless," that is, extends to infinity. Yet, hell is infinite only in one direction. It is described, on the one hand, as a "Bottomless pit," but also as a "dungeon," "den," or "prison": that is, it has an entrance which is not also an exit. In contrast to the Chain of Being from which it is excluded, and which spans the metaphysical distance from matter to pure spirit, hell has no ultimate limit, and hence no gradations enabling progress to that limit. In other words, then, Milton's hell is a receptacle which has a threshold, an upper limit which appears to be the ultimate one, the crossing of which renders all limits meaningless.

This metaphysical structure is reflected as a state of mind. The "gloom" the devils try to "purge" is not only the "palpable obscure" surrounding them, but also psychological depression. The "deep" gloom or darkness in the external landscape of hell corresponds to the "deep despair" with which Satan is racked. This correspondence has been termed a "metaphor," assuming that the physical landscape which constitutes the ostensible "vehicle" is semiotically subordinate to the psychological torments which are projected as its "tenor."[28] However, *Paradise Lost* seems to be an attempt to incorporate in one text all spatial dimensions and all elements of human epistemology and psychology, while according an equal degree of reality to them all, and thus precluding the subordination of one dimension to another. Moreover, as C. A. Patrides points out, though Protestant theologians, and Milton among them, affirmed that "all the torments of Hell are accommodated to our understanding," they were not "prepared to assert without qualification that Hell [is] mere metaphor . . . and 'no corporeal place.'"[29] Both reflecting and reflected dimensions, then, both the physical and the psychological torments of hell, are part of the world projected by the poem.

However, these torments are not, as Joseph E. Duncan suggests, "inseparable." The psychological state may exist independently of the site of hell. Or, as J. B. Broadbent puts it, "Hell is not, in this poem, just a scene, but a state of being which overtakes different characters wherever they are all through the story."[30] Satan brings hell with him "whichever way" he flies (IV, 20, 75); and Adam, still in Paradise, expresses the same state of mind when he says, after the fall: "O conscience! into what Abyss of fears / And horrors hast thou driven me; out of which / I find no way, from deep to deeper plunged!" (X, 842–44). For he, too, describes a state one can enter, or be driven into, but out of which there is "no way," and which is constituted of never ending, increasingly "deeper" absence of limits, which engenders "fears and horrors."

Hell, then, is the state of mind produced by transgressing the ulti-

mate moral and hence also psychological limit, after which no more limits exist. It is, to use more modern terms, the psychological wasteland
lying beyond the threshold of psychosis. And it is characterized by the
emotion of gloom or melancholy whose external or "macrocosmic" correlative is darkness.

Furthermore, darkness is also the external correlative of the epistemological state characterizing hell. By rebelling, the fallen angels have
transgressed not only a moral and psychological, but also a cognitive
limit: they have renounced reason. Consequently, when they attempt
to philosophize, they are led only by the emotional "inclination" (I, 524)
to be rid of their depression or find "truce" to their "restless thoughts"
(I, 526); and as it is only reason that can impose "truce" and order on
the contents of the mind, they are lost in "wandering mazes" (I, 561)
of limitless sophistry.

Darkness is, again, one of the metaphysical attributes of Chaos: like
hell, chaos is "darksome," a "dark ocean" (II, 973, 841), "damp and
dark," or a "dark abyss" (X, 283, 371). As in hell, this darkness is an aspect of the lack of limits of order. For Chaos, too, is described as "hollow" (III, 518), "wasteful," a "desert" (II, 961, 973) in which there is
no self-instigated movement toward order. And it too is "illimitable" (II,
892), that is, stretches to infinity. Yet, unlike hell, Chaos is not described
as a bottomless receptacle lying beyond the ultimate limit, but as possessing no limits whatsoever. It is said to be a "vast immeasurable abyss"
(VII, 211) "without bounds" (II, 892), or a "vast unbounded deep" (X,
471). As Robert M. Adams has pointed out, hell, or more precisely, its
upper limit, "gives the cosmos a bottom and [hence] a sense of moral
and physical distance"; while in the unbounded Chaos, "there is nowhere
to fall to."[31]

Moreover, hell is an essentially intransformable state, a pure negative which can generate no positive aspect. Satan is mistaken when he
says that the "mind is its own place, and in itself / Can make a Heaven
of Hell, a Hell of Heaven" (I, 254–55). For the misuse of free will which
entailed Satan's banishment from heaven to hell precluded his ability
to perpetuate any further changes in his being. Or, as Irene Samuel puts
it, the soul in the state of hell "can no more create an external heaven
for itself than it can fail to turn any outer good into a further torment."[32]
The content of Chaos, on the other hand, is described as "devoid of sense
and motion" (II, 151), of the essence of reason — but as capable of receiving it upon itself. It is described in terms of potential life, as the "womb
of nature," whose inner components are "pregnant causes" or "embryon
atoms" (II, 911, 913, 900). And this "wide womb," in turn, is identified

with darkness, with "uncreated night" or "the void profound of unessential night" (II, 150, 439). Hence, the "primordial darkness" of Milton's Chaos may indeed, as Curry writes, "be considered a positive existence" in the sense that it represents the infinite potentiality of matter capable of being molded into form.[33]

As pure potentiality, however, the elements of Chaos, as William H. Boyd points out, have "no intrinsic identity."[34] They cannot be defined intentionally, in terms of essence, for any stipulation of individual identity is already an exclusion from Chaos. Their only possible definition, therefore, is extensional and collective in terms of their participation in an eternal "stri[fe] for mastery" (II, 899). The components of Chaos, then, "ever fight" (II, 914) a battle in which, by definition, there cannot be an orderly division into factions but a constant osmosis and interpermeation. The darkness with which these atoms are equated, therefore, is an expression of "anarchy" (II, 896) as well as of the absence of individual identity, and in that sense, negative.

These metaphysical attributes of darkness in Chaos again correspond to states of the soul. Critics have noted the analogy between Milton's descriptions of Chaos and of psychological turmoils. "Chaos," writes Chambers, "indicates the horrors of internal tumult and confusion that may rage in Satan or in man."[35] The "four champions fierce" (II, 898) which wage the war of contrary qualities in Chaos correspond to the "Torment . . . [and] hateful siege / Of contraries" (IX, 121–22) which rage within Satan's breast. However, Milton's Chaos is also an objective correlative for the destructive drives whose external expression leads to such internal turmoils. The tendency of Chaos toward "havoc and spoil and ruin" (II, 1009) finds an echo in Satan's search for ease "only in destroying" (IX, 129).

However, the psychological aspect of Chaos is represented by Milton not only as a state of turmoil, but also as a situation in which a limitless infinite threatens the psyche with "utter loss of being" (II, 440) because it can suck in the limits constituting it. It is the psychological danger not so much of self-torment, as in hell, but of the dissolution of self. Darkness in Chaos, then, also represents a primeval collective state of the psyche existing as a potential beyond the limits of any individual "I." Chaos, in other words, is "the womb of Nature and perhaps her grave" (II, 911) also in the psychological sense of the matter from which the individual ego is molded, and to which it may, in conditions of transgressing its own limits, dissolve.

Finally, the metaphysical and psychological characteristics of Chaos are mirrored in the epistemological state associated with it. For the acquisition of knowledge requires, first, the limits of the mind of a knower, which constitute him or her as a separate, self-enclosed entity; and second, the apparatus of logic or order to know by. The first of these conditions is precluded by Chaos as a psychological state; the second, by its metaphysical nature. Hence, darkness in Chaos may also be considered an external correlative for the lowest cognitive state, in which knowledge is an impossibility.

In Milton's scheme, the molding of an individual identity on both the metaphysical and the psychological levels is an external imposition of limits rather than an infusion of essence. The Son, who is himself the embodiment of logos, is represented as creating via two further symbols of order: the golden compasses with which he "circumscribe[s]," that is, both limits and brings under control the "formless mass" (VII, 226); and language, with which he "confine[s]" the "vast infinitude" (VII, 711). Consequently, as Northrop Frye puts it, Chaos remains "that into which God's presence chooses not to extend itself [and] creation is that into which his presence has extended itself."[36] Yet, the imposed limits do not totally transform the original darkness, which remains in the created world in two forms.

First, darkness remains in creation as created night in the cycle or "wheel / Of day and night" (VIII, 135-36). In accordance with the poem's principle that "Earth / [is] but the shadow of Heaven" (V, 574–75) — that is, differs from it not in structure but in its containing more darkness — this cycle appears to be a reflection "In darker veil" (V, 646) of the "cave / Within the mount of God . . . / Where light and darkness . . . / Lodge and dislodge by turns" (VI, 4–7) in a regulated schedule. In other words, the equally structured diurnal cycles of heaven and earth follow a pattern of orderly "vicissitude" (VI, 8), or, as Fowler (p. 449) puts it, display a "clockwork regularity, emblematic of their temperance," which restricts original and anarchic darkness.

A further restriction is provided by the fact that, in the created world, darkness is never allowed to appear on its own, but is always accompanied by an agent of reason. The moon, which reflects the light of the sun, the emblem of reason, externally checks the dark by throwing "her silver mantle" over it (IV, 609). Similarly, the stars, as Adam tells Eve, "set and rise; / Lest total darkness should by night regain / Her old possession, and extinguish life / In nature and all things" (IV, 664–68). Finally, night is brought about by Hesperus, a star whose office it is to be an "arbiter" or mediator "twixt day and night" (IX, 50).

These subordinations to the divine order, while not transforming the original darkness, enable it to function as a vehicle of order. In the

war in heaven, darkness, accompanied by silence, imposes "truce," the
limitation of disorder which, uncircumscribed in hell, it represented
the impossibility of: "Now night her course began, and over heaven /
Inducing darkness grateful truce imposed, / And silence on the odious
din of war" (VI, 406–08).

Similarly, it is silence, this same accompaniment to created night,
that the Son evokes as a force of order when standing on the verge of
Chaos following the fall of the angels: "Silence, ye troubled waves, and
thou deep, peace, / . . . your discord end" (VII, 216–17). Silence, then,
is represented as a force of order available to the Son in heaven. Hence,
it is not described as circumscribed, but as attached to darkness in its
pure form, perhaps as a counterbalance to the "loud and ruinous" din
(II, 921) accompanying it in Chaos. Silence in *Paradise Lost*, in other
words, may be construed as an additional positive force imposed upon
primal matter, and providing the orderly gaps which transform its anarchic noise into a symphony, which, as Patrides points out, was, for
Milton as for other Renaissance expositors, a symbol of the perfection
of the natural order.[37]

However, in the created world, silence is represented as a self-
destructive rather than creative force. In the account of night given by
the narrative voice, silence is again associated with darkness:

> Now came still evening on, and twilight grey
> Had in her sober livery all things clad;
> Silence accompanied, for beast and bird,
> They to their grassy couch, these to their nests
> Were slunk, all but the wakeful nightingale;
> She all night long her amorous descant sung;
> Silence was pleased.   (IV, 598–604)

As in *Comus*, where, upon the sound of music, "Silence . . . wished she
might / Deny her nature, and be never more / Still to be so displaced"
(558–60), silence is represented in *Paradise Lost* as a state that wishes
to efface itself, to be replaced by its opposite, sound.

Moreover, shortly afterwards in the poem, Eve, in a speech of obedience which thus reflects the attitudes of Adam and of the organizing
narrative voice, describes night in similar terms:

> sweet [is] the coming on
> Of grateful evening mild, then silent night
> With this her solemn bird and this fair moon;
> And these the gems of heaven her starry train.   (IV, 646–49)

Here, Eve establishes a parallel in the syntax between the "solemn bird," the nightingale, and the moon and stars. For as the moon and stars prevent total darkness from repermeating the universe, the nightingale, which itself also emits light in darkness, prevents total silence from gaining sole precedence in it. Silence, then, is represented in the poem not only as a force of order, but also, like original darkness, as a potential destructive state which creation strives to avoid.

However, the reason underlying these intimations of a negative aspect associated with silence is brought out only in Satan's speech in Eve's dream in Book V, which seems to be a distorted echo of her praise of night:

> Now is the pleasant time,
> The cool, the silent, save where silence yields
> To the night-warbling bird, that now awake
> Tunes sweetest his love laboured song; Now reigns
> Full-orbed the moon, and with more pleasing light
> Shadowy sets off the face of things." (V, 38–43)

Whereas in Eve's speech silence was "pleased" at the sound of the nightingale, Satan says it "yields" to it, and therefore essentially resists it. Moreover, Satan describes the moon's light as "pleasing," not because it is a reflection of the divine light which prevents total darkness from overtaking, but because it "Shadowy sets off the face of things," that is, renders the visual landscape more obscure. Silence and darkness, then, are "pleasing" to Satan in the sense that they are the congenial environment for evil to operate in. Both are states in which little or no information comes in from the senses, and in which man is thus forced to rely on his inner faculties, which are then put to their utmost test. Aside from their presentation as occasions for the acquisition of divine knowledge (respectively, in the second invocation and in the absence of internal exegesis on the Father's Word), silence and darkness in Milton's scheme are potential traps of evil.

For evil, as represented by Milton, is always the "highly attractive" outside concealing the "hideous [and] destructive."[38] It is, in other words, a "fraud" (VI, 121), an "artifice" whose perfect form is a "perverted ordering of the prime substance"[39] because it is but a vial of moral nothingness. In his temptation of his fellow angels, Satan uses the substance of language to create a text which is "ambiguous" (VI, 568) because the perfect rhetoric of its surface is at odds with the absence of morality which constitutes its content. In the war in heaven, he uses swords to create a perfect geometric shape of a "cube" (VI, 552), which hides his "devilish enginery," and is therefore "hollow" morally rather than spatially. Furthermore, Satan's associate, Belial, is described as outwardly seeming "For dignity composed and high exploit," whereas in terms of his inner nature all is "false and hollow" (II, 110–12). And in hell, Pandemonium, the consummate expression of the devils' artistry, "Rose like an Exhalation" (I, 711), or as J. B. Broadbent comments, "like the machinery of a masque — artificial, temporary, illusory, a veil for . . . ugly discomforts."[40] The "type of hell," in Milton's own words, is a "pleasant valley" concealing "Tophet," which, in Hebrew, denotes not only the name of a place, but also infernal agony.

As Peter Fisher points out, since "the form of anything may be destroyed, though not its essence, evil is destructible."[41] However, in external conditions of silence and darkness, the discrepancy between form and content is blurred, and evil presents itself as a perfect, congruent object. Hence, its lure becomes strong enough to draw consciousness toward itself, instead of the required turning toward the "umpire conscience" (III, 195) externally implanted by God in man as "a guide to truth and conduct."[42]

Thus, though silence is presented as a force of order, it is also the condition in which Adam and Eve fall. Eve's withdrawing "from her husband's hand her hand" (IX, 385), in order to garden alone, precludes the possibility of human dialogue and thus provides Satan the necessary substratum for the fabrication of deception, for making "intricate seem straight" (IX, 632). Moreover, this condition is reconstructed on the level of the reading experience. As Mary Niquist points out, "between the last words of Satan's temptation and the first fallen human motion, Eve's desirous gaze," there is a "silent gap . . . bridged only by the narrator's 'He ended, and his words replete with guile / Into her heart too easy entrance won' (IX, 733–34) [which] lets the reader know that . . . Eve has beyond doubt fallen."[43]

Similarly, darkness, though represented as part of an order, is also spoken of as a time for evil. The time "when night darkens the streets" is the occasion for the drunken, insolent riots of "the sons of Belial" (I, 500–03). Later, Adam characterizes night as harboring the activity of deception: the gathering and concealment of evil (V, 207) in an innocent-seeming receptacle. Furthermore, darkness is an environment favorable not only for the construction of incongruous, deceptive objects, but also for the deconstruction of order. What "we by day / Lop overgrown, or prune, or prop, or bind," says Eve, "One night or two with wanton growth derides / Tending to wild" (IX, 209–12). Nature in *Paradise*

Lost, as Fowler notes (p. 868), "has a continual tendency to wildness," to return to its primeval form, which is associated with darkness. This tendency, moreover, is reflected on the psychological level "as a moral temptation" (Fowler, p. 868) which man is required to control as a parallel effort to the attempt to subdue the wilderness without. However, any control furnished by man does not provide a progressive conquest of either the physical or the psychological wilderness: darkness is the situation in which, within an order, the possibility of wilderness or disorder ever perpetuates itself.

Moreover, this nature of darkness as a favorable condition for the growth of evil is obviously the reason for Satan's operating by night. Satan "resolved / With all his legions to dislodge" only "Soon as midnight brought on the dusky hour / Friendliest to sleep and silence" (V, 667–668). Satan "rode / With darkness" (IX, 64), "obscure," "wrapt in mist / Of midnight vapor" (IX, 158–59), which, as Robert R. Craven points out, is itself a traditional Renaissance metaphor for deception.[44] Hence, darkness as prerequisite for evil is repeatedly associated with immorality: Satan is "the Prince of darkness" (X, 383) who has "dark designs" (I, 213), and his followers are the "sons of darkness" (VI, 715).

The first sense in which darkness remains in creation, then, is as a partially transformed and tamed force in an overall balanced system, providing the desired balance only at the price of potentially subverting it. However, darkness remains in creation also in its original form. In the creation from Chaos, the spirit of God "vital virtue infused, and vital warmth / Throughout the fluid mass, but downward purged / The black tartareous . . . dregs / Adverse to life" (VII, 236–39). In other words, part of original darkness remains suppressed beneath the surface of the created world. Consequently, beneath the celestial soil, Satan's followers see "The originals of nature in their crude / Conception" (VI, 511–12). These dregs, Milton emphasizes, are not in themselves evil, but morally neutral, capable of receiving the influence of whatever force makes use of them, be it the sun that "to each inward part / With gentle penetration, though unseen, / Shoots invisible virtue even to the deep" (III, 584–86), or the devils, who use them to create their vehicles of destruction. However, as in Chaos, this same inert material is negative in its psychological and epistemological reflections.

As it is present beneath the surface of the world, original darkness is present beneath the surface of any individual consciousness. Beneath the "government / [of] reason," says Michael in Book XII, lurk "obscure" or dark "inordinate desires" and "upstart passions" (86–89): the potential psychological states of hell and Chaos, of the loss of balance, of all inner limits, or of the very limits of the self. However, the poem presents yet another aspect of potential psychological darkness. The "shadow" (IV, 470) of self that appears in Eve's dream presents a danger to the government of reason not through anarchy or dissolution of limits, but rather through extreme self-enclosure or solipsism. For the shadow, which "return[s]" (IV, 463) or reflects all movements of the self, thus presents itself as a possible completion to it, a completion which would render the self autarchic and in no need of external reliance on external agents such as reason or God's will. However, for Milton, such self-sufficiency is pathological. For in Milton's scheme, any ascent toward self-sufficiency, as Arnold Stein explains, involves "being nearer or tending nearer to God, which means rising toward a higher resignation in his will, which is always external to the creature."[45]

Furthermore, epistemologically, the original darkness is ever present in consciousness as the eternal limit on man's understanding, perhaps the limit dividing discursive reason from the intuitive reason of the angels, which differs from it "but in degree, in kind the same" (V, 490). Hence, man requires divine assistance both to control the dark psychological forces and to rise above the limits of understanding. Such cognitive and psychological aid, it seems, is prerequisite to the attainment of global knowledge, encompassing all moral and ontological principles of the universe, as well as the history enacted in it, knowledge such as attained by Adam through the aid of Raphael and Michael, and such as Milton himself hopes to project. For it is aid to rise above the dark of both ignorance and all forms of potential madness that the poet himself seems to be seeking in the opening passage of the poem, as he implores the spirit of God: "what in me is dark / Illumine, what is low raise and support" (I, 22–23).

God's grace may lift man above the limit his built-in epistemological blindness constitutes, and enable him to apprehend things ordinarily "invisible to mortal sight" (III, 55). However, the most important knowledge gained in this way, ironically, is that of the limitation itself. In Milton's epistemology, in contrast to that of the negative theologians, the ideal is not transcendence of the structures of the mind, but "lowly wis[dom]" (VIII, 173), or, to use the term coined by Nicolas of Cusa, "learned ignorance," the concentration of human cognitive effort within the given limits of human capabilities.[46]

Hence the senses, the organs of man's discursive demonstrative reasoning, become of utmost importance, and the loss of sight a staggering, irrevocable blow. For in a state of external darkness, wisdom is "at one entrance *quite shut out*" (III, 50; italics mine). A blind man, Milton implies, may learn through other senses, or even through God's grace; but one of the few means of being "lowly wise," of exercising the uniquely human form of reasoning, is denied him.

Moreover, sight and speech are not only uniquely human means of acquiring knowledge, but also a distinctly human way of expressing devotion to God. In the definition given by the narrative voice in Book VII, man is said to be:

> self-knowing, and from thence
> Magnanimous to correspond with heaven,
> But grateful to acknowledge whence his good
> Descends, thither with heart *and voice and eyes*
> Directed in devotion.   (VII, 510–14; italics mine).

First, then, the worship of God supreme, in Milton, in contrast to the negative theologians, is to be implemented through the eyes and not in darkness. Second, it is to be with the heart, that is, with full psychological intention, though necessarily with the heart as governed by reason. For "self left," says Milton, the heart is "variable and vain" (XI, 92), or, as Adam puts it, "apt to rove" (VIII, 188). But finally, what is perhaps most illuminating concerning the role of silence in the poem, and contrary to the assumption of negative theologians, devotion to God is not to be shown in silence.

As situation, silence in the poem characterizes a form of obedience which is a result, not of emotional devotion, but of intimidation before authority. The "silence" (I, 561) marking the march of the fallen angels to the council in Pandemonium is an expression of the "united force" — in other words, the conformity — of their "fix'd thought" (I, 560–61). Similarly, their muteness when assembled in Pandemonium is another result of their unified "attention" (I, 618) to their commander. Thus, the occasion in which Abdiel condemns the rebelling angels, but meets with silence in which "his zeal / None seconded" (V, 849–50) — which, according to Mary Niquist's interpretation, "preenact[s] . . . Eve's guilty participation in Satan's subversive reason"[47] — may more plausibly be taken simply as an expression of the angels' collective inertia and inability to resist the authority of Satan.

In contrast, the obedience required of man is both free and individual. It is an expression of inner personal choice and not of identification with a larger social whole. Therefore, it is to be expressed by "voice" (VII, 513), the externalization of the unique self, which may further formulate itself in language, its "daughter" (IX, 653) or image, rather than by silence, which effaces the limits between self and other.

Second, silence in the poem is a form of signification used by non-human entities. In heaven, there seems to be no distinction between silence and speech. After the war in heaven, the saints, who were "eye witnesses" to the Son's "almighty deeds," came out to greet him, and instead of voicing their admiration, stand "silent" before him (VI, 882). The Son uses silent signification as direct continuation to the speech act in which he volunteers to ransom man: "His words here ended, but his meek aspect / Silent yet spake, and breathed immortal love / To mortal men" (III, 266–68). Similarly, when he orders the raging deep, he evokes "silence," yet while doing so, speaks.

Satan retains this suprahuman form of signification through silence even after his fall from heaven. When Satan sees the bridge built by Sin and Death, "Long he admiring stood, till Sin . . . / the silence broke" (X, 352–53). However, silence also characterizes the signification of the entities at the other end of the Chain of Being. All entities which "breathe," or are animate, but which, possessing no intellect, are mere "things," "From the earth's great altar send silent praise / To the creator" (IX, 194–96).

The closest Adam and Eve get to the suprahuman form of nonverbal signification is in a great moment of intimacy almost at the end of the poem, when Eve speaks and Adam is "well pleased, but answered not" (XII, 625). But throughout, the only signification used by Adam and Eve, the only form of expressing admiration, is in speech: "Witness if I be silent, morn or even" say Adam and Eve in their prayer, "To hill, or valley, fountain, or fresh shade / Made vocal by my song and taught his praise" (V, 202–04).

Yet, it seems that though man differs from other creatures in his unique form of vocal expression, for all creatures—angels, fallen angels, and man—silence denotes a psychological state of brooding and introversion. When the Father asks for a volunteer to ransom man, "all the heavenly choir stood mute / And silence was in heaven" (III, 217–18), each angel apparently turning to his own consciousness. Similarly, when Satan asks for volunteers for the journey to earth, "all sat mute, / Pondering the danger with deep thoughts" (II, 420–21). Finally, after the fall, Adam and Eve turn to confront their consciences and are similarly described as "silent, and in face / Confounded long they sat, as strucken mute" (IX, 1063–64).

However, in contrast to the introversion of the angels, this last silence signifies a collapse. Adam's introversion or "inward silence" after the fall is described as something he eventually "broke" (IX, 895). For previously, Adam and Eve had existed through dialogue, with each other, with Raphael, with God. It was thus that they expressed emotion and gained knowledge. Furthermore, Adam's essential role and form of participation in the creation was by naming, which is another extroversion of the self through language. Adam is presented as the endower of "names" (VIII, 344) to the beasts, who, in doing so, gains "sudden apprehension" of "their nature" (VIII, 353). Naming, then, is the task of man within God's creation. The silence following the Fall, therefore, is an expression of the fact that it is not only a divine decree man has betrayed but his own nature and vocation.

Consequently, *Paradise Lost*, as a speech act, the obverse of silence, moves not only toward justifying God to man, but also toward restoring man to his proper vocation. Speech acts, moreover, assume an audience which is part of the act. Both the poet who composed *Paradise Lost* and the reader who interprets his text, then, are involved in an attempt to define the universe through language, and hence to approach the original Adamic situation. Thus, it seems that though Milton balances and juxtaposes silence and darkness throughout the poem, placing them as both conditions for knowledge and conditions of evil — as both good and evil on the psychological, epistemological, and physical dimensions of his universe — he ultimately tilts the balance and projects silence as the greater evil. For, on a metapoetic level, though a blind poet could write so great and enduring a poem of devotion as *Paradise Lost*, silence remained the greatest, most irrevocable curse he could impose on the fallen angels: "Nameless in dark oblivion let them dwell / . . . eternal silence be their doom" (VI, 380, 385).

Tel Aviv University

NOTES

1. Merrit Y. Hughes, "Milton and the Symbol of Light," *SEL* IV (1969), 2–3; Lawrence Babb, *The Moral Cosmos of "Paradise Lost"* (East Lansing, Mich., 1970), p. 116; Walter Clyde Curry, *Milton's Ontology, Cosmogony and Physics* (Lexington, Ky., 1967), p. 15; D. C. Allen, "Milton and the Descent to Light," in *Milton: Modern Essays in Criticism*, ed. Arthur Barker (New York, 1963), p. 184; Jackson Cope, *The Metaphoric Structure of "Paradise Lost"* (Baltimore, 1962), p. 46.

2. Peter F. Fisher, "Milton's Theodicy," *JHI* XVII (1956), 38; Edward J. Zimmerman, *"Light out of Darkness": A Study of the Growth and Structure of Evil in Milton's "Paradise Lost,"* Ph.D. diss., State University of New York at Buffalo, 1970; Abstract in *DA* XXXI (1971), 4741-A.

3. Curry, *Milton's Ontology, Cosmogony and Physics*, pp. 190, 17; Babb, *The Moral Cosmos of "Paradise Lost,"* p. 116.

4. Louis L. Martz, *The Paradise Within: Studies in Vaughan, Traherne and Milton* (New Haven, 1964), pp. xiv, 110, 115, 140.

5. Irene Samuel, *Dante and Milton* (Ithaca, N.Y., 1966), p. 17.

6. Joseph Anthony Mazzeo, *Medieval Cultural Tradition in Dante's "Comedy"* (New York, 1968), p. 104.

7. Samuel, *Dante and Milton*, p. 17.

8. Milton's poetry is quoted throughout from *The Poems of John Milton*, ed. John Carey and Alaister Fowler (London, 1968).

9. Joseph Summers, *The Muse's Method: An Introduction to "Paradise Lost"* (London, 1962), p. 28.

10. Kester Svendsen, *Milton and Science* (New York, 1956), pp. 64, 65, 232, 64.

11. Rosalie Colie, *Paradoxie Epidemica: The Renaissance Tradition of Paradox* (Princeton, N.J., 1966), pp. 519, 32.

12. Colie, *Paradoxia Epidemica*, p. 519.

13. Edgar Wind, *Pagan Mysteries in the Renaissance* (Harmondsworth, Middlesex, 1967), pp. 53–54.

14. See Andrew Louth, *The Origins of the Christian Mystical Tradition* (Oxford, 1981), pp. 32, 83, 87–89, 173.

15. Giordano Bruno, *Eroici Furori*, II, iv, quoted in Wind, *Pagan Mysteries in the Renaissance*, p. 54.

16. Louth, *Origins of the Christian Mystical Tradition*, pp. 32, 83.

17. A. B. Chambers, "Wisdom at One Entrance Quite Shut Out: *Paradise Lost*, III, 1–55," in *Milton: Modern Essays in Criticism*, p. 223.

18. Franklin R. Baruch, "Milton's Blindness: The Conscious and Unconscious Patterns of Autobiography," in *ELH* XLII (1975), 37.

19. Herman Rapaport, *Milton and the Postmodern* (Lincoln, Neb., 1983), pp. 210, 214.

20. Mary Niquist, "The Father's Word/Satan's Wrath," *PMLA* (1985), 190–92.

21. Allen, "Milton and the Descent to Light," p. 191.

22. Curry, *Milton's Ontology, Cosmogony and Physics*, p. 10.

23. Babb, *The Moral Cosmos of "Paradise Lost,"* p. 116.

24. Colie, *Paradoxia Epidemica*, p. 32.

25. Babb, *The Moral Cosmos of "Paradise Lost,"* p. 7; see also William G. Madsen, "Earth the Shadow of Heaven: Typological Symbolism in *Paradise Lost*," in *Milton: Modern Essays in Criticism*, p. 246. The same observation appears also in C. A. Patrides, *Milton and the Christian Tradition* (Oxford, 1966) pp. 9–10.

26. Mary Niquist, "The Father's Word/Satan's Wrath," p. 188.

27. Joseph E. Duncan, "Milton's Four-in-One Hell," *Huntington Library Quarterly* XX (1957), 129.

28. Roland Mushat Frye, *God, Man and Satan: Patterns of Christian Thought and Life in "Paradise Lost," "The Pilgrim's Progress" and the Great Theologians* (Princeton, N.J., 1966), p. 40.

29. C. A. Patrides, "Renaissance and Modern Views of Hell," in *Theological Review* LVII (1964), 223.

30. Duncan, "Milton's Four-in-One Hell," p. 134; J. B. Broadbent, "Milton's Hell," *ELH* XXI (1954), 169–70.

31. Robert M. Adams, "A Little Look into Chaos," in *Illustrious Evidence: Approaches*

to *English Literature of the Early Seventeenth Century*, ed. Earl Miner (Berkeley and Los Angeles, 1975), p. 77.

32. Irene Samuel, *Plato and Milton* (Ithaca, N.Y., 1947), p. 160.

33. Curry, *Milton's Ontology, Cosmogony and Physics*, p. 85.

34. William H. Boyd, "The Secrets of Chaos," *MQ* X (1976), 840.

35. A. B. Chambers, "Chaos in *Paradise Lost*," in *JHI* XXIV (1963), 84; see also Arthur Sewell, *A Study in Milton's Christian Doctrine* (Oxford, 1939), p. 147.

36. Northrop Frye, *Five Essays on Milton's Epics* (London, 1966), p. 44.

37. Patrides, *Milton and the Christian Tradition*, p. 40.

38. David Francis Finnigan, *Dark Designs: The Presentation of Evil in Paradise Lost*, Ph.D. diss., University of Oregon, 1970. Abstract in *DA* XXXII (1972) 387-A.

39. Fisher, "Milton's Theodicy," p. 36.

40. Broadbent, "Milton's Hell," p. 178.

41. Fisher, Milton's Theodicy," p. 36.

42. Douglas Bush, "*Paradise Lost* in Our Time: Religious and Ethical Principles," in *Milton: Modern Essays in Criticism*, p. 161.

43. Mary Niquist, "Reading the Fall: Discourse and Drama in *Paradise Lost*," in *ELR* XIV (1984), 218.

44. Robert R. Craven, "The Mists in *Paradise Lost*," *ELN* XVIII (1980), 21.

45. Arnold Stein, "Milton's War in Heaven: An Extended Metaphor," in *Milton: Modern Essays in Criticism*, p. 281.

46. Pauline Moffit Watts, *Nicolas Cusanus: A Fifteenth Century View of Man* (Leiden, The Netherlands, 1982), p. 40.

47. Niquist, "The Father's Word/Satan's Wrath," p. 193.

READING GOD:
MILTON AND THE
ANTHROPOPATHETIC TRADITION

Michael Lieb

As a crucial part of the chapter entitled "Of God" in his treatise *Christian Doctrine* (I, ii), Milton addresses a concept of major import not only to his own view of deity but to the traditions of theological exegesis dating back to the early church fathers.[1] Known as *anthropopatheia*, this concept focuses upon the nature of God not just as an anthropomorphic presence but as a passible being. Adopting the perspective of divine anthropomorphism, *anthropopatheia* moves logically to the corresponding issue of whether or not God experiences emotions and the extent to which those emotions represent an important index both to what might be called the "personality" of God and the means by which one might better understand the nature of that personality.[2]

Because of the role that Scriptures play in the attempt to arrive at an understanding of the divine personality, a discussion of *anthropopatheia* in the context of the debates over passibility should suggest the way in which the delineation of God in the scriptural text gave rise to a theoretics of reading through which the debates themselves found expression. As was made clear from the earliest attempts to argue on behalf of passibility, on the one hand, or impassibility, on the other, one's view of godhead was largely determined by a willingness (or unwillingness) to take Scriptures at their word. One's stance regarding this crucial issue proved decisive in the determination of not only how God is to be understood in scriptural terms but how the Bible itself is to be read, how it functions as a text, and how the readers should view themselves as interpreters of that text. In order to gain a greater awareness of these issues, we shall first glance at the traditions from which the debate over passibility arose, after which we shall proceed to an analysis of Milton's own views in the context of those traditions. In the course of considering the traditions, we shall become increasingly aware of how a theoretics of reading formed an essential part of the emerging attitude concerning the emotional life of God, particularly as manifested in the notion of *anthropopatheia*.

213

I

As scholars have long recognized, *anthropopatheia* as a concept finds its source in early commentaries concerning the nature of God's attributes. Even before the church fathers addressed themselves to this idea, Philo considered it in his treatise *The Unchangeableness of God*.[3] Approaching the subject from the Hellenistic perspective that he embodied, Philo transformed the biblical deity into a philosophical principle founded upon the idea of immutability. In place of any scriptural suggestions of a passible deity, Philo substituted his own philosophical predilections founded upon the concept of divine permanence.[4] As that which is immutable, God, argues Philo, cannot be "moved," that is, cannot experience emotion, for emotion implies movement, which, in turn, suggests mutability. Accordingly, God "is not susceptible to any passion [*pathei*] at all." Correspondingly, "the parts and members of the body in general" have "no relation to God," who is self-existent principle (XI, 52). To suggest otherwise, Philo observes, is to engage in "the mythical fictions of the impious, who, professing to represent the deity as of human form, in reality represent Him as having human passions [*anthropopathes*]" (XII, 59). But this, as Philo was well aware, is precisely what the Bible does. On the basis of such a recognition, Philo is accordingly put to the expense of devising a rationale for God's delineation as a passible being in the biblical text. Philo does this through a theory of accommodation that amounts to a denigration of those inclined to take the Bible at its word. Granting that Moses did ascribe humanlike characteristics to God in the Bible, Philo maintains that these expressions served only for "a kind of elementary lesson, to admonish those who could not otherwise be brought to their senses" (XI, 52). These are the foolish rabble whose natural wit is dense and dull and who do not have ability to see clearly. "Thus ill-disciplined and foolish slaves receive profit from a master who frightens them, for they fear his threats and menaces and thus involuntarily are schooled by fear" (XIV, 63). Arguing on behalf of a completely immutable and depersonalized deity, Philo has nothing but contempt for the anthropopathetic and anthropomorphic conceptions of God. As these notions are found in the biblical text, they are used negatively and condescendingly to admonish an unbelieving and foolish multitude. The true reader for Philo, then, is one who is able to look beyond the apparent meanings implicit in Scriptures. Seeing through the text, as it were, the reader arrives at a truly philosophical understanding of deity.

It is this notion that found widespread acceptance in the early church, particularly among the Alexandrian fathers.[5] Even those who adopted it, however, did not do so categorically. Especially pertinent in this regard is Origen, in whom one discovers an evolution from a belief in impassibility to the adoption of an idea of God as entirely passible. Moving from a concept of divine *apatheia* in such early works as *On First Principles* and the *Commentary on John*, he begins to show signs of a shift in position in his *Homilies on Numbers*. By the time he reaches his *Homilies on Ezekiel*, however, he has changed his mind completely. Addressing himself in the sixth homily on Ezekiel to the passion of the Son symbolized by the cross, Origen sees this experience as the emotion of love consummated in the Father:

Moreover, does not the Father and God of the universe somehow experience emotion, since he is long-suffering and of great mercy? Or do you not know that when he distributes human gifts he experiences human emotion? . . . Therefore God endures our ways, just as the Son of God bears our emotions. The Father himself is not impassible. If he is asked, he takes pity and experiences grief, he suffers something of love and . . . for our sake he experiences human emotion [*humanas sustinet passiones*).[6]

This passage demonstrates the extent to which the appeal of the emotional life of God exerted an overwhelming influence even on those committed philosophically to the idea of an impassible deity. The concept of a passible God was difficult to resist. In addition to suggesting the influence of passibility on Origen, the passage also raises other points of interest. Origen views the concept of divine passibility in terms of the relationship between Father and Son. Specifically, the suffering of the Son upon the cross is seen to be intimately related to (in fact, a manifestation of) the suffering that the Father undergoes on behalf of man. In a very real sense, Christ's passion is the embodiment of God's passion.[7] God experiences emotion, an experience consummated in that of the Son upon the cross. Although Origen does not elaborate on the idea of precisely how God may be said to feel emotion, the concept is one that engaged an entire range of patristic exegetes from the earliest times onward.

Tertullian may serve as an example. Although seen as the enemy of Patripassianism, the idea that the Father himself suffered and died on the cross in the guise of the Son, Tertullian endorses the notion of passibility in the godhead. So in *The Five Books Against Marcion*, Tertullian defends divine passibility against those (notably philosophers of the Epicurean school) who argue that emotion implies corruption, even in God.[8] The heretics contend that "if God is angry, and jealous, and roused, and grieved, He must therefore be corrupted, and must therefore die." Such, Tertullian argues, is the folly of those who "prejudge divine things from human" and conclude that, "because in man's corrupt condition there are found passions of this description, therefore there must be deemed to exist in God also sensations of the same kind." In order to clarify the matter, Tertullian distinguishes between the emotional life of man and the emotional life of God. Just as the difference between the divine and the human body is great, so, Tertullian observes, it is with the divine and the human soul, even though the sensations of each are designated by the same names. Just as these sensations in the human being are rendered corrupt by the corruptibility of man's substance, in God they are rendered incorruptible by the incorruption of the divine essence. It is absurd to place human characteristics in God rather than divine ones in man and to clothe God in the likeness of man, instead of man in the image of God. It is to be seen as the likeness of God in man, therefore, that the human soul has the same emotions and sensations of God, although they are not of the same kind. Whereas man possesses these emotions in imperfection, God possesses them in perfection. God, Tertullian concludes, is moved by all these affections "in that peculiar manner of His own, in which it is profoundly fit that He should be affected; and it is owing to Him that man is also similarly affected in a way which is equally his own" (II, xvi). What makes Tertullian's observation so interesting is its insistence that passibility may be seen not only as a characteristic of God but as an attribute that God bestows upon his offspring, notably man in the role of *imago Dei*. Although different in kind from that which man experiences, God's emotion is nonetheless as integral to the divine personality as man's emotion is to the human. In Tertullian, then, emotion is accorded a divine psychogenesis, one that legitimates the concept of the "mind" or personality of God.

Tertullian is not alone in having approached the notion of passibility in this manner.[9] Among the church fathers, the one individual who, more than any other, devoted his energies to a defense of passibility is Lactantius. His treatise *The Wrath of God* is a detailed exploration of the issue.[10] Arguing against the Epicureans, who maintained that God experiences no emotion, and the Stoics, who believed that God could be kind but not angry, Lactantius asserts that it is the very nature of divinity to be passible: "What beatitude, then, can there be in God," asks Lactantius, "if quiet and immobile He is ever inactive; if He is deaf to those who pray, if blind to those who worship Him? What is so worthy, so befitting to God as providence? But if He cares for nothing, provides for nothing, He has lost all divinity" (chap. 4).[11] What is true for Tertullian is likewise true for Lactantius: emotion becomes an essential constituent of the divine personality. In both church fathers, one discovers a divinization of emotion as it originates in God. This divinization, moreover, applies not only to emotions such as love and compassion, normally associated with God. It likewise applies to the emotions of anger and hatred, both of which for Lactantius are manifested in the divine personality of God. Addressing himself to that personality, Lactantius observes: "He who loves the good also hates the evil, and he who does not hate the evil does not love the good, because, on the one hand, to love the good comes from hatred of evil, and to hate the evil rises from love of the good. . . . The one who loves, therefore, also hates, and he who hates also loves" (chap. 5). A loving God is also therefore not only potentially an angry God but a God who, under the appropriate circumstances, is capable of hatred as well. Entering the perilous waters of divine passibility, Lactantius does not hesitate to attribute to deity the most extreme of emotions, but even Lactantius has his limits. He will not allow the possibility that God experiences such affections as fear, sexual desire, envy, avarice, or grief. These affections, he feels, are demeaning to God. "What need is there," he asks, "to speak of the human affections to which our frailty yields?" In the case of fear, for example, Lactantius offers the following reason for its absence from the emotional makeup of deity: God, "on whom there falls neither need, nor injury, nor pain, nor death, can fear in no way because there is nothing that can bear force against Him." Corresponding arguments are put forward for sexual desire, envy, avarice, and grief (chap. 15). What determines the criteria of selection that Lactantius adopts finally seems somewhat arbitrary and suggests the potential dangers awaiting those whose view of deity is determined to immerse godhead in the realm of the passible. Although Lactantius realized that it was easier to conceive deity as an entity totally removed from the possible turmoil and uncertainty that such an immersion might entail, his view of godhead was such that the removal of passibility was tantamount to the removal of divinity itself. Granting the questions that his approach was bound to provoke, Lactantius was fully committed to the notion of a passible God.

Needless to say, the views represented by Origen (in his later writings), Tertullian, and Lactantius proved to be the exception rather than the rule. Committed to the kind of outlook manifested in the philosophical schools, the early church adopted the impassibility of God as an established doctrine. In this respect, St. Augustine is the consummate spokesman for the orthodox point of view. In the expression of that point of view, he begins with the human perspective and moves to the divine. Arguing in *The City of God* that *pathos* implies "a commotion of the

mind contrary to reason" (VIII, 17), he concludes that passion, when
uncontrolled and misdirected, is incompatible with blessedness.[12] "It is
in the freedom from all disturbance, from all the weakness and defects
which in human experience are associated with the various phases of the
emotional life, that Augustine sees the divine impassibility."[13] Accordingly, he says, "that which the Greeks call *apatheia,* and what the Latins
would call, if their language would allow them, '*impassibilitas,*' . . . is
obviously a good and most desirable quality, but it is not one which is
attainable in this life." When man shall be without sin, then shall he
be able to realize full *apatheia* (XIV, 9). It is precisely this *apatheia* that
finds true expression in God. In keeping with those philosophical principles that subscribe to the idea of immutability, St. Augustine argues
that God remains impassible, that is, immutable, even when appearing
to undergo pathos. Although pathos is ascribed to God, his impassibility
is such that what we would call emotion in him is of a nature totally
beyond our understanding. So St. Augustine observes in his treatise *On
Patience:*

> Patience is spoken of as belonging even to God. So though God can suffer nothing,
> while patience takes its name from suffering, nevertheless we not only faithfully
> believe, but also healthfully confess, that God is patient. But of what kind and how
> great the patience of God is who can explain, when we speak of Him as suffering
> nothing, yet not as without patience, but rather as most patient? His patience is
> therefore ineffable, even as His jealousy, His anger, and any other similar char-
> acteristics. For if we think of them as though they were ours, none such exists in
> Him. For none of them do we experience without vexation, but far be it from us
> to imagine that the impassible nature of God suffers any vexation. For as He is
> jealous without any envy, is angry without any perturbation, is pitiful without
> any grief, repents without having any evil in Him to correct, so He is patient
> without any suffering.[14]

In effect, St. Augustine has it both ways: God is essentially impassible,
but appears to exhibit passibility in the most exalted and ineffable form.
Whatever that passibility is (or at least appears to be) far transcends our
power to know. One thing is certain, however: that which appears to
us as passibility occurs without any perturbation in the mind of God or
compromising of his divine *apatheia.* "God," says St. Augustine, "does
not repent as does a man, but as God; just as He is not angry after the
manner of men, nor is pitiful, nor is jealous, but all He is He is as God."
By the repentance of God is signified "the change of things which lie
within His power, unexpected by man; the anger of God is His vengeance
upon sin; the pity of God is the goodness of His help; the jealousy of God
is that providence whereby He does not allow those whom He has in

subjection to Himself to love with impunity what He forbids." In short, it is we who read pathos into God: we attribute to him those emotions that we experience as a result of the effects that his actions have upon us.[15]

As with Philo, St. Augustine explains this act of "reading God" through the idea of accommodation. Unlike Philo, however, St. Augustine in *The City of God* does not view the accommodative dimension of Scriptures in a manner that is necessarily demeaning to the reader. The audience for God as accommodated deity encompasses a wide range of abilities but is essentially limited by man's incapacity to go beyond the boundaries of his own nature. Applying such attributes as anger and repentance to God, the Bible "familiarly insinuate[s] itself into the minds of all classes of men, whom it seeks access to for their good, that it may alarm the proud, arouse the careless, exercise the inquisitive, and satisfy the intelligent; and this it could not do, did it not first stoop, and in a manner descend to them where they lie" (XV, 25). If St. Augustine adopts the theory of accommodation, he does so not to suggest that what appears to be pathos in God really is so but to explain that pathos as a literary manifestation of what might be called God's "figurative" presence in Scriptures. In his regard, St. Augustine's view of scriptural language as applied to notions of passibility is essentially rhetorical in nature. The Bible adopts metaphors for deity in order to allow the reader to understand what would otherwise be beyond human comprehension. The reader, in turn, is not to interpret these metaphors literally. To do so would be to violate the figurative dimension of the biblical text. When applied to the notion of passibility, reading God for St. Augustine requires us to distinguish between the way God appears in the text and the way God really is. What appears to be true is so only insofar as it insinuates itself familiarly into the minds of readers in order to promote their betterment, but it does not provide insight into the actual mind of God, which is finally unknowable. For St. Augustine, that unknowability and the fact of God's impassibility are synonymous.[16]

If the kind of outlook that St. Augustine embodied became the norm throughout the Middle Ages, an adherence to the essential impassibility of God was the standard of Renaissance thought on the subject as well.[17] Such is particularly true of Reformation theology. Those among the Reformation exegetes who considered the issue of God's personality generally remained committed to the idea of an impassible deity. In this respect, Calvin represents a case in point. His allegiance to impassibility appears most fully delineated in his *Commentaries Upon the Book of Genesis*.[18] Analyzing Genesis vi, 6 ("And it repented the Lord that he had made man on the earth, and it grieved him at his heart"), Calvin maintains that "the repentance which is here ascribed to God does not properly belong to him, but has reference to our understanding of him. For since we cannot comprehend him as he is, it is necessary that, for our sake, he should, in a certain sense, transform himself." The same reasoning is applicable, Calvin observes, to the notion that God grieves. "Certainly," says Calvin, "God is not sorrowful or sad; but remains for ever like himself in his celestial and happy repose: yet, because it could not otherwise be known how great is God's hatred and detestation of sin, therefore the Spirit accommodates himself to our capacity."

Calvin's observations are interesting for a number of reasons. They suggest that the ascription of emotion of God derives not from God as he really is but from man as he responds to the accommodated presence of deity in the Scriptures. As a being moved by passions of one sort or another, man is prompted by that presence to read his own passibility into God, to create God, as it were, in his own image. This is entirely understandable, Calvin would argue, because man, as a limited creature, indeed, a fallen and sinful creature, cannot conceive of God in any other way. In order to read God, man must, in a sense, misread. As he does so, however, he must also be aware at every juncture that his reading is in fact a misreading. Aware of this misreading, he will know that God is not really passible but only appears to be so. Calvin is no doubt aware of this fact, for, just at the point of advancing the notion of divine *apatheia*, his analysis implicates itself in the very passibility it would dismiss. Arguing that God neither repents nor grieves, his analysis portrays God as a being who exhibits emotions such as hatred and detestation. How does one argue on behalf of *apatheia* and yet refer to God's "hatred and detestation of sin"? For Calvin, as for earlier exegetes, the answer lies in the transformative nature of God's act of accommodation. In Calvin's understanding of that act, God "clothes himself with our affections" in order to "pierce our hearts" more compellingly. This piercing of the heart has the effect of "subdu[ing] in us the love of sin." In accommodated form, God assumes a possible presence for the purpose of heightening our awareness of our own passibility. Such are the spiritual effects of accommodation.

As Calvin was well aware, these effects are intimately bound up with literary dimensions that accommodation assumes in his thought. As a means by which deity makes itself known, accommodation for Calvin is essentially a troping of God. It is a literary act, one in which deity attires itself in the clothing of humanity. As such, accommodation is tantamount to figuration. In fact, Calvin refers to God's "clothing" of himself with man's affections as a trope, a figure distinguished by a particular name. "This figure," he says, "which represents God as transferring to himself what is peculiar to human nature, is called *anthropopatheia*." With this statement, Calvin places himself squarely in the tradition of those who read the fact of God's passible presence in Scripture as a rhetorical event. Determined to reconcile scriptural representation with doctrinal imperative, such exegetes consign passibility to the realm of trope. They rhetoricize passibility in order to avoid compromising any notion of *apatheia*. As a result of this rhetoricizing, the impassible is clothed in passible form. Unlike those for whom the act of rhetoricizing represents a perfectly acceptable means of reconciling the fact of God's *apatheia* with his apparent passibility in Scriptures, Calvin approaches the whole notion of such a rhetoricizing with some trepidation.

His ambivalence is made clear in the *Institutes*.[19] There, he argues that "every figurative representation of God contradicts his being." Among the prophets, Isaiah, for example, "teaches that God's majesty is sullied by an unfitting and absurd fiction, when the incorporeal is made to resemble corporeal matter, [and] the invisible a visible likeness" (I, xi, 2). Accordingly, any image that we conceive in our minds concerning God is "an insipid fiction" (I, xi, 4). Nonetheless, man does not hesitate to imagine God according to his own conception and to express in various forms (notably in works of art) the sort of deity he has inwardly conceived (I, xi, 10). Calvin is not totally opposed to such representations. Works of art, he says, are "gifts of God." But works of art must have a pure and legitimate purpose, one fully aware of their own limitations, and even granting the potential usefulness of such works, Calvin still concludes that it is "wrong that God should be represented by a visible appearance, because he himself has forbidden it and it cannot be done without some defacing of his glory" (I, xi, 12). No matter how God is portrayed, such portrayals are suspect. This, Calvin implies, is true even of scriptural representations. The fault here, however, lies not in God's accommodating of himself to man's limited capacities. Rather, it lies in man's foolish inclination to assume that God's accommodated presence may be interpreted literally. Such, observes Calvin, was the fault of the Anthropomorphites, "who imagined a corporeal God from the fact that Scripture often ascribes to him [God] a mouth, ears, eyes, hands, and feet."[20] This, correspondingly, would be the fault of those who might believe in the passibility of God. In both respects, interpreters who literalize trope do not understand that, "as nurses commonly do with infants, God is wont in a measure to 'lisp' in speaking to us." "Such forms of speaking do not so much express clearly what God is like as accommodate the knowledge of him to our slight capacity. To do this, he must descend far beneath his loftiness" (I, xiii, 1). We, in turn, must be on guard not to read literally what must be interpreted figuratively. To do otherwise is to create false images of God, that is, to misread without being aware that our misreading is precisely that, a belying of the true ineffability of godhead.[21] Then, we would interpret *anthropopatheia* as fact rather than as figure. We would rest content with the clothing of God's anthropopathetic presence rather than removing that clothing in order to perceive the truth of the impassibility that his clothing masks. As one fully committed to the concept of *apatheia*, Calvin looked upon himself as an interpreter determined to preserve the notion of God's impassibility at all costs.[22]

If Calvin fulfilled this ideal in his own work, his adherence to the concept of impassibility became a commonplace of Reformation exegesis. In this respect, William Ames, an acknowledged influence on Milton's own *Christian Doctrine*, is representative.[23] Addressing himself to the issue of "God and His Essence" in *The Marrow of Theology* (I, iv), Ames makes clear his position on the subject of impassibility.[24] True to the title of his work as a "marrow" or *medulla*, the mode of expression that Ames adopts provides the quintessence of prevailing thought on the subject. Pithy and declarative, this mode of expression assumes the form of *topoi* or theological commonplaces that by their very nature suggest the extent to which impassibility itself became a Reformation topos given to bald pronouncement.[25] Ames issues his pronouncements in the context of what he calls "the knowledge of God." "God, as he is in himself," declares Ames, "cannot be understood by any save himself." Those who do attempt to explain "the things which pertain to God" must do so in "a human way." This human way frequently assumes "a manner of speaking called *anthropopatheia*." Because the attribute of passibility implicit in *anthropopatheia* is accessible to "human comprehension," such an idea is applied to God "according to our own conceiving rather than according to his real nature." For the quality which is called "passive" is simply not in God. Indeed, "the affections attributed to God in scripture, such as love, hatred and the like . . . apply to God only figuratively" (pp. 83–87). Once again, we are made aware of the way in which the idea of reading God represents an act of creating God. The reader as author projects his own image, that is, his own passible nature, onto what is inconceivable and uncreatable. This Ames calls the "human way" of reading God, one that speaks of deity according to its "own conceiving" rather than according to what really is. The form assumed by this manner of reading is *anthropopatheia*, which in Ames, as in Calvin and his forebears, is a figure of speech, a rhetoricizing of the divine. Here, as elsewhere, *anthropopatheia* becomes a troping of God, an understandable misreading, given man's limitations, but a misreading nonetheless. For Ames, the concept of emotion as a divine attribute loses any real meaning: it is simply metaphor. The God of Ames remains distant and aloof in the blissfully untouched and untouchable realm of *apatheia*. Nothing out of the ordinary here: the views embodied in Ames's *Marrow* simply reflect the acknowledged beliefs of the Church of England, institutionalized in the Thirty-nine Articles and reiterated in the Westminster Confession: "There is but one only living and true God, who is infinite in being and perfection, a most pure spirit, invisible, without body, parts, or passions, immutable, immense, eternal, [and] incomprehensible."[26] As expressed here in institutional form, such a statement codifies the prevailing Reformation view regarding God's impassibility, a view shared not only by Ames but by a host of other theologians as well.[27]

II

The foregoing should suggest something of the milieu (both medieval and Renaissance) out of which Milton's own treatment of divine passibility emerged in *Christian Doctrine*. There, the subject receives full consideration. Because Milton's treatment, like that of Ames, falls under the larger heading of "knowing God" ("*cognoscendo Deo*"), this aspect requires initial attention. In his discussion of knowing God, Milton argues that because God far transcends man's limited powers of comprehension, it is impossible to speak of knowing him in any absolute sense. Despite these limitations, however, God makes a point of revealing as much of himself as the mind of man can conceive and the weakness of his nature can bear. God's principal mode of self-revelation is through the sacred writings ("*in sacris literis*"). To know God as he wishes himself to be known is to read him in Scriptures. It is there that God most fittingly "accommodates" himself to our capacities ("*ipse se ad captum accommodans nostrum*"). Encountering God as he has authorized his appearance in the sacred text, we, in turn, should "form such a mental image of him [*mente nostra concipere*], as he, in bringing himself within the limits of our understanding, wishes us to form."[28] Attending in this manner to God's portrayal of himself in the scriptural text, we shall be spared the errors of those tempted to extend their reach beyond the "the written authority of scripture," only to find themselves lost in the "vague subtleties of speculation" (YP VI, pp. 133–34; CM XIV, pp. 31–33).[29]

Immediately at issue is the nature of God's self-revelation. In Milton's thought, this phenomenon assumes a distinctly textual bearing. The sacred writings for Milton are the vehicle through which God authorizes his own presence.[30] To use the language of *Paradise Lost*, one might say that in the Bible God becomes "author to himself" (cf. III, 122). Acting in his capacity as author, God appropriates the Bible as the text in which his accommodated presence is to be most fully and effectively understood. At the heart of Milton's hermeneutics is this all-important emphasis upon intentionality. Reading the Scriptures becomes for Milton an exercise in the discovery of God's intentions, of forming a mental image of him corresponding to that which he, in bringing himself within the limits of our understanding, desires us to form. Responsive to God's authorized presence, Milton's hermeneutics is a hermeneutics of intentionality.[31] A misunderstanding of intentions can become a particularly risky enterprise, because, as a sacred text, the Bible deals in matters of belief. To read God is in effect a religious act: one must be careful to avoid the perils of misinterpretation. Although Milton was well aware that these perils were compounded by the questionable state in which the sacred writings were preserved, he nonetheless believed that between the writings as they had been transmitted to his own times and the Holy Spirit as a guide to God's intentions, the reader had sufficient warrant to know God as the deity revealed himself in his own writings, in that text of which he himself was supreme author.[32] For Milton, this fact bestowed upon the text a primacy that refused to allow its message to be compromised by "vague subtleties of speculation." Responding as we should to what Scriptures actually say — that is, to what they have been authorized to proclaim — we should behold them "protesting their own plainnes, and perspicuity" in all matters essential to be known and especially that concerning God's portrayal of himself in his own text.[33]

This view of Scriptures is fundamental to Milton's treatment of *anthropopatheia* in *Christian Doctrine*. There, Milton appears initially to dismiss the notion of divine passibility, only afterward to reintroduce it in another form. He dismisses it as a trope through which theologians presume to come to terms with God's unknowableness and reintroduces it as a fact through which God's unknowableness is manifested in accommodated form to man's limited capacities. This paradoxical maneuver is one that does away with the rhetorical dimensions of passibility while preserving its substantive dimensions. Having argued for the self-sufficiency of the biblical text as a means of knowing God, Milton accordingly ventures the following observation:

In my opinion, then, theologians do not need to employ anthropopathy, or the ascription of human feelings to God. This is a rhetorical device thought up by grammarians [*quam figuram Grammatici*] to explain the nonsense poets write about Jove. Sufficient care has been taken, without any doubt, to ensure that the holy scriptures contain nothing unfitting to God or unworthy of him. . . . So it is better not to think about God or form an image of him in anthropopathetic terms, for to do so would be to follow the example of men, who are always inventing more and more subtle theories about him. Rather we should form our ideas with scripture as a model, for that is the way in which he has offered himself to our contemplation. We ought not to imagine that God would have said anything or caused anything to be written about himself unless he intended that it should be a part of our conception of him. (YP VI, p. 134; CM XIV, p. 32)

The observation is unequivocal in its expression of Milton's argument on behalf of scriptural self-sufficiency. Responding to the biblical text, the reader need not "invent" God through the attribution of characteristics that are nothing more than a rhetoricizing of God's presence. To do so is tantamount to making of him a pagan deity whose actions are comparable to those one finds indecorously portrayed not only in myths of various sorts but implicitly in the traditions of exegesis dating back to the early church and extending into his own times. Countering those traditions, Milton endorses a theoretics of reading that refuses to secularize the sacred writings. This is what he feels happens in any attempt to explain God through the use of *anthropopatheia* conceived in rhetorical terms, that is, as a trope by which what is otherwise inexplicable is domesticated, brought down to the level of man. So conceived, *anthropopatheia* explains away, rather than explains, and the reader as *rhetor* creates God in the image of man. God becomes an *imago hominis*, rather than man an *imago Dei*. Avoiding this trap, Milton advises against following the example of men, who are always inventing more and more subtle theories about God; rather, he advocates following the example of God, through whom appropriate care has been taken to insure that the text of the Bible is a sufficient vehicle for the revelation of God's will. When meaning flows from author (God) to reader (man) and not the other way around, *anthropopatheia* as a rhetorical device is obviated.

Given this theoretics of reading, what then does Milton say about the passibility or impassibility of God? The immediate assumption might well be that in his dismissal of *anthropopatheia* Milton calls passibility itself into question. Precisely the opposite is true. Having done away with *anthropopatheia*, he not only intensifies the idea of passibility but bestows upon it renewed significance. For lack of a better term, this new form of passibility might be called *theopatheia*, as opposed to *anthropopatheia*. Milton generates the concept of *theopatheia* through a reassertion of the divine intentionality that underscores his theoretics of reading. "On the question of what is or what is not suitable for God," Milton observes, "let us ask for no more dependable authority [*auctorem*] than God himself." This appeal to the author to come forth and speak on his own behalf leads Milton to invoke an entire series of instances in which the passibility of God is authorized in the biblical text. "If *Jehovah repented that he had created man*, Gen. vi. 6, *and repented because of their groanings*, Judges ii. 18, let us," Milton says, "believe [*credamus*] that he did repent." "If *he grieved in his heart*, Gen. vi. 6, and if, similarly, *his soul was grieved*, Judges x. 16, let us believe [*credamus*] that he did feel grief." "If it is said that God, after working for six days, *rested and was refreshed*, Exod. xxxi. 17, and if he *feared his enemy's displeasure*, Deut. xxxii. 27, let us believe [*credamus*] that it is not beneath God to feel what grief he does feel, to be refreshed by what refreshes him, and to fear what he does fear. For however you may try to tone down [*lenire*] these and similar texts about God by an elaborate show of interpretive glosses [*interpretationis ambitus*], it comes to the same thing in the end" (YP VI, pp. 134–34; CM XIV, pp. 33–37). In this recitation of proof texts that establish the validity of *theopatheia*, Milton emphasizes time and again both the primacy of the text as the vehicle of intentionality and the function of the creator in authorizing his presence in that text. Reading is believing: "let us believe [*credamus*]," Milton reiterates throughout. *Credamus:* let us believe, no matter how disturbing we may find the notion that deity by its very nature experiences such emotions as repentance, grief, and fear.[34]

To allay any doubts about the nature of the emotions that God experiences, Milton makes it perfectly clear that they are of a different order from those experienced by man. In the case of repentance, for example, Milton says, "let us not imagine that God's repentance arises from lack of foresight, as man's does" (YP VI, pp. 134–35). Although Milton does not elaborate further on the issue of precisely in what manner God repents or feels any other emotion he is said to undergo in the biblical text, it is quite evident from what Milton does say that his theology is founded upon a divinization of the passible. Reflecting an outlook made evident in exegetes as early as Tertullian, this divinization accords the passible a legitimacy, indeed, a sanctity, as compelling as any of the other attributes customarily associated with God.[35] So Milton observes that "those states of mind [*affectus*] which are good in a good man, and count as virtues are holy in God" (YP VI, p. 135; CM XIV, p. 34). With this statement, Milton reclaims the passible as a phenomenon that proved disturbing from the very point at which the early Church sought to come to terms with the personality of God. Relying upon the authority of the biblical text as an index to that personality, Milton dismisses the kind of latitudinarian approach that seeks to tone down (*lenire*) and make palatable the passible dimension of God's character. As a rhetorical fabrication of the exegetes given to such latitudinarianism, *anthropopatheia* will therefore not suffice for Milton. Only *theopatheia*, as that which implies the true emotional life of God, will do.

If such is the case, Milton's advocacy of *theopatheia* raises corresponding issues as well. Despite the fact that the divine nature by definition cannot be known or defined in any absolute sense, Milton does not hesitate to concern himself with the states of God's mind, that is, with the psychogenesis of the passible in the *animus Dei*. Recalling once again those early church fathers who took Scriptures at their word, Milton combines the psychogenetic approach with one that takes into account not just the mind of God (what Milton would call the "internal form") but the body of God (what Milton would call the "external form") as well.[36] Associating these two, Milton maintains that "if *God is said to have created man in his own image, after his own likeness*, Gen. 1. 26, and not only his mind but also his external appearance [*idque non animo solum sed forma etiam externa*]," and "If God attributes to himself again and again a human shape and form, why should we be afraid of assigning to him something he assigns to himself, provided we believe that what is imperfect and weak in us is, when ascribed to God, utterly perfect and utterly beautiful." Both in mind and in body, then, God's accommodated presence as revealed in the biblical text is one in which deity is conceived as a being who not only experiences a full range of emotions but who is portrayed in a manner that corresponds to the shape and form of man as *imago Dei*.[37] Perfecting the image of God in himself, man becomes a fit reader of the biblical text when he is sensitized to the way in which God as creator of that image accommodates himself to man's understanding. "Let there be no question about it," Milton says, "they understand best what God is like who adjust their understanding to the word of God, for he has adjusted his word to our understanding, and has shown what kind of an idea of him he wishes us to have."

This is as much a hermeneutics of reciprocity as it is a hermeneutics of intentionality. As God accommodates himself to man, man adjusts himself to God. The author reaches down; the reader reaches up. The author's intentions are validated in and through the text; the reader's understanding is revealed in its ability to grasp those intentions. Reading is sharing as well as believing. If we refuse to share, that is, if we arrogate meaning to ourselves, we break that hermeneutical circle so fundamental to the concept of reciprocity that Milton endorses. We cannot presume to impose our will upon the text, to create the text. In doing so, we not only violate our role as readers, we misconceive God, who,

Milton insists, "has disclosed just such an idea of himself to our understanding as he wishes us to possess." "If we form some other idea of him,"
Milton concludes, "we are not acting according to his will, but are frus-
trating him of his purpose, as if, indeed, we wished to show that our
concept of God was not too debased, but that his concept of us was" (YP
VI, pp. 135–36; CM XIV, pp. 37–39). The assumptions are clear enough:
as the embodiment of the *imago Dei*, we should not assume that God
debases himself in appearing to be like us; rather, we should ennoble
ourselves in attempting to be like him. We should understand God the
way he understands us. Only by fulfilling the dynamics implicit in this
hermeneutical circle will we do justice to the text in which God's self-
disclosure occurs.

Because of Milton's refusal to rhetoricize (and thereby secularize)
God's presence in the biblical text, then, accommodation for him is an
ennobling experience, not a demeaning one, as it was, say, for Philo,
who admonished that foolish rabble incapable of moving beyond the
world of trope. Dismissing that world as inapplicable to the real nature
of God's accommodated delineation, Milton endorses a hermeneutics of
passibility (and therefore a theoretics of reading) that aligns him with
such exegetes as Tertullian and Lactantius (as well as the later Origen),
through whom the passible was divinized and Scriptures taken at their
word. Recalling these figures — and, in fact, going beyond them in extending the range of emotions attributable to God — Milton broke not
only with the orthodox traditions of the early Church but with the reformed dogmatics of his own time. Doing so, he provoked the kind of
critical debate to which *Christian Doctrine* was customarily subjected
after its publication in 1825.[38]

In this respect, a review that appeared in *The Evangelical Magazine* in 1826 is representative.[39] According to the author of the review,
Milton's attribution of divine emotions to God in *Christian Doctrine* is
nothing more than "a striking example of the power of poetical feeling
over-balancing the dictates of a cool and rigorous judgment." In other
words, by succumbing to the temptation of divine passibility, Milton for
this reviewer abandons the rigors of true theology and writes as a poet.
Having argued that those who subscribe to the anthropopathetic view
of deity are themselves guilty of a kind of poetical excess, Milton would
no doubt find the reviewer's charge somewhat perplexing. Milton would
argue that not he but the reviewer has been taken in by the impulse to
abandon the rigors of theology and to align himself with those exegetes
who rhetoricize and thereby secularize Scriptures. In fact, this is precisely what the reviewer does in his criticism of Milton. From those bibli-

cal passages (notably in the earlier books of the Old Testament) in which "the mutable affections of the human mind, and even the form and members of the human body, are *figuratively* applied to the Infinite Being," Milton, the reviewer charges, would have us conceive God "according to the *literal* meaning of those expressions" (my italics). Such a criticism, of course, makes no allowances for the distinctions Milton himself draws between human passibility and divine passibility. For the reviewer, both are the same. Collapsing the distinction between human and divine, the reviewer then presumes to reveal the shortcomings of the Miltonic point of view:

If the Deity be in reality susceptible of disappointment, grief, regret, change of purpose, the relinquishing of old plans upon an unwelcome discovery of their failure, and the setting to work of new ones, with the hope of better success; — it is impossible to avoid the inference that he is a being limited in both knowledge and power, ignorant of many things which are of the first importance that he should know, embarrassed in his views, thwarted, perplexed, and defeated by unexpected circumstances, and, in fine, a being unutterably distressed and unhappy. (Pp. 92–93)

Although Milton would hardly have acceded to these charges as in any sense applicable to his notion of deity, the reviewer's concern over the potential dangers that lie in wait for those who endorse the concept of passibility is one of which Milton would have been very much aware in his own reading on the subject. Milton knew that in an imperfect form passibility led to all those shortcomings that distinguish human nature from the divine. Despite his awareness of these shortcomings and the concerns that they provoked, Milton was determined not to compromise his view of deity by underestimating the significance of the passible as authorized by God himself in Scriptures. If such is true of Milton's treatment of deity in his theological tract, it is no less true of his handling of deity in his poetry. Both as theologian and as poet, Milton is consistent in his incorporation of the passible into his delineation of godhead. Among his poems, *Paradise Lost* in particular provides dramatic evidence of this fact.

III

As I have argued elsewhere at some length, the figure of God in *Paradise Lost* is portrayed as a fully passible being. In him are embodied an entire spectrum of emotions, ranging from compassion and love to anger and even hate.[40] Although these assertions would appear to be self-evident, the state of Milton criticism at this time is such that Milton's God is still viewed more nearly as abstract principle than as fully realized character. In the very essay in which Irene Samuel argues on behalf of a dramatic reading of God she maintains that he is essentially "Total Being," "Primal Energy," the "Voice of Reason." As an embodiment of "the toneless voice of the moral law," Milton's God, "speaks simply what is." For Roland M. Frye, he is "pure intellect, pure reason, unmixed with passion."[41] Such an outlook is the rule rather than the exception. What makes this outlook so interesting is the extent to which it reflects the antipassible point of view that became the theological norm from the period of the early church up until Milton's own time. The critics of *Paradise Lost* have adopted the role of those earlier exegetes who insisted upon reading the portrayal of God in the scriptural text as the embodiment of *apatheia*. When Milton took this view to task in *Christian Doctrine*, it is almost as if he were responding to the future critics of his own poem.

In modern criticism, one of the most influential and brilliant spokesmen for the antipassible point of view has been Stanley Fish. Adopting the perspective of those who argue on behalf of *apatheia*, Fish conceives God as a being totally removed and fully aloof, an abstraction void of dimensionality. Whatever tonal qualities one discovers in God's voice are the result not of what is there but of what the reader ascribes to or "reads *into*" that voice. The entity that projects this voice is, in turn, devoid of both ethos, the quality that constitutes personality, and pathos, the quality that constitutes the emotional substratum of personality. These qualities emerge as the result of the meaning that arises from the reader's encounter with deity: they are bestowed by the reader onto deity rather than inhering in deity itself.[42] Responding to Milton's God in this manner, Fish explains the presence of the passible by transferring emotion from God as portrayed in the text to the reader as he interprets the tonalities that appear in the voice of God. Such a transferral of the passible from text to reader corresponds in effect to that which occurs among the theologians who invoke the device of *anthropopatheia* to explain God's apparent passibility in the Bible. Reading the passible into God, the reader for Fish in effect creates God in his own image. In Fish as in those theologians committed to an anthropopathetic notion of deity, God becomes an *imago hominis* rather than man an *imago Dei*.[43] As a result of this occurrence, all concepts of the passible in Fish are rhetoricized, "toned down," to use Milton's phrase, and made palatable.

As we have seen, such a view is precisely the opposite of that which Milton held as a theologian who sought to reclaim the passible as a category of deity. Legitimating the passible, Milton divinizes the emotional

life by viewing it as an essential attribute of God. Doing so, Milton refuses to rhetoricize God as the product of an anthropopathetic world view.
He will not consign the passible to the realm of trope. For Milton, the
emotional life of God is real and indeed holy. It originates in God, in-
heres in him, and is bestowed upon his offspring as manifestations of the
imago Dei. From this theological perspective, Milton might well have
responded to the anthropopathetic trend in modern criticism in terms
reminiscent of his answer to the anthropopatheticists in *Christian Doctrine:* "In my opinion, critics do not need to employ anthropopathy, or
the ascription of human feelings to God. This is nothing more than a
rhetorical device thought up by grammarians to explain the nonsense poets
write about Jove." Invoking (in somewhat altered form) his statement
in *Christian Doctrine* and applying it to the modern critics, he would
then have effectively divorced himself not only from the prevailing anthropopathetic reading of God in Scriptures but from the current anthropopathetic reading of God in *Paradise Lost.* In the process, he would
have distinguished his exalted conception of God in his poem from the
"nonsense" the pagan poets write about Jove in theirs. Aligning his poem
with the sacred writings, he would have suggested the kind of hermeneutics most appropriate for his poem, a hermeneutics consistent with
that which was to be applied to the Scriptures.

What Milton says in *Christian Doctrine* about the act of reading
God as rendered in Scriptures might then be accordingly applied to the
act of reading God as rendered in *Paradise Lost.* "It is better not to think
about God or form an image of him in anthropopathetic terms, for to
do so would be to follow the example of men, who are always inventing
more and more subtle theories about him." Rather, we should rely on
the way in which God is actually depicted in Milton's poem, for (to adapt
Milton's statement to our present purposes) "sufficient care has been taken
without any doubt, to ensure that *Paradise Lost* contains nothing unfitting to God or unworthy of him." If such is the case, we shall read the
God of Milton's epic theopathetically rather than anthropopathetically.
If Milton's God is said to be angry, we shall grant him that anger; if
he is said to hate, we shall grant him that hatred; if he appears to be
compassionate, we shall grant him that compassion; if he appears to be
jocular, we shall grant him that jocularity.[44] "For however you may try
to tone down these and similar texts about God by an elaborate show
of interpretive glosses, it comes to the same thing in the end." What is
true of Milton's view of Scriptures is true of the view he holds of his own
poem: the text protests its self-sufficiency, indeed, its primacy as the
vehicle of intentionality. *Credamus:* reading is believing.

Granting the alignment that Milton makes between Scriptures, on the one hand, and *Paradise Lost*, on the other, a major dilemma none-theless presents itself in any attempt to derhetoricize the Miltonic por-trayal of deity in his epic. That dilemma has to do with the accommo-dative assumptions on which the Miltonic portrayal is based. In keeping with the discussion that falls under the heading of "cognoscendo Deo" in *Christian Doctrine*, Milton argues, we recall, that because God far transcends man's limited powers of comprehension, it is impossible to speak of knowing him in any absolute sense. Accordingly, God reveals as much of himself as the mind of man can conceive and the weakness of his nature can bear. God's principal mode of self-revelation is through the Scriptures. It is there that he most fittingly accommodates himself to our capacities. Encountering God as he has authorized his appearance in Scriptures, we, in turn, should "form such a mental image of him, as he, in bringing himself within the limits of our understanding, wishes us to form." Given such an outlook, it is one thing to argue for an au-thorized representation of deity on the basis of scriptural self-sufficiency; it is quite another to make the same claim on the basis of poetic reenact-ment. Milton's epic, after all, is not the Bible, nor can it be said that God authorizes his presence in *Paradise Lost* in the same manner that he does in Scriptures. Milton may dismiss as nonsense what the poets write about Jove, but he was well aware that in presuming to accommodate the transcendent and unknowable to the limited capacities of his fellow mortals, he himself was treading on dangerous ground, risking the pos-sible "ruin" of "sacred Truths to Fable and old Song."[45] The question remains, then, in what manner the accommodative formulation of deity is to be understood in Milton's epic, and by what authority Milton as a poet presumes to undertake such a formulation. The answer to this question should help to clarify the way in which the God of *Paradise Lost* is to be conceived in general and how the theopathetic dimensions of that presence are to be understood in particular.

Milton himself might be said to provide his answer to this question in the angelic hymn of celebration that culminates the celestial council scene in Book III of *Paradise Lost*. There, the angelic hosts, accompa-nied by the music of their harps, sing a "sacred song" in praise of Father and Son (III, 372–415). The song is executed in such a way as to sug-gest not only the theopathetic bearing of God's nature but the means by which his presence is made known in accommodated form. The first part of the song (III, 372–82) celebrates the Father through a recapitulation of those attributes that Milton himself ascribed to godhead in *Christian*

Doctrine. As an entity that defies all attempts at conceptualization, god-head is celebrated in the following terms:

> Thee Father first they sung Omnipotent,
> Immutable, Immortal, Infinite,
> Eternal King; thee Author of all being,
> Fountain of Light, thy self invisible
> Amidst the glorious brightness where thou sit'st
> Thron'd inaccessible.   (III, 372–77)

It is the attributes of immutability, immortality, and infinity that to-tally remove deity from any possibility of conceptualization. By means of these attributes, the "self" of God is made invisible to any that would attempt to discern it. Enveloped in brightness, deity overwhelms any inclined to comprehend its meaning. It is this failure of comprehension that the language underscores through a kind of *via negativa* that at once conceives deity metaphorically and is made to confront the fact of its own incapacity to do so:

>   but when thou shad'st
> The full blaze of thy beams, and through a cloud
> Drawn round about thee like a radiant Shrine,
> Dark with excessive bright thy skirts appear,
> Yet dazle Heav'n, that brightest Seraphim,
> Approach not, but with both wings veil thir eyes.   (III, 377–82)

So totally "inaccessible" is deity, the angels proclaim, that even when it shades the full blaze of its beams, the brightest seraphim dare not ap-proach but veil their eyes with both wings (cf. Isa. vi, 1–6; Rev. iv, 1–8). Enshrined in its own unknowability, deity blinds with its brilliance: it is "Dark with excessive bright." At the very point that the language de-nies accessibility, however, it invites conceptualization. Deity may be "Thron'd inaccessible," but it is also the "Author of all being" and the "Fountain of Light." As such, it is the generative source of all that it bestows upon those who are the beneficiaries of its illumination. Bestow-ing this illumination upon those it engenders, it embodies itself in all those who seek to know it and understand it, in all those, that is, who are the recipients of the *imago Dei*. In the dissemination of this imago, the unknowable is at once the source of all life and the source of all knowledge. Within the accommodative context of Milton's poem, we might say that that which is the author of all being is also the author of all meaning: the two are synonymous.

The most fully discernible form they assume in the manifestation

of their presence is that of the Son. So the angelic hosts next celebrate
the first "of all Creation":

> Begotten Son, Divine Similitude,
> In whose conspicuous count'nance, without cloud
> Made visible, th'Almighty Father shines,
> Whom else no Creature can behold; on thee
> Impresst th' effulgence of his Glorie abides,
> Transfus'd on thee his ample Spirit rests.   (III, 383–89)

As the visible manifestation of God's embodying of himself in discernible
form, the Son represents the way in which deity as the author of all
being is also the author of all meaning. Implicit in the Son's presence
is that categorical imperative by which the Father authorizes himself in
the text. In the self-consciously literary (as well as theological) terms that
the language adopts, the Son accordingly becomes a "Divine Similitude."
If this is in any sense a troping of God, it is a form of troping that calls
upon the *topoi* of rhetoric in order to suggest the inability of the rhetorical to sustain the weight of what the Son truly signifies. The Son is not
simply metaphor (similitude). Or if he is metaphor, he represents an entirely different order of troping from that customarily associated with
rhetoric as secular enterprise. To use the language of Milton's God, he
is "My word, my wisdom, and effectual might" (III, 169–70). He is the
logos of God, the word of God's text and the text of God's word.[46] In
him as in a text is "impresst" or engraven the effulgence of God's glory.
In his countenance is made "conspicuous" (from *specere*, "to look at" or
"behold") the Almighty Father as visible entity, "Whom else no Creature can behold." On the Son is transfused the spirit of God, that which
moves the Son to enact the Father's will. So the Father at another point
celebrates his Son as the "Effulgence of my Glorie, Son belov'd, / Son
in whose face invisible is beheld / Visibly, what by Deitie I am / And
in whose hand what by Decree I doe" (VI, 680–83). This "whatness,"
this "beingness," is that which the Son manifests both in his appearance
and in his actions. In him is embodied all that is otherwise unknowable
in God. If such is true of God's essential ineffability, it is especially true
of his passible nature. In this respect, the Son is a primary vehicle for
the expression of *theopatheia*.

   As embodied in the figure of the Son, it is this theopathetic dimension that constitutes the primary focus of the remainder of the angelic
song (III, 390–410). In the expression of *theopatheia*, the Son becomes
the means by which the Father's vengeance, on the one hand, and his
mercy, on the other, are manifested. As the product of indignation and

wrath, the Father's vengeance is that to which the angels first allude. So they recall the way in which the Son "threw down / Th'aspiring Dominations": "thou that day / Thy Fathers dreadful Thunder didst not spare, / Nor stop thy flaming Chariot wheels" (III, 392–94). In the execution of the Father's vengeance, the Son declares to his Father: "whom thou hat'st, I hate, and can put on / Thy terrors, as I put thy mildness on, / Image of thee in all things," after which his countenance changes into terror as he goes forth in his chariot of vengeance to overwhelm the rebel angels (VI, 734–36, 825–27). Doing so, he is, in the words of the angels, "Son of thy Fathers might, / To execute fierce vengeance on his foes" (III, 398–99). All that the Father experiences in the form of indignation and wrath is transfused into the Son as the veritable embodiment of divine passibility, the vehicle of *theopatheia*.

What is true of the Father's indignation and wrath in the celestial battle is correspondingly true of his pity in the celestial council. Here, God becomes "Father of Mercie and Grace," one moved by "pitie." It is in response to this expression of *theopatheia* that the Son adopts his sacrificial role. Thus, the angels sing:

> No sooner did thy dear and onely Son
> Perceive thee purpos'd not to doom frail Man
> So strictly, but much more to pitie enclin'd,
> He to appease thy wrauth, and end the strife
> Of Mercy and Justice in thy face discern'd,
> Regardless of the Bliss wherein hee sat
> Second to thee, offerd himself to die
> For mans offence. O unexampl'd love,
> Love no where to be found less then Divine.   (III, 403–11)

The lines are immensely illuminating for what they tell us about Milton's version of the theopathetic process. That process begins with the perception of God's motives (that which "moves" God) as revealed in a genuine conflict, indeed, an actual "strife" that the Son beholds occurring on the face of his Father. Like those who "read" God in Scriptures, the Son reads his Father in the text of his "beingness." Although the Son is the only one who can read his Father in this manner, the angels acknowledge in their song that such a reading has occurred. The fact of its occurrence attests both to the primacy of *theopatheia* as a phenomenon for Milton that actually transpires in godhead and to the incorporation of that phenomenon as an event in Milton's epic. That event ultimately leads the Son to offer himself as a sacrifice for man. "O unexampl'd love, / Love no where to be found less then Divine." This is the ultimate demonstration of pathos, one that eventuates in what Milton himself calls a *Christus patiens*, [47] through which mankind is redeemed and as a result of which the Son, along with those who are saved, will return after long absence to see God's face, "wherein no cloud / Of anger shall remain, but peace assur'd, / And reconcilement." Then, "wrauth shall be no more" but in God's presence only "Joy entire" (III, 261–65). In this manner, then, the theopathetic dimensions of the Father are consummated in the Son. As a being who experiences indignation and wrath, on the one hand, and pity, on the other, the Father is one in whom the passible is divinized: he is the source of emotion at its most perfect, indeed, at its most sacred. Both in his theological writings and in his poetry, Milton did not hesitate to urge this belief home in the most compelling manner. Because of its emphasis upon the Son of God as the embodiment of the passible in its sublimest form, *Paradise Lost* is a testament to the importance that the Son assumes in Milton's epic.

The fact of this importance is sounded in the final lines of the angelic hymn:

> Hail Son of God, Saviour of Men, thy Name
> Shall be the copious matter of my Song
> Henceforth, and never shall my Harp thy praise
> Forget, nor from thy Fathers praise disjoin.   (III, 412–15)

These lines are significant not only because they attest to the centrality of the Son to Milton's poetic enterprise but because they suggest the function that the poet himself assumes in the act of celebrating both Father and Son as the source of poetic enactment. In both respects, one discovers a renewed emphasis on the nature of identity. To praise the Son, to make him the copious matter of one's song, is to praise the Father. The quatrainal coda to the angelic song of praise represents a reuniting of identities "disjoined" momentarily for the purpose of suggesting how the ineffability of the divine nature finds expression in, indeed, is embodied in that word, that name, through which it makes itself known in the transmission of its unknowableness. Beyond this, the quatrainal coda represents the establishment of a new identity in the sudden shift from the third person references to the angelic hosts ("they sung") to the first person reference to the poet himself ("my Song"). The shift is quite a remarkable one but also a very significant one. What it signifies is not just a joining of one's voice unto the "angel quire" or a uniting of one's voice with the "celestial consort," although, of course, such a joining or uniting is certainly implied. In the shift from third person to first person, the poet goes further than this. His solemn music is one in which the poet in effect appropriates the "sacred song" of the angelic doxology and makes it distinctly his own ("my Song"). If such is the case, then all that occurs within the song of praise to which this quatrain is a coda provides the occasion by which the poet is textualized as a real presence within his own poem. His voice is literally that of the angels. Their song is his poem; their identity one with his. What they know, he knows; what is communicated to them on this sacred occasion is communicated to him. This means that the poet no longer stands on the outside as he writes a poem about what transpired in the celestial realms. Having appropriated to himself both the voice and identity of the angelic hosts that surround the thrones of God and the Son, the poet places himself in the profoundly unique position of offering his poem as the vehicle through which the voice of God is able to speak. By means of the poet, the accommodative presence of deity as it is transmitted from Father to Son is able to be made known. Replicating in large what the angelic doxology enacts in small, the poet is thereby authorized to delineate "what surmounts the reach / Of human sense" in a manner that permits the unknowable to manifest itself in poetic form.[48]

Paradise Lost is not the Bible, and Milton's God does not possess the same authorized presence as he does in the Bible. As far as Milton is concerned, however, his poem is the most authoritative reenactment of what happens in the Bible as one can possibly imagine. In the process of that reenactment, the possibility of God is accorded a new and distinctly compelling status, one in which a sublimely feeling, indeed, passionate deity becomes the focal point of all the creative energies that Milton's poem is able to marshal.[49] Bestowing upon the theopathetic a renewed legitimacy, *Paradise Lost* thereby represents Milton's poetic response to the theological traditions through which the ongoing debates over the passibility of God assumed paramount importance both in the early Church and in his own times. As they are addressed in Milton's theological tract, on the one hand, and in his epic, on the other, these debates provide Milton the occasion to demonstrate the way in which one should go about "reading God" as a fully passible being.

University of Illinois at Chicago

NOTES

1. References to Milton's prose by volume and page number in my text are to the *Complete Prose Works of John Milton*, 8 vols., gen. ed. Don M. Wolfe et al. (New Haven,

1953–82), hereafter designated YP. Corresponding references to the original Latin (and on occasion to the English translations) are to *The Works of John Milton*, 18 vols. ed. Frank Allen Patterson et al. (New York, 1931–38), hereafter designated CM. References to Milton's poetry are to *The Complete Poetry of John Milton*, 2nd ed. rev., ed. John T. Shawcross (Garden City, N.Y., 1971).

2. The concepts of divine passibility versus divine impassibility have received extensive treatment both historically and theoretically. A brief but informative discussion is Robert S. Franks, "Passibility and Impassibility," in *Encyclopaedia of Religion and Ethics*, 12 vols., ed. James Hastings (New York, 1917–22), vol. IX, pp. 658–59. The fullest historical study is John K. Mozley, *The Impassibility of God: A Survey of Christian Thought* (Cambridge, 1926). See also G. L. Prestige, *God in Patristic Thought* (London, 1952), esp. pp. 1–15; Robert M. Grant, *The Early Christian Doctrine of God* (Charlottesville, Va., 1966), pp. 14–33, 111–14; Richard E. Creel, *Divine Impassibility: An Essay in Philosophical Theology* (Cambridge, 1986).

3. In *Philo*, 10 vols., trans. F. H. Colson and G. H. Whitaker (London, 1960), vol. III, pp. 10–101.

4. The kinds of ideas that Philo as Neoplatonist has in mind are discernible in the discussion of God's immutability in the *Republic* (II, 380–81).

5. Represented by church fathers such as Clement of Alexandria and Origen, the Alexandrian school refashioned God in an attempt to construct a Christian philosophy of religion. In his *Stromata* (V, 11), Clement, for example, maintains that God, as that which is totally immutable, is "without passion, without anger, without desire." Following the example of God's impassibility, the Christian gnostic should rise above all emotions, which bind him to this world. See Mozley, *Impassibility of God*, pp. 52–59.

6. Cited by Grant, *Early Christian Doctrine*, p. 30. See Grant's entire discussion, pp. 28–31. See also Mozley, *Impassibility of God*, pp. 60–63.

7. According to Grant, *Early Christian Doctrine*, p. 31, Origen here reflects the influence of Ignatius, who often speaks of the suffering of Christ as a manifestation of the "passion of God." Ignatius, in turn, is in keeping with Tatian and Clement of Rome. For additional elaboration, see Mozley, *Impassibility of God*, pp. 7–8; and Prestige, *Patristic Thought*, p. 6.

8. In *The Ante-Nicene Fathers*, 10 vols., ed. Alexander Roberts and James Donaldson (New York, 1908), vol. III. For a discussion of Patripassianism, see Tertullian's *Treatise Against Praxeas*. See also Mozley's treatment of Modalistic Monarchianism, in *Impassibility of God*, pp. 28–37; and the entry on Patripassianism in the *New Catholic Encyclopedia*, 15 vols., ed. CUA staff (New York, 1967), vol. X, p. 1103.

9. See also Novatian's discussion of the anger, indignation, and hatred of God in his *Treatise Concerning the Trinity*, chap. 5, in *The Ante-Nicene Fathers*, vol. V, p. 615. In the next chapter, Novatian addresses the notion of God's body (V, 615–16).

10. In *The Fathers of the Church*, 53 vols., gen. ed. Joseph Deferrari (Washington, D.C., 1965), vol. LIV. For the influence of Lactantius on Milton, see Kathleen E. Hartwell, *Lactantius and Milton* (Cambridge, Mass., 1929).

11. In this respect, Lactantius is at odds with his putative teacher Arnobius of Sicca. See Arnobius's *The Case Against the Pagans*, 2 vols., trans. George E. McCracken (Westminster, Md., 1949), esp. pp. 197–207.

12. St. Augustine, *The City of God*, trans. Marcus Dods (New York, 1950), p. 263. All future references are to this edition. My treatment of St. Augustine's views follows Mozley, *Impassibility of God*, pp. 104–09.

13. Mozley, *Impassibility of God*, p. 104.

14. Cited from ibid., p. 107.

15. Cited from ibid., p. 106.

16. This theory of reading is reinforced by St. Augustine's discussion of scriptural tropes in *On Christian Doctrine*. There, he distinguishes between sign and that which is signified by sign. In the expression of the relationship between sign and signified, Scripture makes use of literal renderings that are clear and direct and figurative renderings that are often obscure. It is the figurative renderings about which one must be careful, especially those that describe God. To interpret these expressions as literal is to find oneself in bondage to the sign. Such figurative expressions include the presence of passions in deity. St. Augustine even goes so far as to assert that one in whom faith, hope, and love are perfected needs neither the literal nor the figurative interpretations that the Bible offers. In fact, such a person does not need Scriptures at all. See, in particular, Book I, chapters 2, 39; Book II, chapters 6, 10; and Book III, chapters 9, 10, and 11 in *On Christian Doctrine*, *A Select Library of the Nicene and Post-Nicene Fathers of the Christian Church*, ed. Philip Schaff, first series, 14 vols. (Buffalo, 1886–89), vol. II, pp. 523, 534, 537, 539, 560, 561.

17. On the views of such scholastics as Scotus, Anselm, and Aquinas, see Mozley, *Impassibility of God*, pp. 109–19.

18. Trans. Rev. John King, 2 vols. (Edinburgh, Scotland, 1847). References in my text are to the sixth chapter of the opening commentary, vol. I, pp. 248–49.

19. References are to the *Institutes of the Christian Religion*, 2 vols., ed. John T. McNeill and trans. Ford Lewis Battles (Philadelphia, 1960).

20. Founded in the fourth century by Audius in Mesopotamia, this sect taught that because man was made in the image of God, God possesses a human form (see the note to *Institutes* I, p. 121). Interestingly, Luther was more accepting of the Anthropomorphites. In his *Lectures on Genesis*, in *Luther's Works*, ed. Jaroslav Pelikan (St. Louis, Mo., 1958), vol. I, pp. 14–15, he observes: "A papal decree condemns the Anthropomorphites for speaking about God as if they were speaking about a human being, and for ascribing to Him eyes, ears, arms, etc. However, the condemnation is unjust. Indeed, how could men speak otherwise of God among men? If it is heresy to think of God in this manner, then a verdict has been rendered concerning the salvation of all children, who think and speak of God in this childlike fashion. But even apart from the children: give me the most learned doctor — how else will he teach and speak about God?" Luther then goes on to suggest that in Scriptures, "when God reveals Himself to us, it is necessary for Him to do so through some such veil or wrapper and to say: 'Look! Under this wrapper you will be sure to take hold of Me!'" Judging by the foregoing, Luther's view of accommodation provides a greater latitude for conceiving God in anthropomorphic terms, but his view of passibility, although not given extended treatment in his works, would be essentially in agreement with Calvin's. Such Lutherans as John Gerhard, however, are much more outspoken in their adherence to impassibility. See Mozley, *Impassibility of God*, pp. 121–25.

21. Proper reading as a religious act meant a great deal to Calvin, who cited with approbation Cicero's association of the word "religion" with the word for "reading" (*Institutes* I, p. 117). See Cicero's discussion in the *De natura Deorum* (II, xxviii, 72–73), likewise concerned in part with the way the gods are represented in human terms. In this work, Cicero maintains that the term "religious" is ultimately derived from the idea of reading or rereading (*legere* and *relegere*). Although the accuracy of this etymology is open to question, it does suggest the way the ancient commentators emphasized the association between religion and reading. See *De natura Deorum* in *Cicero*, trans. H. Rackham (Cambridge, Mass., 1951), pp. 192–93.

22. In the language of contemporary hermeneutics, Calvin advocates "demytholo-gizing" the rhetoric of God's passibility in order to declare with full assurance the fact of his *apatheia*. For a discussion of the principles of such an approach, see especially Rudolf Bultmann, *New Testament and Mythology*, ed. and trans. Schubert M. Ogden (Philadelphia, 1984). For an enlightening analysis of the demythologist point of view, see Paul Ricoeur, "Preface to Bultmann," in *Essays on Biblical Interpretation*, ed. Lewis S. Mudge (Philadelphia, 1980), pp. 49–72. The demythologizers assume that it is not possible to rely on the literal meaning of Scriptures, because they are dependent upon a "mythical world picture" that is no longer believable and essentially "naive." Finding it impossible to "repristinate" Scriptures, they strip away "the mythological garments" of the older conceptions in order to recapture the message or *kerygma* embodied in scriptural proclamation (Bultmann, *New Testament*, pp. 2–3, 41, 98–99, 161). Demythologization thereby enacts a deconstruction of the text, "a cutting into the letter by taking off the mythological wrappings." Under the wrappings, this deconstructive hermeneutics presumes to "discover the summons which is the primary meaning of the text" (Ricoeur, "Preface to Bultmann," pp. 57–59). Nothing could be further from Milton's hermeneutical outlook. For a cogent analysis of Milton and the contexts of Bultmann's program for demythologization, see Thomas Merrill, *Epic God-Talk: "Paradise Lost" and the Grammar of Religious Language* (Jefferson, N.C., 1986).

23. See Milton's *Christian Doctrine* (II, vii), which cites Ames as "*Amesius Noster*" and discusses a passage from Ames's *Marrow* (CM XVII, p. 172; YP VI, p. 706). In his biography of Milton, Edward Philips identifies Ames as an influence. For additional discussion, see, e.g., Maurice Kelley, "The Composition of Milton's *De Doctrina Christiana: First Phase*," in *Th'Upright Heart and Pure*, ed. Amadeus Fiore (Pittsburgh, 1967), pp. 35–44. Among other influences on Milton, Johannes Wollebius skirts the issue of passibility entirely. See his discussion of "The Knowledge of God" in *Compendium of Christian Theology*, trans. John W. Beardslee III in *Reformed Dogmatics* (New York, 1965). The whole issue of passibility goes unnoticed in Heinrich Heppe's encyclopedic *Reformed Dogmatics*, trans. G. T. Thomson (London, 1950).

24. References are to *The Marrow of Theology*, trans. John D. Eusden (Durham, N.C., 1968).

25. Such an approach is consistent with Renaissance theological treatises of the same type, among them the *Loci communes* of Melanchthon and Peter Martyr Vermigli. For a discussion of the form, see John M. Steadman's excellent entry on Milton's *Christian Doctrine* (under the heading "De Doctrina Christiana") in *A Milton Encyclopedia*, 9 vols., gen. ed. William B. Hunter, Jr. (Lewisburg, Pa., 1978–83), vol. II, pp. 118–19.

26. The Westminster Confession of Faith (chapter 2), in *Creeds of Christendom*, 3 vols., comp. Philip Schaff (Grand Rapids, Mich., 1977), vol. III, p. 606. Compare the statement in the Thirty-nine Articles (I): "There is but one lyuyng and true God, euerlastiyng, without body, partes, or passions" (III, p. 487). The Westminster Confession elaborates by maintaining that God, although passionless, "hat[es] all sin."

27. For additional examples, see such works as Roger Hutchinson, *The Image of God or Layman's Book* (1550), in *The Works*, ed. John Bruce, The Parker Society (Cambridge, 1842), and Thomas Jackson, *A Treatise of the Divine Essence and Attributes* (London, 1628). In many respects, Jackson's treatment of the subject is among the wisest and most balanced that the literature produced. See esp. pp. 226–32.

28. Milton's concept of accommodation has been much discussed. See, in particular, Roland M. Frye, *God, Man, and Satan: Patterns of Christian Thought and Life in "Paradise Lost," "Pilgrim's Progress," and the Great Theologians* (Princeton, N.J., 1960),

pp. 9–13); C. A. Patrides, *"Paradise Lost* and the Theory of Accommodation," *TSLL* V (1963–64), 58–63; Patrides, *Milton and the Christian Tradition* (Oxford, 1966), pp. 9–11 and *passim;* Patrides, *"Paradise Lost* and the Language of Theology," in *Language and Style in Milton,* ed. Ronald David Emma and John T. Shawcross (New York, 1967), pp. 102–19; and William G. Madsen, *From Shadowy Types to Truth* (New Haven, Conn., 1968), pp. 70–74 and *passim.*

29. As Milton avers in *Christian Doctrine* (I, xxx): "Each passage of scripture has only a single sense," although Milton does allow for other senses under particular circumstances. See the major statement by Hugh MacCallum, "Milton and the Figurative Interpretation of the Bible," *UTQ* XXXI (1962), 397–415. Also important is Theodore Huguelet, "Milton's Hermeneutics: A Study of Scriptural Interpretation in the Divorce Tracts and in *De Doctrina Christiana,"* (Ph.D. diss., University of North Carolina, 1950).

30. On Milton's sense of the poet as authorizing presence in his own works, see John Guillory, *Poetic Authority: Spenser, Milton, and Literary History* (New York, 1983).

31. For a full statement of this idea, see John T. Shawcross, *With Mortal Voice: The Creation of "Paradise Lost"* (Lexington, Ky., 1982).

32. See Milton's important discussion of the Old and New Testaments in *Christian Doctrine* (I, xxx). There, he discusses the texts of these documents, the nature of their preservation; and how they are to be interpreted (YP VI, pp. 574–92).

33. As early as *Of Reformation,* Milton declared: "The very essence of Truth is plainnesse, and brightnes; the darknes and crookednesse is our own. The *Wisdome* of *God* created *understanding,* fit and proportionable to Truth the object, and end of it, as the eye to the thing visible. If our *understanding* have a film of *ignorance* over it, or be blear with gazing on other false glisterings, what is that to Truth? If we will but purge with sovrain eyesalve that intellectual ray which *God* hath planted in us, then we would beleeve the Scriptures protesting their own plainnes and perspicuity" (YP I, p. 566). A similar idea is put forward in *Christian Doctrine* (I, xxx).

34. So Milton says in *Christian Doctrine* (I, xxx), "No inferences should be made from the text [of Scriptures], unless they follow necessarily from what is written. . . . What we are obliged to believe are the things written in the sacred books, not the things debated in academic gatherings." "The rule and canon of faith, therefore, is scripture alone." Despite the importance of the text of Scriptures, "the preeminent and supreme authority, however, is the authority of the Spirit, which is internal, and the individual possession of each man" (YP VI, pp. 580–88). As important as this emphasis upon the Spirit as supreme authority is for Milton, the Spirit nonetheless does not replace the text of Scriptures. If that text is understood correctly, it is because the Spirit is responding in accord with the text and vice versa.

35. These include (among others) the fact that he is infinite, eternal, immutable, incorruptible, omnipresent, omnipotent, omniscient, and incomprehensible (YP VI, pp. 139–52). Such attributes (especially immutability) in no way compromise for Milton the fact of God's passibility. Unlike other theologians, Milton sees no contradiction in holding that God is at once passible (in other words, subject to being "moved") and immutable (that is, "unmovable").

36. For further treatment of the concept of form as internal and external, see the chapter "On Form" (I, vii) in Milton's *Art of Logic* (YP VIII, pp. 231–35).

37. For detailed discussions of this concept, see Hugh MacCallum, *Milton and the Sons of God: The Divine Image in Milton's Epic Poetry* (Toronto, 1986), esp. pp. 113–32, and *passim;* and Anthony C. Yu's important study, "Life in the Garden: Freedom and the Image of God in *Paradise Lost," Journal of Religion* LX (1980), 247–71.

38. See Francis E. Mineka, "The Critical Reception of Milton's *De Doctrina Christiana*," *Studies in English . . . The University of Texas 1943* (Austin, Tex., 1943), 115–47, and the discussion in YP VI, pp. 5–10.

39. [John Pye Smith], "On Milton's Treatise on Christian Doctrine," *The Evangelical Magazine*, n.s., IV (1826), 92–95. Although the editors of the Yale *Prose* VI, p. 136*n* attribute this piece to Smith, I could find no reference to a specific author.

40. See the chapter, "The Dialogic Imagination," in my book *The Sinews of Ulysses: Form and Convention in Milton's Works* (Pittsburgh, 1989), pp. 76–97, as well as my essay "'Hate in Heav'n': Milton and the *Odium Dei*," *ELH* LIII (1986), 519–30.

41. Irene Samuel, "The Dialogue in Heaven: A Reconsideration of *Paradise Lost*, III, 1–417," in *Milton: Modern Essays in Criticism*, ed. Arthur E. Barker (New York, 1965), pp. 233–45; rpt. from *PMLA* LXXII (1957), 601–11. Roland M. Frye, from entry on "The Father," in *A Milton Encyclopedia*, vol. III, p. 98. Although Dennis Danielson, *Milton's Good God: A Study in Literary Theodicy* (Cambridge, 1981), doesn't deal specifically with God as a fully conceived figure in Milton's epic, his study is implicitly predicated on the assumption of God as principle. See, however, William Empson's classic study, *Milton's God* (London, 1961).

42. See Fish's seminal study *Surprised by Sin: The Reader in "Paradise Lost"* (London, 1967), pp. 57–91, and *Is There a Text in This Class: The Authority of Interpretive Communities* (Cambridge, Mass., 1980). In *Surprised by Sin*, Fish maintains that God's adoption of what to us are emotionally laden words (such as "ingrate") are tantamount to "scientific notation[s] with the *emotional* value of an X or a Y" (p. 65).

43. Even for those who hold to some form of passibility, emotion is conceived anthropopathetically. Georgia B. Christopher's excellent book *Milton and the Science of the Saints* (Princeton, N.J., 1982) is representative. Although apparently disagreeing with Fish's contention that God's language is "purely scientific and denotative," she maintains that "the angry voice of God in Book III, which has elicited so many critical attempts to justify or ameliorate its tone, belongs not to God as he *is* but to God as the sinner perceives him." As a result of that perception, the reader in effect "creates God" as he moves from the first to the final presentation of deity as a character. Essentially, Christopher views God as progressing from a figure of wrath to a figure of tenderness and love. What amounts to an anthropopathetic reading of God is tied by Christopher to the prevailing Reformation views of deity explored above (pp. 114–19).

44. These emotional extremes make themselves felt throughout Milton's epic. Having explored a number of them in depth in earlier studies (see above, note 40), I simply allude to some of them here. Based upon Psalm ii, the laughter of God, for example, rings throughout the war in heaven: "Mightie Father," the Son declares, "thou thy foes / Justly hast in derision, and secure / Laugh'st at thir vain designes and tumults vain" (V, 735–37; cf. II, 731; XII, 59). Manifested in the council scene, the anger of God is likewise discernible in the celestial warfare (VI, 56–59). God's sternness is seen in his warning to Adam not to eat the fruit of the forbidden tree (VIII, 333–34).

45. The reference, of course, is to Andrew Marvell's commendatory poem "On Paradise Lost" that prefaced the 1674 edition. Addressing the theory of accommodation implied by the association of *Christian Doctrine* and *Paradise Lost*, William G. Madsen voices similar concerns: "Unless we are willing to grant that John Milton was literally inspired," there seems to be no meaningful way to relate the idea of accommodation as delineated in *Christian Doctrine* to that implied in Milton's epic. As a viable alternative, Madsen opts to read the concept typologically. Although such a reading is possible, I still feel that it is necessary to interpret accommodation in accord with Milton's own discussion of the

subject in his theological tract. See Madsen's *From Shadowy Types to Truth: Studies in Milton's Symbolism* (New Haven, Conn., 1968), pp. 73–74 and *passim.*

46. For some of the Reformation contexts of this idea, see Christopher, *Milton and the Science of the Saints,* and Robert L. Entzminger, *Divine Word: Milton and the Redemption of Language* (Pittsburgh, 1985).

47. See Milton's outlines for tragedies in the Cambridge Manuscript (CM XVIII, p. 240), and his early but unfinished poem "The Passion."

48. Compare Raphael's classic statement: "what surmounts the reach / Of human sense, I shall delineate so, / By lik'ning spiritual to corporal forms, / As may express them best" (III, 571–74). In effect, this is what the poet does in his own depiction of God throughout.

49. Embodied in deity as a divinized attribute, the passible, of course, finds apt contrast with the debased form it assumes in fallen creatures, both human and satanic. There, it results in the overcoming of the rational faculties by the emotional and the discovery of oneself "in a troubl'd Sea of passion tost" (X, 718). It is this sea into which man is plunged after he succumbs to the temptations of the Adversary. Although a discussion of these matters lies well beyond the purview of the present undertaking, they are germane to it. For a treatment of the psychological dimensions of such matters in the Renaissance, see J. B. Banborough, *The Little World of Man* (London, 1952).

TYPOLOGY AND *PARADISE LOST*, BOOKS XI AND XII

William Walker

I

STANLEY FISH tells us that the primary intent of his survey of criticism of the final books of *Paradise Lost* is "to take the history of literary criticism seriously by demonstrating that the questions one can ask and therefore the answers one can receive and therefore the details one can see and the accounts one can give are the functions of conditions prevailing in the profession."[1] More crudely stated, Fish attempts to accomplish the feat of persuading us that some literary critics of the past wrote what they did not because they were stupid or inexplicably blind, but because they were rigorous and intelligent within a set of conditions that differ from those of today. More abstractly stated, he is attempting to teach how to recognize, and so respect, critical power in time. If one finds oneself persuaded by this teaching and so denied both the unqualified sense that one is more rigorous than previous critics and the convention of opening critical essays with catalogues of the inexplicably blind, one may resort to introductory speculations about the conditions which affect one's belief that even if previous critics were neither weak nor blind, they are in some sense inadequate. In connection with criticism of the final books of *Paradise Lost*, one feature which Fish's survey suggests may presently demand and reward attention is the understanding of Milton's vision as a typological one. Fish points to the appearance of typological interpretive strategy in Milton criticism during the sixties as the perfect tool for the "completion" of the critical rehabilitation of the final books which found its theoretical premises in both new criticism and the myth criticism of Cassirer, Frye, and others (p. 55). That typology has been so pervasively invoked over the last twenty years in Milton criticism to *complete* a critical project works to locate a consideration of this accomplishment on what Fish refers to as criticism's invisible list of things to do. And recent theoretical interrogations of modes of figurative representation of history such as allegory may incline one to suspect that, as another such mode, typology may be more complex than is evident in its new critical, mythic, and rehabilitative implementations.

245

Evidence of this different critical and theoretical project is already visible. In a collection of articles edited by himself and Geoffrey Hartman, Sanford Budick argues that both standard typological theory and Milton's version of it in *Paradise Lost* are in part constituted by a hermeneutic that closely corresponds to one form of Midrash. The implication for Milton criticism is that "in *Paradise Lost*, [Milton] demonstrates that a Christian exegetical poetry can forcibly express interpretive necessities in which the fulfillment associated with one kind of typology is significantly deferred." While reaffirming the importance of typology as "the correct general approach to Milton's interpretive meanings," Budick points to revisions which differentiate Milton's typology "from a typology of fulfillment and closure."[2] In an article on Auerbach's *Mimesis*, Timothy Bahti also focuses on difficulties in typological theory, and outlines the extraordinary conceptual workings required to accommodate the "tensions" within Auerbach's account of it.[3] While Milton criticism has recognized various degrees of complexity in typological theory and in Milton's version of it, Budick and Bahti are interrogating typology at the limits of its coherence and comprehensibility. I find what follows to partake in a motion, evident in Bahti and Budick, which is responsive to, among other things, the prominence of typology in Milton criticism and changes in the contemporary theoretical scene. It is not a project of diminishing the centrality of typology to the final books of *Paradise Lost*, but of further determining the ways in which that centrality is constituted and what it means. By observing how specific features of Milton's history conform with typological theory as stated by Auerbach, I propose to reaffirm the centrality of typology to these books, but then turn on the claim that this centrality effects a coherent vision of history as an image of eternity.

II

In spite of some qualifications recently urged to it, Eric Auerbach's account of typology remains an authoritative and intriguing statement. He claims in *Mimesis* that the church fathers began to systematize methods of figural interpretation of historical events described in the Bible in an attempt to bring large historical contexts, especially Roman history, into line with what they felt was the biblical account of history.[4] In an earlier classic essay, "*Figura*," which is the foundation of much in this major later work, Auerbach explains that

figural interpretation establishes a connection between two events or persons, the first of which signifies not only itself but also the second, while the second encompasses or fulfills the first. The two poles of the figure are separate in time, but both, being real events or figures, are within time, within the stream of historical life. Only the understanding of the two persons or events is a spiritual act, but this spiritual act deals with concrete events whether past, present, or future, and not with concepts or abstractions; these are quite secondary, since promise and fulfillment are real historical events, which have either happened in the incarnation of the Word, or will happen in the second coming.[5]

This figural interpretation of history, according to Auerbach, emerges unqualifiedly victorious in western culture over the classical conception of history as a comprehensible, causally linked sequence of events.

The victory consists in both a new concept of human experience in time, and a new language: within the context of figural interpretation, the connection between two widely separated temporal events such as the sacrifice of Isaac and the sacrifice of Christ

can be established only if both occurrences are vertically linked to Divine Providence, which alone is able to devise such a plan of history and supply the key to its understanding. The horizontal, that is the temporal and causal, connection of occurrences is dissolved; the here and now is no longer a mere link in an earthly chain of events, it is simultaneously something which has always been, and which will be fulfilled in the future; and strictly, in the eyes of God, it is something eternal, something omni-temporal, something already consummated in the realm of fragmentary earthly event. This conception of history is magnificent in its homogeneity, but it was completely alien to the mentality of classical antiquity, it annihilated that mentality down to the very structure of its language, at least of its literary language, which — with all its ingenious and nicely shaded conjunctions, its wealth of devices for syntactic arrangement, its carefully elaborated system of tenses — became wholly superfluous as soon as earthly relations of place, time, and cause had ceased to matter, as soon as a vertical connection, ascending from all that happens, converging in god, alone became significant. Wherever the two conceptions met, there was of necessity a conflict and an attempt to compromise — between, on the one hand, a presentation which carefully interrelated the elements of history, which respected temporal and causal sequence, remained within the domain of the earthly foreground, and, on the other hand, a fragmentary, discrete presentation, constantly seeking an interpretation from above. (*Mimesis*, pp. 64–65)

By dissolving the temporal and causal connections between events, and by discounting earthly relations of place, time, and cause, typological thinking and representation radically disrupt any conception of history as a series of events which unfolds like a story. Auerbach's sensitivity to how this disruption occurs on a linguistic level allows him to observe that, in a work such as Augustine's *City of God*, the battle is not just between classical and Christian typological senses of history, but also between the vocabularies and syntaxes that to some extent make those senses possible.

Critics of the final books of *Paradise Lost* ally Milton with typological tradition by observing that in centering his presentation of history on the figures of Cain, Noah, Abraham, Moses, Enoch, and Christ, the poet is following Hebrews x, 13 and the commentary attached to it which identified these figures as types of Christ. Typology, moreover, is regarded as the basis for the general vision of history as "an image of eternity" (Fish), "a time that is intersected by eternity" (Madsen), and temporal events in their eternal context (Tayler).[6] Auerbach's formulation of typological theory allows us to add that several other features of Milton's description of history are accountable in terms of this theory. It is a commonplace that the style of the final books is austere, cold, and simple, but it seems just as obvious that this is the immediate fallout of the demand for a "discrete presentation" of history. A simple and flat style is what is left after a typological theory of history has annihilated the ingenious and subtle conjunctions, the wealth of syntactic devices and system of tenses of classical historiography. The notable fragmentariness of the final narration of human experience is also answerable to this view of history. The strangely distinct visions of Book XI, loose or nonperiodic sentences consisting of clause piled on clause (see especially the Nativity account, Book XII, lines 348–71), repetitions and apparent sequence reversals in the account of Moses crossing the Red Sea, frequent interpolations of references to the Incarnation and descriptions of apocalypse and Paradise regained — these features disrupt narrative continuity in the final books, discourage any attempt to understand human experience in terms of a causally connected linear sequence, and seek an interpretation from above.

A further feature of Milton's presentation of history which is also consistent with a typological vision of history is the marked denial of definitiveness to those "events" such as the incarnation, the crucifixion, and the apocalypse which are the fulfillments or antitypes of the Old Testament types. By avoiding any articulation which would incline us to regard the typological fulfillment as a specific event which happens at a particular point in time, Milton seems to be insisting on the "homogeneity" of history as it is understood through figural interpretation. A good instance of Milton's deemphasis of the fulfillment as an event is the remarkably brief, understated, and conditional mode of his account of the birth of Christ:

> at last they seize
> The Sceptre, and regard not David's Sons,
> Then lose it to a stranger, that the true
> Anointed King Messiah might be born
> Barr'd of his right; yet at his Birth a Star
> Unseen before in heav'n proclaims him come,
> And guides the Eastern Sages, who enquire
> His place to offer Incense, Myrrh, and Gold.   (XII, 356–63)

Nowhere do we find the assertion that Christ is born. The event is merely suggested or implied by "might be born" and the adverbial phrase "at his Birth," which acts only as an indicator of the occasion for the appearance of a star and the coming of the magi — Milton leaves the proclaiming of Christ's birth up to the star. Similarly, the account of the crucifixion strangely liquidates the event by having two adjectives without a noun at its center and immediately substituting Christ for his nation as the crucifier:

> For this he shall live hated, be blasphem'd,
> Seiz'd on by force, judg'd, and to death condemn'd
> A shameful and accurst, nail'd to the Cross
> By his own Nation, slain for bringing Life;
> But to the Cross he nails thy Enemies,
> The Law that is against thee, and the sins
> Of all mankind, with him there crucifi'd,
> Never to hurt them more who rightly trust
> In this his satisfaction.   (XII, 411–19)

"Where is the body? A shameful and accursed what?" we ask, as any expectation of details of Christ's punished body is forced to find satisfaction in nothing or the bare initial pronoun "he." Like the nativity, the crucifixion here seems to slip through our fingers if we try to grasp it as a single, definite, temporal event.

Though it is of course crucial to the way in which history can be fulfilled and fulfilling, the apocalypse, conceived as a definitive, final, and climactic event, poses a problem for one who is concerned to detach us from an understanding of history as a sequence of thrilling events or duels. Typology itself is in a basic sense antieschatological, antiteleological, antiapocalyptic, simply because within its assumptions there is ultimately no beginning, telos, or ending of any process or thing, but only one eternal omnitemporal shape. As Auerbach puts it in "*Figura*," figures "point not only to the concrete future, but also to something that

always has been and always will be; they point to something which is
in need of interpretation, which will indeed be fulfilled in the concrete
future, but which knows no difference in time" (p. 59). But while there
is absolute unity from God's perspective and in his providence, the appearance of story enables expectations of action from man's perspective,
and it is for this reason that man's interpretive engagement with God's
signs is important. This engagement leads man out of the latter perspective toward the former, as do some of the ways we see Milton dealing
with the problem of how to describe the Second Coming not as a definitive
act or stroke but, like the victory of the babe in "On the Morning of Christ's
Nativity," simply as an expression of what Christ is. First of all, the fact
that the Second Coming is described at least three times in the course
of Book XII not only makes the typological insistence on its omnipresence,
but detracts from its uniqueness, its singularity as an event. Next, like
the Nativity, Christ's Second Coming is described not as a duel, but as
a curiously calm and even casual moment. It is mentioned seemingly by
chance when we learn that it is not Moses who leads the Israelites into
Canaan,

> But *Joshua* whom the Gentiles *Jesus* call,
> His Name and Office Bearing, who shall quell
> The adversary Serpent, and bring back
> Through the world's wilderness long wander'd man
> Safe to eternal Paradise of rest.
> Meanwhile . . .   (XII, 310–15)

Jesus' quelling of the serpent and bringing back long-wandered man safe
to eternal paradise of rest is here referred to only, it seems, as a gloss
on who Joshua is, and on the fact that the Gentiles happen to call him
Jesus. It is notable, too, that the grammar allows Joshua and not Jesus
to be the performing agent, and that the verbs "quell" and "bring back"
are remarkably pale in comparison with the lurid language of Revelation. The "meanwhile" which follows the account resembles the move
Milton makes in the Nativity ode when, after describing the return of
truth and justice to men and the opening of heaven's gates, he stops us
short: "But wisest Fate says no, / This must not yet be so" (149–50). The
function of this "meanwhile" is to put a lid on any expectation Adam
(though likely not the reader) may have of the imminence of the definitive
moment (the "But first" at Book XII, line 331 does the same thing in relation to the Nativity).

Another brief account of the apocalypse is given at the conclusion
of the narration of Christ's career, and is again markedly lacking in verbs

of identifiable action: Christ will come to judge, reward, and receive into bliss (XII, 458–65). This event is further attenuated by Milton's blatant refusal to take a stand on what was a political issue both during and after the revolution, namely, whether Paradise was possible on earth. By saying that Christ will receive the faithful "Whether in Heav'n or Earth" (XII, 463), Milton concludes this apocalyptic account with a notable indifference to details thought to be crucial to a vision of the end.[7] Adam then cries *felix culpa,* and we learn how bad the world will be from the Resurrection until the end that was just described and is once again described:

> so shall the World go on,
> To good malignant, to bad men benign,
> Under her own weight groaning, till the day
> Appear of respiration to the just,
> And vengeance to the wicked, at return
> Of him so lately promis'd to thy aid,
> The Woman's seed, obscurely then foretold,
> Now amplier known thy Saviour and thy Lord,
> Last in the Clouds from Heaven to be reveal'd
> In glory of the Father, to dissolve
> Satan with his perverted World, then raise
> From the conflagrant mass, purg'd and refin'd
> New Heav'ns, new Earth, Ages of endless date
> Founded in righteousness and peace and love,
> To bring forth fruits Joy and eternal Bliss.   (XII, 537–51)

The definitiveness of the Second Coming is here weakened by the non-periodic syntactic form of the sentence which poses the possibility of closure at the end of each clause, but denies it as further clauses are added to the initial ones. And the Second Coming is here not so much an act of Christ as the revelation, the "apocalypse," of what he is: the three main verbs "to dissolve," "raise," and "To bring forth" are only tenuously connected to Christ as the agent, and are made subordinate to another act which is really not an act — the revelation of Christ in the glory of the Father. Christ does not dissolve, raise, and bring forth; he simply is, and is revealed to be what he is. That is sufficient to have Satan dissolved, to have new heavens and earth raised, to have joy and bliss brought forth. These actions are not described as being performed by Christ, but as effects of his return and the revelation of what he is.

The word "till" that introduces the account of apocalypse and which is a common word in the poem is hence misleading if it is read as a herald of definitive action. But the opening of Book XI has already warned us not to read it as such. Here God tells the heavenly host of his decree that man be sent "from the Garden forth to Till / The Ground whence he was taken, fitter soil" (XI, 97–98). Michael dutifully announces the decree to Adam and Eve: "to remove thee I am come, / And send thee from the Garden forth to till / The ground whence thou wast tak'n, fitter Soil" (XI, 260–62). Moreover, the first thing Adam sees, when Michael tells him to "first behold / Th' effects which [his] original crime hath wrought" in his corrupted progeny, is "a field, / Part arable and tilth, whereon were Sheaves / New reapt, the other part sheep-walks and folds" (XI, 429–31). In a fundamental sense, to be in postlapsarian history is to till. In Books XI and XII, the word "till" is strongly established as God's imperative to man to live in a fallen world and as the word that describes the work and exertion that will be required of him in this world. When, then, we read of history till apocalypse, of the world groaning "till the day / Appear of respiration to the just," of, as Adam puts it, "the Race of time, / Till time stand fixt" (XII, 539–40, 554–55), or, in retrospect, of "all our woe, / With loss of Eden, till one greater Man / Restore us" (I, 4–6), we know not to read that "till" as the unqualified herald of apocalyptic change or action. Rather, at precisely the moment that the word invokes the expectation of the ultimate action, we sense it commanding us to be patient, to bear the mild yoke, to work. As such, it chastens our fallen impulse to conceive of our history in terms of plot or story, and urges us to consider it as an omnitemporal shape which is made comprehensible to us by means of figural interpretation.

III

The understanding of Milton's congruence with a typological view of history must, however, come to terms with the conceptual problematic which has characterized typological theory from the start. In an excellent article on Auerbach's *Mimesis*, Timothy Bahti points to the possibility of such a problematic when he observes "the implied tension in the concept of *figura* as a relation between two signs, both of which are to remain real and historical, but the latter of which is to be the truth of the former's mere prefiguration."[8] For Bahti, however, this tension is not fundamentally disruptive but accountable in terms of Auerbach's connection with Hegel. By observing Auerbach's description in "*Figura*" of the antitype as what "fulfills and annuls" and what "unveils and preserves" the *figura*, Bahti confirms his claim, made convincingly in a prior essay on Vico and Auerbach,[9] for the importance of the Hegelian notion of sublation to Auerbach's understanding of typology. By recourse to the notion of sublation, Bahti explicates the "tension" between the antitype

as truth and the type as prefiguration whose truth and concrete historical reality would seem to be compromised by the assignation of truth
to the antitype:

Within the *figura*, then, the operation of cancelling-and-preserving the literal-
historical event in the production of a spiritual sign seems to obey the economy
of sublation. In the same manner, the *veritas* or fulfillment of this historical *figura*
follows the pattern of the Hegelian "idealization" of phenomenal and historical
experience, and so the *veritas* cancels-and-preserves the historical reality of the
previous *figura* in fashioning truth through this elevation-and-negation. Yet that
initial *figura*, as we have seen, itself displays the double structure of the figurative sign, that is, it is both literal and figurative. What would it mean for the *veritas*
to cancel-and-preserve this sublation of the literal into the figurative which occurs *within* the very *figura* which the *veritas* fulfills? What is sublated, what is
cancelled-and-yet-preserved, is precisely this first rhetorical sublation of the historical, the very double structure already at play within the beginning *figura*.
Whatever the prior historical event might be, when it is taken to prefigure some
later meaning, it becomes doubled (literal and figural), but the later "fulfillment"
of the former's prefigural meaning must at once preserve the former's figural
character — as the latter's sign, after all, as its prefiguration — *and* cancel it, render it nothing but a mere *littera*, annihilate it into a non-thing, a dead letter or
a corpse. (P. 133)

I would like to suggest that there are further "tensions" in statements
of typological theory which are not accountable by recourse to the powerful and refined understanding of sublation which Bahti shows to be op-
erative in Auerbach's project. The first involves the problem not of the
historicity of the *figura*, but its status as a copy/archetype. That this is
a problem can only be expected given the radical ambivalence in the
classical usage of the Latin *figura* and Greek *typos*, two of the major
terms which were used by the authors of the Bible and the church fathers in their articulation of the typological theory of history. In connection with *typos*, Clark tells us that

The word initially meant either a "blow" or a "mark left by a blow," such as the
marks left on Christ's hands by the nails (John 20:25). Moreover, *type* could also
mean not only the "impression" or "image," such as that on a wax seal, and "cast"
or "replica," such as that of a sculpted figure, it could also mean the "die" making the mark, and even "archetype" or "pattern." In the Old Testament, Amos
refers to the image (5:26) and Exodus to the model (25:40). The first of the classic
passages from Romans refers to a prefigure (4:14), the second to a moral exemplum
(7:17). *Type* thus remains potently ambiguous: an Old Testament type has full,
substantive, inherent, and predictive values but simultaneously it is only a substantial copy of spiritual reality.[10]

Similarly, Auerbach's comprehensive tracing of the word *figura* in Terence, Varro, Lucretius, Cicero, Ovid, Quintilian, Tertullian, and the church fathers reveals an impressive array of meanings for the term. Lucretius, for instance, invokes *figura* because only it "could serve for [the] play on model and copy" which Auerbach observes in his usage (p. 16). And during the Roman Empire when *figura* was "firmly ingrained in the language of philosophy and cultivated discourse," it was the poets "who were most interested in the shades of meaning between model and copy, in changing form and the deceptive likenesses that walk in dreams." Though several other terms such as *ambages, effigies, exemplum, image, similitudo, species,* and *umbra* were employed for figuration in the place of *figura,* "none of these words combined the elements of the concept as fully as *figura:* the creative, formative principle, change amid the enduring essence, the shades of meaning between copy and archetype. Hence, it is not surprising that *figura* should have been most often and most widely used for this purpose" ("*Figura,*" pp. 48–49).

It is also no surprise that the play on model and copy enabled by this term raises the question of the coherence of the "concept" it ostensibly designates. As we shall see, this problem is chronic in Protestant articulations of typology, but it is also evident in Auerbach's summation. For his language repeatedly posits a continuum between meanings and concepts which are ostensibly opposites. How do we conceive of the figure or type if it cannot be categorized as model or copy but only as the play or shaded continuum between them? Explaining that the Latin *figura* was chosen over the Greek *typos* to designate prefiguration, Auerbach writes that "*figura* more or less consciously evoked all the notions involved in its history, while *typos* remained an imported, lifeless sign" (p. 48). How does one conceive of the figure or type if *figura* evokes *all* the notions which Auerbach shows to be involved in its history — imprint, seal, corpse, spirit, ghost, similitude, truth, form, newness, permanence, grammatical form, geometric outline, figment, style, deception, position (in lovemaking), rhetorical figure, show? It seems that besides the model/copy polarity, a number of other conceptual oppositions such as that between life and death, seal and impression, substance and shadow, truth and falsity, real and unreal must be rethought as shaded continuums in order to conceive of the type.

A specific and crucial instance of this kind of conceptual difficulty arises in Auerbach's designation of the historicity of type and fulfillment. Auerbach insists on the historicity, the reality, the concreteness of both type and antitype throughout "*Figura.*" Discussing figural interpretation in relation to allegory, for instance, he writes: "Since in figural interpretation one thing stands for another, since one thing represents and signifies the other, figural interpretation is 'allegorical' in the widest sense. But it differs from most of the allegorical forms known to us by the historicity both of the sign and what it signifies" (*Figura*," p. 54). But the nature of this criterion of the historicity of sign and signified is made problematical throughout the essay by its subjection to expressions of degree and quantity. In Tertullian, sometimes the type and sometimes the antitype possesses "a higher degree of historical concreteness" (p. 32); the figure sometimes has "a lesser force of reality" and sometimes "greater concreteness" (p. 33). Tertullian's interpretation is "more historical and realistic" than Origen's, and Augustine's thinking was "too concrete and historical to content itself with pure abstract allegory" (p. 37). After the distinction between allegory and typology is drawn, Auerbach adds that the typological sign represents "a definite event in its *full* historicity" (p. 54; my emphasis). This type of qualification persists when Auerbach describes the late antiquity practice of stripping texts, events, and natural phenomena of their historicity and interpreting them "allegorically or on occasion somewhat figurally" (p. 55). Under the allegorical method of interpretation which persists in the Middle Ages, "the text loses far more of its concrete history than in the figural system" (p. 55). But the figural system predominates, and its success "paved the way for less concrete schools of allegorism" (p. 56). What Auerbach's language in these passages implies is that historicity is something of which a text or event can have more or less. To the extent that an interpretation grants more of it to an event, the interpretation is figural; to the extent that an interpretation grants less of it to an event, it is allegorical. But what kind of thing is historicity or concreteness if an event can have more or less of it? And what kind of thing is an event that can have more or less concreteness and historicity? Instead of being either historical or nonhistorical, concrete or abstract, it seems an event can be a little of both. Just as *typos* and *figura* posit what we take to be antithetical concepts as two distant points on a shaded and shared continuum, so Auerbach is here positing the historical and the nonhistorical as different quantities or degrees of the same thing.

Another version of this peculiar seepage of conceptual definition into difference of degree is evident in a remarkable occurrence in the history of typological theory and Auerbach's account of it. Commenting on the church fathers' understanding of how the antitype "fulfilled" the type, he writes,

But the "heavenly" fulfillment is not complete, and consequently, as in certain earlier writers but more definitely in Augustine, the confrontation of the two poles, figure and fulfillment, is sometimes replaced by a development in three stages: the Law or history of the Jew as a prophetic *figura* for the appearance of Christ; the incarnation as fulfillment of this *figura* and at the same time as a new promise of the end of the world and the Last Judgment, and finally, the future occurrence of these events as ultimate fulfillment. (*"Figura,"* p. 41)

One may wish to pause here to consider what it means for the events which are to fulfill the Old Testament types suddenly to be deprived of their definitiveness as fulfillments and to become, in fact, only more types which require the "complete" and "ultimate" fulfillment of the apocalypse. One difficulty which this "developmental typology" obviously poses is that of establishing the extensive analogy or correspondence between Revelation and the two testaments that had been established between the two testaments. As Auerbach notes in connection with the initial formulation of figural interpretation in Tertullian, the relation between type and antitype "is revealed by an accord or similarity" (*Figura,"* p. 29), and this relation of correspondence or similitude clearly remains as an essential criterion for identifying typological connection throughout the history of typological theory. Within the premises of this theory, the Second Coming could fulfill Old Testament types and New Testament antitypes (which become types) only if a whole set of similarities was established between Revelation, on the one hand, and the rest of the Bible on the other. How could all of the analogies between the Old Testament and the New Testament (minus Revelation) find a further analogy in Revelation alone? The apparently casual move "sometimes" made of replacing the confrontation of the two poles of type and antitype with a three-stage development must either exert tremendous pressure on the notion of similitude as the ground for identifying type and antitype, or simply leave many corresponding events in the two testaments as unfulfilled types.[11]

This reconception of polarity as a tripartite chain poses a more fundamental problem regarding the nature of fulfillment. The account of the antitype as a new type obviously compromises the understanding of the antitype as fulfillment, truth, and meaning—the antitype is no longer the real reality, the fulfilling fulfillment, the true truth, the complete completion. Indeed, how could it be? How could the life of Christ be the pure and absolute fulfillment and meaning of history if, after him, history seemed to continue just as badly as ever, if history obstinately remained history? In his recent writing on typology which remarkably shows no recognition whatsoever of Auerbach's work, Frye refers to "the difficulty that the continuation of history posed for Christianity. As century after century passed without a second coming, the Church developed a progressive and forward-moving structure of doctrine, one that carries the typology of the Bible on in history and adapts it to what we have called second-phase, or metonymic, language."[12] What Auerbach narrates as a revision sometimes made in the development of typological theory and what Galdon vainly attempts to regard as an innovation best left alone is recognized by Frye to be demanded by the fact that history was experienced as continuing after its ostensible fulfillment in Christ. Because things continued past the ostensible fulfillment, that fulfillment had to be downgraded into a fullfilment/promise which prefigured the real, ultimate, and complete fulfillment. That this revisionist typology threatens to exclude history altogether as the site of fulfillment is evident in Frye's further claim that, "in practice," it meant that "the doctrines of Christian theology form the antitypes of which the stories and maxims in the Bible, including those of the New Testament, are types" (p. 85). As opposed to any historical event such as the Second Coming, Frye sees *doctrine* as what revised typology identifies as the ultimate fulfillment of the history of types which is now the referent of the Bible in its entirety.

Auerbach seems to concede the centrality of these problematical revisions in his summary to the third section of "*Figura*," "Origin and Analysis of Figural Interpretation," where he refers to the move "sometimes" made as one which is in fact constitutive of typological theory in general:

Figural prophecy implies the interpretation of one worldly event through another; the first signifies the second, the second fulfills the first. Both remain historical events; yet both, looked at in this way, have something provisional and incomplete about them; they point to one another and both point to something in the future, something still to come, which will be the actual, real, and definitive event. This is true not only of Old Testament prefiguration, which points forward to the incarnation and the proclamation of the gospel, but also of these latter events, for they too are not the ultimate fulfillment, but themselves a promise of the end of time and the true kingdom of God. Thus history, with all its concrete force, remains forever a figure, cloaked and needful of interpretation. In this light the history of no epoch ever has the practical self-sufficiency which, from the standpoint both of primitive man and of modern science, resides in the accomplished fact; all history, rather, remains open and questionable, points to something still concealed, and the tentativeness of events in the figural interpretation is fundamentally different from the tentativeness of events in the modern view of historical development. (Pp. 58–59)

In so recognizing an ostensibly casual revision in typological theory as a constitutive moment, Auerbach, too, precludes any historical moment from being "the actual, real, and definitive event." Because history "remains *forever* a figure, cloaked and needful of interpretation," because "*all* history" is open and pointing to something still concealed, no historical event can ever really, truly, ultimately, and completely fulfill the figures and types that history endlessly and always constitutes — if history is fulfilled in history, even by God, it is not fulfilled. Although Auerbach insists on the historicity of both type and antitype in his account of typological theory and insists that this is what distinguishes typology from allegory and symbol, he ultimately postulates the fulfillment of history as a nonhistorical event, the *end* of history or, more strictly, what is beyond the end. The reconception of the type/antitype polarity as a chain of types which Auerbach documents in his history of typology contests a premise of the theory by positing history as a temporal tract of ever-increasing and, in an absolute sense, unfulfilled promises and events. Central to the establishment of typological theory and Auerbach's own statement of it is a rift between this designation of history as the site of endlessly unfulfilled promise which finds real fulfillment only in what terminates and purely transcends it, and the attempted designation of history as the site of its own fulfillment and meaning in the historical immanence of God.[13]

All of these problems are evident in the Protestant articulation of typological theory. Although, like most Milton critics, she never sees the coherence of typology being questioned or threatened, Barbara Lewalski spells out the Reformer's ambivalence over the issue of whether Christ's first coming was really the fulfillment of Old Testament types:

Of course, the Protestant exegetes declared that Christ has fulfilled the types, and they insisted, none more vigorously, that Old Testament ceremonies and practices have been abrogated. Yet, partly because of their doctrine of the sacraments as signs rather than conduits of special grace, Protestants saw the spiritual situation of Christians to be notably advantaged by the New Covenant but not different in essence from that of the Old Testament people, since both alike depend on signs which will be fulfilled in Christ at the end of time. The Old Testament is still *figura*, but in the sense of a real historical time of preparation for and expectation of the future. And the Christ of the *eschaton* rather than the incarnate Christ of the Gospel is the ultimate antitype for all the types.[14]

That the Protestant ambivalence over the antitype may not leave intact a coherent typology, but work to impose a conceptual problematic comparable to that which afflicts Auerbach's statement, is made clear if we turn to a passage from what Lewalski regards as the schematization of mid- and late seventeenth-century typological theory, Samuel Mather's *The Figures and Types of the Old Testament*. After a preliminary discourse on the ways of God's preaching to man, Mather moves to a direct consideration of typology. He writes:

> 1. There is in a *Type* some *outward* or *sensible* thing, that represents an higher spiritual thing, which may be called a *Sign* or a Resemblance, a *Pattern* or *Figure*, or the like. Here is the general Nature of a *Type*; it is *a Shadow*. It hath been the Goodness and the Wisdom of God in all times and ages, to teach Mankind *Heavenly* things by *Earthly*; spiritual and *invisible* Things, by outward and *visible*; as *Job* 3. 12.
>
> 2. There is the *thing shadowed* or represented by the *Type*, And what is that? *Things to come*, faith the Apostle, *Col.* 2. 17. and good things to come, Heb. 10. 1. The good things of the Gospel, *Christ and his Benefits; but the body is of Christ*, as *Col.* 2. 17. This we call the *Correlate*, or the *Antitype*; the other is the *Shadow*, this the *Substance: The Type* is the Shell, this the kernel; the *Type* is the Letter, this the Spirit and Mystery of the *Type*. This we are still to look at, and to search into in every *Type*; we must look beyond the Shadow, to the Substance, to the Truth and Mystery of it: And this is Christ and the gospel, as future, and hereafter to be exhibited. This may be called the *Prototype*, or the Pattern, out of which, and according to which the other is drawn; as Pictures from the Man, whose Visage they represent.[15]

Initially it looks as though the type/antitype opposition will be congruent with the sensible/spiritual, outer/inner oppositions. But no sooner has the outer, sensible nature of the type been asserted than it is questioned by the adjectival phrase "which may be." The play on model and copy has already begun since, though it seems this phrase is modifying the type, the grammar also allows the higher spiritual thing to be the modified noun. As if in recognition of the major difficulty already at hand, Mather attempts to shut it down with the authoritative "Here is the general Nature of a *Type*; it is a *Shadow*." But this only compromises both the outward sensible nature of the type and the inner, spiritual nature of the antitype initially affirmed — though a shadow is outward and sensible, is not the substance that casts it also (if not more) outward and sensible? The final substitution of "visible" for "sensible" confirms the attenuation of the "outward or sensible" type and further skews the correspondence between the type/antitype difference and the inner/outer,

sensible/spiritual oppositions. But with the assertion in number 2 that
there is the thing shadowed or represented by the type, the type seems
to regain its materiality, for it is material substance that casts a shadow
or shadows forth — the implication now, however, is that the antitype
is the immaterial shadow. Only momentarily, for Mather goes on to say
that it is not the type but the antitype that is the substance in relation
to the shadowy type, as if substance is the more heavenly, spiritual, inner,
and invisible thing. Though affirming once more that the antitype is the
spirit of the type, Mather returns to his privileging of substance and again
identifies it with the truth and mystery of the type. Moreover, it seems
that the antitype is what is visible, for we are to look at it in every type
and look beyond the shadow to the substance. The sudden introduction
of a new term for the antitype, "the Prototype," and the occurrence of
"Pattern" not as a designation of the type, as it seems to be in number 1,
but of the antitype, only further obfuscates the issue. And the concluding
statement does not resolve but reiterates the problem, since, by drawing
an analogy between typology and visual representation, Mather is obliged
to designate both type and antitype as sensible (visual). The attempted
valorizations of the spiritual, invisible, and inner over the sensible, visible,
and outer are once more negated by an assignation of priority to one
sensible thing over another sensible thing.

In this passage from Mather, we can sense the alterities of *figura*
and *typos* in full force. In that things which are spiritual invisible patterns are superior to things which are sensible visible copies, and in that
Christ is superior to the Old Testament types, Mather needs his term for
the figure or type to mean sensible visible copy. But he also needs it to
mean nonsensible pattern or model. This is because, first, as what precedes the antitype, as what prefigures it, as what promises, prophesies,
and shadows forth the antitype, the type must in some sense be a pattern
of the antitype. The second reason is evident in the rhetorical question
Mather poses at the conclusion of his work: "For is not the Substance
better than the Shadows?" (p. 539). Because substance is better than
the shadow, because substance is the origin or model which precedes
the shadow and produces it or shadows it forth, and because Christ is
better than Moses, Mather needs his term for type or figure to mean a
nonsensible thing, at least a thing less sensible and substantial than the
antitype. Mather's account of the type, then, evinces the conceptual over-
determination which Auerbach senses to be evoked and born by the key
terms in the history and development of typological theory. But Mather's
rhetorical confidence and Auerbach's designation of the various "elements"
involved in comprehending typology as components of a coherent "con-

cept" of the type neglect how deeply counterintuitive this concept is. Mather and Auerbach are compelled to problematical formulations of not just the notion of the type, but of the notions of historicity, an event, and fulfillment in their attempts to formulate or record a coherent typological theory of history.

Miltonists have not been unaware of the difficulties in these statements of typological theory, but they have designated them as benign paradoxes within a theory whose consistency and comprehensibility remain securely intact. Instead of presupposing the legitimacy of these notions that fundamentally challenge conceptual oppositions, it is more reasonable to recognize them as powerful challenges to the intelligibility of typological theory. This recognition calls for further scrutiny of those accounts of human experience, such as Books XI and XII of *Paradise Lost*, which have been regarded as typological presentations of history. While these accounts may straightforwardly conform with some features of typological theory, they should be expected to manifest the problems which afflict the theory itself.

IV

In the case of the concluding books of *Paradise Lost*, we can see that some features of Milton's presentation of history insist not on the explanatory value of the theory, but precisely on the difficulties of its articulation. Michael first tells Adam that by ordaining law to man on Mount Sinai, God informs them "by types / And shadows, of that destin'd Seed to bruise / The Serpent, by what means he shall achieve / Mankind's deliverance" (XII, 232–35). But the sense in which Christ is the fulfillment or meaning of these types is attenuated when Michael then says,

> So Law appears imperfet, and but giv'n
> With purpose to resign them in full time
> Up to a better Cov'nant, disciplin'd
> From shadowy Types to Truth, from Flesh to Spirit,
> From imposition of strict laws, to free
> Acceptance of large Grace, from servile fear
> To filial, works of Law to works of Faith.   (XII, 300–06)

It is as if a disciplinary power resides in the type itself, as if it is not the fulfillment of the type that matters most, but the human engagement with the type as law which disciplines man to the point of allowing him to accept the new covenant. Moreover, the resignation to and acceptance of the new covenant, the discipline from shadowy types, flesh, and law to truth, spirit, and grace only instigates a new interpretive project of discerning the truth of the new covenant constituted in the New Testament. This is because after the death of the apostles, grievous wolves will taint the truth with superstitions and traditions: the truth will be "left *only* in those written Records pure, / Though not but by the Spirit understood" (XII, 513–14; my emphasis). Even after man has been disciplined from types to truth and Christ has in some way fulfilled the types, man must engage with the record of that fulfillment in order to comprehend the truth of his new condition, the truth of his Truth. If typological fulfillment issues in a different condition of human being, the understanding or consciousness of that condition is mediated by an interpretive engagement with the authorized description of that fulfillment.

Besides teaching us not to expect meaning in history in the form of a definitive act or duel, Milton's marked attenuation of events such as the Nativity and the Crucifixion interrogates these events as typological fulfillments. And even the "real" or "complete" fulfillment to be achieved by the apocalypse is, as we have clearly seen, made to have something casual, unfulfilling, even open about it. The attenuation of the antitype, be it the first or second coming, works to negate Adam's (and possibly our own) expectations of duels and to establish the homogeneity of history, but it also questions how any historical event could fulfill history, how any event could have the distinction of being a fulfillment. Indeed, as opposed to a single totalizing shape that embraces both history and eternity, Michael's figural presentation of history appears to Adam as a world or race *beyond* which eternity opens as an abyss:

> He ended; and thus Adam last repli'd.
> How soon hath thy prediction, Seer blest,
> Measur'd this transient World, the Race of time,
> Till time stand fixt: beyond is all abyss,
> Eternity, whose end no eye can reach.   (XII, 552–56)

Unless Adam is mistaken yet again, it seems that eternity is resolutely beyond history, that history is irrevocably the realm of types which, even if in some sense fulfilled, remain signs of what utterly transcends them. Milton's presentation of history, then, may be said to be typological in the comprehensive sense of conforming with standard typological procedures and embodying the conflicting designations of fulfillment and history which mark attempts to articulate a coherent typological theory. In so manifesting the difficulties within the theoretical framework governing the comprehension of human experience, Milton's typology finally questions the adequacy and possibility of this understanding.

McGill University

NOTES

1. Stanley Fish, "Transmuting the Lump: *Paradise Lost*, 1942–82," in *Literature and History: Theoretical Problems and Russian Case Studies*, ed. Gary Saul Morson (Stanford, Calif., 1986), pp. 55–56. Further references included in the text.

2. Sanford Budick, "Milton and the Scene of Interpretation: From Typology Toward Midrash," in *Midrash and Literature*, ed. Geoffrey Hartman and Sanford Budick (New Haven, Conn., 1986), pp. 195–205.

3. Timothy Bahti, "Auerbach's *Mimesis*: Figural Structure and Historical Narrative," in *After Strange Texts*, ed. Gregory Jay and David Miller (Tuscaloosa, Ala., 1985), pp. 124–45. Further references are included in the text.

4. Eric Auerbach, *Mimesis*, trans. Willard Trask (1953; rpt. New York, 1957), p. 64. Further references are included in the text.

5. Eric Auerbach, "*Figura*," trans. from German text in *Neue Dantestudien*, Istanbul, 1944, by Ralph Manheim, in *Scenes from the Drama of European Literature* (1959; rpt. Minneapolis, 1984), p. 53. Further references are included in the text.

6. See H. R. MacCallum, "Milton and Figurative Interpretation of the Bible," *UTQ* XXXI (1962), 397–415; J. Summers, *The Muse's Method* (London, 1962); Barbara Lewalski, "Structure and the Symbolism of Vision in Michael's Prophecy, *Paradise Lost* Books XI–XII," *PQ* XLII (1963), 25–35; Stanley Fish, *Surprised By Sin* (Berkeley and Los Angeles, 1967); William G. Madsen, *From Shadowy Types to Truth* (New Haven, Conn., 1968); J. M. Evans, *"Paradise Lost" and the Genesis Tradition* (Oxford, 1968); H. R. MacCallum, "Milton and Sacred History: Books XI and XII of *Paradise Lost*," in *Essays in English Literature from the Renaissance to the Victorian Age*, ed. M. MacLure and F. Watt (Toronto, 1974), pp. 149–62; Edward Tayler, *Milton's Poetry: Its Development in Time* (Pittsburgh, 1979).

7. On revolutionary and Restoration eschatological discussion, see, for example, Christopher Hill, *The World Turned Upside Down* (London, 1972), and J.G.A. Pocock, *The Machiavellian Moment* (Princeton, N.J., 1975).

8. Bahti, "Auerbach's *Mimesis*," pp. 131–32.

9. Timothy Bahti, "Vico, Auerbach and Literary History," *PQ* LX (1981), 239–55.

10. Ira Clark, *Christ Revealed* (Gainesville, Fla., 1982), p. 6. For another account of *typos* in the Bible, see K. J. Woollcombe, "The Biblical Origins and Patristic Development of Typology," in *Essays on Typology* (Chatham, U.K., 1957), pp. 60–62. Woollcombe observes that the term usually means "pattern" or "matrix" in the New Testament.

11. For the importance of correspondence or similarity between events as a criterion for identifying them as type and antitype and as a rule that prevented "subjective allegorizing," see Joseph A. Galdon, *Typology and Seventeenth-Century Literature*, (The Hague, 1975), pp. 46–53. Galdon seems to recognize but then dismiss the problem I am pointing to here: in reference to "the triple typological structure which is seen in many of the early Fathers and especially in Augustine," he writes, "it is impossible, for example, to verify the reality of the third element, and therefore the metaphysical correspondence and the notion of fulfillment are difficult to determine. The eschatological antitype can hardly be said to be phenomenal or actual. The present 'unreality' of this third element also opens the door once again to every variety of subjective allegory. Therefore it is perhaps best to consider typology as existing only in two terms — the Old Testament type and the New Testament antitype" (pp. 48–49). It is worth noting that in the following chapter of the book Galdon refers to the Eschaton as one of the "three elements which stand as the foundation upon which any meaningful typological interpretation of scripture is to be built" (p. 67). "Typology," he continues, "is actually the relationship which unites the

Old and the New Testaments and the final eschatological end of all time" (pp. 67–68). That is to say that Galdon ultimately does not consider typology as existing in two terms but finds he must accept the triple typological structure whose problems he leaves unresolved.

12. Northrop Frye, *The Great Code* (New York, 1982), p. 85. Madsen also points to this problem, in *From Shadowy Types to Truth*, p. 108.

13. Another way of putting this is to say that the conflict Madsen observes between the Platonist who regards history as being meaningless in itself and the Christian typologist who asserts the validity of history in fact resides within the Christian typological position. See Madsen, *From Shadowy Types to Truth*, pp. 100–01. I am also led to differ with Budick's claim that Auerbach's account of typology clearly distinguishes it from Philo's hermeneutic, which Budick sees as "symptomatic of a desire to describe a delayed messianic coming." Auerbach's recognition of the revisions in typological theory, and his account of typology as a hermeneutic which designates *all* history as open and unfulfilled, demonstrate his understanding of typology as, in part, symptomatic of the desire to describe a delayed messianic coming. Auerbach does not, however, recognize the problems posed by the reconception of the antitype (Christ's first coming) as another type and the reconception of fulfillment as what occurs outside of history. Though Budick points to the practice of Christian typologists of incorporating Philo's interpretations in typological ones, he does not point to what I sense to be the major theoretical inconsistencies underlying this practice. See Budick, "Milton and the Scene of Interpretation: From Typology Toward Midrash," p. 208.

14. Barbara Lewalski, *Protestant Poetics and the Seventeenth-Century Religious Lyric* (Princeton, N.J., 1979), pp. 125–31.

15. Samuel Mather, *The Figures and Types of the Old Testament*, 2nd ed. (London, 1705), p. 52.

MILTON AND THE POETICS OF EXTREMISM

Steven C. Dillon

Prove all things, hold fast that which is good. — 1 Thess. v, 21

I BEGIN WITH a note and some queries. Satan's last words in *Paradise Lost* are "full bliss" (*PL* X, 503),[1] where "full" echoes back to the conclusion of the satanic opening books:

> In close recess and secret conclave sat
> A thousand Demi-Gods on golden seats,
> Frequent and full. After short silence then
> And summons read, the great consult began. (I, 795–98)
>
> Thither full fraught with mischievous revenge,
> Accurst, and in a cursed hour he hies. (II, 1054–55)

The echo is certain, but what does it mean?[2] What is the status of last words in *Paradise Lost?* Are last words related to last things?

In this essay I wish to consider what I call Milton's poetics of extremism, by concentrating on last moments which are scattered throughout *Paradise Lost*. I will discuss, in specific, moments of threshold, book endings, last words, and the way all these critical moments tend to accumulate force through allusion. In addition to studying Miltonic extremes — the firsts and lasts are without end — I wish also to remark on what happens to the "middle" in the wake of such a procedurally apocalyptic mind. Spenser is always "in the middest," writing an "endlesse worke" that is lifelike for always being between.[3] One major problem for Milton's readers is to relate themselves to a work that intends "no middle flight" (I, 14) and does not hit the middle ground until the end.

I

The two poets who have most in common with Milton's literary practice — although neither of them share his extremist mind — are Virgil and Spenser. Virgil uses his book endings in ways very similar to Milton, and Spenser teaches Milton a crazy threshold pun (though it appears also in Virgil). Dante ends each *canticle* of the *Commedia* with "stelle" ("stars"), but this is a rigorously medieval Alexandrianism, like the clear, schematic ordering of the *Inferno*.[4] The manner of Virgil and Milton is more suggestive and resonant, although a Virgilian irony — as when

265

Aeneas's last words to Dido in Hades echo their parting words on earth —
will always be more pathetic and less clear than the Miltonic.[5]

Virgil's book endings are important thematically: words or phrases
point around to other places in the poem, assuring us of their importance.[6] Book III, for instance, makes an end of Aeneas's two-book story
by hearkening back to "conticuere," the first word of Book II: "conticuit
tandem factoque hic fine quievit" ("At last he ceased, and here, making
an end, was still"). As E. L. Harrison observes, however, "quievit" also
looks forward with a sudden irony toward Dido's unquiet in Book IV:
"nec placidam membris dat cura quietem" ("and the pang withholds calm
rest from her limbs," IV, 5). Turnus's death at the end of Book XII looks
back toward Dido's at the end of Book IV, as tragedy inexorably repeats
itself.[7] In the same way, the image of Aeneas at the end of Book II, carrying his father, changes to that of Aeneas bearing the shield at the end
of Book VIII ("genitor" becomes "nepotes," "father" becomes "grand-
children," as Troy becomes Rome). "Condit" at the end of Book XII,
when Aeneas "buries" his sword in Turnus ("ferrum . . . sub pectore condit," XII, 950), echoes ironically "conderet" at the beginning ("dum conderet urbem," I, 5), just as wandering Aeneas, "fato profugus" (I, 2) turns
to fleeing Turnus at the close, "fugit . . . sub umbras" (XII, 952). And
so much is, more or less, critical commonplace. Scores of classical phi-
lologists have taught us that Virgil's Alexandrianism works like this. Yet
Virgilian criticism has still to comment on less direct kinds of repetition,
such as "cessi" (II, 804) and "recessit" (IV, 705; Aeneas leaves Troy and
Dido dies), or such as "ignarus" Aeneas at the end of Book VIII, who
parallels "haud inscius" Mezentius at the end of Book X (Aeneas is unaware of his prophetic dimensions, while Mezentius knows perfectly well
why he is doomed).

And there is still another kind of echo which has gone unreported,
and which is in any case nearly invisible without Spenser and Milton
coming after. This has to do with what I call a threshold pun, where
the language self-consciously observes that it is in a threshold position.
"Crinem secat" ("Juno shears the lock," IV, 704) is a thematic version
of this, where the "cut" enforces the cut-off nature of this most isolated
book in the *Aeneid*. But the most gaudy version of this threshold pun
occurs at the ends of Books I, II, and finally, VI, when the strangeness
of threshold is then most strikingly confirmed:

> nam te iam septima portat
> omnibus errantem terris et fluctibus aestas.

[For it is now the seventh summer that bears thee over the sea] (I, 755–56).

> Danaique obsessa tenebant
> limina portarum, nec spes opis ulla dabatur.
> cessi et sublato montis genitore petivi.

[And the Danaans held the blockaded gates, nor was any hope of help offered. I gave way and, taking up my father, sought the mountains.] (II, 802–04)

> ille viam secat ad navis sociosque revisit;
> tum se ad Caietae recto fert litore portum.
> ancora de prora iacitur; stant litore puppes.

[Aeneas speeds his way to the ships and revisits his comrades; then straight along the shore sails for Caieta's haven. The anchor is cast from the prow; the sterns rest upon the beach.] (VI, 899–901).

We should observe the repetition of the morpheme "port": in Book I it means "carrying," in Book II it means exactly "portal," and in Book VI "portum" puns very cleanly towards "porta" above (Aeneas goes out that critically remarkable ivory gate, "portaque emittit eburna," VI, 898). A ninth-century *Aeneid* manuscript reads "limite portum" for "litore portum" (VI, 900), a reading toward which I am inclined (with Bentley, Heine, Henry, and Mackail), not only because it avoids a repetition of "litore" (VI, 900, 901), but also because it triggers again a threshold wordplay. Now "limite" sounds with "limina" ("limina portarum," II, 803). "Portat" in Book I is by itself not a pun, but in sequence with the others it is; threshold accumulates the uncertainty and playfulness that is poetically necessary for Aeneas to pass through the gate of false dreams toward Rome and victory.

Spenser does not exploit his book and canto endings in this way, which in fact furthers the sense of an "endlesse work." But he deploys several times a threshold pun that will be important for Milton, and which continues Virgil's play on "port." Ignaro, for instance, is the keyholder to the castle where Redcrosse is imprisoned, and "gate" marks his threshold status:

> At last with creeping crooked pace forth came
> An old old man, with beard as white as snow,
> That on a staffe his feeble steps did frame,
> And guide his wearie gate both too and fro:
> For his eye sight him failed long ygo,
> And on his arme a bounch of keyes he bore,
> The which unused rust did overgrowe:
> Those were the keyes of every inner dore,
> But he could not them use, but kept them still in store. (I, viii, 30)

The only ideal, truly courteous porter in *The Fairie Queene* is Humilta, whose paradigmatic aspect is stressed not only by the threshold topos from Matthew vii, 13–14, but also by the pun on "gate":

> He was an aged syre, all hory gray,
> With lookes full lowly cast, gate full slow,
> Went on a staffe his feeble steps to stay, [and]
> Hight Humilta. They passe in stouping low;
> For streight & narrow was the way, which he did show.   (I, x, 5)

The Squire of Dames looks toward Malbecco's castle with an ironic play—"to yonder castle turne your gate" (III, viii, 51)—since the problem of Book III, canto ix is precisely that the gate will not turn: Malbecco is the one who beckons badly.[8] Finally, Spenser hints toward a crisis at the house of Radigund by reinvoking Virgil's portal play: "So forth she came out of the citty gate, / With stately port and proud magnificence" (V, v, 4).

Milton, in his turn, concentrates clearest of all on the verbal highlightings of threshold. Portress Sin is a "Sign / Portentous" (*PL* II, 760–61). At the end, as Adam and Eve turn from the "Eastern Gate" toward the world, Michael inspires Eve with a pacific pun: "Her also I with gentle Dreams have calm'd / Portending good" (XII, 595–96). In a less fortunate ending-port, Satan is angel-handled thus at the end of Book IV (whose book-ending expulsion, as we shall see, sums echoes throughout the poem): "And with them comes a third of Regal port, / But faded splendor wan; who by his gait" (IV, 869–70). Threshold self-consciousness accumulates its most dire effect when Eve parts from Adam; here is the liminal, last moment par excellence:

> Thus saying, from her Husband's hand her hand
> Soft she withdrew, and like a Wood-nymph light,
> Oread or Dryad, or of Delia's Train,
> Betook her to the Groves, but Delia's self
> In gait surpass'd and Goddess-like deport.   (IX, 385–89)

In an important essay on Coleridge's thresholds, Angus Fletcher writes, "few poets of major stature remain long interested in the material aspect of the threshold." Spenser and Milton are both more interested in mind than material body: "From Spenser, Milton learns the iconographies of mental shift."[9] Yet the materiality of language that is consistently evoked by threshold wordplay suggests that materiality as such has not been completely transcended. Milton in fact very much wants to emphasize the materiality of threshold: it is a crisis place, a place of division; it is frequently a wall. The Miltonic act of internalization at the end of *Paradise Lost* is one more act of division, as much a psychological consolation as a thematically typical exclusion. Internalization divides man from the serious materiality of both the body and Paradise. Miltonic threshold is emblematic of Miltonic continuity, which is why thresholds turn to ends, betweenness to extremes. Milton's poetry is based on discontinuity and an aiming toward ends; the emphasis on form and language in *Paradise Lost* helps to materialize the way transition in Milton becomes much more troubling than in Spenser or in Virgil. To adopt Fletcher's language, the poetry of Milton, unlike that of the circularly wandering Spenser, tends toward motionless, central *templum*, rather than displaced, wandering labyrinth.[10]

II

Paradise Lost, Book IV, is Milton's book of ideal paradise, and he marks its boundaries with absolute divisions. Book IV begins with a cry for apocalypse and ends with an allusion to the last line of the *Aeneid*. Milton's poetics is based on divisions and ends.[11] The continual process in *Paradise Lost* is to divide and to reconsolidate, repulse and repair, from the expulsion of the rebel angels from heaven, and of man from Paradise, to the addressed fit audience ("drive far off the barbarous dissonance / Of Bacchus and his Revellers," VII, 32–33), to the little clearings-out of Eden ("Those Blossoms also, and those dropping gums / . . . Ask riddance, if we mean to tread with ease," IV, 630, 632), to the expulsion of Satan from Eden at the end of Book IV. Reparation occurs as the heavenly wall rolls closed (VI, 879), as Adam "clears" Eve of her devilish dream (V, 95–136), and insofar as the remaining audience *is* fit. Satan disregards boundaries ("At one slight bound high overleap'd all bound," IV, 181), whereas God constantly circumscribes his endlessness by measurement and judgment ("Love hath abounded more than Glory abounds," III, 312). *Paradise Lost*, Book IX, which formally balances Book IV, defines man's tragedy by the emptiness and endlessness of its last sentence: "And of thir vain contest appear'd *no end*," IX, 1189, my emphasis).[12]

Book IV ends by providing Satan with a clear warning sign:

> Satan, I know thy strength, and thou know'st mine,
> Neither our own but giv'n; what folly then
> To boast what Arms can do, since thine no more
> Than Heav'n permits, nor mine, though doubl'd now
> To trample thee as mire: for proof look up,
> And read thy Lot in yon celestial Sign

> Where thou art weigh'd, and shown how light, how weak
> If thou resist. The Fiend lookt up and knew
> His mounted scale aloft; nor more; but fled
> Murmuring, and with him fled the shades of night.   (IV, 1006–15)

Satan flees like Turnus ("vitaque cum gemitu fugit indignata sub umbras," *Aeneid* XII, 952), yet *with* the shades, not *to* them. "Murmuring" here means "complaining" — Satan is no "murmuring" brook (IV, 260). Indeed, Satan packs with him all kinds of Edenic parody: "murmuring," "shades," and "light," just as Book III ended by recalling God's light (1) in Satan's landing ("till on Niphates' top he lights," III, 742).[13] The "celestial Sign" (IV, 997) refers to God's Homeric scales, but also echoes in this Virgilian context the "insigne" of Pallas's belt — "umeris inimicum insigne gerebat" ("and now [he] wore on his shoulders his foeman's fatal badge," XII, 944). Milton recalls Virgil's ending and also reverses it: whereas the "sign" of his dead friend makes Aeneas leave off his hesitation and strike down Turnus, God's sign prevents what seems to be certain and chaotic violence.

The end of Book IV is the end of an ideal idyll, and so quite reasonably, its end is paradigmatic for *Paradise Lost*. Notice the formal and structural resonances waiting and available. Satan is weighed: he is not "full" but rather *plenus illi*. He is light ("levis") not light ("lux"). "For proof look up" (IV, 1010) recalls Ithuriel's direction to earth, "Look downward" (III, 722); Satan's gaze is as emblematic as Mammon's, whose "looks and thought / Were always downward bent" (I, 680–81). The cosmic stage with Satan surrounded by angels plays formally against Abdiel surrounded by rebel angels at the end of Book V, just as Satan dragged by two angels inverts the iconography of one angel leading out Adam and Eve at the end of Book XII (and confirming once more those threshold puns, "port" and "gait," IV, 869–70). The angels surround Satan with a virtuoso display of limitary language:

> While thus he spake, th' Angelic Squadron bright
> Turn'd fiery red, sharp'ning in mooned horns
> Thir Phalanx, and began to hem him round
> With ported Spears, as thick as when a field
> Of Ceres ripe for harvest waving bends
> Her bearded Grove of ears, which way the wind
> Sways them; the careful Plowman doubting stands
> Lest on the threshing floor his hopeful sheaves
> Prove chaff.   (IV, 977–85)

In this doubtful threshold moment "ported" speaks for itself; but what is most important is that the liminal as threshold moment always moves to an extreme. The middle space becomes a beginning or an end. In a moment heaven will "ponder," weighing Satan, and, as Geoffrey Hartman puts it, "God overbalances the balance."[14] The field of Ceres takes its momentary revenge for the endless wandering caused by "gloomy Dis" ("which cost Ceres all that pain / To seek her through the world," IV, 270–71). And what seems about to *prove* chaff will become absolute, celestial *proof*.

And consider that moon, sharp and angry; it could be a middle, but is has appeared previously at the ends of Books I, II, and III.[15] In Book I there is the famous moon from Virgil, hanging over a similarly georgic "plowman" ("Whose Midnight Revels . . . some belated Peasant sees / Or dreams he sees, while overhead the Moon sits arbitress," I, 782–85).[16] Book II ends with Satan's vision of "This pendant world, in bigness as a Star / Of smallest Magnitude close by the Moon" (II, 1053–54); and the end of Book III depicts a remarkably Christ-like moon, which "fills and empties to enlighten the earth":[17]

> That place is Earth the seat of Man, that light
> His day, which else as th' other Hemisphere
> Night would invade, but there the neighboring Moon
> (So call that opposite fair Star) her aid
> Timely interposes, and her monthly round
> Still ending, still renewing through mid Heav'n
> With borrow'd light her countenance triform
> Hence fills and empties to enlighten the Earth,
> And in her pale dominion checks the night.   (III, 724–32)

The moon is caught up in a measured system of checks and balances. The language is of comparison, weight, and number: "fills and empties" (we recall "full" at the ends of Books I and II, "vain" ["vana"] at the end of Book IX); "the pendant world" (we recall the Homeric scales at the end of Book IV). Book VI will remind man to keep his balance ("remember, and fear to transgress," VI, 912) just as Book VII concludes "if else thou seek'st / Aught not surpassing human measure, say" (VII, 641).

Christian lessons of temperance have something to do with all this weighing and measuring, of course, but Milton, unlike Spenser, teaches a *via media* above ground, always looking to the end.[18] The insistence on division is essentially a metaphysical substitution of all kinds of little ends before the last one. We wait not so much by standing as by weighing. Adam's last words juxtapose apocalypse with temperance, so that the cry for revelation ("O for that warning voice!") may be assuaged by constant though earlier than last judgments:

> And thus Adam last repli'd.
> How soon hath thy prediction, Seer blest,
> Measur'd this transient World, the Race of time,
> Till time stand fixt: beyond is all abyss,
> Eternity, whose end no eye can reach.
> Greatly instructed I shall hence depart,
> Greatly in peace of thought, and my fill
> Of knowledge, what this Vessel can contain;
> Beyond which was my folly to aspire.   (XII, 552–60)

I will analyze in the next section the last words of each major character, and so attend in more detail to Adam's last reply. We might for now simply reiterate our earlier problem, which is, why is Satan associated with "full"? To be sure, there is clear parody involved: "full" balloons Satan into a spiritually empty figure like Orgoglio (*FQ* I, vii), as in the description of Satan's journey at the end of Book II:

> And now with ease [he]
> Wafts on the calmer wave by dubious light
> And like a weather-beaten Vessel holds
> Gladly the Port, though Shrouds and Tackle torn;
> Or in the emptier waste, resembling Air,
> Weighs his spread wings.   (II, 1041–46)

Here Satan's port-tending vessel, "full fraught" with revenge, is an easy demonic counterpart to Adam's temperate "vessel" filled with knowledge.

The point, however, is that "full" is a word like Empson's "all" — a complex word that extends the chain to all/fall/full — and it has more than merely satanic implications.[19] For Adam should be full too — but not to excess — and with knowledge not revenge. The fullness of "full" is made most explicit in Satan's last speech and also at the end of Book X. Satan's "full bliss" is, on the one hand, straightforward dramatic irony, as he listens for plenitude and hears only absence:

> What remains, ye Gods
> But up and enter now into full bliss.
>   So having said, a while he stood, expecting
> Thir universal shout and high applause
> To fill his ear, when contrary he hears
> On all sides, from innumerable tongues
> A dismal universal hiss.   (X, 502–08)

Instead of full *bliss*, an empty *hiss*. On the other hand, we should observe that Satan's last act is precisely that of making an end: the demonic desire is that nothing remains. What is vexing—and this is always the case with satanic imitation—is that God's divisions and Satan's are precariously near. But fullness is *not* Satan's problem; it is instead, finally, Milton's sarcastic mark and remark. Like the stairs God lets down from the borders of heaven, only to "aggravate his sad exclusion from the doors of bliss" (III, 525), Milton puts a "full" at every possible demonic end—and laughs serenely at Satan's emptiness.

Milton will allow a human fullness—neither God's nor godlike—at the end of Book X:

> Both confess'd
> Humbly thir fault, and pardon begg'd, with tears
> Watering the ground, and with thir sighs the Air
> Frequenting, sent from hearts contrite, in sign
> Of sorrow unfeign'd, and humiliation meek.   (X, 1100–04)

Book X ends with a broad, hymnic repetition, as lines 1098–1104 repeat lines 1086–92. Now closure is patient and perfect. Adam and Eve give the sigh *and* the sign, in contrast to Satan's well-warned *gemitus* at the end of Book IV. Most clearly, "frequenting" means "filling" and occurs in the same line position as "frequent" in the satanic "frequent and full" (I, 797).[20] Adam and Eve fill the air with their own signs, and thereby undo forever the empty endlessness of Book IX's tragedy.

The puritanical vision of God is unmediated; the emphasis is on origins and ends, with an effort to drive off the middle. A master himself of dialectical mediation, Geoffrey Hartman writes, "The Reformation . . . produced, in its purity, a most awesome concentration of human consciousness on a few existentials. The space filled by boughten mercies and mediations is collapsed into a direct, unmediated confrontation of the individual and his God."[21] The "process of speech," as Boyd M. Berry describes, is always toward an end; Adam's last speech "dismisses the human concerns of time and history and the exploits of men, resting rather on the absolute, immutable, eternal will of God."[22] Paradoxically, although Dante's epic takes place in a world utterly beyond, and Milton's epic takes place in an earlier protoworld, Dante's Catholicism very evenly balances body, city, and history with the mysteries of allegorical soul and eternity, while Milton consistently overthrows the balance.[23] Thus C. A. Patrides frames the poem as follows: "the story told is not a sentence in the history of the world, it is a parenthesis in eternity."[24] Though history's revolution has failed, Milton ignores history, and he writes an apocalyptic poem, a poem absolutely obsessed by ends.

III

Eve has the last human speech in *Paradise Lost* and the last word is "restore": "By mee the Promis'd seed shall all restore" (XII, 623). Eve is in between, at once devilish, as she repeats Satan's temptation ("though all by mee is lost") and also restorative, Christ-like. Eve's last word specifically echoes back to the appearance of Christ in the opening sentence, where "restore" moves from the end of the line to the beginning: "till one greater Man / Restore us, and regain the blissful Seat" (I, 4–5). We hear not only Eve as Christ in line 5, but also an inverted Eve-as-Satan. Full bliss *remains* instead of a bliss-full seat *regained*. Keeping in mind the threshold attention to diction and theme discussed so far, I will turn now to the last words of major characters. As we shall continue to notice, there is a definite tendency for last words to echo first words, last words, or other extremist moments. We know already that Milton's poetry is filled with thematic key words, such as "wonder," "wander," and "fruit," but these ending echoes constitute a much more severe and programmatic repetition. Only a poetics of extremism can account for such a relentlessly detailed interest in last things.

God's last words are words of division:

> So send them forth, though sorrowing, yet in peace:
> And on the East side of the Garden place,
> Where entrance up from Eden easiest climbs,
> Cherubic watch, and of a Sword the flame
> Wide waving, all approach far off to fright,
> And guard all passage to the Tree of Life:
> Lest Paradise a receptacle prove
> To Spirits foul, and all my Trees thir prey,
> With whose stol'n Fruit Man once more to delude.   (XI, 117–25)

Paradise is at an end; and the most authoritative threshold figure in the poem is immediately linked with the dissolution of Paradise:

> He ceas'd; and th' Archangelic Power prepar'd
> For swift descent, with him the Cohort bright
> Of watchful Cherubim; four faces each
> Had, like a double Janus, all thir shape
> Spangl'd with eyes more numerous than those
> Of Argus, and more wakeful than to drowse,
> Charm'd with Arcadian Pipe, the Pastoral Reed
> Of Hermes, or his opiate Rod.   (XI, 126–33)

God orders man cut off from Paradise, and a threshold chariot, "like a double Janus," moves out to do his bidding. That God's last word is "delude" is quite remarkable, though I take it that this is another instance of the strict Miltonic — not Callimachean — play (Lat. *ludus* = play). The only other instance of "delude" in *Paradise Lost* occurs in Book X, where the devils feast upon false apples; as a literal exchange for the forbidden tree a multitude of trees are "to delude them sent" (X, 554). We should make two observations. First, the trees become important thematically, by repetition, and we shall meet them again. Second, God's manner is characterized not only by prohibition and division, but also by this bitter sense of humor. God divides, or purifies away what is corrupt, but — by keeping up his spirits, as it were — he does not miss what is lost. "Delude" is a queerly hopeful word for God to end with, since it is at once both angry and assuredly playful.

If God's last words divide, then Christ's last words repair, a distinction which also applies to the final words of Adam and Eve. The observation itself may not seem altogether surprising, but the clarity, both verbal and formal, which patterns each of the final speeches is to my mind particularly noteworthy. Christ's last words look forward to the Last Judgment, when "All my redeem'd may dwell in joy and bliss, / Made one with me as I with thee am one" (XI, 43–44). But this is now precisely what man is punished for, as God makes clear in the first words of his last speech: "O Sons, like one of us Man is become" (XI, 84). God drives man out "Lest Paradise a receptacle prove" to foul spirits (XI, 123), whereas Christ offers himself as a receptacle: "Accept me, and in mee from these receive / The smell of peace toward Mankind" (XI, 37–38). Christ intercedes to pray for man (24, 32) with fruits more pleasing than "all the Trees / Of Paradise could have produc't" (XI, 28–29), while God closes by preventing the satanic repetition, when "all my Trees [would be] thir prey" (XI, 124).

Adam's last words repeat in a number of ways his first words. These echoes work not only to "undo" what has come before, but also to reveal the human cost of this final reorganization. Adam's first speech (IV, 411–37) is taken up with doctrine, as he reminds Eve of the easy charge of Paradise:

> not to taste that only Tree
> Of knowledge, planted by the Tree of Life,
> So near grows Death to Life, whate'er Death is,
> Some dreadful thing no doubt. (IV, 423–26)

Adam's last speech "undoes" this forsaken warning, by considering not the tree of knowledge, nor by association all those trees with which the devils are deluded, nor the Tree of Life from which mankind is excluded —

though these are all part of a chain formed by last words — but instead
by contemplating the "*Gate* of Life" (XII, 571; my emphasis). The Tree
of Knowledge is the Tree of Death, as Adam understands in his first
speech, and it stands next to the Tree of Life in the middle of Paradise.
But Adam's last speech turns middles into ends, ends into beginnings,
and the trees of life and death into the gate of death and life. Small
things and large, temperance and apocalypse, will afford a final, better
threshold:

> Henceforth I learn, that to obey is best,
> And love with fear the only God, to walk
> As in his presence, ever to observe
> His providence, and on him sole depend,
> Merciful over all his works, with good
> Still overcoming evil, and by small
> Accomplishing great things, by things deem'd weak
> Subverting worldly strong, and worldly wise
> By simply meek; that suffering for Truth's sake
> Is fortitude to highest victory,
> And to the faithful Death the Gate of Life.   (XII, 561–71)

The correct reorganization of death and life, from tree to gate, is apparent — but the pathos, the human cost of such reordering, is immense.
With an ideology of ends, what happens to those middles — what happens in particular to Eve? Adam will now concentrate "solely" on God.
Adam's first speech — though it is no less didactic — begins "Sole partner
and sole part of all these joys," and ends with a wonderful drawing of
Eve into the picture:

> But let us ever praise him, and extol
> His bounty, following our delightful task
> To prune these growing Plants, and tend these Flow'rs,
> Which were it toilsome, yet with thee were sweet.   (IV, 436–39)

In Adam's last speech, however, he *only* praises divinity: his speech is
framed rigorously by "seer blest" (XII, 553) and "my Redeemer ever blest"
(575). There is a pitiable sense of Eve's exclusion. The Fall enforces the
distance not only between God and man, but also between man and
woman; after Eve's concluding speech, Adam "answer'd not" (XII, 625).

Only Eve *could* have spoken the last words. Given the hierarchy
of our world parents, she is nearest the world toward which they move.
She is God's last creation, "heav'n's last best gift" (V, 19), who also speaks
the last words before the fall — "but *Eve* / Persisted, yet submiss, though
last" (IX, 376–77). As the first to fall, her last words lend her a poetic

dignity like that of Dido, who spurns Aeneas in the underworld to return his own silence earlier in Carthage. Once more last words undo and reply to what has come before. Eve wakes as she awakes in Book V, to find Adam returned; and we observe that there is in each scene of consolation a curious verbal mark. Adam tells Eve to "be not sad" (V, 116) while he is sad himself ("thus *Adam* answer'd sad," V, 94); Michael foresees a life "in one faith unanimous though sad" (XII, 604) while Eve wakes "with words not sad" (XII, 609). Neither consolation is perfect, or perfectly smooth, I gather, insofar as they are insufficiently internalized. The beautiful point of Eve's last words is that they end with her, alone with herself, with a recognition of self-reliance and self-worth that cancels out the narcissistic:

> This further consolation yet secure
> I carry hence; though all by mee is lost,
> Such favor I unworthy am voutsaf't,
> By mee the Promis'd Seed shall all restore.   (XII, 620–23)

This final speech very specifically disabuses Eve of the narcissistic overtones of her opening monologue (IV, 440–91), since she now accepts the guide instead of lingering:

> But now lead on;
> In mee is no delay; with thee to go,
> Is to stay here; without thee here to stay,
> Is to go hence unwilling.   (XII, 614–17)

Wonderfully, these lines not only reply to the Ovidian context of Eve's opening speech, but they also translate Ovid even better than that oft-studied passage:

> What thou seest,
> What there thou seest fair Creature is thyself,
> With thee it comes and goes: but follow me,
> And I will bring thee where no shadow stays
> Thy coming.   (IV, 467–71)

> quod petis, est nusquam; quod amas, avertere, perdes!
> ista repercussae, quam cernis, imaginis umbra est;
> nil habet ista sui; tecum venitque manetque;
> tecum discedet, si tu discedere possis!

[What you seek is nowhere; but turn yourself away, and the object of your love will be no more. That which you behold is but the shadow of a reflected form and has no substance of its own. With you it comes, with you it stays, and it will go with you—if you can go.] (III, 433–36)

"Tecum venitque manetque" is exactly "with thee to go, / Is to stay here," but the echo of Narcissus turns a shadow into Adam.[25] Adam's first words hold Eve within the scheme, but his last words programmatically divide her from him; Eve at first shuns Adam as less fair than her own self, but at last, incorporating Adam, Eve represents the entirety of man's hope.

IV

"If Spenser is the Renaissance reproduced, Milton is the Renaissance understood," writes William Kerrigan.[26] I believe that we all feel the *Fairie Queene* to be a much more experiential, lifelike poem, on C. S. Lewis's terms, in pointed contrast to *Paradise Lost*, which is so much more a book *about* life. This formulation is of itself sufficient to explain why Milton has no middles:

You remember the golden bird in Yeats's poem — it sang of what was past and passing and to come, and so interested a drowsy emperor. In order to do that, the bird has to be "out of nature"; to speak humanly of becoming and knowing is the task of pure being, and this is humanly represented in the poem by an artificial bird.[27]

To be, as with Spenser or Satan, is to be vivid and *full*, but to know is necessarily to leave something out. Milton images the problem most precisely at the beginning of Book III, where he is "from the cheerful ways of men / Cut off" (46–47). It is important to notice that Milton employs a threshold figure: "wisdom [is] at one entrance quite shut out" (III, 50). Milton receives "celestial Light" in compensation for a missing world, just as innocent, sharp-eyed Ithuriel lets Satan pass to earth — "suspicion sleeps / At wisdom's gate" (III, 686–87, about fifty lines from the other end of Book III). These thresholds are once again more like dividing walls than opening gates, and they divide absolutely human wisdom from divine. William Kerrigan's *Sacred Complex* is one of the best books on Milton, and its Freudian title immediately and quite properly implies that sacred knowledge will come only in terms of blindness and insight.

Patricia Parker's chapter in *Inescapable Romance* is one of the best essays on Milton, but not because its overall descriptions ring true (as Kerrigan's so often do). Romance is as inescapable as life or as literature because of a common middle, mediated threshold status. She discusses many of the topics of the present essay in sections such as "This Pendant World" and "The Fullness of Time." But she does not take into account the chain of measure and division to be found at crucial ending places; she does not ask why a threshold should be a middle rather than a beginning or an end. Eve's "staying" at the mirroring waters (IV, 449) is an important figure for romance deferral or hesitation, but it needs to be emphasized how quickly "a voice thus warn'd" Eve (IV, 467), echoing the apocalyptic opening of Book IV, and ending Eve's fixated moment. Pondering is not so much wandering or semiotic suspension — it isn't "hanging around" — as it is a constant measuring, an alert, knowing balance. Parker does not seem to account for the vast differences between the full, endless poetics of Ariosto and Spenser, the oxymoronic, collapsed habit of thought in Keats, and a Milton who avowedly wants to escape romance (see the invocation to Book IX). "The characteristic Miltonic focus is on the process rather than on the product" (p. 142) — but if Milton is not a poet of extremes, who is? At least Parker should say that Milton is, since least obvious, her most interesting test case. *Only* Satan changes gradually — Parker's example of process — and this is not only because sin is seen in terms of continuity, but also because Satan is a narrative, romance figure, and absolutely divided from representations of divinity.[28] Virtue, like Milton's poetry, is based on difference, not deferral, balance not suspension, division and then repair. Milton is wonderfully illuminated by Spenser and Keats, but not at all because he is ultimately very much like them.

The burden for the reader of Milton's extremist poetics, however, remains immense. Knowing full well that Milton looks always to ends, Kerrigan concludes his book with the poignant effort to make Milton's "second home" serve as ours: the place of rest at the end of the poem must be sufficient unto itself. Kerrigan argues that God is excluded ("no gods, no angels, no demons"), that dogma and polemic are past, "things are as they are," and "man is all in all."[29] Similarly, Patricia Parker reaches the conclusion that *Paradise Lost* ends inescapably with romance: "The end of the poem is finally open-ended, not definitively either evening or morning, but both."[30] I will close, however, by attempting to reopen the argument. It is, after all, still not clear that Dr. Johnson was so very wrong to say that *Samson Agonistes* has no middle. We may have to return to that notion — which makes a good deal more sense than a kind of novelistic, romance process — and also to consider what it means that *Paradise Regained* is Milton's *Georgics*.[31] As middles and romances become ends and Christian epic, just so, Milton makes a number of very specific and stern gestures of closure at the end of the poem, in order to confound its possibly satanic, howsoever lifelike openness. In a word, the end is a restrained beginning but not an opening or a middle.

Michael's last words ask Adam and Eve to meditate "on the happy end": we are constantly asked to look through the middle toward an extreme. Eve's dream "portending good" (XII, 596) sounds the moment of threshold, and from here on all we hear is ending: "with meditation on the happy end. / He ended, and they both descend the Hill; / Descended" (XII, 605–07). Michael catches hold of Adam and Eve—between them—but then the middle vanishes:

> In either hand the hast'ning Angel caught
> Our ling'ring Parents, and to th' Eastern Gate
> Led them direct, and down the Cliff as fast
> To the subjected Plain; then disappear'd.   (XII, 637–40)

Adam and Eve fall "down the cliff" with a rather frightening haste (Hopkins's "cliffs of fall"), and they find themselves divided from Paradise with a recollection of Milton's blinded threshold (Milton is "cut off" from the "cheerful ways of men" and the "human face divine"):

> They looking back, all th' Eastern side beheld
> Of Paradise, so late thir happy Seat,
> Wav'd over by that flaming Brand, the Gate
> With dreadful Faces throng'd and fiery Arms.   (641–44)

The depiction is horrible enough that De Quincey uses it to stand for the opium nightmares at the end of his *Confessions*. Is the poem, here, "where we are"?

In the exact middle of the first line of *Paradise Lost* is "Disobedience"—"Of Man's First Disobedience, and the Fruit": to be in the middle is to be disobedient. Satan waffles like Aeneas, caught between relentless contraries, but God divides and Christ unifies. Christ may be a mediator, but it makes little sense to think of him in the middle; Christ moves from one extreme to the other, now with God, now God-in-man. And the last lines of *Paradise Lost* have no middle:

> The World was all before them, where to choose
> Thir place of rest, and Providence thir guide:
> They hand in hand with wand'ring steps and slow,
> Through Eden took thir solitary way.   (XII, 646–49)

"Providence" is now the long word among monosyllables, but it has shifted to the right. Most strikingly, each of the last four lines begin with "th," so that beginnings rather than middles are emphasized at the end. The strict repetition works, however, precisely to counteract wandering; such formality resists to the end "open-endedness."

The last word is a thematic, threshold pun. We have seen how last words in previous books and speeches had to do with measuring, fullness, or division. The matter is clear enough that Marvell ends his introductory poem thus: "Thy verse created like thy Theme sublime, / In Number, Weight, and Measure, needs not Rime." Measure in Milton's poem replaces the unsubtle, as unchosen, ends of rhyme — and everywhere — right down to the last word. With all the talk of fullness, vessels, ports, ends, and choosing it is clear that "way" sounds with "weigh."[32] The poem ends by calling to mind responsibility even more than possibility: it would be too easy, and assuredly un-Miltonic, to say that they are even.

Bates College

NOTES

1. All quotations from Milton follow Merritt Y. Hughes's edition, *John Milton: Complete Poems and Major Prose* (New York, 1957). I also cite from the following editions of Virgil, Ovid, and Spenser: *Virgil*, trans. H. Rushton Fairclough [Loeb Edition], 2 vols., (Cambridge, Ma., 1954); Ovid, *Metamorphoses*, 2 vols., Loeb Edition, trans. Frank Justus Miller (Cambridge, Ma., 1971); Edmund Spenser, *The Faerie Queene*, ed. Thomas P. Roche, Jr. (New Haven, Conn., 1981).

2. A study to which I am indebted for its analysis of figurative echo is John Hollander's *The Figure of Echo: A Mode of Allusion in Milton and After* (Berkeley and Los Angeles, 1981). The Miltonic difference occurs in his use of transumption, or "echo metaleptic." Insofar as it elides middles, as I hope to show, this figure is typically Miltonic: "There is a general sense that it is a kind of meta-trope, or figure of linkage between figures, and that there will be one or more unstated middle terms which are leapt over, or alluded to, by the figure" (p. 114).

3. "When I say that [*The Fairie Queene*] is like life, I do not mean that the places and people in it are like those which life produces. I mean precisely what I say — that it is like life itself not the products of life. . . . The things we read about in it are not like life, but the experience of reading it is like living," writes C. S. Lewis, *The Allegory of Love* (Oxford, 1936), pp. 357–58.

4. For the Callimachean Dante, see John Kevin Newman, *The Classical Epic Tradition* (Madison, 1986), pp. 244–81.

5. To further the comparison: Miltonic ambiguities, such as those adumbrated by Stanley Fish, *Surprised by Sin* (Berkeley and Los Angeles, 1967), tend to go away, no matter how caught up we are momentarily by syntax or enjambment. But Virgilian ambiguity tends to be permanently ambivalent; in *Aeneid*, Book IV, line 449, "lacrimae vulvuntur inanes," we shall never know whether the tears belong to Dido or Aeneas.

6. See E. L. Harrison, "The Structure of the Aeneid: Observations on the Links between the Books," *Aufstieg und Niedergang der Römischen Welt*, ser. 2, vol. XXXI, no. 1, ed. Wolfgang Haase (Berlin, 1980), 359–93.

7. See Michael C. J. Putnam, *The Poetry of the "Aeneid": Four Studies in Imaginative Unity and Design* (Cambridge, Ma., 1966), pp. 151–201.

8. The advertisement to Book III, canto ix begins "Malbecco will no straunge knights

host." "Malbecco" has been etymologized as "male goat," which is clunky and un-characteristic, however apt, since all other "mal" prefixes translate to "bad." As an equally likely and equally thematic possibility, then, I translate Malbecco as "bad beckoner."

9. "'Positive Negation': Threshold, Sequence, and Personification," in *New Perspectives on Coleridge and Wordsworth*, ed. Geoffrey H. Hartman (New York, 1972), pp. 136–37. For a loosely conceptual framework relating liminal moments to experiential extremes, see Albert Cook, *Thresholds: Studies in Romantic Experience* (Madison, 1985).

10. "Paradise, the garden, is the original *templum* for the Hebraic, Christian tradition, while the desert is the archetypal profane space," writes Fletcher, *The Prophetic Moment: An Essay on Spenser* (Chicago, 1971), p. 60; on thresholds, see pp. 47–49.

11. See Sanford Budick's excellent *The Dividing Muse: Images of Sacred Disjunction in Milton's Poetry* (New Haven, Conn., 1985). I would want to expand on Budick's analysis by observing that Milton's poetry is based on division and then reparation, a movement which has nothing to do with dialectic, either Ramist or Hegelian.

12. See Kay Gilliland Stevenson, "'No more . . . No End': *Paradise Lost* IX," *Renaissance Papers* (1983), pp. 103–09.

13. "Book Two ends with the punning verb 'hies' [sounding toward "High" of Book II, line 1] as Book Three ends with the punning 'lights,'" writes Thomas Greene, *The Descent From Heaven* (New Haven, Conn., 1963), p. 388.

14. Geoffrey Hartman, "Milton's Counterplot," in his *Beyond Formalism: Literary Essays 1958–1970* (New Haven, Conn., 1970), p. 123.

15. "The moon has always been known to poets for its changes, its continuous waxing and waning" (Fletcher, "'Positive Negation,'" p. 153).

16. For an excellent analysis of this passage see John Guillory, *Poetic Authority: Spenser, Milton, and Literary History* (New York, 1983), 140 to 145.

17. See Dustin Griffin, "Milton's Moon," in *Milton Studies*, vol. IX, ed. James D. Simmonds (Pittsburgh, 1976), pp. 151–68.

18. Temperance is a problem most explicitly in the strongly Spenserian *Comus*, and even there the Lady's chastity often seems more extreme than mediating. Arthur Barker, *Milton and the Puritan Dilemma 1641–1660* (Toronto, 1942, 1971), pp. 10–13, makes this point and later adds that the virtue "exemplified by Spenser's knight is sometimes less Aristotelian temperance than Puritan renunciation" (p. 97).

19. On "all" in Milton, see William Empson, *The Structure of Complex Words* (Totowa, N.J., 1951, 1977), pp. 101–04.

20. "Frequent" means "full" (OED, v, 6); "frequent and full" is idiomatic (OED, a, 1), as in "the assembly was full and frequent according to summons," *Complete Prose Works of John Milton*, ed. Don M. Wolfe et al. (New Haven, Conn., 1954–82), vol. V, p. 378. Subsequent references to this volume will be cited as YP.

21. Hartman, "Milton's Counterplot," p. 348.

22. Boyd M. Berry, *Process of Speech: Puritan Religious Writing and "Paradise Lost"* (Baltimore, 1976), p. 266.

23. And it does not hurt to remind ourselves that Dante, contrary to Milton, has a purgatory between his heaven and his hell. On body, city, and history, see Giuseppe Mazzotta, *Dante, Poet of the Desert: History and Allegory in the Divine Comedy* (Princeton, N.J., 1979).

24. C. A. Patrides, *Milton and the Christian Tradition* (Oxford, 1964), p. 262.

25. On the "shadow" in Book IV's Ovidian imitation, see Richard L. DuRocher, *Milton and Ovid* (Ithaca, N.Y., 1985), p. 92.

26. William Kerrigan, *The Sacred Complex: On the Psychogenesis of "Paradise Lost"* (Cambridge, Ma., 1983), p. 233.

27. Frank Kermode, *The Sense of an Ending*, (New York, 1967), p. 3.

28. As Budick, *The Dividing Muse*, p. 91, shows, Satan's fixated delusions result from the incapacity to divide himself from heaven: "I give not Heav'n for lost" (II, 14). Raphael's chain of being (V, 470–503) is best thought of in terms of difference, as discrete stages, root, stalk, flower, fruit. This movement is "contiguous" rather than "continuous" (see Milton's use of these terms in *Areopagitica*, YP, p. 744).

29. Kerrigan, *The Sacred Complex*, pp. 296, 297.

30. Patricia Parker, *Inescapable Romance: Studies in the Poetics of a Mode* (Princeton, N.J., 1979), p. 158.

31. See Louis L. Martz, *Poet of Exile: A Study of Milton's Poetry* (New Haven, Conn., 1980), pp. 293–304.

32. Spenser leaves Book VI open by letting loose the Blatant Beast in the present day (a *huge* figure of opening), but he is also interested in a counteractive decorum: "Therefore do you my rimes keep better measure, / And seek to please, that now is counted wisemens Threasure" (VI, xii, 41).